European Populism in the Shadow of the Great Recession

Edited by

Hanspeter Kriesi and Takis S. Pappas

Cover: © Daniel Pudles

First published by the ECPR Press in 2015

This paperback edition published in 2016

The ECPR Press is the publishing imprint of the European Consortium for Political Research (ECPR), a scholarly association, which supports and encourages the training, research and cross-national co-operation of political scientists in institutions throughout Europe and beyond.

ECPR Press
Harbour House
Hythe Quay
Colchester
CO2 8JF
United Kingdom

Typeset by the ECPR Press

Printed and bound by Lightning Source

British Library Cataloguing in Publication Data

A catalogue record for this book is available from the British Library

HARDBACK ISBN: 978-1-785521-24-9

PAPERBACK ISBN: 978-1-785522-34-5

PDF ISBN: 978-1-785521-37-9

EPUB ISBN: 978-1-785521-38-6

KINDLE ISBN: 978-1-785521-39-3

www.ecpr.eu/ecprpress

ECPR Press Editors
Peter Kennealy (European University Institute)
Ian O'Flynn (Newcastle University)
Alexandra Segerberg (Stockholm University)
Laura Sudulich (University of Kent)

You may also be interested in:

Spreading Protest: Social Movements in Times of Crisis
Edited by Donatella della Porta and Alice Mattoni
ISBN 9781785521638
Which elements do the Arab Spring, the *Indignados* and Occupy Wall Street have
in common? How do they differ? What do they share with social movements of
the past? This book discusses the recent wave of global mobilisations from an
unusual angle, explaining what aspects of protests spread from one country to
another, how this happened, and why diffusion occurred in certain contexts but
not in others. In doing so, the book casts light on the more general mechanisms
of protest diffusion in contemporary societies, explaining how mobilisations
travel from one country to another and, also, from past to present times.

Constitutional Deliberative Democracy in Europe
Min Reuchamps and Jane Suiter
ISBN 9781785521454
European institutions have introduced different forms of deliberative democracy
as a way to connect citizens back in. These empirical cases are emblematic of a
possibly constitutional turn in deliberative democracy in Europe. The purpose
of this book is to critically assess these developments, bringing together
academics involved in the designing of these new forms of constitutional
deliberative democracy with the theorists who propagated the ideas and evaluated
democratic standards.

Political Violence in Context: Time, Space and Milieu
Lorenzo Bosi, Niall Ó Dochartaigh and Daniela Pisoiu
ISBN 9781785521447
Context is crucial to understanding the causes of political violence and the form
it takes. This book examines how time, space and supportive milieux decisively
shape the pattern and pace of such violence. While much of the work in this
field focuses on individual psychology or radical ideology, Bosi, Ó Dochartaigh,
Pisoiu and others take a fresh, innovative look at the importance of context in
generating mobilisation and shaping patterns of violence.

Europeanisation and Party Politics
Erol Külahci
ISBN 9781907301223
A sophisticated theoretical framework and up-to-date analysis of the
Europeanisation of domestic party systems and political parties' policy stances.
This book covers a range of contemporary topics: party systems, policy stances
of political parties, opposition/co-operation over European integration, cleavage
theory of party response to European integration, domestic depoliticisation and
EU representation. It presents a sophisticated political analysis of Europe, and an
exceptional amount of factual information about European countries and parties.

New Perspectives on Negative Campaigning
Alessandro Nai and Annemarie Walter
ISBN 9781785521287
This unique volume presents for the first time work examining negative
campaigning in the US, Europe and beyond. It presents systematic literature
overviews and new work that touches upon three fundamental questions:
What is negative campaigning and can we measure it? What causes negative
campaigning? And what are its effects?

**Please visit www.ecpr.eu/ecprpress for up-to-date information about new
and forthcoming publications.**

Contents

List of Figures and Tables

Tables

List of Contributors

PARIS ASLANIDIS is a PhD researcher at the University of Macedonia, Greece, studying the nexus between populism and social movements during the Great Recession. He has a background in engineering and philosophy of science.

LAURENT BERNHARD is a postdoctoral researcher at the University of Zurich (Switzerland). His PhD thesis focused on the campaign strategies adopted by political actors in the context of direct-democratic campaigns. Together with Marco Steenbergen (University of Zurich) and Hanspeter Kriesi (EUI, Florence), he currently leads a project that deals with populism in Western Europe in the framework of the research program NCCR Democracy.

HANS-GEORG BETZ is currently Adjunct Professor in political science at the University of Zurich. Previously he taught at York University, Toronto, Johns Hopkins University, Washington, DC and Koc University, Istanbul. He is the author of several books and articles on radical right-wing populism in Europe.

GIULIANO BOBBA is Assistant Professor in the Department of Cultures, Politics and Society at the University of Turin. His research interests include: political communication and election campaigns; primaries elections; the evolution of political parties and leadership in Western democracies; the European integration process and the development of a European public sphere. He has published in particular on elections campaigns, media and politics in Italy and France.

ZSOLT ENYEDI is Professor at the Political Science Department of Central European University. He is the 2014–15 Austrian Marshall Plan Fellow at SAIS, Johns Hopkins University.

JOHN FITZGIBBON is senior lecturer in politics at School of Psychology, Politics and Sociology, Canterbury Christchurch University. His main areas of interest are Euroscepticism, European Political Economy, Social Movements, Referendums, the use of Simulations in Political Science Education.

MATTHEW GOODWIN is Associate Professor at the School of Politics and International Relations, University of Nottingham. He has run numerous research projects for the Economic and Social Research Council, the Leverhulme Trust and British Academy and is most recently the co-author of *Revolt on the Right: Explaining Support for the Radical Right in Britain* (with Robert Ford, 2014).

VLASTIMIL HAVLÍK is a research fellow at the International Institute of Political Science, Faculty of Social Studies, Masaryk University (FSS MU) and

Assistant Professor at the Department of Political Science, FSS MU. His teaching and research activities include populism, party politics in the Czech Republic and Europeanisation. He is also the managing editor of the *Czech Journal of Political Science*.

ANN-CATHRINE JUNGAR is a senior lecturer at Södertörn University in Stockholm. She holds a PH D from Uppsala University, has worked as a research leader and director of Studies at the Centre for Baltic and East European Studies.

ANDERS RAVIK JUPSKÅS is a research fellow at the Department of Political Science, University of Oslo. He is currently finishing his PhD on populist persistence, which is part of a larger research project on party change in Norway funded by the Norwegian Research Council.

HANSPETER KRIESI holds the Stein Rokkan Chair in Comparative Politics at the European University Institute in Florence. Previously, he has been teaching at the universities of Amsterdam, Geneva and Zurich. He was the director of a Swiss national research programme on the 'Challenges to democracy in the 21st century' from 2005–12.

KURT RICHARD LUTHER is Professor of Comparative Politics at Keele University, UK and at Tongji University, Shanghai. He chairs the ECPR Standing Group on Political Parties. His current research includes party organisation and strategy and party-interest group links. He also continues to specialise on Austria and holds the Austrian Cross of Honour for Science and Arts.

DUNCAN MCDONNELL is a Senior Lecturer in the School of Government and International Relations at Griffith University, Brisbane. He was previously a Marie Curie Fellow at the European University Institute in Florence. He is the co-author (with Daniele Albertazzi) of *Populists in Power* (Routledge, 2015) and the co-editor of *Twenty-First Century Populism* (Palgrave, 2008).

EOIN O'MALLEY is senior lecturer in politics at the School of Law and Government, Dublin City University. He has published over thirty journal articles mainly on questions relating to Irish politics, parties and prime ministers. He is author of *Contemporary Ireland* (Palgrave 2011) and co-editor of *Governing Ireland* (IPA 2012).

TAKIS S. PAPPAS is Associate Professor at the University of Macedonia, Greece, and during this project, was a Marie Curie Fellow at the European University Institute in Florence. His most recent book is *Populism and Crisis Politics in Greece* (Palgrave 2014). He currently works on a new book project under the tentative title *Democratic Illiberalism: How Populism Grows*.

TEUN PAUWELS works at the Flemish Ministry of Education and Training and is scientific collaborator at the Université Libre de Bruxelles. His research focuses on populism, ideologies and voting behaviour. He is the author of *Populism in Western Europe*, comparing Belgium, Germany and The Netherlands (Routledge, 2014).

MATTHIJS ROODUIJN is postdoctoral researcher at the Amsterdam Institute for Inequality Studies (AMCIS) and lecturer in the Department of Political Science at the University of Amsterdam. He studies populism, radicalism and voting behaviour in Western Europe.

BEN STANLEY is Marie Curie Intra-European Research Fellow in the School of Law, Politics and Sociology at the University of Sussex, and Lecturer at the Cardinal Stefan Wyszyński University, Warsaw. His main research interests are the theory and practice of populism, the comparative analysis of voting behaviour, the comparative analysis of party-system and cleavage formation, and the political entrepreneurialism of elites in new democracies. He has published articles in the *Journal of Political Ideologies, Communist and Post-Communist Studies, Europe-Asia Studies, and Party Politics*, as well as contributing a number of chapters in edited volumes.

PETER UČEŇ works as the Senior Programme Officer with the Europe Programme of the International Republican Institute (IRI). He has been working in the field of democracy assistance since 1999 focusing on enhancing capacities of political parties, party foundations and training institutes. In his research he specialises in populism, anti-establishment politics and new political parties in Slovakia and East Central Europe.

STIJN VAN KESSEL is lecturer in Politics at Loughborough University, UK and Alexander von Humboldt Foundation Postdoctoral Fellow at the Heinrich Heine University Düsseldorf, Germany. He completed his doctoral research at the University of Sussex in 2011 and is the author of the monograph '*Populist Parties in Europe: Agents of Discontent?*' (Palgrave MacMillan, 2015). He has further published in edited books and journals, including *Government and Opposition, Acta Politica* and *Journal of Political Ideologies*.

EDWARD WEBER is a PhD Student at the University of Zurich and since 2013 working for the Swiss national research programme on, 'Populism in the context of globalisation and mediatisation'.

TUOMAS YLÄ-ANTTILA is the co-founder and co-director of the Helsinki Research Group for Political Sociology at the University of Helsinki. He has published on globalisation, politics of climate change, social movements and populism.

TUUKKA YLÄ-ANTTILA is a doctoral researcher with the Helsinki Research Group for Political Sociology at the University of Helsinki. His work focuses on the relationship of populist argumentation and political cultures.

Preface

The European University Institute (EUI) in Florence is one of those great academic institutions that brings together members of disparate scientific communities in informal and unanticipated encounters. We met for the first time at the EUI, while one of us was a Marie-Curie Fellow and the other a new member of the faculty of the social and political sciences. In December 2012, we organised a small, exploratory conference on 'Studying Europe's Populism by Regional Country Clusters', which, in addition to us two future editors, brought together a small group of like-minded scholars, who formed the nucleus for the emerging project. The invitation to that first meeting stated that:

> [...]we scholars of populism are like the proverbial group of men in the dark touching an elephant to learn what it is like. Only that, in our case, darkness is due to the fact that we either try to draw general conclusions on the basis of one, or very few cases, that we happen to know best, or that we engage in large-scale comparisons of diverse countries without substantive knowledge of all the cases involved.

The original hunch of the conveners was that in Europe there may be as many shades of populism as there are geographic regions: Nordic populism, Alpine populism, Benelux populism, British populism, etcetera. Accordingly, the proposal discussed at this workshop was to study European populism by focusing on regional clusters rather than on individual country cases or even small groups of countries.

The members of the group did not really buy into this idea of different types of regional populisms. They agreed with the proposal that we lack an overview of what populism is really like across Europe. It was decided, however, that a step back should be taken and that the first priority should be to take stock of the phenomenon of populism in as many individual European countries as possible. At the same time, it was suggested that the focus of this stock-taking should be the question of whether and how the Great Recession has influenced manifestations of populism in Europe, with respect to their incidence, magnitude and expressive forms. With this idea in mind, we planned a larger conference with prospective authors on 'The Impact of the Great Recession on Manifestations of Populism in Europe'. This conference, which took place in Sofia during autumn 2013 and was graciously organised by Dobrinka Kostova, brought together most of the contributors of this volume and some more colleagues who presented first drafts of country chapters. In March 2014, at a follow-up conference at the EUI in Florence, the final group of contributors met once again to discuss more advanced drafts of the individual chapters and to prepare the final volume that you hold in your hands. While still in line with the idea of stock-taking in the individual countries, this volume is essentially based on country chapters. These chapters are grouped into geographical regions and the conclusion makes an attempt to take up the original idea of regional groups of countries sharing some similarities with respect to the phenomenon under study.

We would like to thank all the contributors to this volume for the sustained effort they have put into this joint endeavour. As the pre-history of this volume suggests, we put considerable demands on our contributors. We are particularly grateful to Dobrinka Kostova and her staff for organising our conference in Sofia, as well as to Maureen Lechleitner, who helped us to organise the conference at the EUI and with preparing the manuscript. We would also like to thank the PhD students and colleagues - Jovo Bakic, Lars-Erik Berntzen, Blagovesta Cholova, James Dennison, Mathilde van Ditmars, Jonas Draege, Mladen Lazic, Philip Rathgeb and Lyuba Spasova, who have contributed to the debates and discussions at the two conferences. Last, but certainly not least, we would like to thank the institutions which have contributed to financing our joint endeavour: without the generous support by the Robert Schuman Centre for Advanced Studies at the EUI, the Swiss National Science Foundation (Project IZ74Z0_137483/1: *'Democracy and Debate: The Shadows of Totalitarianism and Populism'*), the Stein-Rokkan-Chair of the EUI, the ERC-grant 338875 (POLCON) and the Marie-Curie Fellowship Programme, this volume would not have seen the light of the day.

Hanspeter Kriesi and Takis S. Pappas
Florence and Strasbourg
April 2015

Chapter One

Populism in Europe During Crisis: An Introduction

Hanspeter Kriesi and Takis S. Pappas

Populism and the crisis

This volume aspires to be the first large-scale comparative work on the impact of the early twenty-first century's Great Recession on European populism. At a time when the former Italian Prime Minister Mario Monti appealed to electorates to avoid 'a return to populism', the French President Francois Hollande warned against 'dangerous populist excesses', and former European Union (EU) President Herman van Rompuy sent alarming messages about the 'winds of populism' threatening Europe, we propose an assessment of whether, and to what extent, populism has interacted with the crisis. Furthermore, distinguishing between the economic and the political aspects of the crisis, and remaining sensitive to the timing of events in each of our country cases, we attempt to assess the different effects of the crisis on populism at both a national and EU level. Finally, we hope to be in a position to offer a theoretically robust and dynamic evaluation of contemporary European populism.

In the aftermath of the Lehman Brothers' bankruptcy in September 2008, populist arguments have been made in political discourse throughout Europe, and populist short-cut solutions have been proposed. As austerity became the new policy norm, economic and social inequalities grew larger, and as European integration appeared to many constituencies as a hopeless project, newly emergent populist leaders rose in some countries to defend the powerless people against sinister elites including politicians (both at national and the EU levels), bankers and industrialists – in short, the powerful and the wealthy. In some countries, formerly mainstream political formations went into decline, some irreversibly, and new populist parties appeared, some of which skyrocketed to electoral success.

The economic crisis included three intertwined dimensions (Shambaugh 2012): First, a competitiveness crisis, which caused the slowing down of economic growth in most of Europe; second, a banking crisis, due to undercapitalisation of banks and their consequent lack of liquidity/solvency; and, third, a sovereign debt crisis, especially in countries that could no longer fund public debt on their own because of rising bond yields. To be sure, the economic crisis was not uniform in terms of its causes, manifestations and outcomes. Not all European countries endured all three dimensions, nor was the crisis felt in the same way throughout the continent. A few countries (most notably Norway and Switzerland), did not really experience a crisis at all, while others were spared some of its dimensions. For those countries faced with an excessive sovereign debt, the problem became the most acute. Unable to refinance their respective governments' debts, some of them (including the herein examined Greece, Hungary and Ireland) had to be bailed out by the IMF or by the so-called 'Troika' (consisting of EU, ECB and IMF).

Although the crisis initially appeared as a purely economic one, it also had important political consequences. However, one has to distinguish between degrees of political and social disturbances. In most countries, the crisis led to the punishment of incumbent governments – a phenomenon widely observed across Europe. Only in very few countries (most notably Germany and Sweden) incumbents were able to maintain their position. In several countries, new political actors emerged forcefully during the crisis on both the radical right and the radical left (e.g. SYRIZA in Greece or the True Finns in Finland), while already established parties of the radical right were reinforced (e.g. FN in France). In addition, some countries saw the rise of new populist contenders rallying against the old political order (e.g. Beppe Grillo's M5S in Italy, or Jon Gnarr's 'Best Party' in Iceland). Everywhere, the crisis contributed to the erosion of existing party systems. In the countries hardest hit, the economic crisis developed into a deep political crisis. In some countries, it gave rise to intense social unrest, including mass mobilisation and the occasional use of street violence, and even led to the rise of political extremism on both the right and the left (most ominously in Greece and Hungary). In other countries, it caused tectonic changes in the established party system architecture (as, for instance, in Italy and Ireland) and even party system collapse (most obviously in the case of Greece).

We should not forget, however, that populism has not been the unique product of the Great Recession in Europe (Kriesi 2014). In Western Europe, the rise of populism has been a long-term process that has already been well underway at the time of the intervention of the Great Recession. This process has, for some time, been driven by the malfunctioning of representative democracy, especially by the deficiencies of the party system, the main intermediary system linking the citizens to political decision-making (*see* Mair 2002). These deficiencies of representative democracy, in turn, have different origins, depending on the countries we are looking at. In Western Europe, mainstream political parties have been less and less able to mobilise the voters: indicators are declining party membership and party identification, declining voter turnout, increasing volatility of the vote and declining shares of voters who choose the mainstream parties. Mair (2009) attributed this erosion of the mainstream parties' representation function to the increasing tension between 'responsibility' and 'responsiveness', i.e. the tension between the parties' role as representatives of the national citizen publics, and their role as governments being responsible to a range of domestic, inter- and supranational stakeholders. According to this view, the lack of responsiveness of the mainstream parties to specific new demands from society provided new challengers who appeal to the unrepresented demands arising from socio-economic change with the opportunity to mobilise successfully.

In particular, the lack of responsiveness of established parties to the plight of the 'globalisation losers' provided a chance for their mobilisation by the new populist right. As Kriesi *et al.* (2006, 2008, 2012) have argued, globalisation has transformed the basis of politics in Western Europe by giving rise to what they have called a new 'integration-demarcation' cleavage: processes of increasing economic, cultural and political competition linked to globalisation created latent structural potentials of globalisation 'winners' and 'losers'. According to their analyses, the mobilisation of the group of 'losers' by parties of the new populist right and by transformed established parties of the liberal and conservative right has provided the key impetus for the transformation of the party systems in the six West European countries they had studied. As they also showed, the success of the new challengers was mainly due to their appeal to the cultural anxieties of the 'losers', which, given the 'losers'' heterogeneous economic interests, provided the least common denominator for their mobilisation. The long-term tide of populism was, in other words, not driven in the first place by economic, but by cultural motives. It is an open question to be analysed by the contributors of this volume whether the Great Recession has added economic fuel to the cultural fire.

For different reasons, Central and East European party systems have also been characterised by a considerable estrangement between the citizens and the established political elites long before the economic crisis intervened. In Central and Eastern Europe, party systems have not yet produced stable mainstream parties that reliably represent their constituencies: in contrast to the party systems of Western Europe, the party systems in Central and Eastern Europe have never been institutionalised to the same extent. In other words, in this part of Europe, parties have not yet developed stable roots in society, their organisation has been unstable, and they are hardly considered legitimate by the citizens of their countries. The most important empirical evidence for the lack of institutionalisation of these party systems comes from Powell, and Tucker (2014), who show that the very high level of volatility in these systems since the democratic transition has above all been due to the entry and exit of parties, and not to switches between established parties.

In Central and Eastern Europe, the low level of institutionalisation of the party systems has provided a general opportunity for the rise of new populist challengers. This opportunity became all the more important, given the widespread dissatisfaction of the Central and Eastern European publics with their political elites. The high costs of economic transition and the low level of political and administrative performance have contributed to the constitution of anti-elitist sentiments which provide a general breeding ground for populist challengers. Thus, a strong majority in all Central and Eastern European EU member states perceives public officials as acting in a corrupt manner when exercising their power. The levels of public distrust in political authorities are especially high in Bulgaria, Romania, Lithuania and Slovakia. Across Central and Eastern Europe, there is a deep-seated disenchantment of citizens with democratic politics, which is, as Linde (2012) shows, largely explained by perceptions of corruption and feelings of unfair treatment by authorities. As a result of this particular combination of circumstances, 'centrist' populist mobilisation, i.e. a 'pure' version of populism that is reduced to anti-establishment posture without any other ideological element (Učeň 2007: 54a), has characterised Central and Eastern Europe already before the crisis. These 'centrist-populist' parties have 'largely arisen as a reaction to the general disappointment of East European electorates with mainstream parties and the high cost of economic reforms' (Pop-Eleches 2010: 232).

The most general question we try to answer in this volume is whether and to what extent the Great Recession has served to enhance these overall trends and contributed to the general ascendancy of populism across Europe. At the outset of our endeavour our hunch is similar to that of the politicians we cited at the beginning of this introduction: whether of a rightist, leftist or centrist hew, represented by old as well as brand new parties, we expect populism in its many manifestations to have been a beneficiary of crisis at the expense of liberal democracy as it developed during the long postwar decades.

Definitions

Of course, populism needs clear defining. Remaining fully aware of the term's slippery nature, the contributors to this book rely on well-tested concepts of populism. We define populism as an 'ideology' that splits society into two antagonistic camps, the virtuous people and some corrupt establishment, effectively pitting one against the other (Canovan 1999: 3; Laclau 1977: 172–3; Mudde 2004: 543; Wiles 1969: 166). More specifically, following Mudde (2004: 543), we conceive of populism as an ideology which 'considers society to be ultimately separated into two homogenous and antagonistic groups – 'the pure people' versus the 'corrupt elite', and which argues that politics should be an expression of the 'volonté générale' (general will) of the people'. This definition includes:

—   the existence of two homogenous groups – 'the people' and 'the elite';
—   the antagonistic relationship between the two;
—   the idea of popular sovereignty; and
—   a 'Manichean outlook' that combines the positive valorisation of 'the people' with the denigration of 'the elite'.

As has been pointed out by Stanley (2008) and Stanley and Učeň (2008), this conceptual core is distinct, but 'thin', in the sense established by Freeden (1998: 750) of an ideology unable 'to provide a reasonably broad, if not comprehensive, range of answers to the political questions that societies generate'. Populism's 'thinness' is a product of the vagueness and plasticity of its core concepts, which allows it to be combined with a variety of 'thick' ideologies, such as conservatism or socialism, that add more specific content to it. As Stanley and Učeň (2008: 8) observe:

Conceiving of populism as a thin ideology resolves the persistent problem of how to account for the variety of political content associated with manifestations of populism whilst simultaneously positing a set of common elements, but it also illustrates the dependent relationship of populism on 'fuller' ideologies that project a more detailed set of answers to key political questions.

For populists, 'the people' is paramount and whatever their specific view of the people, they share a 'monolithic' conception of the people. As Canovan (2002: 34) points out, the concept of the people is always conceived as a homogenous category, a unity, a corporate body capable of having common interests and a common will – a *volonté générale*. All populists also share the notion of the people as sovereign, and all of them deplore that democracy is not working because the sovereignty of the people has been eroded and is threatened with being ever-further eroded. In addition to this conceptual core notion and depending on the 'thick' ideology with which the 'thin' ideology of populism is combined, 'the people' may also be conceived as 'the nation' (right-wing populism) or as the 'common man', the 'little guys', the 'poor', the '99 per cent' or the 'exploited' (left-wing populism).

The monolithic conception of the people as a homogenous unity not only implies the antagonism between the people and the elites, but also opens the possibility of the 'exclusion of others' – non-elite groups who do not belong to 'the people'. Depending on the 'thick' ideology that is complementing the thin populist core, specific groups of 'others' may be singled out as scapegoats who, in addition to or in combination with the elites, are to be blamed for the predicament of 'the people'. Examples of groups excluded by right-wing populists comprise all kinds of ethnic minorities (e.g. Roma or Jews), immigrants and the undeserving beneficiaries of the welfare state (those who benefit from social security without having contributed to it).

While populism is 'a shadow cast by democracy' (Canovan 1999: 3) and populists see themselves as true democrats, it is important to keep in mind that their 'thin' ideology implies quite a specific 'illiberal vision of democracy' (Pappas 2013, 2014b). We can identify three illiberal components of the populist vision of democracy: it takes 'government by the people' literally and rejects liberal checks and balances (the 'constitutionalist dimension of democracy' in the terms used by Mény and Surel 2002); it is hostile to intermediaries between the people and the decision-makers, especially to political parties (Pasquino 2008: 21), and pleads for a more direct linkage of the masses to the elites (Taggart 2002: 67); and it is also illiberal because of its monolithic (or unanimous), and, we should add, predetermined conception of the will of the people, which leaves no room for pluralism or deliberation (Mastropaolo 2008: 34f.; Urbinati 2014: 132ff.).

Populism as an ideology manifests itself in specific discursive patterns for identifying foes and solidifying the community of friends. Jagers and Walgrave (2007) and Hawkins (2009) have introduced the conception of populism as a discursive pattern or political communication style. This notion does not add another theoretical element to the definition of populism, but it is very helpful for attempts to operationalise populist ideology. Populist ideology becomes visible in the political communication strategies or discursive patterns of the populist actors. Conceiving of populism as a communication style is complementary to the definition of populism as an ideology. The populist communication style puts an emphasis on the fundamental role of the people, claims that the people have been betrayed by those in charge, i.e. the elites are accused of abusing their position of power, and that the primacy of the people has to be restored (Mény and Surel 2002: 11f.). Several authors have usefully proposed indices to operationalise populism based on an analysis of its core themes as they appear in both the political discourse and the political literature of populist parties (such as party manifestos, speeches or press releases) (*see* Aslanidis 2014, Bruhn 2012, March 2012, Rooduijn *et al.* 2014, Rooduijn and Pauwels 2011, Pauwels 2011b).

From populism as an ideology or a discourse we should distinguish populism as a political strategy. Some authors, most notably authors writing about Latin America, conceptualise populism as a specific way of competing for and exercising political power. Thus, Weyland (2001: 14) has argued that populism is best defined as a political strategy through which a personalistic leader (our emphasis) seeks or exercises government power based on direct, unmediated, uninstitutionalised support from large numbers of mostly unorganised followers. According to this definition, the connection between the people and the leader is mostly based on direct quasi-personal contact, not on organised intermediation. More recently, Urbinati (2014) has suggested that 'populism can hardly exist without a politics of personality' (p.131) and that 'without the presence of a leader or a centralised leadership that seeks control of the majority a popular movement that has a populist rhetoric[...]is not yet populism' (p.129). For her, populism is 'a project of power whose aspiration is to make its leaders and elected officials use the state to favour, extend and consolidate their constituency' (p.131).

We do not adopt this definition of populism in terms of political strategy, but we would like to point out that populist discourse is most commonly expressed by a personalistic leader in Europe, too. Typically, this personalistic, populist leader does not belong to the established political elites, but is an outsider (a new challenger), who incarnates the demands of 'the people'. He (it is most often a man, although not always (*see* Marine Le Pen, Pia Kjärsgaard, Siv Jensen)) has direct, unmediated access to the people's grievances, and acts as the spokesperson of the *vox populi* (Abts 2011: 930). The leader as the spokesperson of the *vox populi* is, in fact, one with the people whose deepest feelings he or she articulates. The direct, populist form of representation by a personalistic leader promises to make politics transparent by offering 'a short-cut that bypasses philosophical disputes and institutional niceties' (Canovan 2002: 34). The monolithic conception of the leader (there is only one) and of the leader's (hierarchically structured and centralised) political organisation (if there is one) corresponds to the monolithic conception of 'the people'. In this very specific sense, populism as an ideology and as a political strategy are complementary, and tend to go together.

The main, although not exclusive, organisational vehicle for populist ideology and discourse is a political party, and populist leaders typically create new or transform existing parties in order to win elections and to gain power. Accordingly, we are focusing in our study of European populism in the shadow of the Great Recession on populist parties, and we are sensitive to and trying to analyse populism-during-crisis in two specific modalities: discourse and electoral outcomes. First and above all, we want to detect populism through the detailed analysis of its *discursive patterns* before and during the crisis. Second, we shall also evaluate the electoral success of populism by examining electoral contests during the crisis and assessing the transformative power of old or upcoming populist parties on each country's overall political and party system.

Guiding hypotheses

Having defined our key object of analysis, we aim in this volume to examine *where*, *when*, *how* and *how much* populism profited during, and because of, Europe's Great Recession. For some authors, populism is intrinsically linked to crisis. Thus, for someone like Laclau (1977, 2005a, 2005b), populism simply cannot emerge without crisis (*see* Moffitt 2014). For him, it is a political crisis – a crisis of representation, which is at the root of any populist mobilisation. Similarly, Roberts (1995: 113) maintains that populism 'is a perpetual tendency where political institutions are weak. However, it surges most strongly in contexts of crisis or profound social transformation'. Other scholars focusing on Latin America argue in the same way. While we do not want to go as far as to suggest that populism may only arise in crisis situations, we expect that populism will benefit from crisis. Given its essentially anti-elitist orientation, populism can be expected to thrive on popular dissatisfaction with the elites. Such dissatisfaction can have different origins, depending on the national context, but it is certainly expected to increase in crisis situations. Let us hasten to add that a crisis is not necessarily exogenous to the development of populism. If crises provide an opportunity for populist mobilisations, they are in turn aggravated and brought to a climax by the populists' mobilisation themselves. This has been argued most forcefully by Moffitt (2014: 2), who suggests that 'rather than just thinking about crisis as a trigger of populism, we should also think about how populism attempts to act as a trigger for crisis'.

When discussing the impact of crisis on populism, we believe it is important to distinguish between economic and more narrowly political crises. First, we suggest that a deep economic crisis enhances the antagonism between 'the people' and some political or economic elites, which serves to intensify populist mobilisation, i.e. populism-*qua*-discourse and electoral success of populist parties (H1). Where the economic crisis creates socio-economic misery and deepens economic inequality, populist discourse falls on fertile ground. In other words, we expect the Great Recession to enhance the long-term trends that have been giving rise to right-wing populism for the past decades. In addition to enhancing right-wing populists, the Great Recession also provides an opportunity for left-wing populism, which has always been framing its anti-elitism in economic (class) terms. We expect left-wing populism to get its chance especially in the countries hardest hit by the crisis.

Right-wing populists, as we have already argued, mobilise their constituency mainly in cultural terms, which means that they emphasise the negative consequences of cultural diversity and political integration, and reframe economic conflicts in cultural terms. For example, they attribute the loss of jobs not to economic globalisation but to the influx of migrants. The fact that the Great Recession in Europe manifested itself mainly as a sovereign debt crisis actually provides right-wing populists with a golden (discursive) opportunity to reframe economic conflicts in nationalistic terms. Typically, the elites attacked by populists are domestic elites, but given that the sovereign debt crisis has led to a conflict between 'debtor' and 'creditor' countries in the Eurozone, the elites that come to be the object of populist attacks may also be supranational elites (e.g. the 'Troika') and/or elites from other nation states (e.g. the German Chancellor, Angela Merkel, for the Greeks). Moreover, given that the programmes to solve the European debt crisis require increasing solidarity between European 'states-peoples', they tend to create 'others' in terms of nationalities. Thus, some peoples of 'creditor' states (e.g. the Finns) turn against the peoples of 'debtor' states (e.g. the Greeks). Note that the inverse does not seem to have taken place so far: the peoples of 'debtor' states did turn against the 'creditor' states' governments, but not (yet) against their peoples.

Second, as we have already pointed out for the Central- and Eastern European countries, populism not only thrives on economic, but also on political crises. A political crisis is the result of poor governance in general, not just of poor economic performance. It results from corruption and partiality, lacking rule of law, and general ineffectiveness of government. One manifestation of poor governance is large-scale scandals. The emphasis here is on 'large-scale': although national elections are increasingly held in the shadow of political scandals, these events have typically been inconsequential for voter satisfaction. Only major scandals, involving more than one party tend to have an impact on the voters (Kumlin and Esaiasson 2011). Another, much more serious form of political crisis is a crisis of representation and the eventual breakdown of mainstream parties and even the collapse of entire party systems. The Latin American experience shows that mainstream party breakdown occurs when two conditions are jointly met (Lupu 2012, Roberts 2013): a) the dilution of the party's brand, which weakens the voters' attachments to the party, leads to de-alignment and, eventually, to a breakdown of programmatic linkages, and b) poor performance of the party in office, which, in combination with a) leads to an extraordinary sanctioning by economic voting. The dilution of the party brand, in turn, is a function of inconsistent signals of the party to the voters and/or of ideological convergence of the mainstream parties. Both inconsistency and convergence may be the results from an exogenous shock like the euro crisis that forces the parties in government to renege on their programmatic commitments. This is what happened to some Latin American mainstream parties from the left in the 1980s and 1990s, which, when in government, had to implement austerity programmes imposed by the Washington consensus. This is what also seems to have happened to the Greek socialists of PASOK, who, when in government, were forced to implement an austerity programme that was entirely incompatible with their programmatic commitments and electoral promises that they had made only a few months before.

Political crises create anti-elitist sentiments on which populists feed. In other words, we expect more intense populism in countries characterised by a political crisis (H2). The political crisis may occur independently of an economic crisis, but the political crisis may also co-occur with an economic crisis. The political crisis may precede the economic crisis and contribute to it, or a deep economic crisis may serve as a catalyst for the development of a political crisis. Indeed, when the economic crisis combines with a political crisis, we expect the joint effect of the two crises to be particularly conducive to populism (H3). This hypothesis is supported by empirical findings, which show that electoral punishment of poor governance (corruption in particular) is conditional on the economic performance in many, although not all countries. When the economy performs well, citizens do not tend to punish the executive for corrupt behaviour; conversely, citizens are more punitive when incumbents are perceived to be corrupt and incapable of delivering economic performance (Zechmeister and Zizumbu-Colunga 2013; Manzetti and Wilson 2007). As the experiments of Klasnja and Tucker (2013) suggest, there may be exceptions to this generalisation: while the conditional relationship holds in a new democracy like Moldavia, voters seem to be unforgiving with respect to corruption under all circumstances in an established democracy like Sweden. Quite generally, however, not only economic performance, but also corruption moves up on the voters' agenda in times of crisis (Singer 2013).

Finally, in the countries least hit by the economic crisis, we expect populism to develop according to the long-term trends and to vary in the short term according to more narrowly political factors. Among the latter, we consider the question of whether the populists were part of the government or not as a crucial consideration. In several West-European countries, populist challengers have become the dominant party in government (e.g. pre-crisis PASOK in Greece, Berlusconi's FI/PdL in Italy, or, since 2010, *Fidesz* in Hungary), a minority partner in the government (e.g. the Italian LN, the Swiss SVP, the Austrian FPÖ, or the Norwegian Progress Party) or they have been supporting the government coalition without having become formally part of it (e.g. the Dutch PVV or the Danish People's Party). Our fourth hypothesis suggests that, when in power, populists tend to tone down their populist discourse, behave more like mainstream parties and, accordingly tend to benefit less from an economic or political crisis (H4). This hypothesis is in line with recent findings of Roodujin *et al.* (2014) who show that 'populist parties do adjust their political programmes once they have experienced electoral growth'. The authors suggest that they do so in an attempt to become an acceptable coalition partner to mainstream parties.

Selection of cases and operationalisation of the crises

The chapters of this book cover 17 countries, that is to say, most of the European countries where populism has been a significant political phenomenon before and during the crisis. They include four Nordic countries (Denmark, Norway, Sweden and Finland), five countries from Western Europe (Austria, Belgium,

The Netherlands, France and Switzerland), two countries from Southern Europe (Greece, Italy), four countries from Central and Eastern Europe (Czech Republic, Slovakia, Hungary and Poland), plus two Anglo-Celtic countries (UK and Ireland).

We shall use three indicators to characterise the economic development of these countries since 2000: unemployment rates, growth rates and public debt. For unemployment and growth rates, Figures 1.1 and 1.2 present quarterly data, while yearly data are presented for the public gross debt in Figure 1.3. Figure 1.1 shows that, with the exceptions of Norway and Poland, the growth rates collapsed in all the countries in 2009. Hungary is exceptional to the extent that its economy already slowed down to a considerable extent before the Great Recession set in. Generally, the European economies recovered rather rapidly after 2009, with the notable exception of the Southern European countries and Ireland. By 2010, they were growing again. But growth was not sustainable in most of the countries. Already in 2011, it started to decline again and several of the countries had fallen back into a recession by 2012.

While growth rates display a lot of similarity, the unemployment rates presented in Figure 1.2 point to great differences with respect to the economic trajectory of the various countries. In the hardest hit countries – Greece and Ireland, unemployment has grown enormously. In Italy, unemployment has increased as well, but more slowly and at a lower rate than in the other Southern European countries. By contrast, unemployment has been relatively stable in Continental Western Europe, except for The Netherlands where it has considerably increased, but from a low level. Among the Nordic countries, Denmark in particular experienced rising unemployment rates and unemployment rates rose in Central- and Eastern Europe, above all in Slovakia and Hungary. Gross public debt generally increased in the course of the crisis, but in some countries, Greece, Ireland and the UK, it literally exploded. As shown in Figure 1.3, the increase of public debt was also rather accentuated in France, Italy, Hungary, The Netherlands and the Czech Republic. Hungary is again exceptional to the extent that public debt started to increase long before the crisis set in.

To summarise these trajectories, we take the difference between the average quarterly rates for the pre-crisis period 2001Q1–2008Q3 (or the average annual levels for 2001–08) and the corresponding rates for the post-crisis period 2008Q4–2013Q2 (2009–12). We then submit these three differences to a factor analysis. The results are displayed in the first part of Table 1.1. The three indicators equally contribute to the underlying factor that corresponds to the impact of the crisis on the national economy in the 17 countries. The resulting factor is our summary indicator for the economic crisis in a given country.

For the characterisation of the political crisis, we follow the lead of Mainwaring et al. (2006), who have suggested some measures for the 'crisis of democratic representation' in Latin America. We shall use one behavioural and two attitudinal indicators. Our behavioural indicator refers to electoral volatility. More specifically, we measure electoral volatility for the last national election before the crisis and for the most volatile post-crisis election. In calculating electoral volatility, we followed the procedures of Powell and Tucker (2014),

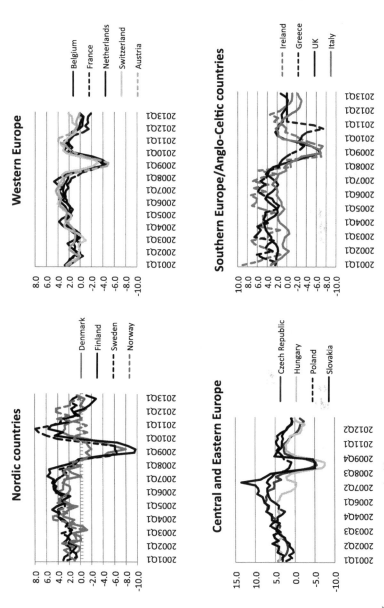

Figure 1.1: GDP – growth, quarterly data, seasonally adjusted compared to corresponding period of previous year[1])

[1] *Source:* Eurostat [namq_gdp_k].

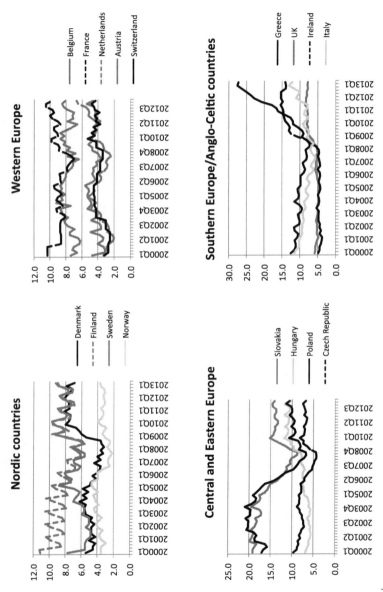

Figure 1.2: Level of unemployment, quarterly data (2000Q1 – 2013Q1: percentage[1])

[1] Source: Eurostat [lfsq_urgan].

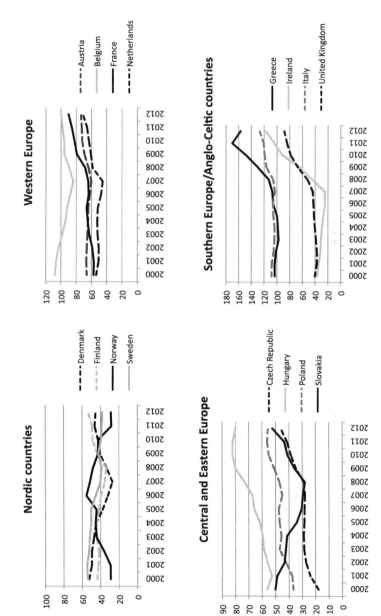

Figure 1.3: General government gross debt (as percentage of GDP[1])

[1] Source: Eurostat [tsdde410].

Table 1.1: Factor analysis of the indicators for the two types of crises

Economic crisis	Factor loading	Factor score
d_unemployment	0.74	0.26
d_growth	−0.76	−0.28
d_debt	0.84	0.47
EV	1.82	N=17
Political crisis		
d_volatility	0.88	−0.20
d_swd	−0.91	0.15
d_trustparl	−0.66	0.06
volatility2012	0.96	−0.31
swd2012	−0.91	0.21
trustparl2012	−0.86	0.15
EV	4.50	N=17

who distinguish between two types of volatility. But we only use total volatility here. In most countries there was just one post-crisis election, but in some cases there were two or, as in Greece, even three post-crisis elections up to and including the first quarter of 2013, the last quarter covered by our analysis. We use as our indicator the difference in volatility between the pre- and the most volatile post-crisis elections. An increase in volatility serves as an indicator of the destabilisation of the party system in the course of the crisis, while a decrease in volatility serves as a sign of party system stabilisation and suggests that the party system might have been going through an unstable period before and unrelated to the Great Recession. The first graph in Figure 1.4 shows that the countries that suffered most from the economic crisis also tend to have the highest electoral volatility in the aftermath of the crisis. Thus, electoral volatility has increased enormously in the Southern European countries and Ireland, as well as in Hungary and the Czech Republic. By contrast, volatility has considerably decreased in the first post-crisis elections in Poland and Norway. In the other countries, volatility has not changed that much.

Our two attitudinal indicators for a political crisis refer to trust in parliament and satisfaction with the way democracy works in one's own country. We have again pre- and post-crisis measures for these indicators. The pre-crisis measurement comes from the Eurobarometer 68.1, which went into the field in September–November 2007; the post-crisis measurement is from the Eurobarometer 77.3, fielded in May 2012.[1] For each country, we measure the share of respondents

---

1. We have no measures of SWD and trust in Parliament for Norway and Switzerland, given that they are not covered by the Eurobarometers. As a proxy, we attributed both countries the mean values for Denmark, Finland and Sweden. We shall not interpret these figures, however.

Figure 1.4: Indicators of political crises

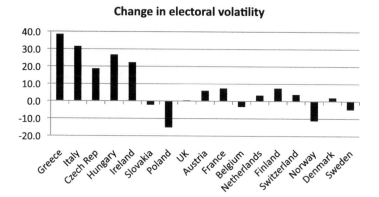

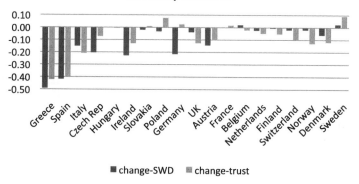

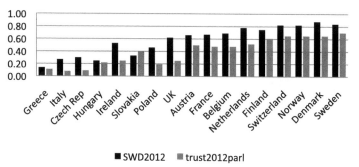

who trust their national parliament as well as the share of respondents who are very or fairly satisfied with the way democracy works in their country (SWD). The second graph in Figure 1.4 shows the difference between pre- and post-crisis measures of trust in parliament and SWD. Both SWD and trust in parliament have decreased across Europe during the crisis years. The only exceptions to the general pattern are Poland and Sweden, where trust in parliament has actually increased. The greatest loss of trust and satisfaction occurred in Greece, Italy, the Czech Republic and Ireland. In Hungary, another country hit hard by the crisis, there was no loss of trust or satisfaction, but as is shown in the third graph in Figure 1.4, this is because both were already at very low levels. Note also the Austrian decline in SWD, as well as the decline in trust in parliament in the UK (where it was already rather low), Austria and Denmark.

To summarise our six indicators for political crises – the three differences and the three levels in 2012, we perform again a factor analysis. The results are presented in the second part of Table 1.1. The six items all belong to the same underlying factor, which suggests that they are all indicators of a political crisis. As it turns out, both types of crises are closely correlated ($r=.71$): economic crises tend to go together with political crises. However, the correlation is not perfect.

Table 1.2: Summary indicators of economic and political crisis by country: countries ordered according to gravity of economic crisis

Country	Economic crisis	Political crisis
Poland	−0.98	−0.30
Norway	−0.94	−1.13
Switzerland	−0.75	−0.87
Sweden	−0.72	−1.07
Belgium	−0.65	−0.57
Austria	−0.45	−0.34
Denmark	−0.33	−0.96
Slovakia	−0.25	0.08
Finland	−0.13	−0.45
France	−0.10	−0.23
Netherlands	−0.10	−0.48
Italy	−0.08	1.54
Czech Rep	0.14	1.20
Hungary	0.57	1.08
UK	0.73	−0.37
Greece	1.80	2.24
Ireland	2.23	0.64
Total	0.00	0.00

Table 1.2, which provides the country-scores on the two indicators, sorted according to the gravity of the economic crisis, confirms that the two crises tend to go together. There are only two countries, Italy and Slovakia, which have not been as hard hit by the Great Recession as the five countries that took an above average hit, but which have suffered from a serious political crisis. On the other hand, there is only one country, the UK, which has not experienced a political crisis according to the indicators used here, although it has been relatively hard hit by the economic crisis.

Combining the two indicators provides us with a typology of countries according to the incidence of the two crises. For this typology, we dichotomise each summary indicator at its respective mean. This procedure implies that we perceive a domestic crisis relative to the situation in the other countries of our sample. Table 1.3 presents the typology. Given that the two types of crises tend to occur together, the majority of the countries are located in the main diagonal of concordant combinations. Ireland, Greece, Hungary and the Czech Republic belong to the group of countries that cumulate both types of crises. The UK just had an economic crisis; Slovakia and Italy are classified as having experienced only a political crisis. According to this rough classification, the remaining ten countries experienced neither a sharp economic, nor a serious political crisis: Austria, Belgium, Denmark, Finland, France, The Netherlands, Norway, Poland, Sweden and Switzerland.

This classification is exclusively based on the limited number of elements we used here. With respect to political crises, additional criteria, which are more country-specific, may have also played a role. Among them are political scandals or government crises. Thus, Finland experienced a major political scandal concerning election finances in 2008–11, which has certainly added to crisis perceptions in the crucial 2011 crisis election. In Belgium, the problems of government formation caused a serious political crisis, which we do not capture by our indicators either: after the 2010 elections, government formation took a record number of 543 days. In the final analysis, whether a country experiences an economic or political crisis crucially depends on the public's perception of the situation in a given country. And the perception, in turn, very much depends on the standard of comparison. The standard of comparison our typology rests upon does not take into account country-specific criteria. The perception of a crisis may, however, be determined relative to a given country's experience rather than in internationally comparative terms. Thus, if the French compare the

Table 1.3: Typology of crises

Economic crisis	Political crisis	
	Weak impact	**Strong impact**
Weak impact	AU, BE, DK, FIN, FR, NL, NO, POL, SWE, SWI	ITA, SLK
Strong impact	UK	CZ HU, GR, IRE

economic situation in their own country with that of Germany, they may sense a deep 'malaise', even if their country has fared rather well compared to the overall mean. The country chapters will build on our admittedly rough typology and, based on more detailed knowledge of the country-specific situation, may modify the overall assessments which we propose here.

Organisation of the volume

For each country, we have asked the authors to construct a 'timeline of crisis' from mid-2008 to late 2013. After locating the peaks of the crisis and all significant events associated with it (such as elections, mass mobilisations, or other social disturbances) each author will analyse the discourse of the parties identified as populist, thus producing a 'barometer of populism' during the long crisis. When that barometer shows high 'pressure', the authors look at whether new populist parties have emerged or old mainstream parties have turned into populists. They also examine the intensity of populism and try to assess the relative weight of the populist appeals. For, as Stanley (2008: 108) notes: 'At any given point, certain [populist] parties and social movements will be 'more populist' than others' and some may even develop populism as a 'full ideology'. Be that as it may, we aim at a qualitative description of populist phenomena during crisis based on the following sources of political communication: speeches by party leaders, party manifestos, press releases and other materials from party websites, party newspapers and depending on author selection, twitter messaging. The authors of the country chapters have resorted to different ways of assessing the quality of the populist discourse of the protagonists in their respective countries. Some have used more qualitative, others more quantitative measures. All, however, have tried to gauge the development of populist discourse throughout the period covered.

In each country case, the authors proceed at four steps:

— *Populism until 2008.* They (a) map the populist parties/forces in the respective country by 2008 and assess their electoral strength; (b) make sense of the variation within the country; (c) examine the political discourse used and key messages transmitted by such populist parties up to that point.

— *Economic crisis, 2008 onwards.* They (a) establish variation relative to the crisis' economic impact; (b) examine post-2008 patterns of political crisis in the country.

— *Post-crisis populism.* They (a) examine whether/how old populist parties reacted to the crisis; (b) examine whether/which new populist forces have emerged because of the crisis; (c) analyse the new political discourse used by the new populists as enriched by crisis-related themes. Who is to blame for the crisis?

— *New electoral politics.* They (a) examine post-crisis electoral politics as the chief manifestation of new populist politics in Europe; (b) assess both the nature and strength of new populist parties/forces; (c) discuss the reasons of success/failure of such parties by placing particular emphasis on the interplay between economic *and* political factors.

The country cases are presented by region. We begin with the two regions, where right-wing populist parties have risen long before the Great Recession intervened as a result of the 'demarcation-integration' conflict that we have already mentioned – the Nordic and West European countries. Compared to the European average, for both groups of countries the impact of the Great Recession has been rather benign. We follow with the two Southern European countries in our sample, which have been particularly hard hit by the Great Recession. In both of these countries, populism has already been rampant before the intervention of the Great Recession, too, but for reasons which are different from North-Western Europe: in Greece, populism represented the predominant mode of politics as it had permeated all major parties, while the Italian populism has been a product of the profound economic and political crisis in the early 1990s, which provided a particularly fertile ground for the populist reconstruction of the party system. Next, the experience of the Central and Eastern European countries is presented, before we come to the quite contrasting experience of the two Anglo-Celtic countries in our selection. We conclude by a systematic comparison of the country-experiences at the regional and, ultimately, at the European level.

PART I

THE NORDIC REGION

Chapter Two

Institutionalised Right-Wing Populism in Times of Economic Crisis: A Comparative Study of the Norwegian Progress Party and the Danish People's Party

Anders R. Jupskås

Introduction

It is widely held that different kinds of crises – political, economic or cultural – fuel populist support (e.g. Mudde 2004: 547; Laclau 1977: 196). Taggart (2004: 275), for example, argues that 'populism tends to emerge when there is a strong *sense* of crisis and populists use that sense to inject an urgency and an importance to their message'. The argument is that a crisis tends to delegitimise the existing political parties, which in turn creates a window of opportunity for new untainted political players claiming to represent the will of the people rather than the interests of the established elites. But how are populist parties affected by the existence of a crisis if they are already fairly integrated in the respective party system at the time that the crisis emerged?

This chapter compares the impact of an economic crisis on two institutionalised right-wing populist parties, namely *Fremskrittspartiet* (The Progress Party, FrP) in Norway and *Dansk Folkeparti* (Danish People's Party, DF) in Denmark. More specifically, the chapter will analyse how these two parties were affected discursively and electorally by the international financial crisis which emerged in late 2008. Moreover, while the study is primarily concerned with the impact of the crisis, the Danish and Norwegian cases also allow for an intra- and interparty comparison of the electoral and discursive effects of government participation. While the DF moved from being a stable support party of the Danish government to a clearer role as an opposition party in the post-crisis period, the FrP moved the other way entering office for the first time.

Following the general guidelines given in the introduction of this edited volume, this chapter proceeds as follows. The first section briefly sketches out the general evolution, ideological legacy and degree of institutionalisation of FrP and DF in the pre-crisis period. Then, the impact of the international financial crisis in Norway and Denmark will be systematically assessed based on standard economic indicators such as growth rates, unemployment and public debt. However, acknowledging that crises tend to be evaluated in relative terms, the development of the economy of these two countries will also be seen from a European and regional perspective. The third section focuses on the discursive development – the populist elements as well as other core ideological features – of the two right-wing populist parties in the post-crisis period, including a comparison of the period in which these parties were in government (or supporting the government) with the period in which they were in opposition. Since the DF has not published any new electoral manifestos in the post-crisis period, the data are primarily internal party magazines (i.e. *Dansk Folkeblad* for the DF and *Fremskritt* for the FrP). The fourth and final section considers the complex interplay between the international financial crisis, the discursive reaction of the populist parties, their position inside or outside the government and their electoral development. Some of the main findings will be summarised towards the end of the chapter.

Populism until 2008: Institutionalised right-wing populism

Prior to the financial crisis, right-wing populism in Scandinavia was in contrast to many, if not most other countries in Europe, characterised by long-lasting presence and high level of institutionalisation, which means that the parties existed as 'social organisation apart from its momentary leaders' and that they demonstrated 'recurring patterns of behaviour valued by those who identify with it' (Janda 1970: 88). Populism, defined as a specific thin ideology which pits the ordinary and virtuous people against the corrupt and ignorant elite (Stanley 2008; Mudde 2004) and which is often led by a charismatic leader (Zaslove 2008), emerged as a political force already in the so-called 'electoral earthquakes' in 1973 in both Denmark and Norway (e.g. Andersen and Bjørklund 1990). While *Fremskridtspartiet* (The Progress Party, FrPd) gained 15.9 per cent in Denmark, Anders Lange's *parti til sterk nedsettelse av skatter, avgifter og offentlige inngrep* (Anders Lange's Party for a Strong Reduction in Taxes, Duties and Public Intervention, ALP) gained 5 per cent of the votes in Norway.

As part of what von Beyme (1988) calls the 'second wave' of far right mobilisation in postwar Europe, these parties were primarily anti-tax movements rather than nationalist parties. Both FrPd and ALP were organised around rather charismatic leaders who frequently committed a breach of established political etiquette; tax lawyer Mogens Glistrup and editor Anders Lange in Denmark and Norway respectively. Programmatically, they were opposing rising taxes, growing bureaucracy, expansion of the Scandinavian welfare state and foreign aid. The two leaders were particularly hostile towards the established parties, though Glistrup also criticised bureaucrats and intellectuals (Bjørklund 1981: 4).

Contemporary right-wing populist parties are either an organisational continuation with a different name (as in Norway) or a split party (as in Denmark) of the parties which entered the party systems in the early 1970s. In Norway, the ALP changed its name to FrP a few months before the national election in 1977. At this point, the party had already experienced a temporary party split; abysmal results in the sub-national elections in 1975; and demonstrated low levels of parliamentary cohesion. The party elite was profoundly divided as to what extent a more traditional organisational structure was needed, and without Lange who died unexpectedly in 1974, the party dropped out of parliament in 1977.

The electoral loss created a 'window of opportunity' for Carl I. Hagen, a former secretary of the ALP, who was elected chairman in 1978 and remained so until 2006. With Hagen as a media-savvy and charismatic chairman, the party slowly regained its electoral strength and started building a traditional organisation combining the logic of mass party and business firm (Jupskås 2014). The ideological appeal, however, remained fairly constant, though the party drifted towards Kitschelt's (1995) famous winning formula in the 1980s – namely, a comprehensive and explicit neoliberal, xenophobic and authoritarian position (Bjørklund and Andersen 2002). While this appeal seemed to be electorally successful, it simultaneously reinforced – together with the increased saliency of the European Union (EU) question in the Norwegian public debate in the early 1990s – existing tensions between a liberal, a nationalist, and a Christian-conservative faction. Internal disagreements were repeatedly played out in public, and popular support decreased rapidly. After an agonising party convention in 1994, the liberal faction – including part of the party leadership, a majority of the youth organisation, and four members of parliament – left the party.

In contrast to the Danish party, which was never able to recover from a similar though not identical party split in mid-1990s (*see* next section), the Norwegian party rapidly re-gained its electoral and organisational strength. Ideologically, the party became more pro-welfare at the beginning of the 2000s, while simultaneously remaining the most right-wing oriented party in Norway on most economic issues (e.g. taxes, privatisation, economic incentives, labour market and trade unions) and, with a few exceptions, the most authoritarian on cultural issues (Jungar and Jupskås 2014: 9). The paradoxical position of being in favour of more welfare and drastic tax cuts at the same time was mainly resolved by suggesting that Norway should spend more of the income from the oil industry today, rather than saving the revenues for future generations and growing welfare expenses. In terms of Norwegian membership in the EU, the party has no official position as it remains fundamentally divided among voters, members, and members of parliament (Jupskås 2013: 217–18).

In this period, the party also became (more) institutionalised, at least according to the indicators suggested by Janda (1970: 88–89). Electoral support and legislative representation were stabilised, and even though the leadership succession from Carl I. Hagen to Siv Jensen in 2006 did not involve 'an overt process of criticism' (Janda 1970: 89), the party proved to be fully capable of survival without its longstanding chairman and party builder. Actually, with Jensen as chairman, the party increased its electoral support in the subnational elections in 2007.

When the financial crisis emerged towards the end of 2008, the FrP was the dominant right-wing party in Norway. In fact, according to opinion polls, the party was twice the size of the Conservative Party. Yet it was the only parliamentary party without governmental experience. Although the FrP had been office-seeking since the early 2000s, it was not perceived as *salonfähig* by the other non-socialist parties in 2001 or 2005. Suffering from limited influence in opposition and experiencing a generation shift among party elites, however, the non-socialist parties gradually accepted the FrP as governing party. Thus, when the incumbent left-centre coalition lost in 2013, all four non-socialist parties joined the government negotiations resulting in a minority government with the Conservatives and the FrP.

The DF is a more recent party formation than the FrP, but the legacy connects it to the political earthquake in the early 1970s. The party was founded in 1995 after several prominent MPs defected from the FrPd, most notably the former chairman, Pia Kjærsgaard. Initially, the main difference between the two right-wing populist parties in Denmark was not related to ideology, but related to party organisation and parliamentary behaviour; the party elite in DF wanted a party with a more centralised organisation and reliable behaviour *vis-à-vis* other non-socialist parties (Ringsmose and Pedersen 2005; Meret 2010). However, the DF also gradually developed a new ideological position. The party adopted a more explicit nationalist position: anti-immigration and Euroscepticism became two of the party's core issues. Moreover, it slowly abandoned the anti-tax and anti-welfare position promoted by FrPd (Meret 2010: 102ff).

DF quickly replaced the FrPd as the dominant right-wing populist party at the Danish electoral arena. Already in 2001, the FrPd failed to pass the electoral threshold, whereas the splinter party increased its electoral support to 12 per cent (up from 7.4 per cent in 1998). And even though the party was probably still quite leadership-dependent prior to the financial crisis (e.g. Andersen and Borre 2007), it had become quite institutionalised (again according the indicators suggested by Janda). Most importantly, the DF did not experience any organisational discontinuity (although one MP defected in 2007), and both the legislative and electoral stability were remarkable compared to the FrPd, especially since the early 1980s. In the national elections in 2005 and 2007, the party gained 13.2 and 13.8 of the votes respectively, and the number of MPs have only varied between twenty-two (in 2001) and twenty-five (in 2007).

This process of institutionalisation is perhaps all the more impressive knowing that the party simultaneously was a stable support party of the Danish right-wing minority government which seized office after the national election in 2001. Although the party did not hold any government portfolios, it was included in almost all legislation including the preparation of the bills. Moreover, the government consistently passed the annual state budget with DF's support – ten in total between 2001 and 2011 (Christiansen 2012). In the mainstream media, the government was symbolically labelled the VKO-government, which represents the Liberals, the Conservatives and DF respectively. In the first years of the financial crisis, the DF was therefore closely linked with the incumbent government and expected to support (at least some of) the policies proposed by the Liberals and the Conservatives. However, this political situation changed when the right-wing block (i.e. Liberals, Conservatives and DF) lost its majority in the first post-crisis election in 2011, and was replaced by a centre-left government (i.e. Social Democrats, Socialists and Social Liberals). Consequently, DF lost its pivotal position as government support party.

To summarise briefly, then, both Norway and Denmark had right-wing populist parties that were electorally successful and institutionalised prior to the outbreak of the international financial crisis. They were both characterised by legislative and electoral stability, as well as organisational continuity. And while the DF to some extent remained a highly personalised party though not a 'personal party' (McDonnell 2013), the FrP had demonstrated its ability to outlive its long-standing chairman and 'party builder'. Ideologically, the two parties were both characterised by anti-immigration policies, anti-establishment rhetoric and a pro-welfare position. However, only the Norwegian party promoted a neoliberal economic agenda with massive tax cuts, privatisation and less bureaucracy, and only the Danish party promoted a soft Eurosceptic position. Before analysing the extent to which these two institutionalised right-wing populist parties have been affected discursively or electorally by the emerging international financial crisis, the next section will briefly assess the domestic economic development in the two Scandinavian countries in the post-crisis period.

Diverging patterns of economic crisis

To what extent has there been an economic crisis in Denmark and Norway since the beginning of the international financial crisis in 2008? The answer obviously depends on how we conceptualise and operationalise 'an economic crisis'. Generally speaking, an economic crisis refers to a situation in which there is a rapid and profound slowdown of the national economy. This kind of crisis is well captured by economic indicators such as (1) annual growth of the gross domestic product (GDP), (2) unemployment rates, and (3) the level of public debt (*see* also the introductory chapter of this edited volume). However, in addition to these objective indicators measuring the current situation of the national economy, there is also a subjective or relative aspect inherent in the notion of a being in a state of crisis. Given that the baseline for evaluating the economic situation in a particular country is usually affected by previous experience and/or the situation in 'similar countries' (e.g. countries in geographical proximity, same size or shared cultural legacy), there might be a feeling of crisis even though the national economy performs relatively well. This relative aspect of the crisis is particularly important when assessing the Danish development.

Being two small and open economies, neither Denmark nor Norway were unaffected by the international financial crisis in 2008. The economic activity in both these two countries is highly interwoven with other countries, most notably in Europe and North-America.[1] Despite the economic openness, however, only Denmark experienced an economic crisis based on the aforementioned indicators,

---

1. In 2012, Denmark's most important trading partners were Germany, Sweden, UK, US, Norway and The Netherlands, whereas Norway's most important partners were UK, Germany, The Netherlands, France, Sweden and US (CIA World Fact Book, 2012).

though the Danish economy was never equally weakened as the ones in the PIGS-countries (i.e. Portugal, Italy, Greece and Spain). The Norwegian economy, on the other hand, remained exceptionally strong.

In Norway, the GDP annual growth first decreased from 2.7 per cent in 2007 to around zero in 2008, before turning negative in late 2008 and early 2009 for the first time in many years (e.g. Cappelen and Torbjørn 2010). Yet, in contrast to almost all other countries which experienced a temporary setback, the Norwegian economy recovered rapidly and the annual growth exceeded 2 per cent in 2012. Furthermore, the unemployment rate remained at a very low level throughout the crisis. While there was a small increase between April 2008 and April 2010, the unemployment rate never exceeded 4 per cent between 2008 and 2013. The only social group which was strongly affected by the international crisis was foreign workers in the construction industry (Ekeland *et al.* 2009). In fact, some of public policies implemented by the incumbent government improved rather than aggravated the economic situation for many Norwegians (e.g. those burdened with large interest payments) (Jenssen and Kalstø 2012).

Last but not least, due to the large sovereign wealth fund owned by the government, the public debt in Norway continued to be insignificant. While most other countries have experienced a substantial increase in the level of gross public debt (as percentage of GDP) since 2009, it has actually decreased in Norway (from 51.5 per cent in 2007 to 29.5 per cent in 2013). Moreover, if we calculate the net government debt, taking the large sovereign funds into consideration, the Norwegian economy is in a league if its own, even compared to other countries which were largely unaffected by the financial countries, such as Switzerland (*see* Figure 1.3).

In contrast to the Norwegian experience, the Danish economic development resembles the general patterns observed elsewhere in Europe. Most notably, the trajectory of the GDP growth rate reflects the general trajectory of the EU as a whole: limited decline from 2007 to 2008 (+1.6 to -0.8 per cent), extensive setbacks in 2009 (-5.7 per cent); slow recovery in 2010 and 2011 (1.4 and 1.1 per cent respectively) followed by a limited setback in 2012 (-0.4 per cent), before the growth rate again turned positive in 2013 (+0.4 per cent). Similarly, unemployment increased rapidly in 2009. From a stable and comparatively low level of between 3.1 and 4.2 per cent unemployment in the pre-crisis years, it doubled to more than 7 per cent throughout 2009 and remained above this level in the post-crisis years. In 2013, the unemployment rate decreased somewhat – especially in comparison with the overall trend in the EU – yet it was still above 7 per cent at the end of the year.

However, while these indicators – low or negative GDP growth in combination with rising unemployment – suggest a crisis of competitiveness, Denmark did not experience any sovereign debt crisis. Although public debt increased between 2008 and 2011, it was initially quite limited and since 2012 it has actually (slowly) decreased again (from 46.4 to 44.5 per cent). According to objective indicators, the Danish development may therefore not qualify as a state of crisis, at least not in a European perspective. The gravity of the economic crisis was much stronger in other European states, not only the PIGS-countries but also countries like The Netherlands (*see* introductory chapter). Moreover, as observed by Andersen (2013: 51), the Danish economy differed from Southern European economies in at least two important ways. First, Denmark had a strong balance-of-payments surplus and, secondly, there was a solid savings surplus in the private sector. Consequently, the creditworthiness of the Danish state remained strong in a comparative perspective.

Yet, from a national perspective, the Danish recession had historical dimensions. The 6.4 per cent decrease in GDP growth from 2008 to 2009 was three times larger than during the oil crisis in 1974–75 and 1980–81, and the harmonised unemployment figures (from OECD) were exceptionally high (Andersen 2013: 46–47). Moreover, compared to the neighbouring Scandinavian countries (Norway and Sweden), and perhaps also Finland (*see* Figure 1.3), Denmark's economy was performing poorly. This is due to the fact that the economic crisis in Denmark was not exclusively caused by the international financial crisis, but also related to domestic policies (e.g. Andersen 2011). The Danish economy had substantial problems even before the crisis: economic growth had been significantly low in comparison with other Nordic countries since the early 2000s and the country was already experiencing a growing housing and credit crisis when financial crisis emerged (Andersen 2013: 46). When the international crisis reached Denmark, these problems were reinforced and private consumption fell significantly by 3.2 per cent from 2007 to 2011 (Andersen 2013: 50). Only in Southern Europe, Iceland, Ireland and UK did private consumption decrease more. In sum, then, the Danish development may nevertheless qualify as crisis, even though the country did better than Southern Europe.

Post-crisis populism in Scandinavia

How and to what extent did the FrP and DF react discursively to the international financial crisis? In short, we would expect the reactions to be related to at least three factors: (1) the impact of the crisis, (2) the ideological legacy of the parties and (3) government participation. This means that DF is expected to pay more attention to the crisis than the FrP, not only because Denmark experienced an economic crisis (or at least an economic recession) whereas Norway did not, but also because the popular resentment in the wake of the financial crisis could be mobilised more easily using DF's ideological framework (i.e. soft Euroscepticism and centrist economic policy) than FrP's position (i.e. EU-ambivalence and neoliberal populism). However, given that government participation put constraints on the anti-elitist and redemptive aspect of the populist discourse, we would expect the DF's discourse to be fairly moderate until the party returned to opposition after the 2011 election. The FrP, on other hand, is expected first to be discursively unaffected (as there was no crisis) and then to tone down its populist rhetoric as party entered government in late 2013.

When the economic crisis reached Denmark, DF had been a stable support party for the Danish government for many years. Its self-presentation in the party magazines suggests that it tried to maintain the image of a 'responsible party' concerned with the welfare of the Danish people. For example, the state budget for 2009 was presented as success despite unfavourable 'economic realities' (Dansk Folkeblad 2008/6: 4). According to the party, it had been able to combine responsible economic policies with favourable policies for Danish household and basic welfare arrangements, most notably healthcare and geriatric care. And rather than exploiting the crisis to distance the party from its liberal-conservative coalition partners, Kjærsgaard called for cross-partisan cooperation among right-wing parties in order to fight rising unemployment and lack of economic growth (Dansk Folkeblad 2010/2: 3).

Before the elections in 2011, the party continued to emphasise its 'responsible' behaviour during the crisis. Tax cuts, which had been decided upon in 2009–10, were re-negotiated upon in order to 'find money to cover the holes that the international crisis had created in the Danish economy' (Dansk Folkeblad 2011/2: 2). Moreover, whereas the left-liberal opposition (Social Democrats, Socialist People's Party and Social Liberals) was accused of having a completely unrealistic economic plan, DF campaigned on the need for a 'tight political control of Denmark's finances'. As argued by Kjærsgaard, 'this is no time for political and economic experiments – or economic fantasy solutions' (Dansk Folkeblad 2011/4: 3).

More generally, the crisis was explicitly used by DF to promote traditional policies and ideological positions. The negative impact of the financial crisis was at least partly connected to a failed common currency in Europe (the euro) (Dansk Folkeblad 2009/special issue: 16–17), as well as it, according to DF, reinforced the need for strict immigration policies and welfare chauvinism (Dansk Folkeblad 2010/1: 2): 'Foreigners in Denmark are an economic burden, and the more of them, the less resources for welfare to those who legitimately deserves it'.

Furthermore, even though DF has drifted leftwards in terms of economic policies and has become more pro-welfare in recent decades, the party did not interpret economic problems as a symptom of a failed capitalist system. In fact, according to the party, capitalism is not even 'a system' or 'an ideology' – it simply means 'freedom' (Dansk Folkeblad, 2009/1: 1). Instead of calling for more regulations and state control, the party warned against left-wing parties trying to exploit the crisis to re-introduce socialist economic policies (e.g. economic democracy at the workplace and nationalisation of the banking sector) (Dansk Folkeblad 2009/1: 1). According to DF, the economic crisis in Denmark was best explained by various international events and irresponsible behaviour of the chief executives of certain Danish banks. For example, the director of the Danish bank Roskilde, the first bank to be saved by the state, was presented as a selfish, upper-class leader unable to take responsibility for the damage he had created (Dansk Folkeblad 2013/2: 16).

After the party lost its pivotal position in the Danish parliament in 2011 and Kjærsgaard was replaced by Kristian Thulesen Dahl as the party chairman, it seems as if the party's discourse became somewhat more focused on economic issues and anti-establishment oriented. As a new chairman, Thulesen Dahl highlighted two policy areas in which DF should play an important role: immigration policies and saving the Danish economy (Dansk Folkeblad 2012/5: 3). Kjærsgaard also underlined Thulesen Dahl's competence in economic issues when he was elected (Dansk Folkeblad 2012/5: 7). At the party convention in 2012 addressing those who argued that Thulesen Dahl was an uncharismatic political 'geek', she rhetorically asked: '[...]is it not good to know something about the (state) economy when we need to be in control of it and fight unemployment?'

In recent years, DF has repeatedly attacked the left-liberal government – the 'Radikale misregimente' as Kjærsgaard calls it (Dansk Folkeblad 2012/5: 7) – or the political elite in Brussels. The domestic government has been presented as an agent working for the interests of multinational companies rather than small-scale Danish industry and as a political agent completely uninterested in the situation for Danish workers who have lost their jobs due to poor economic growth. Moreover, DF has argued that the government actively facilitates the import of cheap labour from Eastern Europe reinforcing an already difficult situation for Danish workers. The current Prime Minister Helle Thorning Schmidt (the Social Democrats) is presented as 'a European at heart' rather than a politician who defends the interests of the Danish people (Dansk Folkeblad 2012/5: 7).

The other main enemy in DF's discourse is the EU elite. Indeed, the euro crisis and political situation in Southern Europe (most notably in Greece) has reinforced DF's soft Euroscepticism. The economic crisis in general and in Southern Europe in particular is explained as the consequence of a common currency and lack of economic reforms. The main elites to be blamed are the following: 'the EU-elite', the Central Bank in Frankfurt, 'intellectuals' who try to replace a national identity with a European identity (Dansk Folkeblad 2010/2: 15–16), the European Parliament (Dansk Folkeblad 2012/2: 17) and 'follower parties' (i.e. pro-EU parties).

According to Messerschmidt, the party's MEP, the EU suffers from 'democratic schizophrenia' in the sense that it promotes democracy only when its serves the purpose of the elite in Brussels (Dansk Folkeblad 2010/2: 16). Messerschmidt has also argued that the current EU-elites are driven by 'ideology' rather than 'common sense': due to an unrealistic and national-hostile dream of a United States of Europe, the elites have developed 'tunnel vision' and allegedly lost all contact with the reality. The European Parliament is depicted as a group of politicians aiming for 'draining the nation-states of political and economic content – the faster, the better' (Dansk Folkeblad 2012/2: 17). Especially the 'Fiscal Compact' signed by all member states in 2012 (except UK) is seen as the first step towards the 'United States of Europe' (Dansk Folkeblad 2012/2: 17). However, DF continues to promote soft rather than hard Euroscepticism; the party does not want Denmark to leave the EU, but rather that the EU should be transformed from within and that its powers should be reduced to its minimum. European collaboration should be restricted to maintenance of the 'internal market' (Dansk Folkeblad 2013/3–4: 14). Moreover, the European Parliament should be dissolved and the EU should only address challenges that due to their nature cannot be dealt with nationally (Dansk Folkeblad 2010/2: 16).

In general, DF is more concerned with the elite in Brussels than with other kinds of people in the EU. However, MEP Messerschmidt has warned against so-called 'welfare tourism' and social 'shopping' as potential consequences of having Bulgaria and Romania entering the EU (Dansk Folkeblad 2013/3–4: 15). Moreover, he – and presumably the party – is against giving more money to what he calls a 'bottomless Greek hole'. The only solution, according to Messerschmidt, is that the Greek state should be declared bankrupt (Dansk Folkeblad 2011/3).

As to be expected, the financial crisis and economic development in the EU receives much less attention by the FrP compared to DF. Initially, when the financial crisis was still discussed in Norwegian politics, the FrP tried to challenge the conventional interpretation of the crisis. After all, the crisis had been interpreted as the result of dysfunctional neoliberal policies, a policy position which had been associated with the FrP. According to former party chairman Carl I. Hagen, this interpretation was completely wrong: the crisis was not the result of too little regulation, but the result of too much regulation, that is, too much left-wing policies. More specifically, Hagen argued that 'a combination of congress politicians (especially Democrats), academics, social activists, regulation institutions and the Clinton government' should be blamed for the collapse of the Lehman Brothers (Fremskritt 2008/22: 16). In a similar vein, another prominent MP, Christian Tybring-Gjedde, claimed that Prime Minister Stoltenberg engaged in 'history forgery' when he criticised 'the market' and that he was 'lying' about the causes of the financial crisis (Fremskritt 2010/11: 7). According to Tybring-Gjedde, the crisis was caused by too much state intervention, not by market failures. Other youth party members have repeatedly presented similar arguments (e.g. Fremskritt 2012/7: 9). One youth member even argued that the popular reaction against the financial crisis (particularly in the US) was in fact a reaction against communism rather than capitalism (Fremskritt 2011/6: 17).

FrP also tried to undermine the role played by the centre-left government in diminishing the impact of the crisis on the Norwegian economy and labour market. According to party representatives, the good management was the least to be expected. Hagen, for example, argued that the government would have had to be composed by 'idiots' (*pappskaller*) in order not to manage the Norwegian economy safely through the international crisis (Fremskritt 2010/19: 6).

Similar to the Danish case, FrP reacted predictably to the crisis as it tried to present itself as the only truly responsible party. It suggested that massive tax cuts (twenty-nine billion kroner) would ensure that Norway would get through the crisis without rising unemployment figures (Fremskritt 2008/22: 14). The financial spokesman argued that the emerging crisis in Europe reinforced the need for FrP's policies: work longer, reduce social benefits, reward work efforts, spend less and invest more, create incentives for investments, and focus on relevant vocational education (Tybring-Gjedde in Fremskritt 2013/6: 12), whereas the vice-chairman claimed that Norway should decrease taxes to secure the country's competitiveness (Solvik-Olsen in Fremskritt 2013/5: 15). All these right-wing policies were presented as particularly beneficial for 'ordinary people' and the 'business sector'. However, at least at one point in time, the crisis was instrumentally used by the

FrP to promote social populism. In 2008, when there was still uncertainty about the impact of the crisis in Norway, the party suggested that the poorest in society should be offered 2,000 kroner each before Christmas (the proposal was estimated to cost around 100 million euros) (Fremskritt 2008/23: 3).

Furthermore, FrP tried to present itself as the only responsible party (Fremskritt 2012/4: 12). Against the backdrop of economic problems in Europe, vice-chairman Per Sandberg argued that the FrP was the only party that would invest more of Norwegian oil fund in 'the future', namely infrastructure and education. The Prime Minister, on the other hand, was accused for having 'created a false safety'. (Interestingly for a party that normally opposes economists, Sandberg's argument was almost exclusively based upon the arguments of Professor Erik Reinert). The incumbent government was also presented as being more concerned with 'political fads' than listening to the experts (who happened to agree with some of the policy proposals from the FrP) and the victims of the crisis. Siv Jensen, the party leader, even speculated that Prime Minister Jens Stoltenberg (Labour Party) was intentionally avoiding any measurements against increasing unemployment due to vote-seeking strategies (Fremskritt 2008/22: 14).

The economic crisis was also used to warn against increased 'welfare exportation', immigration from Eastern Europe and rising criminality (Fremskritt 2012/7: 13; 2012/4: 4). Against the backdrop of the final report from the Government-appointed Welfare and Migration Committee (Brochmann-utvalget), the FrP suggested to decrease the level of welfare benefits to labour immigrants. MP Robert Eriksson said that Norway cannot become 'Europe's office for social security' (Fremskritt 2012/18: 19) in times of crisis and he continued in an alarmist fashion: 'it has been said that 500 million people in Europe are ready to milk money from the Norwegian government. I'm not paranoid, but the possibility is there'.

The enemies in the FrP's discourse are more or less identical with the pre-crisis enemies. Most importantly, the party opposes 'socialist parties' or 'the left-wing' (Fremskritt 2011/6: 17). However, vice-chairman Per Sandberg specifically mentioned the following four enemies: Prime Minister Stoltenberg who portrays himself as 'an economic gift from god', the Labour Party which 'governs Norway in the trench with open eyes', and the bureaucracy which is 'strangling the Norwegian house and the Norwegian model' and the Schengen agreement which turns Norway into a welfare 'buffet' (Fremskritt 2013/5: 12). Party leader Jensen continued to frame politics in a populist fashion: the FrP will 'challenge established parties; speak up against the powers, and be the defender of the little man' (Jensen quoted in Fremskritt 2013/5: 6). The enemies of the people are journalists, pundits and political opponents. According to Jensen, the FrP has 'never been a party which has listened to technocrats and bureaucrats'. On the contrary, the FrP 'listen to people who live ordinary lives, with ordinary challenges'.

After the FrP entered government in late 2013, the party became significantly less anti-establishment oriented. While it continued to present itself as the party for *'folk flest'* (ordinary people) (Fremskritt 2013/16: 2–3, 15), the traditional criticism of political and/or other kinds of societal elites have rarely been expressed, at least in the magazines. In fact, there have been only a few sporadic statements that could be interpreted as a populist critique of the elite (e.g. claims that the previous government was hiding unpaid bills; and that the pundits and experts completely underestimated the FrP's ability to govern). Instead, the party elite seems to have been predominantly preoccupied with lowering the expectations of the activists, partly by repeating what they have already achieved in terms of policy change on key issues (e.g. law and order, immigration, care for the elderly, and road constructions), and partly by stressing that government participation involves compromises and political losses (Fremskritt 2013/15: 2–3; Fremskritt 2013/18). To summarise briefly, the post-crisis populist discourse of DF and the FrP does not differ much from the pre-crisis discourse. On the contrary, the crisis has primarily sought to reinforce traditional policies advocated by these two parties: Euroscepticism in the case of DF and neoliberal populism in the case of the FrP. The enemies of the parties follow a recognisable pattern: social democratic prime ministers and left-wing/socialist parties. The elites in Brussels (or Frankfurt) are also important figures in DF's discourse. None of the parties viewed the crisis as a symptom of failed capitalist policies. Instead, they warned against traditional left-wing policies and especially the FrP promoted neoliberal populism as a political solution to the crisis. With regard to discursive effects of government participation, both parties seem to be less populist while in power (as the FrP since late 2013) or supporting parties in power (as DF before late 2011).

Populist mobilisation in times of crisis?

So far the chapter has only discussed the discursive effects of the international financial crisis on right-wing populist parties in Norway and Denmark. This fourth section will assess to what extent and how the international financial crisis had any impact on the popular support of the FrP and DF comparing the pre-crisis and post-crisis period. However, before addressing the development of these two parties in detail, two remarks should be made concerning the overall electoral and political context in the two Scandinavian countries (*see* Tables 2.1 and 2.2).

First, despite rather substantial differences in economic development in the two countries in the post-crisis period – with relatively poor performance in Denmark and rapid recovery in Norway – both countries were, at least initially, characterised by electoral stability: (1) only two new minor parties (i.e. the Greens in Norway and the neoliberal Liberal Alliance in Denmark) have entered the national parliament, (2) changes in electoral turnout has basically been insignificant, and (3) the levels of gross volatility has either been stable (as in Denmark) or actually decreasing (as in Norway). More recently, however, the stability has been challenged, especially in Denmark. The Social Democrats and the Socialists have been hit hard by popular dissatisfaction with government policies. While the two parties polled more than 40 per cent (the joint support in June 2010 was incredibly 47 per cent) in the months prior to the national election, recent opinion polls show less than 25 per cent support. In fact, in April 2013, they barely passed 20 per cent. Together with the far-left (Unity List), DF seems to be one of the parties which have benefitted the most from the resentment *vis-à-vis* the incumbent centre-left government (e.g. Skadhede 2014).

Table 2.1: General elections in Norway (2005–13) (in per cent)

		2005	**2009**	**2013**	**05–09**	**05–13**
Left-wing	Socialist Left (SV)	8.8	6.2	4.1	−2.6	−4.7
	Labour (Ap)	32.7	35.4	30.8	+2.3	−1.9
Centrist	Agrarian (Sp)	6.5	6.2	5.5	−0.3	−1.0
	The Greens (MDG)	0.1	0.3	2.8	+0.2	+2.7
	Christian People's Party (KrF)	6.8	5.5	5.6	−1.3	−1.2
	Liberals (V)	5.9	3.9	5.2	−2.0	−0.7
Right-wing	Conservatives (H)	14.1	17.2	26.8	+3.1	+12.7
	Progress Party (FrP)	22.1	22.9	16.3	+0.9	−5.8
Turnout		77.4	76.4	78.2	−1	+0.8
Gross volatility*		47	39	39	−8	0

Source: Norway statistics and Aardal *et al.* (2014).

Table 2.2: General elections in Denmark (2007–11) (in per cent)

		2007	**2011**	**07–11**
Left-wing	Unity List (EL)	2.2	6.7	+4.5
	Socialist People's Party (SF)	13.0	9.2	−3.8
	Social democrats (S)	25.5	24.8	−0.7
Centrist	Social Liberals (RV)	5.1	9.5	+4.4
	Christian Democrats (KD)	0.9	0.8	−0.1
Right-wing	Liberal Alliance* (LA)	2.8	5.0	+2.2
	The Conservatives (K)	10.4	4.9	−5.5
	The Liberals (V)	26.2	26.7	+0.5
	Danish People's Party (DF)	13.9	12.3	−1.6
Turnout		86.6	87.7	+1.1
Gross volatility*		32	33	+1

Source: Stubager *et al.* (2013: 27, 30). *Liberal Alliance was called 'New Alliance' in 2007.

Secondly, both countries have experienced government alternation in the post-crisis period. In Denmark, a right-wing government of the Liberals and the Conservatives was replaced by a centre-left government of the Socialist, Social Democrats and the Social Liberals after the national election in 2011.[2] None of the Danish governments have controlled a majority of the seats in parliament and they have been dependent upon parliamentary support from the far-right (as in the first case) or far-left (as in the latter). However, in contrast to the first government which consistently collaborated with DF, the current centre-left government has collaborated both ways (i.e. to the left and to the right, though not with DF). In Norway, the centre-left majority government consisting of the Socialists, Labour and agrarian Centre Party was just barely re-elected in 2009, before it was replaced by a right-wing minority government consisting of the Conservatives and the FrP after the 2013 national election. Lacking a parliamentary majority, the government has established a formalised policy agreement with two centrist parties (the Liberals and the Christian People's Party).

Within the context of electoral stability and government alternation, the two right-wing populist parties have experienced completely divergent trajectories of popular support. The support for the FrP decreased significantly in the polls immediately after Lehmann Brothers was declared bankrupt at the end of 2008 (Narud 2011: 234). While FrP had been Norway's largest party enjoying support from more than 30 per cent of the voters in August 2008, the party received 23–24 per cent in January 2009. In the national elections later the same year, the party gained 22.9 per cent, which despite being an all-time high result was perceived as disappointing given the recent success in the polls. After the national elections, the party continued to drop in the polls, and in April 2011, the FrP fell below 20 per cent for the first time since August 2005. The local elections a few months later turned out to be a disaster for the party. With 11.4 per cent in municipality election, the FrP obtained its worst result since the early 1990s. Almost one third of the party's local representatives were not re-elected. And while the party temporarily re-gained some of the electoral strength at the national level receiving 16.3 per cent in the 2013 national election, recent surveys from early 2014 indicate a further decline in popular support to just below 14 per cent.[3]

In Denmark, the popular support for DF remained fairly stable in the first years of the post-crisis period. Although the party increased its share of votes in second order elections (most notably in the election to the European Parliament in 2009), it consistently polled between 12 and 15 per cent of the votes in surveys at the national level.[4] In the 2011 national election, it received 12.3 per cent, which

---

2. The Socialists, however, left the government in early 2014 due to an internal dispute involving the sale of shares in a state-owned energy company to Goldman Sachs.

3. Opinion polls refer to the mean score of different national polls. These scores are calculated and presented by Professor Bernt Aardal, University of Oslo. URL: http://www.aardal.info/partibarometre.html (accessed 18 July 2014.7.14).

4. Numbers are from TNS Gallup. URL: http://www2.tns-gallup.dk/nyhedscenter/statistik/politisk-indeks.aspx (accessed 18 July 2014).

represented only a small decline compared to the results in the first decade of the 2000s. After returning to opposition in 2011, however, the party has gradually increased its support – at a local, national and, not least, the European level. In March 2014, the party passed 20 per cent at the national level for the first time, and it became the largest party in Denmark with 26.6 per cent of the votes in the recent election to the European Parliament.

Two key factors seem to be crucial in order to explain the diverging patterns of popular support of the two right-wing populist parties: (1) new political opportunity structures caused by the emerging international financial crisis and, in Norway, a large-scale terrorist attack from an extreme-right activist, and (2) government participation. In short, while DF has benefitted from favourable opportunity structure and a more clear-cut oppositional role, the FrP suffered from an unfavourable opportunity structure and, more recently, government participation. In contrast to many other countries, the international financial crisis contributed to increased support for the incumbent government in Norway, and the Labour Party in particular (Narud 2011; Jenssen and Kalstø 2012). The voters reacted positively to the Keynesian counter-cyclical fiscal policies pursued by the government, and as many as 90 per cent believed the government handled the crisis well (Narud 2011: 235). The support was obviously strongest among centre-left voters, but even 82 per cent of the FrP's voters approved governmental policies. It thus became difficult to criticise the centre-left parties for being incompetent and irresponsive. A more long-term perspective on political trust also suggests that Norway may have become decreasingly receptive to populist politics (*see also* Figure 1.4). In 2012, only 10 and 4 per cent had very little trust in politicians and national parliament respectively.

Furthermore, the global crisis effectively reduced the level of support for one of the FrP's key pre-crisis messages, namely that Norway should spend more 'oil money' now rather than saving it for future generations. Whereas a majority (between 56 and 67 per cent) of the voters agreed with the FrP between 1997 and 2005, only one third of the voters supported increased usage of oil money in 2009 (*see* Figure 2.1). In times of economic uncertainty, the FrP's policies seemed to have been disqualified as irresponsible.

Finally, the only development which could have been exploited by a right-wing populist party, namely the general increase in Euroscepticism (from just above 50 per cent in 2008 to almost 80 per cent in 2014 being against Norwegian membership in the EU), is ineffective in a Norwegian context.[5] Not only are European-related issues to a large extent absent from the public agenda, the FrP is internally divided and its current government partner is actually the most pro-EU party in Norway which obviously limits the scope for Eurosceptic mobilisation.

A more unfavourable opportunity structure for the FrP was not only related to the emergence of the global financial crisis and the EU-crisis; it was also the

---

5. Figures on Norwegians attitudes towards EU membership are made available by Professor Bernt Aardal, University of Oslo. Online. Available: http://www.aardal.info/eu2000.pdf (accessed 18 July 2014).

Figure 2.1: Norwegian voters' attitudes towards the usage of 'oil money' (1997–2009) (in per cent)

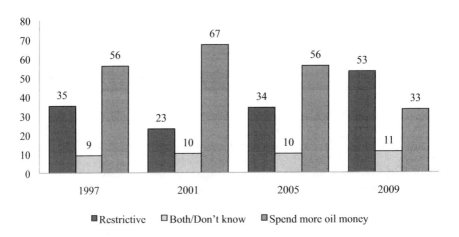

■Restrictive   □Both/Don't know   ▨Spend more oil money

Source: Narud (2011: 238) with correction in 2009.

result of a general shift of political attitudes and the public atmosphere observed in the aftermath of the terrorist attack on 22 July 2011. In the attack, the extreme-right activist, Anders Behring Breivik, killed seventy-seven people and injured more than 200, making it one of the most violent acts by a single individual in modern times. The FrP's general decline in electoral support, and the abysmal result in the 2011 local elections, which took place less than two months after the attack, seemed to be indirectly related to the short-term effects of this atrocity. Most importantly, it has been argued that the nature of the attack – that is, the perpetrator's Islamophobic motivation and his previous membership of the FrP – made Norwegians more tolerant towards immigrants in order to dissociate themselves from his ideas (Jakobsson and Blom 2014: 9) and less attracted by the FrP's controversial immigration policies (Bergh and Bjørklund 2013: 32, 35–37). In fact, the party lost 'ownership' to the immigration issue for the first time in many years. Moreover, the attacks seemed to increase the level of personal and institutional trust (Wollebæk *et al.* 2012a), which probably further diminished the mobilising power of any kind of anti-establishment and/or xenophobic propaganda. Despite these important observations, however, one should not over-emphasise the political impact of July 22nd, at least not the long-term effects (e.g. Jupskås and Wig 2012; Wollebæk *et al.* 2012b). Very few argued, for example, that the FrP was morally responsible for publically cultivating Islamophobic sentiments and the attack was largely depoliticised by all major political parties.

In contrast to Norway, the Danish opportunity structure has been more favourable for right-wing populist mobilisation. Fortunately for DF, given that it was strongly associated with the liberal-conservative government, the electorate did not blame the incumbent government for the emerging Danish economic crisis.

Only 19 per cent attributed the crisis to domestic economic policies, whereas 49 and 63 per cent viewed the crisis as a consequence of US economic policies and risk-prone behaviour of the banks, respectively (Andersen and Hansen 2013: 146). Consequently, neither the two right-wing parties nor DF was punished particularly hard by the voters. Instead, the voters seemed to be increasingly sceptical of centre-left parties' ability to solve the economic recession and uphold key welfare arrangements. While the issue ownership to key economic issues was almost lost already during the election campaign, the actual policies of the centre-left government has made them increasingly unpopular after entering office. In fact, the government has consistently received negative ratings by the Danish electorate on all major policy areas in recent years (Holstein 2014). Not surprisingly, the lack of political trust in Denmark has therefore increased in post-crisis period rather than decreased as in Norway (*see also* Figure 1.4).

With regard to the development of Euroscepticism in the post-crisis period, one of the key mobilising issues of DF, the evidence is more mixed. While some surveys seem to indicate a decline of Euroscepticism (*see* e.g. *Politiken*, 14 April 2014), others suggest that trust in different European institutions (e.g. the parliament, the Commission and the Central Bank) have declined between 2009 and 2013 (Eurobarometer 2009; 2013a). In any case, there seems to be widespread support for some of DF's key Eurosceptic narratives: fear of social dumping (70 per cent), access to Danish welfare arrangements for EU-citizens (two thirds) and opposition to the euro (also two thirds) (Sørensen 2014; Vibjerg *et al.* 2014: Eurobarometer 2013). As the most vocal opponent of the EU and with a clear-cut welfare-chauvinist agenda, DF has successfully mobilised voters who share these fears and attitudes.

Conclusion

This chapter has presented a comparison of how the international financial crisis and government participation has affected two of Europe's most institutionalised right-wing populist parties, the FrP and DF. While the electoral development of these two parties seems to be in line with the general theories of populism and crisis, the discursive development is not.

Rather than intensifying the anti-elitism, populist rhetoric and opportunistically seeking whatever ideological position that might be electorally rewarding, both parties have reacted fairly predictably. As highly institutionalised parties, DF and the FrP have interpreted the crisis according to their ideological framework and have instrumentally used the crisis to promote pre-crisis policies. Moreover, the difference between the discourse of these two parties whether in government (as in Norway since 2013), supporting the government (as in Denmark until 2011) or in opposition, is almost insignificant, though the FrP has indeed moderated the anti-elitist elements of its initial populist ideology. Again, the level of institutionalisation may be a key explanatory factor.

The electoral development of the two parties is, however, more in line with the expectations. In short, the chapter finds that the crisis produced favourable opportunity structures in Denmark, while the non-existing crisis in Norway created unfavorable opportunity structures for right-wing populist mobilisation. Indeed, DF, which has functioned within a context of crisis, has been way more electorally successful than the FrP which has operated within a context of non-crisis. While the post-crisis period in Denmark has been characterised by an economic recession, growing unpopularity of the incumbent centre-left government and widespread support of (parts of) DF's Eurosceptic message, the same period in Norway has been marked by economic optimism, government satisfaction and declining support for 'irresponsible' spending of oil money, which used to be a key mobilising issue for the FrP.

Furthermore, the results indicate that right-wing populist parties – irrespective of the impact of the economic crisis – suffer electorally (as in the Norwegian case) or are unable to benefit electorally from a favourable opportunity structure (as in the Danish case) if they participate in (as FrP) or are closely linked (as DF) with the government. In other words, right-wing populist parties seem to face a hard choice between being responsible and holding office on the one hand, and being responsive and mobilising voters on the other.

Chapter Three

Business as Usual:
Ideology and Populist Appeals
of the Sweden Democrats

Ann-Cathrine Jungar

After several unsuccessful attempts, the Sweden Democrats (SD) won their first seats in the 2010 parliamentary elections. With 5.7 per cent of the vote they passed the 4 per cent electoral threshold and received twenty (out of 349) seats. The era of Swedish 'exceptionalism' had come to an end – Sweden was no longer a 'non-success case' of radical right party parliamentary presence (Widfelt 2008; Rydgren 2002). In the parliamentary elections of September 2014, the SD doubled their vote share to 12.9 per cent and the number of their parliamentary seats rose to forty-nine. It would obviously be tempting to associate the SD parliamentary breakthrough in 2010 with the European economic recession as populist parties are assumed to mobilise on disaffection and political mistrust arising from political and economic crisis. However, the electoral success and parliamentary entrance of SD in 2010 as well as their enhanced success in 2014 had little to do with economic or political crises. On the contrary, the SD obtained their best election results ever at a time when the Swedish economy was doing comparatively well and the citizens' trust in the Swedish political system was at an all-time high.

This chapter is organised as follows: First, we describe the general ideological, electoral and organisational development of the SD. Next, we focus on the economic and political opportunity structure for populist mobilisation in Sweden – the development of standard economic indicators such as economic growth, unemployment and public debt, as well as of indicators characterising the political context. The third section discusses the core elements of the SD's discourse before and after the collapse of Lehman Brothers in 2008. The aim of the detailed analysis of their discourse is to see whether and to what extent this discourse has changed in the more recent past. A variety of sources have been used for this analysis: party programmes, electoral manifestoes, party leadership speeches, the SD magazine *SD-Kuriren*, SD party tweets and personal interviews. In the concluding section, the results are discussed in relation to the hypothesis set out in the general framework of the volume.

Populism before the economic crisis

The Nordic region has been a fertile soil for populism: Agrarian populism developed in Finland in the late 1950s and anti-establishment tax-protest parties have been rising in Denmark and Norway since the 1970s (Jungar and Jupskås 2014). The populism in Sweden, by contrast, developed late and can be considered as part of the long-term trend of the rise of 'new' or national populism since the late twentieth century. The SD were formed in 1988, but until the early 2000s they were a marginal political force. New Democracy, which had been formed in 1991 and was led by two charismatic leaders, proved to be initially more successful. New Democracy was the first party with populist radical right appeals that succeeded in winning seats in the Swedish parliament: In the national parliamentary elections 1991, this party received 6.7 per cent of the vote and twenty-four seats. The party combined anti-immigration appeals with economically liberal positions, which included calls for lower taxes, public welfare restrictions and business-friendly policies (Taggart 1996; Rydgren 2005a). With its combination of anti-immigration policies and anti-tax and anti-state appeals, the party resembled the Danish and Norwegian Progress parties. New Democracy was controlled by two party leaders and was organised on a franchise basis. In the end, the party was not successful in institutionalising an efficient organisation and was troubled by internal conflicts. In the parliamentary elections 1994, the party did not succeed in overcoming the electoral threshold and disintegrated shortly thereafter.

The SD Party emerged out of different nationalist, neo-fascist and neo-Nazi subcultures. The party was formed in 1988 by representatives from three nationalist-minded, interconnected and overlapping political parties and organisations: *Sverigepartiet* (the Sweden Party), *Framstegspartiet* (the Progress Party) and *Bevara Sverige svenskt* (BSS) (Keep Sweden Swedish) (Rydgren 2005b:118; Sverigedemokraterna 2013a). During its twenty-five years of existence, the party has undergone different stages of development. Its first years were characterised by ideological and organisational development. Obviously anti-immigration was the party's most salient issue, but from the beginning the SD made appeals for stricter criminal policies (the re-introduction of the death penalty), traditional family values (restricted abortion rights), animal rights in addition to policies in favour of pensioners. During the first half of the 1990s, the SD radicalised and were plagued by party factionalism. The radicalisation came partly about through the youth organisation, which had been established in 1992, but there were also conflicts over ideology and organisational issues in the mother party. As a result of these internal turbulences, the party lost members and risked falling apart.

It was in the late 1990s that the SD started to distance themselves from their extreme past by renouncing Nazism, banning uniforms at party meetings and changing the party symbol (from a flame to an anemone). The demand for the death penalty was abandoned. In 1996 the party leadership excluded some of its more extreme founding members, who did not distance themselves from Nazism and anti-semitism The excluded veterans formed a new party *Hembygdspartiet*, which later fell apart. Another party-split occurred in 2001, with the founding of the *Nationaldemokraterna* (ND) by a Stockholm-based faction of former SD members.

The historical links of the SD to extreme nationalist and racist groups, as well as internal conflicts and unfavourable opportunity structures were the main obstacles to the party's electoral growth. Until 2002, the electoral fortunes of the SD remained bleak. In the 2002 parliamentary (regional and municipal) elections, however, the SD received 1.4 per cent of the votes and the number of SD representatives in the municipal assemblies increased. Strong internal criticism maintained that the party did not professionalise and organise fast enough. With the election of Jimmy Åkesson as new party leader in 2005, the SD entered a new phase of development. It started to grow rapidly and obtained more success in municipal elections. In the parliamentary election of 2006 it obtained 2.9 per cent of the vote, which entitled it to public funding. Up to this point, the party had to rely on local subsidies, membership fees and donations; from this point on, it had more resources at its disposal for organisational development.

Electoral growth despite unfavourable opportunity structures

As already pointed out, the parliamentary breakthrough came in 2010 with 5.7 per cent of the vote, and in the 2014 European parliamentary elections the SD gained their two first EP mandates with 9.7 per cent of the vote (*see* Figure 3.1 and Table 3.1). In the parliamentary elections of 2014 the SD doubled the vote to 12.9 per cent and became the third largest party of Swedish parliament. As

Figure 3.1: SD vote in parliamentary, regional and municipal elections (in per cent)

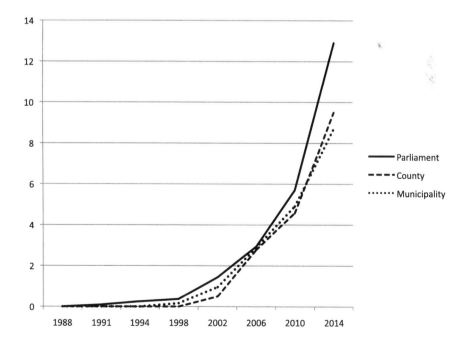

Table 3.1: Election results for the SD (1998–2014)

		National elections	Regional elections	Local elections	European elections	
1998	Vote share	0.4%	N/A	N/A		
	Mandates	0	0	8		
2002	Vote share	1.4%	0.4%	1.4%		
	Mandates	0	0	49		
2006	Vote share	2.9%	2.8%	2.9%	2004	1.1%
	Mandates	0	0	280		0
2010	Vote share	5.7%	4.6%	4.9%	2009	3.3%
	Mandates	20	70	612		0
2014	Vote share	12.9%	9.5%	8.7%	2014	9.7%
	Mandates	49				2

a result of these elections, the SD now occupies a pivotal position that gives it a blackmailing potential: neither the red green bloc (composed of the Social Democrats, the Greens and the Left-wing Party) nor the centre-right alliance control a parliamentary majority.

The electoral growth of the SD in 2010 can neither be attributed to an increase in anti-immigration attitudes nor to a higher degree of political disillusionment, two factors that have been suggested as facilitating the growth of the radical right (Rydgren 2002). In Sweden, anti-immigration attitudes have actually decreased in the 2000s and they were at an all-time low in 2011 (Demker 2012: 95).[1] Moreover, the Swedish voters manifested higher political trust in 2010. According to Oscarsson (2012), 'the trust for Swedish politicians is now at the same level as it was in the 1970s' and 'reflects a real come-back for politics in the 'trustbusiness'. To talk about distrust in politicians in Sweden has always been an exaggeration, now it is incorrect'. Although there has been no increase in these attitudes, anti-immigartion attitudes and political distrust constitute decisive motives for an SD vote. Thus, the SD mobilises the voters who are the most critical of immigration and the least trusting in politics. No less than 94 per cent of the SD voters think that more immigration is a bad idea compared to an overall average of 41 per cent, and only 30 per cent of the SD voters have high or very high trust in politicians, compared to an average of 61 per cent.[2]

---

1. In the SOM 2011 survey 41 per cent agree that more immigration is a very bad or bad idea and 10 per cent perceive immigration as a threat to Swedish culture and values (Demker 2012: 95, 101). The attitudes towards immigration vary between parties. Among the mainstream parties, 20–47 per cent of the sympathisers agree with the statement that more immigration is a bad idea compared to 94 per cent of Sweden Democratic sympathisers.

2. The level of political trust among the other political parties was (in per cent): The Conservatives (73), the Centre Party (81), the Left Wing Party (44), the Social Democrats (57) and the Green Party (71). The SD voters' level of trust is closer to non-voters (35) and to those who voted blank (25).

The electoral growth of the SD can hardly be attributed to the effect of the Great Recession either. On the contrary, the marginal effect of the Great Recession on the Swedish economy and the absence of a political crisis would rather suggest a stagnation of radical right populism in the Swedish case. In economic terms, Sweden was doing comparatively well as a non-member of the Eurozone and opportunities for campaigning on economic disappointment and Euroscepticism were, if not absent, weak. The Swedish economy was certainly also affected by the economic recession but not to the same degree as many other EU member states. Even if the GDP growth rate made a radical downward turn (falling from +4 per cent in 2006 to –6 per cent in 2009), and even if the unemployment rate rose from 6 per cent to over 8 per cent after 2008 Sweden has been doing better than the members of the Eurozone (*see* Figures 1.1 and 1.2). Moreover, Sweden is still one of the most equal countries in the world, even if it has experienced the sharpest rise in inequality among the OECD countries during the past fifteen years.

Not only was Sweden marginally affected by the economic crisis, its political system was also in good shape. Thus, the four party centre-right coalition of the conservative *Moderaterna*, the liberal party *Folkpartiet liberalerna*, the Christian democratic party *Kristdemokraterna* and the centre party *Centern* is one of the few governments which has not been punished by the European voters in the aftermath of the crisis. In the 2010 elections, it repeated its electoral victory of 2006. In Sweden, this was only the second time after 1945 that a non-social democratic government was re-elected for a second term. The coalition did, however, lose its majority status, partly due to the SD parliamentary entrance.[3] The renewed electoral confidence in the centre-right government rested on its economic competence, which was perceived to be higher than that of the opposition (composed of the social democratic party *Socialdemokraterna*, the green party *Miljöpartiet* and the left wing party *Vänsterpartiet* (SCB 2011)). Overall, the SD parliamentary breakthrough can neither be attributed to an economic nor to a political crisis. In a comparative European perspective, the SD have had few incentives to mobilise voters and criticise the government or the established parties for the mismanagement of the economy.

Moreover, it is likely that the '*cordon sanitaire*' applied to the SD discouraged its leadership from opportunism in economic affairs. The pariah status of the SD is motivated by its nationalism and its anti-immigration positions (*see* Ivarsflaten 2006; Van Spanje and Van der Brug 2007). The SD's leadership aspires to overcome this 'pariah' status and to make the SD a legitimate party with governmental credibility: 'Our aim is to grow electorally and assume a position as a political party with real blackmailing power in order to force the other parliamentary political parties to take us into consideration for government formation' (Party leader Jimmy Åkesson, speech, *Sverigedemokraternas framtidsdag*, 11 February 2013). Aspiring to be recognised as a legitimate party the SD has to overcome its historic legacy of extreme nationalism and racism (and contacts with more extreme subcultures).

3. The last time was in 1979.

We would like to suggest that the most important reason for the growth of the populist radical right in Sweden has to do with the overall political opportunity structure which, independently of the crisis conditions, has become more favourable for its mobilisation. First of all, it is well known that ideological convergence between the left and the right facilitates the success of the populist radical right (Kitschelt and McGann 1995; Carter 2005), and it is considered more important for electoral breakthrough than for persistence (Minkenberg 2001). Thus, the SD's electoral and parliamentary breakthrough occurred after a period of ideological convergence in the Swedish political system after 2002. The left-turn of the centre-right conservative party *Moderaterna* is one of the most dramatic changes in Swedish politics during the last decade. As a result, the comparatively high level of class voting (in the working class) in Sweden which has been said to impede SD growth (Rydgren 2002) has decreased, in particular among working class voters who have become increasingly available for the mobilisation by radical right populists. The ideological convergence between left and right that took place in the Swedish political system after 2002, and the simultaneous decrease in class voting among the workers (Demker and Oscarsson 2013) opened up a political space both to the right and to the left, which the SD has utilised.

The ideological positions and the populism of the SD

In this third section the ideological development of the SD as well as the core populist rhetorical elements in its discourse – the people, the nation, popular sovereignty and anti-establishment appeals – are analysed. Continuity has largely prevailed as to the prioritised policies of the SD, and as to how they are framed before and after 2008. Immigration, law and order and welfare (in particular, the pensioners) are the party's, as well as the SD voters' top policy priorities (SCB 2011: 64). To the extent that there were post 2008 transformations in the SD political discourse they are related to the fundamental party goals (Sjöblom 1968; Ström and Mueller 1999): to attract working class and female voters and to lift off the '*cordon sanitaire*' that is applied to it by the other parliamentary parties.

Ideological positions

Nativism, authoritarianism and populism are the three fundamental ideational elements for the populist radical right (PRR) party family (Mudde 2007: 22–239). The mix and hierarchy between these elements vary in the populist radical right party family. For the SD, nationalism is the overarching organising ideological principle, according to which policies are framed. Until 2011 the SD defined themselves exclusively as a nationalist party in their programmes of principles. The nation is defined in terms of loyalty, a common identity, language and culture. The nationalism of the SD is presented as 'open and non-racial', which means that membership in the nation can be accomplished by birth or assimilation. Nationalism encompasses anti-immigration appeals, opposition to multiculturalism as well as welfare chauvinism. It has been claimed that the SD – past and present – are still a single-issue party since they frame other policy issues predominantly in nationalist terms, that is, in terms of problems arising from immigration and multiculturalism. However, more recently, the SD can no longer be called a single-issue party since they attempt to mobilise voters on several issues and particularly economic issues unrelated to immigration. Moreover, the SD voters' core concerns include other issues than immigration, such as law and order, gender equality and economy (Erlingsson *et al.* 2013: 10).

At the 2011 party convention social conservatism was – after heated debates – added to the party's ideological profile: 'The Sweden Democrats are a social conservative party with a nationalist outlook that considers value conservatism and solidary welfare as the most important tools for building the good society' (*Sverigedemokraternas Principprogram* 2011). Social conservatism is claimed to complement nationalism as 'the central aim of conservatism is to safeguard well functioning and deeply rooted communities. The nation is, besides the family, the primary example of such a community' (*ibid.*). The inclusion of, or rather the explicit reference to social conservatism in the party programme is aimed at moderating the party profile by stressing other elements on the liberal-authoritarian dimension, such as traditional family values and gender. The broadening of the ideological base of the SD has little to do with any crisis – political or economic – but is more likely to reflect the party leadership's strategy to downplay the nationalism by social conservative ideas.

The socio-economic dimension has traditionally been most salient in Swedish politics. Politics – electoral competition and government formation – has primarily been structured along the socio-economic left-right dimension, with most other issues aligning themselves along this continuum (Oscarsson 1998; Rydgren 2010). It has been argued that the Swedish political system has been among the most uni-dimensional ones in Western Europe implying that political competition could be reduced to a single left-right dimension (Benoit and Laver 2006). The SD have challenged the 'traditional' left-right political continuum by combining conservative values with centre-leftist economic policies. Since their formation in 1988, they have developed both in a more authoritarian and leftward direction. This (counterintuitive) transformation appears when the position of the SD on the most salient socio-economic left-right dimension and the value-based liberal-authoritarian dimensions are mapped out based on their electoral manifestoes according to the CMP-coding. All the SD party manifestoes, except for the electoral manifesto of 2010 have been coded by us according to Comparative Manifesto coding criteria as only parties with parliamentary representation are included in the publicly available CMP database (Manifesto Data project).

The SD have always been situated on the authoritarian end of the value-based dimension and, between 1989 and 2010, they gradually moved further towards the authoritarian end, in particular after 2002 (*see* Figure 3.2). Given that the party simultaneously excluded extremist groups, this transformation seems counterintuitive. However, the authoritarian dimension does not exclusively tap immigration and multiculturalism, but also other issues of relevance for a populist radical right party, such as spending on the military, law and order and moral issues.

Figure 3.2: Policy changes over time

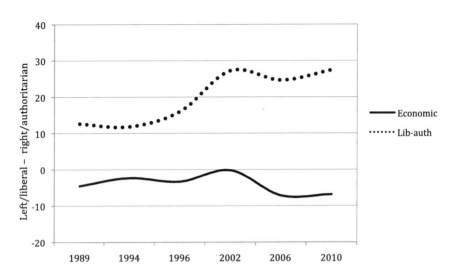

Notes: Changes along economic left-right (solid line) and libertarian-authoritarian (dashed line) policy dimensions. Positive values mean right/libertarian positions and negative values mean left/libertarian, with zero being neutral.

As a matter of fact, there is a greater emphasis on security, law and order after 2001. On the socio-economic left-right dimension, the SD have been firmly anchored in the centre. In this respect, there has been some fluctuation over time, but taken together the economic left-right balance is fairly stable over time. There has been a small turn leftward between 2002 and 2006, but between 2006 and 2010 the position does not change at all.

An analysis of the party's Twitter accounts indicates that the parliamentary entrance in 2010 has impacted on the SD since the party has had to formulate new policies in fields where it previously held no positions (interview with Björn Söder, 18 April 2013). As there is a great personal overlap between the parliamentary group and the party council and executive, the parliamentary entrance has not resulted in party-internal power dispersion (Jungar 2014).[4]

---

4. The Sweden Democrats started tweeting regularly on its official party Twitter account (@sdriks) in January 2010. Most of the tweets during the 2010–11 period are headlines that link to party press releases. During much of the first year, the tweets were dominated by references to unfair treatment of the SD by other political parties and the media (victimisation in Figure 3.1). While not disappearing entirely, the frequency of such tweets then dropped significantly when the SD gained parliamentary representation in the fall of 2010 and stabilised at around 10 per cent. The other initially dominating category refers to immigration, which made up 20–30 per cent of tweets during the first year, but then decreased steadily as the party started addressing a broader range of policies. The most salient policy issue on Twitter for 2011 was crime, with an average of 16 per cent. Other policy issues with increasing saliency include economic policy, healthcare, culture and the EU, meaning that the broadening of issues being addressed by that party can be seen not just in CMP data (i.e. increasing number of categories) but also on Twitter.

Another indicator of the perceived necessity to formulate more distinct policies to act upon is that in 2011 four new specific policy platforms were formulated: labour market policies, criminal policies, energy policies and education policies. The party is currently elaborating specific platforms for agriculture and business/enterprise. No general policy changes directly related to the economic crisis are discernible in the material, but the observed changes are much rather related to the fact that the SD became a parliamentary party.

People-centrism

As noted in the introductory chapter, in the populist thin ideology the people is 'the' central concept. The political community is conceptualised as a united and homogenous people. Populism thus engages in constructing a united people that is contrasted to the political establishment (the democratic people, the 'demos'), other peoples and cultures that are perceived to threaten the traditions and ways of life of the proper 'people' (our people, the nation, the ethos) and lastly, the 'ordinary', 'common' representing common sense, genuine values and virtues of a (lost, depreciated and/or bygone community, i.e. 'a heartland' (Taggart 2000), or 'deserving' people like pensioners ('who have built the nation') or (native) families with children ('the future of the nation'). The SD have made use of all these conceptualisations of the people, as is exemplified by the party secretary Björn Söder at the party congress of 2008:

> Our Swedish nation is a result of an emotional and cultural community, which has evolved over thousands of years [...] We guard the common sense and our thousand year long self-determination, we take care of the elderly and protect our children. The safe decent society that we defend stands in opposition to the multiculturalism, the dissolution of norms and EU-federalism of the other political parties.
> (Björn Söder, party congress 2008)

The primary conceptualisation of the people is the 'nation', which is in line with the party's nativist origin. The people is conceptualised as the national community: 'The Sweden Democrats consider the nation to be the most important, oldest and natural community after the family' (SD 2011). The Swedish nation is defined as 'loyalty, a common identity, a common language and culture. One can become a member of the Swedish nation either by being born into it or later in life by actively choosing to become a part of it' (*ibid.*). The ethno-cultural conceptualisation of the people has been strengthened as Swedish identity no longer is exclusively attached to kinship ('Sweden and Nordic'), but to the knowledge of language, identification with Sweden and a way of life that conforms to 'Swedish' norms and values. Repatriation (for foreigners) was removed from the party programme in 1999 and until 2002 the SD advocated a ban on adoption of non-European children (Widfelt 2008). In the Swedish programme of principles of 2003 it is stated that 'a Swede is someone who has a predominantly Swedish identity and recognises him/herself and is recognised by others as a Swede'. According to the programme of principles of 2011 it is stated that one can become a Swede by means of assimilation. In the present programme of principles (of 2011) the SD elaborated in somewhat greater detail what is meant by a 'native' or assimilated Swede:

> As a native Swede, we consider those who are born in Sweden or who are adopted at an early age by Swedish-speaking parents, with a Swedish or Nordic identity, and as assimilated to the Swedish nation we consider those with a non-Swedish background who speak fluent Swedish, see themselves as Swedish, live in accordance with the Swedish culture, consider Swedish history as their own and feel a greater attachment to the Swedish nation than to any other nation.

The concepts of democracy and the welfare state are rooted in the nation. The SD have recycled the politically established Swedish concept of '*folkhemmet*' or 'the people's home' (Ekströmvon Essen 2003). The originally conservative idea, which was imported from Germany, had been taken over by the Swedish Social Democrats in the 1930s. The concept of the 'people's home' evokes a community based on a welfare state that is ingrained in a national community. The welfare state is the expanded family providing care for its citizens (*see* for instance Hellström 2010). The metaphor of the 'people's home' and the nostalgic evocation of the past is an argument in favour of a homogenous state and stands as a symbol of Swedish democracy and solidary welfare. According to the party leader, the SD are 'here to re-establish the people's home that is eroding' (Åkesson 2013). With the 'people's home', the SD attempt to root its welfare chauvinism and anti-immigration position in a political concept which resonates with Swedish, and in particular, social democratic political culture.

The SD have also conceptualised the people by the 'othering' of Islam. The threats posed by Islam have been present in the party's discourse since its inception: since the early 1990s the party has supported and organised demonstrations and protests against the construction of mosques in various municipalities (Ekman and Poohl 2010: 247). After 9/11 the SD, like other European PRR parties, increasingly started evoking the dangers of Islam, which was contrasted with Swedish democracy, freedom and gender equality. Since 2009 the focus on Islam has increased: The SD organised its first anti-Islam meeting (in 2009) and the international secretary Kent Ekeroth has been one of the leading persons to connect the SD with international anti-Islamist networks in Europe and in US. The anti-Islam and (pro-Israeli) sentiments of the present leadership are not shared by the sympathisers of the older nationalist factions within the party and the youth section. The party leader Jimmy Åkesson sided with the Islam-critical section and in a televised interview in TV 8 in 2009 Islam and Muslims were the main topics of the discussion. The party leader stated that 'we do not criticise specific groups or individuals, but we are against the development we have had, it has been going too fast. The Muslim population, the Muslim minority has become too large in too a short time' (interview with Jimmy Åkesson, TV8 Adaktusson 29 January 2009). Non-European, that is, Muslim immigration must be restricted, because it constitutes 'a threat to the Swedish national identity as Muslims tend to distance themselves from the Swedish society' (*ibid.*). In short, they do not assimilate. The anti-Islam mobilisation occurred post-2008, but is unrelated to any crisis, but rather a result of the party leadership's ideology and priorities.

The sovereign people

The 'sovereign people' is less talked about in the SD, and then often related to the anti-establishment critique (*see* more below). The democratic people is evoked in relation to the EU, to which the domestic political elites have delegated powers:

> [...]instead of doing what they are elected to do, to cherish the nation, to preserve the Swedish people's interests, our needs, our desires, they have made every effort not to appear bigoted or prejudiced in front of their colleagues sitting on the really high chairs in Brussels.   (Jimmy Åkesson 1 May 2004)

The political leadership is criticised for having sacrificed its own people for its own self-interest. The SD support direct democracy and the greater use of referenda in order to involve the people in the decision-making: 'We advocate stronger elements of direct democracy and support an increased use of decisive referenda, at the local, regional and national level'. Moreover, the SD state that 'decisions on important and cross-cutting issues should be preceded by municipal referenda, citizen consultations and examinations' (SD 2012b). The party supports institutional innovations that allow citizens to influence policies (referenda, citizen initiatives and agenda initiatives) and technical innovations that facilitate participation (e-voting). After 2011 when a reformed municipal initiative entered into force the SD have been the only party that systematically voted in favour of holding a referendum (but it has also been the party that always has been in opposition) (Jungar 2013). The SD have frequently used agenda-setting initiatives to press for their pet policies (building of mosques, public support to (multicultural) cultural centres) in the municipalities.

The 'common people' have been a recurrent reference of the SD. They speak on behalf of the 'ordinary' and 'honest' people who 'represent opinions that are aired during coffee breaks, but never are allowed to be expressed in public debates' (Åkesson, televised interview TV 8, 9 May 2005). There is an interesting ambiguity in what 'ordinary' refers to. In the early days, the SD were associated by the public with skinheads, outright racists and neo-Nazis, and the faction of modernisers within the party considered this an impediment to electoral growth and party development (Widfelt 2008). The recurrent reference to ordinary people may have been used as a rhetorical 'normalisation' strategy to make clear that ordinary people hold (ordinary) anti-immigration opinions (and may be voters of or feel sympathy with the SD): 'We are ordinary people with ordinary opinions'.

The party has traditionally paid a lot of attention to its so-called 'deserving groups' – pensioners and families who have been juxtaposed to immigrants: 'Politics is about priorities. If you give priority to immigration it will affect other public activities. It will affect the welfare, families with children, childcare, it affects the school, the pensioners, those who are sick, those who are disabled' (Jimmy Åkesson, speech 28 April 2008). The SD have targeted new groups after 2008. Just as the recycling of the 'people's home' serves as a rhetorical device to combine nationalism with a tax-based solidary welfare state, the inclusion of the 'wage-earners' indicates that the SD increasingly articulated a 'leftist' critique of immigration and the free movement of labour in their discourse. This reflects a more pronounced SD vote-seeking strategy aimed at targeting dissatisfied social democratic voters. The Social Democratic Party had already initiated and pursued stricter immigration policies from the late 1960s to the 1980s and they had questioned the capacity of the 'people's home' to make room for more immigrants (Hinnfors and Spehar 2012). The dangers of excessive immigration were lower salaries, social benefits and weakened trade union, in addition to abuse of welfare entitlements. As late as 2004 the Swedish social democratic Prime Minister Göran Persson warned against 'social tourism' as a consequence of the Eastern enlargement of the EU. More recently, the SD have added this 'old' social democratic frame against immigration to their nativist discourse: the free movement of labour is said to put downward pressure on the salaries and EU-legislation to allow foreign companies to outcompete Swedish companies by allowing them to retain the social benefits of their country of origin (SD 2013b). The SD criticised proposals of special incentives for employing immigrants as the discrimination of Swedish wage-earners. 'If it is cheaper for enterprises to employ an immigrant then Swedish employees are out-competed on salary. We think that this is wrong. It is a discrimination of Swedish wage-earners' (interview Jimmy Åkesson SVT 24 at the SD party congress 2009).

This argument that immigration and free movement is a threat to the workers is spiced with critique of the social democrats, who no longer take the interests of their 'old' voters in consideration. The SD have criticised the other political parties in parliament for letting down the wage-earners when they had the possibility – with the support of the SD – to vote against the government to increase the unemployment benefits. Moreover, the social democrats are said to let their core constituency down as a consequence of their principled opposition to the SD:

> The social democrats have once again proved that it is more important not to talk and co-operate with the Sweden Democrats than to realise the policies they have campaigned on. It is a betrayal of the Swedish wage-earners and those who voted for the party.
> (Björn Söder, SD parliamentary group leader, press release, 2011)

The SD are like many other radical right populist parties – male dominated both among their voters and their representatives (Jungar 2014). After the elections in 2010 the SD have intensified their attempts to attract women voters. The party leader has since 2010 paid attention to women employed in the public sector (healthcare and childcare) and referred to them as the 'everyday heroes': 'We cannot accept that the everyday heroes employed in the public health care are consumed prematurely only because Anders Borg (the Swedish finance minister) is greedy and rather invests money in increasing mass immigration and cheap hamburgers' (Jimmy Åkesson, Almedalen June 2013). That is, female workers in the public welfare sector are set against immigration. The SD have proposed reforms for improved working conditions for this group of (low-paid) women, i.e. the right to full-time work (many are only employed part-time). Unlike the feminists, the SD addressed the 'ordinary' women who want to live according to traditional gender roles, and oppose public regulation of a balanced division of tasks between the father and mother for child care, educational programmes for raising gender awareness, and quotas for women in public and private companies. Changes in the post-2008 SD discourse targeting the 'ordinary people', workers and women, are part of a more pronounced vote seeking strategy to attract new segments of voters: People critical of immigration who do not necessarily hold nationalist ideological views, social democratic voters fearing competition from immigrants and lower social benefits, as well as low-wage women in the public sector.

Anti-elitism

An antagonistic relationship between the people and the elite(s) is part of the thin populist ideology. The fundamental societal divide according to populism runs between the elite and the (united and homogenous) people, whereas class and interest based conflicts are downplayed. The anti-establishment discourse of the SD (once again) mirrors the party's (dominant) nationalist ideology. The establishment is defined as those who do not see the negative consequences of immigration and multiculturalism, but rather embrace them. More precisely, the SD's anti-establishment appeals target the 'social-liberal' political establishment and/or cultural/Marxist/feminist elites who do not recognise the concerns of ordinary people stemming from immigration and multiculturalism. The elite targeted by the SD are primarily domestic and there are few references to the EU-elite in Brussels, or international capital and international organisations other than the EU. Nor is the elite accused of abuse of power (except for the political isolation of the SD, *see* next section) or corruption. Even though the SD comments upon the high salaries and benefits of politicians, their arguments rather concern social representation. That is, the socio-economic differences between those who claim to represent the people and the people themselves are considered to be an obstacle to true representation:

> The Sweden Democrats are not part of the establishment. Unlike the newly formed populist parties (i.e. Junilistan) our party does not consist of multimillionaires with a background in the top echelons of society. The Sweden Democrats are a party of and for common people.
>
> (Åkesson, Jimmy, SD-kuriren 66/2005 1 June 2013)

In the corpus of documents, three different rhetorical anti-establishment discourses can be found. First, the party targets the entire (social-liberal) political elite, who is blind to the consequences of immigration and multiculturalism experienced by 'ordinary' people. The political elite is considered unrepresentative of and unresponsive to the people, whereas the SD talk 'truth to power'. 'It does not matter whether it's a socialist or non-socialist government[...]both socialist and bourgeois governments have quite clearly shown that they prioritise mass immigration before welfare' (Jimmy Åkesson, speech Vellinge 26 April 2008). The argument of the hegemonic political establishment is constant and recurring:

> This opinion is symptomatic for the Swedish social-liberal hegemony – an unholy alliance between liberals and socialists who are too extreme and ideological and do not listen nor give any value to honest people but are misled by elites in the media, lobbyists and special interests.
> (Jimmy Åkesson, summer speech at SD meeting 2012)

Secondly, after 2009, the anti-establishment discourse expanded to the cultural establishment, and in particular to feminists and the media. The feminists are accused of not defending what had been accomplished with regard to gender equality in Sweden. Since the early 2000s, the SD have included in their party platform violence against women – and in particular so called 'Swedish-inimical' (*sverigefientligt*) violence such as rape committed by foreigners (*hedersvåld*). (*Sverigedemokraterna* 2013b). By 2010 the feminists were held responsible for the negative development that had occurred in Swedish society according to the SD: 'The feminists turn a blind eye to violence against women[...]because it is sensitive. And it is a consequence of mass immigration. They do not react, they are silent' (Jimmy Åkesson, the annual summer speech 2012). The anti-feminist turn is related to party strategy and has again nothing to do with the economic crisis. After the parliamentary elections of 2010, the SD formed the women's organisation '*SD-Kvinnor*' (SD Women) as a 'complement to the Sweden Democrats, clarifying, deepening and developing the party's policies from a women's perspective'. (*SD Kvinnor* http://www.sdkvinnor.se/om-sd-kvinnor/).

The third anti-establishment discourse has been fuelled both, by the already mentioned '*cordon sanitaire*', which the mainstream parties applied to the SD, and by the 'unfair' treatment of the SD by the media. The establishment consists of the parties that do not recognise the SD as a legitimate and credible party. This type of 'victimisation' rhetoric increased after 2008 and peaks during the parliamentary election campaign of 2010, only to decrease immediately after these elections and the SD's entrance into parliament. This again suggests that it is not directly related to the economic crisis. According to this line of reasoning Åkesson maintains that:

> The other parties unite in order to prevent us from having any influence. They clearly show who constitutes the real opposition in Swedish politics. They consequently refrain from talking to us. They rather give up their own policies

than talk to us. Never has the establishment been so united and has had such an obvious opponent. We Sweden Democrats challenge the establishment, and the establishment senses the challenge.

(Jimmy Åkesson, 2010, speech at SD Kommunkonferens 2010 12 April)

The media are also criticised for treating the party unfairly and differently from the other political parties: in the spring 2010, before the start of the electoral campaign for the parliamentary elections (in September), Åkesson wrote an open letter to the editors of the news media asking for fair media treatment:

I hope to be able to communicate my message to the voters under the same conditions as other political parties, and test the confidence in the Sweden Democrats in open and honest competition[...]This requires a real possibility to communicate my message editorially and in advertisements. And it requires that the ethical rules of the press are respected and that the respect for a democratic and open debate is mutual.

The letter in itself signals a lack of trust in and casts doubts on the democratic ethos and the impartiality of the media. They are suspected to side with the established political parties by isolating and excluding the SD.

Conclusion

Neither the European economic recession nor a domestic political crisis had an impact on the policies or the populist appeals of the SD. Continuity has largely prevailed before and after the economic recession as to their general ideology and the populist discourse. Given the comparatively well-performing Swedish economy and the citizens' general satisfaction with the political system, both the economic and political opportunity structures were unfavourable for populist mobilisation. That is, Sweden constitutes a least likely case for increased success of populists of any kind. To the extent that the SD repositioned itself ideologically during the crisis, this has not been a reaction to the crisis, but rather a result of party strategic concerns – of vote-seeking, i.e. the expansion of the electoral base to wage-earners and women, and of the attempt to become a respectable parliamentary party that no longer has a 'pariah' status. The SD now combines nationalist and social conservative policy positions with a centre-left economic position. Their populist discourse conceptualised as people-centrism, anti-elitism and popular sovereignty has undergone some minor transformations after 2008. The nation and the 'ordinary Swedes' are the 'imagined' people of the SD. The older generation (pensioners) has throughout the party history been recognised as 'the' group worthy of particular treatment and protection. However, workers and women employed in the public sector have increasingly been considered in the party discourse after 2008. The SD have increasingly made use of 'leftist' arguments (wage cuts, workers' rights) against immigration and the free movement of companies and persons. They have added this 'old' social democratic frame against immigration to their previously predominantly nativist discourse. The 'gender policies' of the SD are concerned with women's rights for self-determination and protection from ('anti-Swedish' male) violence. The framing of women empowerment policies of the SD is both dressed in nationalist, conservative as well as socio-economic terms (labour conditions, childcare, parental leave) and is rooted in stereotypical gender conceptions. The authoritarian appeal with demands for a strictly ordered society, the maintenance of law and order, harder penalties for criminals remains unchanged. Overall, the SD's entrance in parliament has contributed to issue expansion and more distinct policy position taking.

The SD's parliamentary breakthrough in 2010 and the continued electoral growth in the parliamentary elections of 2014 are not in line with the three hypothesis of the volume, that is, they cannot be attributed to any economic, political or combined economic-political crisis. Rather, more long-term trends, such as the effect of the general demarcation-integration conflict making itself more distinctly felt in Sweden, mainstream party convergence and party dealignment, as well as a more efficient SD party organisation are the factors that are more likely to explain the SD's electoral growth.

Chapter Four

Exploiting the Discursive Opportunity of the Euro Crisis: The Rise of the Finns Party

Tuomas Ylä-Anttila and Tuukka Ylä-Anttila

For the two decades preceding the economic crisis of 2009, the Finnish party system was notably stable, dominated by 'The Big Three': Social Democrats, the Centre Party (formerly Agrarian League) and the moderate-right National Coalition. The populist Finns Party (*Perussuomalaiset*, PS)[1] made some progress, but remained marginal until the crisis election of 2011, where their vote share skyrocketed (up to 19.1 per cent from 4.1 per cent in 2007) and they became the largest opposition party, illustrated in Figure 4.1. In this chapter we examine the role of the euro crisis in the rise of the PS, and argue that between 2007 and 2013 the party exploited the crisis discourse by moving from their agrarian populist roots towards radical right populism.

Considering populism as a 'thin-centred' ideology that is combined with complimentary ideologies to form a complete ideological base (Mudde 2004: 544), in line with this volume's premises, we will argue that in the PS's ideology 2007– 13, 1) the populist defence of the common people against corrupt elites is combined with 2) a left-populist defence of the welfare state against market-led policies promoted by elites and 3) increasingly, a nationalist defence of the sovereignty and unity of the Finnish people against immigration and federalist tendencies of the European Union (EU), typical of radical right populism (*see* Saukkonen 2003). In 2007, these themes hardly resonated with the general campaign debate, but in 2011, fuel for populist anti-corruption talk and nationalist EU-criticism was abundant. A political crisis following a national corruption scandal implicating the established parties, and the economic crisis of the Eurozone that required Finnish taxpayer money to bailout Ireland, Portugal and Greece, were served to the PS on a silver platter. We will argue that the discursive opportunities (Koopmans and Olzak 2004) brought on by the economic crisis, and the party's willingness to exploit them, have been crucial to their success.

Simultaneously with making EU critique a central part of their discourse, the party also accommodated a new, rising anti-immigration movement, originating from web discussion forums and blogs (*see* also Arter 2012). The integration of this new group of party members and supporters was done by downplaying

---

1. Perussuomalaiset, previously often translated as the True Finns, Ordinary Finns or Basic Finns, adopted the official English name 'The Finns' in August 2011, after receiving international media attention (HS 21 August 2011). The prefix 'perus' refers to fundamental ordinariness as a virtue, similarly to expressions such as 'down to earth' or 'straightforward'.

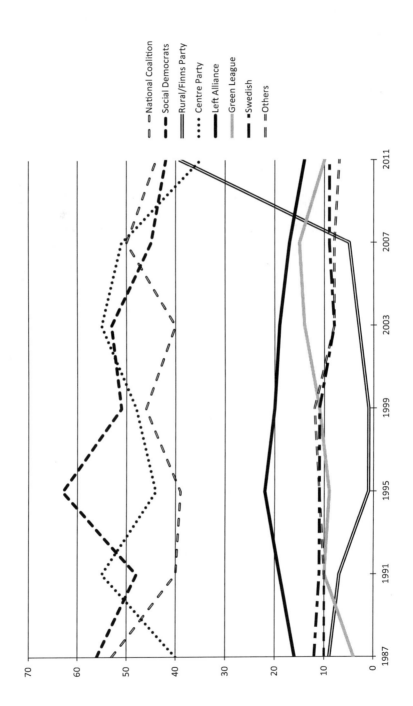

Figure 4.1: Parliament seats won, 1987–2011

the left-populist defence of the poor (ideological tenet two) and emphasising nationalist, anti-immigrant and anti-EU elements of the party ideology (tenet three). The left-populist rhetoric emphasising the distress of the underprivileged had been typical of the party's predecessor, the Finnish Rural Party (Suomen Maaseudun Puolue, SMP), moderately successful in the 1970s and 1980s (Helander 1971). However, the party seems to be moving further away from its SMP roots and towards radical right populism. Defence of the welfare state is still an important part of their ideology, but it is now phrased in a more nationalist tone, as welfare chauvinism: in order to save the welfare state, immigrants must be excluded and payments to the EU, especially the countries in need of bailouts, must be rejected.

This chapter proceeds chronologically. We focus first on the 2007 parliamentary and 2008 municipal elections before the euro crisis, followed by an analysis of the implications for the crisis on Finland. Next, we study the 2011 landslide elections at the height of the crisis and the 2012 post-breakthrough municipal elections. The presentation is based on a qualitative content analysis of the electoral manifestos for the 2007, 2008, 2011 and 2012 parliamentary and municipal elections, along with pre-election issues of the party newspaper, *Perussuomalainen* (The True Finn), read alongside key statistics about the Finnish economy. As the parliamentary elections were held in March 2007 and April 2011, we selected the newspaper issues published since the beginning of the election year until the election, two for 2007 and six for 2011, consistent with the importance of the 2011 elections for the party. For the municipal elections of October 2008 and October 2012, we selected two pre-election issues for each. Additionally, for a glimpse into the future, we look at 2013 issues of the party youth organisation's newspaper *Rahvas* (The Common People) and briefly review the party's performance in the 2014 European elections.

Pre-crisis populism 2007–08: Peripheral and struggling

The campaign for the 2007 parliamentary elections was, in a word, dull. That, at least, is the conclusion of two major reports on the elections (Pernaa, Niemi and Pitkänen 2007; Borg and Paloheimo 2009a). Since the start, polls predicted that the governing coalition would easily renew its mandate (Moring and Mykkänen 2009: 28), and differences in opinion between the three biggest parties were mild (Borg and Paloheimo 2009b: 19). Television coverage focused on the leaders of the 'Big Three' – the Centre Party, the Social Democrats and the National Coalition – and in the last TV debates the three leaders even openly stated that they had already said everything they had to say several times over (Pernaa 2007: 25). In this context, the PS got little media coverage and very little chance to influence the political agenda. However, the speaking skills of the party chairman (since 1997) Timo Soini, as well as his opinions which differed from the consensus of the Big Three, were positively noted by commentators (Saarikko 2007: 66).

Reading the manifesto, it is apparent that the 2007 PS campaign was based on a populist view of democracy (e.g. Canovan 1999; Mudde 2004; Taggart 2004). The manifesto speaks not of democracy (*demokratia*) but *kansanvalta*, literally 'rule by the people', starting with its title 'For justice, well-being and rule by the people!' (*Oikeudenmukaisuuden, hyvinvoinnin ja kansanvallan puolesta!*). The 'people' whom the party sets out to defend refers to 'the ordinary people', especially 'the most forgotten ones: the elderly, the disabled and the homeless'. With this focus on the most downtrodden, the party positions itself at the margin, reinforced by calls for the marginalised to 'protest so they can feel it!' A boxed text in the party newspaper asserts that 'the heartless policies of the government weaken the basic security of people with small and medium incomes, pensioners, families with children, the sick, the handicapped, the unemployed, the precarious workers, students and single parents', and exclaims in large bold typeface: 'YOUR social security is in danger!' The orientation is to secure the votes of the most disadvantaged and incite protest from the margins of society – an attitude that later changes markedly.

'Corrupt cognac drinkers'

Notably, much more colourful language is used to describe those whom the party is opposed to – the elite – than is used to define 'the people'. Two elite groups are singled out in particular: politicians and bureaucrats on the one hand, and business elites on the other. The political elite is described as 'old parties', 'the other parties', 'the big parties' or 'the ruling parties'. Particularly targeted is the Centre Party, from which the predecessor of the PS, the SMP split off in 1959. This implies that the main voter base targeted at this point is lower and lower middle class conservative voters in the countryside and small towns. According to the manifesto, the old parties are 'cheating the pensioners' like they 'cheated the students', their representatives 'raised their own salaries' and voted to 'lower the taxes on the rich'. They are 'the parties in power who only remember the rich, the stock option predators and the EU big spenders'. They are teamed up with 'EU and domestic bureaucracy', and their policies support the second elite group, business elites, described as 'big money', 'rentiers, machine millionaires and cognac drinkers'. At this stage, the elites targeted are mainly national, even though the EU also gets its share of blame.

'Away with poverty!'

The populist discourse of the party in 2007 is supported by a left-wing economic discourse. Most stories in the party newspaper, including editorials, columns of the party leadership as well as quotations of parliamentary speeches by their three MPs, focus on economic justice issues. Headings include: 'Away with poverty', 'Where does Finland's money go?' and 'Child poverty is a national disgrace'. Party chairman Timo Soini is quoted as demanding that tax policy be the main theme of public debate leading up to the elections: 'I shall demand a change in the current line of overtaxing work and favouring lazy capital gains'.

At times, the left-wing rhetoric even uses terms that were common currency of the Finnish Communist Party in the 1970s: 'In many things, including income distribution, Finland has become an ultra-capitalist exploitation society. Examples are corporate executives' exorbitant stock options and excessive salaries'. This is, again, clearly in the tradition of the party's predecessor, SMP, and dovetails with the party's description of its enemies, the elites, examined above.

Social justice is also focused on in the manifesto. It opens with a defence of the 'traditional Nordic welfare state model', with social and health services guaranteed for every citizen. The Nordic model is contrasted with an Anglo-Celtic liberal view of a minimal state, which is purportedly pushed by the political elite under EU command:

> [...] it is wrong that a broad and functioning Finnish model of welfare state is being cut back due to various EU-led strategies [...] Accepting poverty and exclusion as normal phenomena represents an Anglo-Celtic tradition of thought, in which the most important function of the state is only to guarantee the free functioning of markets.

Additionally, the manifesto demands better care for the elderly and pensioners, and particularly state support for those taking care of elderly family members at home and war veterans.

'Minimal EU'

The third main ideological tenet, nationalism, has been present in the party ideology since the beginning. It has become more important in the recent years, however, we will argue. In the 2007 manifesto, the unity and identity of the Finnish nation is already a typical justification for policies, including critique of the EU, which threatens the sovereignty of the Finnish people. The party has never advocated leaving the EU at once, but rather pressed to discard any federalist plans, restrict expansion and demanded that the union interfere in national legislation as little as possible – all in all advocating a 'minimal EU'.

> Finland's influence in the union has only declined. The only thing that has substantially increased is Finland's membership fee [...] we support any and all propositions to reduce the EU's influence on issues of its member countries. (p. 11)

This call for sovereignty[2] is present in the party newspaper too, but comes clearly second to economic issues. Anti-immigration opinion gets relatively little space in 2007. The summary of the electoral manifesto merely states:

> Finland must carry its share of the world's crises and receive refugees – to the extent that resources permit. Therefore, Finland must fast-track the refusal of unwarranted claims for asylum so that resources can be directed to helping real refugees, and so that attitudes towards refugees would not tighten unnecessarily.

---

2. The party tends to use the less formal term '*itsemääräämisoikeus*', literally 'the right to self-rule'.

More hostile arguments on immigration are brewing in the margins of these more careful statements, however. Towards the end of the manifesto it is stated that 'large-scale immigration' might 'threaten original Finnish culture' (p.20). The demands of the party's newly established youth organisation include 'valorisation of national culture – no to multiculturalism!' Ex-boxer and wrestler Tony Halme had already been elected MP in 2003 on a strongly anti-immigrant protest campaign, and this rhetoric will later become more central to the party's argumentation.

'Poverty populism' wins 4–5 per cent of the vote

In sum, the 2007 PS was populist, rooting for the 'common sense' of the 'common people' to fight oppression by corrupt elites. This was combined with left-wing rhetoric, defending the Nordic welfare state model, resisting poverty and advocating redistributive tax policy. Nationalist discourse is there, but appears to play second fiddle.

In the 2007 election, the party achieved 4.1 per cent of the vote and five out of 200 parliamentary seats. This was already a success for the party, as the previous parliamentary elections of 2003 had left them with only 1.6 per cent. It was noted as a victory both by the party itself, with leader Soini citing 'a historical breakthrough' in *Perussuomalainen* 3/2007, and by researchers (Borg and Paloheimo 2009b: 19). With only five seats, however, the party's influence was marginal.

Despite the growth slump of late 2008, the economic crisis was nowhere to be found in the fall 2008 municipal electoral manifesto of the party. On the contrary, the manifesto celebrates 'fast economic growth' and 'good economic standing', which make the 'ever-expanding poverty and exclusion', which runs alongside it, all the more lamentable. Some media accounts even claimed the party had taken a left-populist turn (Yle 6 October 2008). The results saw the party continue their gradual rise in success, receiving 5.4 per cent of the vote. Although party leader Soini received the second-most votes nationally for any candidate of any party, PS activists claimed the result 'demonstrates we are not a one-man show' (Yle 26 October 2008).

An economic crisis, buffered

Was Finland hit hard by the economic crisis, which began globally in full effect after the fall of Lehman Brothers in September 2008? Looking at the first indicator of an economic crisis used in this volume, Figure 4.2 shows that the dip in GDP growth in 2009 was dramatic, deeper than in any other country studied here, including the countries that experienced the worst crisis overall, such as Greece and Ireland (*see also* Figures 1.1–1.3 in the introduction). This is due to the fact that the Finnish economy is heavily dependent on cyclical export industries, producing investment goods such as paper mills and mining machinery, for which demand drops sharply when a global crisis hits. During this crisis, Finnish

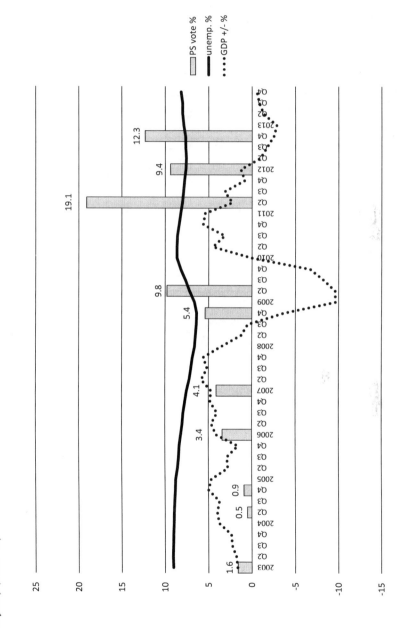

Figure 4.2: Finns Party (PS) vote share, unemployment rate (12-month moving average) and GDP growth rate (compared to same quarter of previous year) (2003–13)

industrial exports slowed down more than in any other OECD country (Rouvinen and Ylä-Anttila 2010: 11).

However, looking at our second crisis indicator, the rise in unemployment caused by the GDP drop was less severe than elsewhere. In fact, average unemployment for the pre-crisis period (2001 Q1–2008 Q3) is slightly higher than for the crisis years (2008 Q4–2013 Q2)! The first explanation for this stability of the job market is that there was a widespread understanding among big businesses that recovery would be quick (EK 2014). This belief proved to be justified at first; by the end of 2010 GDP growth had been restored to the relatively high pre-crisis level of 5 per cent per annum, even if only briefly, before the second phase of the crisis in 2011. Secondly, the age structure of the Finnish population is strongly tilted towards the currently retiring generation, especially compared to Southern European countries. Businesses foreseeing the effect of the retirement boom were less likely to begin mass layoffs, fearing that in the near future when growth would pick up again, they were to face competition for scarce labour resources.

Turning to our third indicator of an economic crisis, the level of sovereign debt did rise as a consequence of the crisis, but the starting level, 33.9 per cent of GDP in 2008 (Eurostat 2014a), was very low. In fact, the rise in debt during the first years of the crisis was due to a conscious decision of the government to engage in deficit spending to stimulate the economy and to provide welfare benefits for those hit by the downturn, something that it could well afford at this stage (Alho 2010).

Taken together, the stability of the job market and the enduring capacity of the state to provide welfare benefits, buffered the impact of the economic crisis on Finnish voters. Therefore, the rise of populism in the Finnish case cannot be explained by the concrete effects of the economic crisis: rising unemployment and decreased capacity of the state to provide safety nets.

However, as Figure 4.2 shows, the PS's success does strikingly coincide with the crisis. Even though the party's 9.8 per cent result in the European Parliamentary elections 2009 was a significant success, it did not yet have much to do with the euro, and was very much a personal triumph of party leader Soini, the only candidate of the party to win a seat. The global economic downturn of 2009 had not yet resulted in much trouble for the common currency and thus did not attract attention to the PS's EU critique (Pernaa 2012b: 20). It was the revelation in early 2010 that Greece was on the brink of bankruptcy that did.

Crisis populism 2011: A right-wing success

The rise of populism was not a direct consequence of the economic crisis on Finnish voters. Rather, it was a consequence of a combination of a national political crisis and the discursive opportunity generated by the economic crisis elsewhere in Europe. These two most important political topics of the campaign spoke directly to two of the PS ideology's main tenets, populism and nationalism. First, their populist claim that the political elite is corrupt gained resonance with an election funding scandal implicating all major parties in 2008–11

(Kantola, Vesa and Hakala 2011). Second, their anti-EU nationalism was well served by the euro crisis, which dominated Finnish media during the campaign. Additionally, the party's nationalist rhetoric expanded towards a more overt anti-immigration stance, with new members of the party crucial for starting a debate on immigration. Content analyses show that these three issues were the most reported in the media before the election (Pernaa 2012a, 2012b).

First, the political crisis began when, during 2008, it was gradually revealed that a group of businessmen had funded the campaigns of certain business-friendly politicians, who had then supported permits for specific property development plans, including a shopping centre and a snowmobile factory. Even taxpayer money had been channelled through the state-owned gambling monopoly to fund the Centre Party's campaign. Several claims against Prime Minister Matti Vanhanen were investigated but he was not charged, eventually resigning for 'personal reasons' in 2010. Party loyalty in the 2011 elections was exceptionally low. Some 40 per cent of voters reported voting for a different party than before. Over half of PS voters stated that the election funding scandal affected their vote 'to some extent' or 'significantly' (Väliverronen 2011: 142). The Centre Party was hit hardest. A total of 72 per cent of survey respondents said that their view of the party had changed for the worse. The Centre Party was also the biggest loser of the elections, crashing from 24.7 per cent to 15.8 per cent. The PS, in contrast, was granted the opportunity to push its discourse of integrity against 'corrupt mainstream parties'. A total of 30 per cent of respondents said their view of the PS had changed for the better, the largest number for any party. The scandal provided them an exceptional public confirmation for their thesis of the mainstream parties being 'corrupt', enabling them to represent 'the honest common people'. These findings of media content analyses and voter surveys strongly suggest that the situation can be characterised as a political crisis. This despite the fact that the general indicators used in this book to characterise political crises – electoral volatility, trust in parliament and satisfaction with democracy – do not place Finland in crisis territory. The crisis may not have been as severe as in Hungary or Greece. But in the Finnish context characterised by an exceptionally stable party system and persistently high trust in parliament, it was interpreted as a severe crisis by the media, the voters, and the PS, which used it as a campaign weapon, as we will show below.

Second, the European economic crisis and bailouts dominated headlines in 2010–11 (Pernaa 2012b: 21–22). Whereas The PS had been fiercely critical of the EU since day one, the theme had lacked salience. However, the revelation that Greece's economy would need EU support, a proposition that would have to be accepted by the Finnish parliament, instantly made the issue top priority. Mainstream parties were tied to their commitment to the EU project (Railo 2012: 231), whereas the populist contenders, in opposition, had no such burden, and could denounce any aid to foreign countries. This position enjoyed broad support from the Finnish electorate (Pernaa 2012b: 20–22). The media dominance of the euro crisis (Railo and Välimäki 2012a: 35–36) was reflected in voting: it was quoted as the most significant issue by voters (Borg 2012b: 246), particularly for PS voters.

Third, the immigration debate was largely started by PS candidates, especially the councilman and blogger Jussi Halla-aho, a fierce critic of multiculturalism. Among the issues debated were the public costs of refugee policy, cultural integration and urban segregation, immigrant criminality and Roma travellers. Immigration was the most reported issue in *Helsingin Sanomat*, the largest daily newspaper, in early 2011 (Railo and Välimäki 2012a: 35–38). The issue was seen as 'owned' (Petrocik 1996) by the PS, with their candidates seen as competent on the issue (Railo and Välimäki 2012b: 132). However, it was also one of the most divisive and controversial issues, with several candidates accused of racism.

The fourth major campaign issue was the rise of the PS itself. The media eagerly reported on the party's rise in opinion polls, promising the most interesting elections in years, giving the party a publicity boost and spurring the phenomenon onwards (Railo and Välimäki 2012b: 127–130). This intensified after the polls of summer 2010 indicated over 10 per cent for the rising party, as the Greece bailout furor was raging (Pernaa 2012b: 21).

In the PS manifesto 2011, '*Best suited for a Finn*' (*Suomalaiselle sopivin*, PS 2011), the first thing to note is its length of sixty-seven pages. It is clearly not written only for voters, but also for party activists themselves: to define, specify and record the growing party's ideology in detail. Populism is clearly the main tenet of this manifesto. While populism in 2007 was implicit, the 2011 manifesto offers a precise definition for the word. The PS is now a self-proclaimed populist party: 'The Finns Party is for a populist model of democracy, which means one based on the will of the people, instead of an elitist, that is, bureaucratic model of democracy' (p.6).

The 'populist view of democracy' is defined at length – perhaps not surprising in the light of the fact that Vesa-Matti Saarakkala, leading the manifesto working group, holds a BA in politics, and party chairman Timo Soini obtained his MA in politics with a dissertation on populism. The party agrees with the scholarly view that populism is combined with other elements: 'Populism is not a global ideology like socialism and capitalism, but always bound to a particular culture and national character' (p.7). In the 2011 manifesto, it is most clearly intertwined with nationalism.

'Democracy needs a nation'

In 2007, the PS's flavour of populism was mostly seasoned by what we have called the second tenet of their ideology – a left-wing social justice discourse – denouncing 'heartless policies' towards the poor, while 'the people', defended by the party, were equated with the disadvantaged. This placed the party at the margins. In 2011, this left-wing discourse is moderated, and what we have described as the third tenet of its ideology, nationalism, is now tightly connected to the populist core. This permits the party to portray itself as the defender of not only the poor, but the entire Finnish people.

What the party opposes now are not only the national elites, but increasingly other nations: the Greek and the Portuguese who have allegedly mismanaged their finances and do not 'deserve' the Finnish bailout money, as well as immigrants who do not 'deserve' Finnish jobs or social security, and whose presence is incompatible with the idea of the Finnish people deciding about its own affairs.

> The Finns Party wants to defend the popular sovereignty of Finns, which means that the people and the people only, which constitutes its own nation, separate from other nations, has an eternal and unlimited right to always freely and independently decide about all of its own issues. (p.7)

In the principles section of the manifesto, the key concept is 'kansanvalta'. As already pointed out, this literally means 'rule by the people'. The party prefers the term to 'demokratia', perhaps because of the possibility to use it interchangeably with 'populism'. As in the Finnish language, the word 'kansa' refers to both 'people' and 'nation', the concept of 'kansanvalta' enables the party to portray nationalism as necessary for true democracy. Their nationalist conception of democracy is 'rule by the nation' just as much as 'rule by the people'. The nation is equivalent to the people, which must be the sovereign ruler – there can be no democracy other than nationalist populist democracy. This is consistent with Mudde's (2007: 19) notion of nativism – the belief that the state primarily 'belongs' to its native group – as a core concept of 'populist radical right' parties. Mudde also notes that '[t]he step from 'the nation' to 'the people' is easily taken, and the distinction between the two is often far from clear' (2004: 549). In Finnish, this is all the more true. The nation-people of the PS's populism is a 'community' with 'shared values and norms'. 'Community is very much based on shared values and norms, which allow for the development of community into a society [...] Democracy is rule by the people, and is not possible without a nation'.

Both other nations, with their distinctive national cultures, and the domestic political elite, are posited as 'constitutive outsiders' or 'others' to this sovereign nation-people (e.g. Laclau 2005a: 73–83). 'Certain original ingredients, such as language, customs, art, conceptions of justice, nature, myths and beliefs affect the identity of each nation. These are unique to each nation, which exactly makes for diversity and richness' (p.8).

This is a typical argument of the contemporary radical right, whether labelled 'ethno-pluralism' (Spektorowski 2003), 'identitarianism' (Betz and Johnson 2004), 'cultural racism' (Wren 2001) or 'differentialist racism' (Taguieff 1993). It opposes immigration and multiculturalism by arguing that a plurality of cultures is best preserved by preventing them from mixing. Instead of the category of 'race' of traditional racism, the concept of 'culture' is used, but cultures are defined similarly to races, as separate and monolithic natural entities. The right of other cultures to exist is acknowledged, but mixing of cultures denied. This makes it possible to defend exclusionary policy by a seemingly 'liberal' justification, diversity of cultures.

'Cheaters and liars of the Eurozone'

The principle of nationalist populism is also used to ground the party's opposition to the EU. In their populist version of democracy, based on the 'general will' of a nation-people, democratic governance on a European scale is impossible.

> To assume that the EU could develop into a system of popular rule [...] we would also need to assume that Europeans could in the long run become a unified people. The Finns Party believes this to be utter madness. (p.32)

The EU is illegitimate because it is supranational, not 'international'. On this basis, the party does not advocate dismantling the EU, but strongly limiting its competencies.

> The Finns Party advocates cooperation between governments of independent nation-states. Our ultimate goal is to regain power from the EU back to nation-states. [...] We want a better EU through having less EU. (p.32)

Regarding the euro crisis, the manifesto is indirect and formal and does not mention Greece or Portugal, likely because it does not seem to be addressed to the voters, but rather to the party organisation itself. In other party communication, however, the euro crisis is everywhere. Chairman Soini demands on TV that Finland 'must stop shoveling money under the palm trees' in Southern Europe, a phrase that begins a life of its own. In his blog entry titled 'Greece', he writes: 'You lied and cheated to get into the Eurozone [...] You knew you were cheating. What does it tell about the EU if they, indeed, did not notice?' Vice-chair Saarakkala links the more abstract criticism of EU democracy with the Union's current financial problems:

> Democracy can never be supranational, which means that the EU is always anti-democratic. This has led, especially in the countries using the Euro, to the final erosion of political morality, because in the EU system, those who should be responsible for their decisions are not. Instead, the innocent, like the Finns, are made to pay for the silliness of the others.

This rhetoric fell on fertile ground. Voter surveys showed that the euro crisis was the most important issue for voters (Borg 2012b: 246), especially PS voters. Exploiting the discursive opportunity created by the euro crisis was crucial to their success in 2011.

'Somali welfare parasites'

The categorisation of 'populist radical right' has been debatable in the case of the PS (Arter 2010; Koivulaakso, Brunila and Andersson 2012). However, an anti-immigration bloc entered the PS in full effect for the 2011 elections and plays an ever larger role, lending more credence to such a classification.

The immigration-focused politicians tend also to take notably right-wing (libertarian) economic stances (Ylä-Anttila 2012; 2014).

The central figure of the anti-immigration politicians is blogger Jussi Halla-aho, who had already been a candidate (without party membership) in 2007, but did not get exposure in party materials. After fame in mainstream media in 2008 as the main critic of immigration policy, he joined the party and got to publish his own piece in the party paper. His rhetoric here is very careful compared to some of his blog remarks, the latter including suggestions that Somali immigrants come to Finland to 'casually rob passers-by' and 'to live as welfare parasites' – for which he was convicted for racist agitation in 2009. He and other new party members belong to nationalist organisations such as Suomen Sisu, which opposes the 'unnatural mixing of peoples' (Suomen Sisu principles 2006).

Such radical positions are not present in official party material. However, the theme of restricting immigration occupies significantly more space in 2011, as anti-immigration candidates have joined the party. Vesa-Matti Saarakkala chairs the party's manifesto committee but is also one of the signatories of an unofficial anti-immigration manifesto and a 'resignation from the ideology of multiculturalism', signed by thirteen PS candidates. Many candidates not previously identified with anti-immigration opinions have now begun to talk about the issue. Ten of the forty candidates presented in the election issue of the party newspaper list immigration as one of their main themes. The long-time editor of the paper now laments:

> The Greens and the Swedish People's Party are the main culprits for the fact that we now get 26,000 immigrants every year to generate wealth (for the rich). Taxpayers' money is spent on uniting immigrant families, even for their plane tickets. The poor of our own country have been forgotten and their constitutional rights trampled on.

The party's five parliamentarians issued a statement to the media asserting that 'Finland must not become the place to store asylum seekers whose applications have been deemed unfounded by other countries', adding that 'in the recent weeks and days big crowds of such asylum seekers have entered Finland. A news-like item in the paper cites a prison guard saying that 'Finnish prisons are no deterrent for foreign thieves, part of whom openly brag that a Finnish prison is like a five-star hotel in their own country'. Another story presents a model immigrant whom the party warmly welcomes to Finland: Igor is Ingrian (from the area that Finland lost to Russia in the Second World War), has a Finnish surname and Finnish roots, and is presented as clearly fitting Finland culturally. He is also a small entrepreneur who works hard 'but still can't even afford a car and only makes 1,000–1,500 euros per month'.

We have argued that there is a shift from populism 'thickened' by a left-wing social justice discourse to populism 'thickened' by anti-EU and anti-immigration nationalism within the PS. It must be noted that the left-wing discourse has not disappeared completely. A major section of the 2011 manifesto calls for the upkeep of a 'traditional Nordic welfare state' with no major privatisations or cuts (pp.11–12). This is to defend the least well off and support income equality, but also to support 'the unity of the people' (pp.46–47). However, living on benefits should not be allowed and the propensity for work should always be rewarded (p.22). 'Ordinary Finns' stand against 'big capital and international finance' (p.44):

> The Finns Party believes that big capital and international finance must pay for the financial crisis, not ordinary Finns. [...] We must look into the possibility to employ taxes on financial transactions, currency transactions, banks and credit institutions. (pp.44–45)

Despite their 2011 landslide victory, the party excluded itself from government negotiations by sticking to its policy of unconditionally rejecting any euro bailouts. This position was untenable for the mainstream parties committed to EU cooperation, leading to a rainbow coalition of Conservatives and Social Democrats with four smaller parties, dubbed the 'six-pack'.

2012–14 and beyond

Even though PS voters are more focused on the party leader than other voters (Kestilä-Kekkonen and Söderlund 2014), in the presidential elections 2012 Soini, as PS candidate, failed to muster support even remotely comparable to the party's recent success. He only received 9.4 per cent. As presidential elections are naturally candidate-focused, neither the protest against the 'old parties', nor opposition to EU or immigration were on the agenda here. Moderate right-wing candidate Sauli Niinistö carried the election by a wide margin, predictable after his narrow loss six years before.

A similar story can be told about the municipal elections of October 2012, where the discussion largely revolved around issues of an administrative and economic nature, lacking any serious potential for large-scale protest. The PS tried to play the anti-EU card again. Their manifesto depicts an old car, number plate FIN-12, representing Finland. Its roof is stacked with boxes, a burden weighing it down, labelled 'developmental aid', 'euro bailouts', 'Greece loans', 'EU membership fees', and 'Green directives'. The party accused previous governments of 'committing Finland to saving foreign big banks' and assert that 'to fund these obligations, the government is cutting funding for municipalities'. The PS, in contrast, is for local democracy and local identities: 'The foundation of a municipality is a home region, where its people want to live and work'. The party obtained 12.3 per cent, not much when compared to the 19.1 per cent in the general election, but still a significant increase from their previous municipal result of 5.4 per cent. EU-critique proved difficult to exploit at the local level.

A look at the party youth newspaper shows a move further towards the right, now also in terms of economic policy. For example, in March 2013, the youth chairman Simon Elo writes that 'the Finns Party youth must drive a tax rebellion into the party!' This 'tax rebellion' refers to 'redefining' the welfare state by 'cutting public spending where we can', lowering corporate tax, and 'gradually lowering taxes for the middle class'. This, he states, would 'fit our national-liberalist economic policy perfectly'. For April 2013, they invited libertarian youth politician Henri Heikkinen as columnist, advocating a decentralisation of the school system to help top achievers to succeed.

The party have also founded a think tank, 'Suomen Perusta' (Foundation for Finland), with Simo Grönroos as its manager – a 29-year old member of the nationalist organisation *Suomen Sisu*, supporter of the anti-multiculturalist MP Jussi Halla-aho, and a fan of United States Republican politicians Ron Paul and Patrick Buchanan, according to his website. The think tank produced a report in February 2014 advocating privatisation of municipal services, in contrast with the mainstream party policy. The report also called to stop all developmental aid and 'humanitarian immigration' and for drastic cuts of social benefits, particularly for two groups: immigrants and drug abusers. Socially conservative, economically libertarian – this seems to be the way forward for the new generation of the party. And the youth wing is gaining support from current members of parliament. In February 2014, Teuvo Hakkarainen, an older MP known for racist remarks, somewhat surprisingly revealed his own suggestions for public-sector cutbacks. 'The public sector will burst like a toad filled with water', he claimed, demanding that '[it] must be cut back with a heavy hand, cut the administration, cut the bureaucracy' (*Verkkouutiset* 27 February 2014). The party's two MEPs elected in 2014, Jussi Halla-aho and Sampo Terho, both represent the party's right wing, also regarding economic policy. After negotiations, they joined the European Conservatives and Reformists Group (ECR), known as the group of the Conservative Party of the United Kingdom, together with the MEPs of the Danish People's Party (DFP).

The party owes it success in 2011 largely to floating voters (Arter and Kestilä-Kekkonen 2014), creating a difficult starting point for lasting support (Borg 2012a: 209). Indeed, its poll success has declined in anticipation of the April 2015 general election (HS 18 August 2014), but it still is the third largest party in the polls. For the time being, the party seems to have established its position as a mainstream player (Arter and Kestilä-Kekkonen 2014), catering to a populist constituency that had long existed (Kestilä 2006).

Conclusion: Populism can exploit crisis discourse

We have argued that the PS ideology can be analysed via three tenets: 1) the populist defence of the common people against corrupt elites, 2) a left-populist defence of the welfare state against market-led policies promoted by EU and national elites and 3) a nationalist defence of the sovereignty and unity of the Finnish people against federalist tendencies of the EU and immigration. Populist democracy, or '*kansanvalta*' (rule by the people), as the party calls it, takes as its input the unfiltered general will of the common people, who know in their hearts what is right. Politics is a matter of morality and conscience, of right and wrong, not of administration and bureaucracy. According to the PS, for this general will to emerge, the democratic unit needs to be consistent with the nation. Constitutive outsiders ('others') such as immigrants and elites, both domestic and European, must be excluded, or democracy cannot function.

The focus of the party, however, has turned from the second tenet above (social justice) to the third (national sovereignty and unity). The party has shifted from opposing the domestic elite – which was the bread and butter of SMP, the PS's predecessor (1959–95) – to opposing foreign threats, namely the EU and immigration. This also means that the definition of 'the people' has shifted from the disadvantaged to all (ethnic) Finns, that is, from people as class to people as nation. While Mudde (2004: 549) correctly observes that '[t]oday, populism is again mainly associated with the (radical) right', because of the conflation of the 'people' of populism with the nation; we have argued that until the economic crisis, the PS's 'people' was largely based on class. However, the move from agrarian populism of the periphery towards radical right populism helped the party to gain massively at a time of political and moral crisis – with the established parties accused of corruption and Southern EU countries accused of immoral economic policy. This brings the PS ideology more in line with the mainstream of current European radical right populist parties and brings it out of the margins, facilitating its more widespread success. Indeed, it is converging with the other Nordic populist parties, despite its agrarian populist roots, as argued by Jungar and Jupskås (2014).

To conclude, looking at economic indicators, the crisis hit Finland's economy hard particularly due to the composition of its industry, but due to other structural factors (the population's age structure and the state's strong economy), it was not reflected dramatically in the everyday lives of Finns. Despite this, the Finnish polity witnessed an unprecedented populist success. This was fuelled by the discursive opportunity the crisis offered for blaming other EU countries on moral and economic grounds.

Thus, the first guiding hypothesis (H1) of this volume, that economic crisis intensifies populism-*qua*-discourse, gains support in the Finnish case, but only with very specific qualifications: it was not the state of the Finnish economy but the broader European situation that served populist success, by way of creating discursive opportunities. As for the second hypothesis (H2), that political crises also intensify populism, we must again add qualifiers. The Finnish populist mobilisation was indeed partly a reaction to a corruption scandal. Nevertheless, in the context of a remarkably stable polity, even a political crisis deemed as severe by the media, academia, parties and voters, might not be visible in simple indicators of volatility or trust. The third hypothesis (H3), of a combination of economic and political crises being particularly conducive for populism, is also supported by our results, but again with the country-specific qualifications outlined above. As for populists toning down their populism when in power (H4), the Finnish case does not apply, since the only party that can be identified as populist has always been in opposition.

These findings suggest that simple structural explanations and indicators only go so far in explaining populism – cultural and economic specificities are equally important. It is interpretations of crisis that matter, not just crisis in numbers.

PART II

THE WESTERN REGION

Chapter Five

The Revenge of the *Ploucs*:[1]
The Revival of Radical Populism
under Marine Le Pen in France

Hans-Georg Betz

Introduction

In France, the inability of successive governments to solve the severe socio-economic problems engendered by the Great Recession has opened ample room for populist mobilisation. Yet the only party to seize the moment has been the *Front National* (FN) under the new leadership of Marine Le Pen. Attempts by the far left behind Jean-Luc Mélenchon to occupy populist terrain proved largely unsuccessful. Mélenchon's 'meta-populist' discourse was much too highbrow (Cassely 2013), his hesitant bid to advance a radical alternative too timid to capitalise on widespread popular political disenchantment and discontent (Bernier 2014). By contrast, Marine Le Pen's emphatic embrace of populist rhetoric and strategy has proved highly successful.

When Marine Le Pen assumed the party presidency in January 2011, the FN was at a crossroad. The party was in serious financial trouble after a series of significant reversals at the polls following the presidential election of 2002 (Igounet 2014: 403–404). The low point was reached in the 2009 European election, where the FN lost four of the seven seats won in 2004. Organisationally, the FN was significantly weakened after the defection and expulsion of a number of leading cadres. After the 2007 presidential election, the party was in such bad shape that TNS-Sofres decided to discontinue its annual survey on the FN's public image (they resumed in 2010). In this situation, Marine Le Pen had the choice between continuing to serve as the point of reference for the anachronistic obsessions of various extreme-right *groupuscules* (such as Catholic traditionalists, Petainist ultra-nationalists, anti-Semitic conspiracy theorists and racists) or pushing the party in a radically new direction. She chose to embark on a project of organisational rejuvenation and programmatic reform designed to '*dediabolise*' the FN's image and gain political respectability for its new leader. The result has been astounding. Most significantly, Marine Le Pen managed to reverse the FN's fortunes: in the presidential election of 2012, the FN candidate received 6.4 million votes (17.9 per cent of the vote), 1.8 million more than her father had garnered in 2002. In the subsequent legislative election,

---

1.   French term for a hick, yokel or bumpkin.

the FN received 13.6 per cent of the vote and managed to win two seats. Two years later, in the local elections, the party elected a dozen mayors and re-established itself as the third national political force. Finally, in the European elections a few months later, the FN caused a political earthquake when, with roughly 25 per cent of the vote, it outdistanced all other major parties. Secondly, Marine Le Pen established herself as a tough yet personable politician, who increasingly managed to push her ideas and demands onto the political agenda. Last but not least, Marine Le Pen's strong personality did much to improve the party's image, even if the media continued to characterise the FN as a right-wing extremist party (Mestre 2014).

Personality accounts, however, only in part for the FN's political revival. Marine Le Pen also benefitted from the profound economic, political, and particularly psychological crisis that continues to traumatise the country. This crisis allowed Marine Le Pen to reinvent herself as an uncompromising promoter of French sovereignty; an untiring, disinterested advocate of ordinary people against the ravages of globalisation; the only credible alternative to the political establishment; and the sole genuine defender of the country's historical heritage, cultural identity and fundamental values.

In response to the crisis, Marine Le Pen not only shifted the party's programmatic centre of gravity from its formerly preponderant focus on immigration toward broader questions of political economy; she also sharpened its populist profile relentlessly charging the political establishment of perpetuating a system that benefited a small oligarchic elite at the expense of ordinary people (Mestre 2012). At the same time, she adopted a social-populist programme that borrowed heavily from the traditional and dissident left. The explicit goal was to recover the manual and routine non-manual vote (the *couches populaires*) the FN had lost to Nicolas Sarkozy in 2007, broaden the party's electoral appeal, and thus turn the FN into a catch-all party of protest, strong enough to bolster Marine Le Pen's self-proclaimed presidential ambitions (Le Pen 2013).

The remainder of this chapter offers an account of these developments. It starts with a short discussion of the socio-economic impact of the Great Recession in France, followed by an extended analysis of the evolution of the FN's doctrine and programme under Marine Le Pen. The final part of the chapter provides a brief assessment of the main factors accounting for Marine Le Pen's success and its impact on French politics and society.

The Great Recession and French malaise

The immediate impact of the Great Recession of 2008 on France was relatively mild. Output and employment losses were less significant than in Germany and the United States. Unlike the latter, however, France has had a hard time recovering from the crisis. In 2012, French output and employment levels were still below pre-crisis levels. Unemployment continued to rise, France's manufacturing base to decline, and the country to lag behind its main competitors in Western Europe and overseas (Bellone and Chiappini 2014).

The slump brought to light the structural weaknesses of the French economy: stagnating productivity; a deteriorating balance of trade; declining attractiveness for foreign investors; a continued high number of annual bankruptcies; a dramatic increase of the national debt (from roughly 64 per cent of GDP in 2006 to more than 90 per cent in 2013); rising socio-economic inequality (Boulhol and Sicari 2014; Mongereau 2013; Altares 2014; Clerc 2014). Most important of all, the crisis brutally exposed the widening competitiveness gap between France and Germany, reflected, among other things, in the two countries' divergent ability to attract FDI (EY Advisory 2013: 12–16; Visot 2014). This was a function of both French companies' low profitability rate (in 2013 the lowest in the euro area) and high indebtedness and France's overall structural 'weakness in innovation' primarily due to its firms' limited capacity to absorb available knowledge (European Commission 2013a: 9; European Commission 2014: 42).

The economic slump has had a profound psychological impact on large parts of the French population, with growing gloom pervading society. Take INSEE's monthly consumer confidence index, for instance: in mid-2013, four years after the onset of the Great Recession, it was at the same level as in 2008 (INSEE 2013). Opinion polls tell a similar story. In 2012, almost two thirds of respondents rated France's competitive position as bad (Ifop 2012). By comparison, in late 2010, some 75 per cent of German respondents considered their country well-positioned with regard to global economic competition (Perrineau 2011: 82). In 2013, three out of four respondents thought France was 'in decline'; for two-thirds, France was in the midst of a 'crisis without precedent' (CSA 2014: 4–7). A mere 36 per cent said they had confidence in France's future, whereas 75 per cent said the same about Germany's future (Viavoice 2013). As a result, in May 2013, *Le Monde* characterised the French as the 'champions of pessimism in Europe' (Gatinois 2013). Many put the blame on globalisation. In late 2013, more than 60 per cent of respondents considered globalisation a threat to the country (Ipsos 2014). A large number agreed that only protectionist measures could counter the impact of globalisation (TNS-Sofres 2011).

At the same time, the majority of French voters showed little confidence in the established parties, the political class, and the political process in general. For most voters, politicians care little about what ordinary citizens think or want and are easily corrupted (in March 2014, more than two thirds of respondents thought politicians were more and more corrupt [BVA 2013]). A considerable number (50 per cent in 2011) think that politicians lack the power to improve the plight of ordinary people given the structural constraints imposed on them by globalisation, the European Union (EU), and big business (Perrineau 2011: 82). Many are disaffected with representative democracy, yearning instead for plebiscitary forms of democracy or even for a 'strong man' unencumbered by parliament and *elections*.

Under the circumstances, the resurgence of the FN is hardly surprising. The failure of successive governments to deal with the socio-economic impact of the crisis boosted the fortunes of the FN. As political confidence declined, the FN's image improved. In June 2007, Sarkozy's approval rating stood at 63 per cent. At the end of 2011, it had fallen to 29 per cent. François Hollande fared even worse. Between June 2012 and December 2013, his approval rating fell from 55 to 21 per cent (TNS-Sofres 2014a). At the same time, the number of those who thought the FN did not pose a danger to democracy increased from 29 per cent (December 2006) to 47 per cent (January 2013) and the number of those saying they agreed with the FN's ideas increased from 26 per cent to almost a third (TNS-Sofres 2014b). In short, as consumer confidence declined and approval ratings for the president of the republic fell, the FN's public image steadily improved (*see* Figure 5.1).

The republican turn

The Great Recession provoked substantial shifts in the political opportunity structure of the French Republic, which proved highly propitious for the FN. After all, issues such as disenchantment with politics, the inexorable decline of the country, and the threatened loss of national identity had always been central to FN rhetoric. As early as 1985, Jean-Marie Le Pen had made the alleged gap between democratic claim (*'La France est une démocratie'*) and everyday reality (*'La pratique, hélas est différente'*) the lynchpin of his political programme (Le Pen 1985: 17–35). According to FN reasoning, democracy in France had been 'confiscated' by a new 'oligarchy' that occupied every locus of political power. The result was a 'profound gulf' separating the people from their representatives charged with doing nothing to defend the French people

Figure 5.1: French malaise and public perception of Marine LePen and Front National

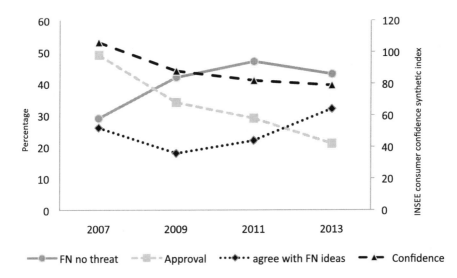

and their national identity (Le Pen 1985: 37). At the same time, Le Pen evoked the spectre of national decline, associated with socialism, immigration, drugs, and corruption. In 1992, the FN advanced '300 measures' supposed to bring about the '*renaissance*' of the country, primarily by reversing the country's demographic decline and thus saving the nation from falling apart (FN 1993).

Under Jean-Marie Le Pen, the FN was long on ideology, but relatively short on concrete policies. Le Pen himself never seemed particularly serious about pursuing the country's highest offices. He was largely content with playing the role of the political maverick, who took great pleasure in launching outrageous verbal provocations meant to shock the educated middle class. When in the late 1990s, Le Pen's right-hand man, Bruno Mégret, attempted to transform the FN into a serious contender for political power, he and his supporters were quickly purged. Mégret's ideas, however, did not disappear. It was Marine Le Pen, who would adopt them as basis for her project of mainstreaming the FN (i.e. *dédiabolisation*). This entailed ridding the party of the remnants of its most radical right-wing extremist elements, particularly the anti-Semitic circles 'obsessed with the Shoah'.[2] In sharp contrast to her father, Marine Le Pen made it clear that for her, the Holocaust represented 'the summit of barbarism' and that therefore there was no room for anti-Semites and racists in the party.[3] Instead Marine Le Pen surrounded herself with (predominantly young) technocrats with expertise in various policy fields.[4]

Mainstreaming the party also entailed curtailing the FN programme's heavy emphasis on immigration, which had led the FN to be seen as little more than a single-issue party. This does not mean, however, that Marine Le Pen abandoned the notion that immigration was central to France's socio-economic woes. Finally, and most importantly, mainstreaming entailed developing a comprehensive and coherent programme that would not only stand the test of outside scrutiny but that also represented a credible alternative to the centre left and centre right.

This strategy rested on two pillars: one, to refurbish the FN as a 'republican party', committed to defending the ideals of the country's republican and 'laicist' tradition (Perrineau 2014: 77–82); two, to put together a comprehensive socio-economic programme offering a credible alternative to the dominant free-market ideology espoused by the political establishment.

Marine Le Pen emphasised her commitment to republicanism as soon as she won the party presidency. In her maiden speech at the 2011 party congress in Tours she vowed that she would restore the traditional values of the French Republic, abandoned and betrayed by the political establishment. In the months that followed, Marine Le Pen repeatedly laid claim to the ideas and positions of Jean-Pierre

---

2.   '2012: Marine Le Pen ira "pour gagner" à la présidentielle', *20 minutes.fr*, 4 December 2010, http://www.20minutes.fr/politique/633823-politique-2012-marine-pen-ira-pour-gagnera-presidentielle.

3.   Alain Soral, a close adviser of Jean-Marie Le Pen for the 2007 presidential election and the leading promoter of virulent anti-Semitism left the *Front National* in early 2009 after falling out with Marine Le Pen (Albertini and Doucet 2013: 286–287; 324–325).

4.   Insiders have maintained, however, that under Marine Le Pen, the FN continued to be pervaded by a climate of racism.

Chevènement, the leader of the republican left – an association, which the latter vehemently rejected. For Chevènement, Marine Le Pen's project represented a hostile takeover of the discourse of the republican left which she used to justify her positions on immigration, multiculturalism and Islam (Chevènement 2011). Chevènement also objected to the fact that the media routinely characterised one of Marine Le Pen's closest advisers, Florian Philippot (since 2012 vice president of the party in charge of strategy and communication) as a young technocrat who had 'passed from Chevènement to Le Pen'. He was particularly incensed that Philippot claimed that Chevènement was 'closer to Marine Le Pen than to Hollande'.[5]

Philippot was instrumental in pushing a major plank of Chevènement's political thinking – *souverainisme*. By putting the question of national sovereignty at the centre of Marine Le Pen's political project, he strengthened her image as a serious candidate committed to restoring France's independence and sovereignty.

Philippot's republican course served several of Marine Le Pen's main objectives. For one, it fed into her catch-all strategy aimed at broadening the FN's appeal across the entire ideological spectrum, even if the party's republican turn was likely to provoke controversy within the party. When party supporters objected to Philippot's repeated tributes to General de Gaulle, Marine Le Pen stressed that the FN was not a *'parti Gaullist'*.[6] Yet she also affirmed that she had no problems making reference to 'some Gaullist ideas' such as the referendum and the defence of national independence and sovereignty. Secondly, it added credibility to Marine Le Pen's strategy of normalisation and accentuated her break with the extreme right. Important extreme right publications, such as *Rivarol* and *Minute*, obliged with vitriolic attacks against the FN's new direction and particularly the man they held responsible for it – Philippot. Thirdly, it provided Marine Le Pen with an ideological foundation for the construction of a serious alternative socio-economic programme that offered concrete solutions to the profound crisis affecting the country. Last but not least, it had the potential to attract intellectuals and experts, who disagreed with the dominant socio-economic rationale and who searched for a new forum that could guarantee them visibility and impact.

Against the dominant doctrine of ultraliberal globalisation

In early 2008, Chevènement stated in *Le Monde* that the left's only chance to regain power was to unite behind a political project that lived up to the challenges of globalisation and appealed to the *'couches populaires'* (Chevènement 2008). Four years later, shortly before the presidential election, an influential socialist think tank issued a report, which strongly suggested that the left, instead of

---

5. Mestre 2012; Mihaely and Boughezala 2012. In late 2011, Chevènement's former *directeur des cabinets*, Bertrand Dutheil de la Rochère, joined Marine Le Pen, who put him in charge of questions pertaining to the republic and laicism.

6. '*Front National*: Marine Le Pen contredit Florian Philippot sur les racines gaullistes du parti', *atlantico.fr*, 12 January 2014, http://www.atlantico.fr/pepites/front-national-marine-pen-contredit-florian-philippot-racines-gaullistes-parti-951717.html (accessed 12 March 2014).

pursuing the *couches populaires*, should assemble a new coalition composed of those social groups – the young, women, the better educated, and French citizens with a migrant background – most likely to support a progressive agenda (Ferrand and Jeanbart 2011). The message was clear: running after the *couches populaires* was a lost cause.

The tenor of the report said much about the programmatic direction taken by the French left since Mitterrand's radical '*tournant de la rigueur*' of 1983, which ended the experiment of an independent socialist economic policy in France. The realisation that in an increasingly globalised world, national governments were losing much of their ability to set an independent economic policy led the French left to focus increasingly on values issues, i.e. gender equality, multiculturalism, anti-racism, and gay rights (Le Goff 2013a). The resulting '*gauchisme culturel*' was far removed from the every-day experiences and worries of ordinary people with regard to the ravages of globalisation, which threatened to destroy 'the protection on which they believed they could count' (Joffrin 2014). For its critics, the inevitable outcome of this programmatic reorientation was to 'accentuate the left's break with the *couches populaires* and destroy its credibility' among the latter (Le Goff 2013a). In the process, the left voided and ceded the political space once occupied by the socialist and communist left. Once the socio-economic preoccupations provoked by the economic crisis assumed centre stage, Marine Le Pen was in an excellent position to fill the void.

Marine Le Pen's response was to accord top priority to the development of a comprehensive, internally consistent socio-economic programme. The result was a set of policies, which represented a marked departure from the market-oriented programme the FN had promoted in the past. Marine Le Pen defended her ideas in numerous speeches, newspaper interviews, and in front of television cameras, often one-on-one with her critics.[7] Charging the political establishment with having led the country into a catastrophic situation, she promoted herself as the only political force capable of affecting a radical change.[8] For Marine Le Pen, this entailed a decisive break with the dominant market ideology, the prevailing subservience to the almighty financial markets and the 'rule of king money', and above all to the blind adherence to the doctrine of globalisation. For globalisation meant rising unemployment, declining standards of living, growing inequality and injustice for the many, astronomical salaries and bonuses, tax free capital gains, and unlimited wealth for the few. While the economic policies of the past caught a growing number of the middle class in a downward spiral of social decline, the

---

7. The most noteworthy was her appearance on *Des paroles et des actes* (23 February 2012) where she refused to debate one of her interlocutors, Jean-Luc Mélenchon, whom she accused of insulting her voters. See http://www.huffingtonpost.fr/2012/02/23/marine-le-pen-des-paroles-et-des-actes_n_1296929.html.

8. For what follows see the following speeches: Tours, 16 January 2011, http://www.nationspresse.info/congres-fn-tours-2011-discours-de-marine-le-pen/; Bompas, 11 March 2011, http://www.nationspresse.info/bompas-34-marine-le-pen-lance-la-vague-sociale/; Saint-Denis, 9 January 2012, http://www.frontnational.com/videos/discours-de-marine-le-pen-a-loccasion-de-la-galette-presidentielle-organisee-a-saint-denis/ (accessed 10 March 2014).

political establishment continued to insist on adhering to the worn-out ultraliberal doctrines, which had caused the present disaster. In sharp contrast, Marine Le Pen presented her presidential candidacy as the beginning of a 'historical and life-and-death fight' for the country's recovery in the name of the 'forgotten' and 'invisible majority' – everyone 'being crushed by a financial system gone mad' and whose suffering was ignored by the political establishment 'because they counted for nothing'.[9]

If they counted for nothing, it was because the established political parties, both right and left, had long abandoned the cause of the people, adopting instead a globalist ideology – *mondialisme*. *Mondialisme* constituted a new 'totalitarian ideology' which, Marine Le Pen charged, aimed at subjugating the people to 'consumption and production for the benefit of a few big enterprises and banks', which reaped all the profits.[10] *Mondialisme* was the new dogma, which stood for 'globalisation without borders, globalisation without limits, without regulation' – in short, the creation of a full-blown world-wide market.[11] The goal was to weaken the nation state and ultimately dissolve it altogether.

It was for this reason, Marine Le Pen explained, that the French political class, conservatives and socialists alike, had supported every step in the process of European integration, including the introduction of the euro, the 'golden calf' of globalisation (Le Pen 2012b: 54). The euro was an artificial currency, meant to pave the way for 'the creation of a federal Europe', even if the people were against it (Le Pen 2012b: 56). This showed, she charged, that *mondialisme* was a 'profoundly antidemocratic ideology', which undermined and weakened 'the natural spaces of democratic life, which are the nations' (Le Pen 2012b: 32). This, of course, posed no problem for France's political establishment, which neither cared nor had any respect for their country. In fact, by relinquishing one part after the other of the nation's sovereignty they showed that they were intent on liquidating France altogether.[12]

The national/social alternative: Le social d'abord

In response, Marine Le Pen promised that if elected she would make every effort to return France to the French people and rebuild 'the pillars of a republican nation' (Le Pen 2012b: 17). Charging those in power of having completely hollowed out French sovereignty, she advanced an economic programme that she claimed would restore France's autonomy and national independence. The programme represented a synthesis of traditional republican/nationalist and traditional left-wing/socialist positions. On the nationalist side, the emphasis was on regaining

---

9.   Metz speech, 11 December 2011, cited in Riché 2011.

10. Bompas speech.

11. Nice speech, 11 September 2011, http://www.frontnational.com/videos/11-septembre-acropolis-nice-%E2%80%93-discours-de-marine-le-pen-videos/ (accessed 12 March 2014).

12. Charenton-Le-Pont speech, 2 December 2011, http://www.nationspresse.info/colloque-defense-discours-de-marine-le-pen/ (accessed 12 March 2014).

national sovereignty as the most effective way to protect ordinary French citizens against the economic and social ravages caused by globalisation. On the socialist side, the emphasis was on reviving the traditional French policies of *dirigisme* and *étatisme*, reflected in a panoply of roles she accorded to the state, ranging from '*L'État protecteur*' to '*L'État stratège*' (Le Pen 2012b: 193ff.).

To achieve full national sovereignty, Marine Le Pen propagated the notion of 'economic patriotism'. It included a call for 'intelligent' protectionism against 'disloyal competition' and the demand that the French state be required by law (*Achetons français*) to award procurement contracts at all administrative levels exclusively to French companies (Le Pen 2012a: 3). Ultimately, however, France would only regain its sovereignty if the French state regained its independence from the financial markets. For this to happen, Marine Le Pen proposed abrogating the 1973 law forbidding the Treasury to borrow directly from the *Banque de France*. This would not only deprive the financial markets of their power to dictate their terms to the state; it would also allow the state to borrow interest-free from the *Banque de France*, which, in turn, would contribute to containing the national debt (Le Pen 2012b: 63ff., 2012a: 3).

Finally, and most important of all, regaining national sovereignty entailed above all abandoning the euro. As her campaign advanced, Marine Le Pen made France's exit from the Eurozone and the reintroduction of the franc the cornerstone of her economic programme. For Marine Le Pen, the euro was not only responsible for asphyxiating French economic growth and destroying whole industries, it was also the cause of the explosion of mass unemployment in France and elsewhere in the EU. Only the return to a national currency would allow France to regain lost sovereignty over monetary policy and flexibility with respect to economy policy. Characterising the euro as 'the instrument of our enslavement', 'our prison, our cage', she maintained that recapturing monetary sovereignty was 'the key to our liberty'.[13] Monetary sovereignty would provide France with room to manoeuvre, above all by allowing the country once again to devalue its currency and thus regain lost competitiveness.[14] At the same time, Marine Le Pen increasingly stressed, however, that the decision to leave the Eurozone could only be made by the French people via a referendum (Le Pen 2012a: 2).

In order to appeal to the 'invisible and forgotten', Marine Le Pen advanced a comprehensive plan of national economic revival. The plan derived its logic from Marine Le Pen's assumptions about the causes and mechanisms of France's economic decline. In her view, the latter was first and foremost due to the dramatic contraction of the country's manufacturing base (i.e. deindustrialisation), a direct result of 'disloyal competition' from developing countries engaging in social and

---

13. Rouen speech, 15 January 2012, http://www.frontnational.com/videos/grand-meeting-de-marine-le-pen-a-rouen-le-15-janvier/ (accessed 12 March 2014). Once again, this was hardly an original position, Daniel Cohen, for instance, in a well-known essay, characterised the euro as a 'gilded prison, which forces the European countries to pursue the same type of austerity, which was practiced during the thirties' and ended in a disaster. *See* Cohen 2012: 154.

14. Marine Le Pen during her appearance on *Des paroles et des actes*, France 2, 23 June 2011, http://www.youtube.com/watch?v=rAxq_4mq9ac (accessed 13 March 2014).

environmental dumping.[15] These practices put French manufacturers at a significant disadvantage in the global market, which led to the loss of manufacturing jobs and thus contributed to mass unemployment.

Marine Le Pen had first-hand experience of this process, derived from her association with Hénin-Beaumont, a once flourishing coal-mining town located in the Nord-Pas-de-Calais region, which had fallen on hard times. Her experience as a regional and municipal councillor in 'the economic badlands along the border with Belgium' (Ames 2014) exposed her not only to the socio-economic consequences of the end of an industrial era; she also witnessed the corruption and nepotism of the local socialist administration, which led a growing number of left-wing voters (and here particularly former communist voters) to defect to the FN (see the account by the former left-wing mayor Gérard Dalongeville [2013] who was sentenced to prison for embezzlement of public funds). This, together with her exposure to the social reality in Hénin-Beaumont, explains at least in part Marine Le Pen's adoption of socio-economic positions traditionally espoused by the left.

In order to reverse the deindustrialisation of France, Marine Le Pen proposed what she called 'a rearmament' of the country 'in the face of unbridled globalisation'. This rearmament would have to be spearheaded by the state. Marine Le Pen reiterated on numerous occasions that her project depended crucially on the reestablishment of a strong French state. In her inaugural speech in January 2011 she declared that it was 'written into our national DNA' to turn to the state as the driving force for regulation, protection, and innovation.[16] In her official economic programme she proposed the development of a 'strategic plan for the reindustrialisation' of France, under the direct supervision of the prime minister.[17] As a further support measure for the French manufacturing and commercial sector she advanced a policy of 'intelligent protection' designed to stop the delocalisation of French firms (Le Pen 2012a: 3).[18]

With respect to social policy, Marine Le Pen charged that the protection of ordinary citizens from the vicissitudes of the economy presumed above all the reestablishment of a strong state, capable of exercising its regulative and protective duties. A strong state meant above all a strong public sector that was in a position to fulfill its central role as a provider of services that guarantee 'the equality of the citizens', as Marine Le Pen put it in early 2011 in a programmatic speech

---

15. *See*, for instance, 'Le Pen defend le "made in France"', *Le Figaro*, 11 April 2013, http://www.lefigaro.fr/flash-actu/2013/04/11/97001-20130411FILWWW00711-le-pen-defend-le-made-in-france.php (accessed 10 March 2014).

16. Tours speech.

17. *Front National*, 'Emploi, réindustrialisation et PME/PMI', http://www.frontnational.com/le-projet-de-marine-le-pen/redressement-economique-et-social/emploi-reindustrialisation-et-pmepmi/ (accessed 12 March 2014).

18. Le Pen 2012a: 3. Here, once again, Marine Le Pen could point to important French economists. Daniel Cohen, for instance, has argued that the euro crisis was considerably exacerbated by the fact that the European Central Bank is forbidden by the treaties to act as a lender of last resort to Eurozone countries in trouble. (Cohen 2012: 15)

that was supposed to launch a 'social wave'.[19] Equality also meant social justice, particularly with respect to taxation, and, thus redistribution. If in the past, the FN had supported lowering taxes, Marine Le Pen called for progressive taxation, i.e. an increase in the tax rate for higher incomes, a reduction for lower ones. At the same time, she called for a revision of the law favouring capital gains over income derived from work. Marine Le Pen justified these measures arguing that the *classes populaires* and the middle class would only truly benefit from growth if 'the financial sector and the stockholders' saw their share of the value-added diminished. This, she added, would lead 'to a lowering of profit rates and a parallel reduction in inequality' (Le Pen 2012b: 41).

At the same time, Marine Le Pen promoted herself as a strong supporter of the welfare state committed to defending France's *acquis sociaux* and guaranteeing their continued availability. For those, as she put it, who have nothing, social services represented 'the only right, the only good' they can claim. The welfare state was a source of 'dignity' as well as the basis of equality – a core republican value.[20] Its future, however, crucially depended on whether or not France would manage to effectively deal with the question of immigration, the major reason for France's socio-economic problems. Social services, she argued, rested on 'national solidarity', 'our consent' to pay taxes 'for each other'. Solidarity, in turn, could only be maintained as long as there was 'a community of values, a common cultural base, within which everyone recognises him or herself'. Mass migration threatened to destroy national solidarity, the foundation of the social welfare state.[21] To defend immigration meant to condemn those on the bottom of society to having to compete for meager resources with those who were even poorer (Le Pen 2012b: 88). It was unacceptable that immigrants lived off services 'thanks to the solidarity of the national community' (de Montvallon and Denis 2011).

To solve the problem, Marine Le Pen advanced a programme of social protectionism – *priorité nationale*: French nationals, including naturalised citizens, should be given priority with respect to employment, social services, and social housing.[22] Family allowances should only be paid to those families where at least one parent was a French citizen or of European origins. By eradicating the incentives ('suction pumps' [*pompes aspirants*]) that made France attractive to migrants, France would regain control over the migration flow. The goal was to radically reduce the annual influx of migrants from the current rate of about 200,000 to a mere 10,000. With this programme, Marine Le Pen offered a new rationale for her party's anti-immigrant position within the larger context of a comprehensive, coherent and internally consistent programme of economic patriotism and *priorité nationale* (*see* Reyniér 2011).

---

19. Marine Le Pen, Bompas speech, published under the title 'Marine Le Pen lance la vague sociale'.

20. Bompas speech.

21. Marine Le Pen, Strasbourg speech, 12 February 2012, http://www.nationspresse.info/?p=168405 (accessed 13 March 2014).

22. *See* Marine Le Pen, 2012, 'Le Projet: Immigration', http://www.marinelepen2012.fr/le-projet/autorite-de-letat/immigration/ (accessed 14 March 2014).

The revenge of the *ploucs*

Since the 2012 presidential election, Marine Le Pen's image has continued to improve. In early 2014, more than 50 per cent of respondents agreed with the statement that Marine Le Pen understood the everyday problems of ordinary people;[23] 40 per cent thought she was warm and personable (*sympathique*); and 40 per cent agreed that she offered new ideas to resolve the country's problems (TNS-Sofres 2014b). Among France's leading politicians, she inspired significantly more confidence (34 per cent) than Hollande (20 per cent), Prime Minister Jean-Marc Ayrault (18 per cent), and Jean-François Copé (13 per cent), the leader of the UMP (OpinionWay 2014). These results confirmed the assessment of otherwise critical observers who conceded that Marine Le Pen not only voiced pertinent questions and concerns stirring society, but also knew how to speak to the people about their precarious situation in their own language, an everyday language that was immediately accessible, and which they understood (Mozet and Perrineau 2014; Mossuz-Lavau 2012). She appealed to those people whose 'suffering' had gone 'unrecognised' by the media and the political establishment and who found themselves and their lived experiences reflected and articulated in her discourse (Wieviorka 2013; Mergier 2011). She gave voice to those 'without a voice' putting in words the 'unbearable sentiment of injustice' of those who thought they were the ones who paid the price of globalisation (Fœssel 2012: 22; Mergier and Fourquet 2011: 55).

In this way, Marine Le Pen managed to gather behind her project significant parts of the *couches populaires*, but also parts of the middle class unsettled by the crisis (Mayer 2012, 2013; Le Bras and Todd 2013: 273–299). What they had in common was less their class consciousness than a 'common perception of the effects of globalisation and the economic and social choices of the ruling class' (Guilluy 2013). Brought together by disparate but shared grievances, they provided fertile ground for Marine Le Pen's populist mobilisation.

From this perspective, Marine Le Pen's success in 2012 and the FN's subsequent electoral resurgence were largely the result of Marine Le Pen's ability to promote herself as a credible politician in tune with the preoccupations of ordinary people.[24] To an extent, it was an expression of a revolt on the part of a large number of French voters from the rural and 'peri-urban' areas of the country, suffering from deindustrialisation and unemployment, often ignored by the political class if not outright dismissed as hopelessly backward, unsophisticated and uninformed *ploucs* (Perrineau 2014: 150–159).

Her self-presentation was in sharp contrast to the political establishment, deemed incapable of dealing with the dramatic deterioration of life chances in the years since 2008 while, at the same time, seen as continuing to serve the interests

---

23. In a different survey, only 23 per cent of respondents said the same thing about Hollande (OpinionWay 2014).

24. In 2012, she managed to recuperate a considerable number of voters who in 2007 had voted for Sarkozy. According to Perrineau, they constituted a quarter of her result, equal to 1.7 million votes (Perrineau 2014: 31).

of the financial markets, big business, the Brussels bureaucracy, and the rich (*see* Fressoz 2012). Not surprisingly, given her rhetoric on globalisation, she did well in the countryside, but lost support in the big cities (Perrineau 2014: 156, 158).

To a significant extent, the revival of the FN was also the result of Marine Le Pen's determination to produce and defend a serious and coherent programme that advanced and proposed concrete solutions to the French malaise. Even if most commentators and experts disagreed with the main policies defended by Marine Le Pen, they agreed to debate her on television and in the print media.[25] In the process, Marine Le Pen used the opportunity to try and seduce dissident thinkers to join her ranks by promoting their ideas in public forums and thus giving them visibility – with occasional success. Thus a few days before the 2014 European election, the economist Philippe Murer, author (together with the left-wing economist Jacques Sapir) of a study that advanced various scenarios for the dissolution of the Eurozone (published on the website of Chevènement's think-tank, *Res Publica*) announced he had joined Marine Le Pen as an adviser.

What distinguished Marine Le Pen's programme was not only its pronounced emphasis on social questions but also that it departed in significant ways from traditional FN doctrine. Whereas in the past, the FN's economic programme was overwhelmingly oriented to the right, with Marine Le Pen, the centre of gravity moved significantly to the left. In fact, by 2012, more than two-thirds of the new programme's propositions were on the left (Ivaldi 2013: 10).

For Marine Le Pen's right-wing and far-rightwing detractors (e.g. the editors of *Minute* and *Rivarol*), the new president was a traitor, her programme a reflection of '*jacobinisme*' or 'outright Marxist' (Letty 2011; Blot 2012; Vouillazère 2013). Not only did they object that in her book, she approvingly quoted Jean Jaurès (the pre-WW I socialist leader and cofounder of *L'Humanité*) and several contemporary left-wing authors; not only were they incensed by the fact that she praised the policies of *étatisme* and *dirigisme* for the prominent role they had played in France's post-war recovery and the economic boom of the *trente glorieuses*. They were also enraged by the fact that Marine Le Pen dared to invoke General de Gaulle and his 'vision' to subordinate the economy to political power, which had laid the foundation for France's post-war mixed economy and which, in turn – thanks to de Gaulle's 'ingenious intuition' – had assured France's sovereignty and independence (Le Pen 2012b: 57).

For Marine Le Pen's catch-all strategy it was paramount to advance a programme that was credible, presented a coherent, and particularly serious, alternative to the dominant liberal ideology, and allowed her to mobilise across the left-right cleavage. This is why she conjured up Charles De Gaulle and with him, France's republican tradition; this is why she preyed upon the thinking of critical left-wing economists such Jacques Sapir and Frédéric Lordon on deglobalisation (who indignantly protested the 'shameless pillage' of their ideas),

25. A prominent example was Pascal Lamy, the general director of the WTO, who, a week before the European election of 2014, debated her in a business magazine on the question of the euro. *Challenges*, 22 May 2014, pp.38–42.

and France's only Nobel economist, the late Maurice Allais, on globalisation and social injustice;[26] and this is why she referred to maverick critics of the establishment left, such as the philosopher Jean-Claude Michéa. At a point where the dominant ideas and their foundations came increasingly under attack, Marine Le Pen clearly saw an opportunity to mount a serious ideological challenge. The result was a programme, which synthesised left- and right-wing populist positions in an extensive project revolving around the defence of both the nation state and the welfare state (Reyniér 2011) while at the same time appealing to feelings of nostalgia for the 'pre-globalisation era' (Frachon 2014).

Evidence suggests that this strategy has been rather successful. For one, Marine Le Pen's economic programme has been taken seriously. She has on numerous occasions been allowed to defend her main demands and proposals on television and on the radio and to comment on current events. In fact, Marine Le Pen has become something of a media star, guaranteeing above-average ratings. At the same time, her propositions have been discussed, commented on, and dissected in the media. And even if her economic programme has generally been dismissed as 'illusionary' if not disastrous for the country (Moatti 2014), the media exposure has gained her a great deal of free publicity – with conspicuous results: According to a recent study, the FN is no longer associated only with the question of immigration and security. Since the presidential election, Marine Le Pen has increasingly gained credibility and acceptance on the question of economic protection, but also on republicanism (Muzet and Perrineau 2014). This suggests that some of the ideas promoted by Marine Le Pen are gaining ground. At the same time, however, core items of her programme, such as France's exit from the Eurozone and the policy of *priorité national*, are largely rejected. In early 2014, for instance, despite widespread Euroscepticism, only 27 per cent of the French public was in favour of leaving the euro (Courtois 2014).

Marine Le Pen certainly seized the opportunity offered to her by the economic crisis not only to establish herself as a serious, professional politician but also to forge a new image for the *Front National*. Under her leadership, the FN has made the transition from a reactionary right-wing extremist party to a modern neo-populist catch-all movement. The latter, however, is still very much a child of the persistent severe socio-economic and socio-political crisis from which France has been suffering since the onset of the Great Recession of 2008. In the shadow of the Great Recession, the FN's programmatic union of economic populism and cultural nativism (i.e. the defence of France's republican values and identity against the challenges posed by militant Islam) has proved its appeal, particularly among lower-class voters. France, however, will eventually recover from its current socio-economic and political crisis. Public confidence is likely to improve. Unless, of course, the crisis of the French model has deeper, structural causes. French economists have noted that France's current difficulties to take

---

26. See particularly the FN's contribution to a volume on globalisation edited by Christine Boutin (Sarkozy's Minister of Housing and Urban Development), which cites Allais in support of the FN's main charge that globalisation is 'the enemy of social justice' (FN 2010: 312).

advantage of globalisation (reflected in France's declining competitiveness, particularly compared to Germany, and its problems to get a foothold in emerging markets such as China and India) are nothing new. Already during the first wave of globalisation, after 1870, France largely failed to 'exploit the opportunities afforded by global economic growth'. It seems France has structural or cultural difficulties to take advantage of intensified globalisation. Under the circumstances, the French public's reservations about globalisation today (reflected in the polls) are a logical response to France's problems in competing successfully in global markets (Becuwe, Blancheton and Charles 2013). Should these structural problems persist, it is unlikely that the appeal of Marine Le Pen's neo-populist project will diminish in the years ahead.

Chapter Six

Populism in Belgium in Times of Crisis: Intensification of Discourse, Decline in Electoral Support

Teun Pauwels and Matthijs Rooduijn

Introduction

The financial crisis that emerged in 2008 has had profound economic, social, and also political consequences. In this chapter we explore whether and how the Great Recession has had an influence on the manifestation of populism in Belgium – both at the level of discourse as well as its electoral strength. As explained in the introductory chapter, the Great Recession might provide a fertile breeding ground for populism at the expense of liberal democracy. At the same time it is also acknowledged that it is difficult to isolate the impact of the financial crisis, as many intervening variables, as well as the specific context in a country might play a role. This is definitely the case in Belgium where the Great Recession coincided with a specific political crisis which had less to do with the economy. Moreover, in a federal country such as Belgium, the party systems of Flanders and Wallonia are very different leading to diverse reactions to the crisis. This makes the analysis complex but also provides interesting insights into how different the outcome of the Great Recession can be, depending on the context.

Populism in Belgium emerged prominently for the first time in the elections of 1991 – also known as 'Black Sunday'. The *Vlaams Belang* (previously *Vlaams Blok* or VB) made its national breakthrough while another protest party, ROSSEM, also gained representation. In the south of Belgium, the *Front National* (FNb) tried to profit from the success of its French example led by Jean-Marie Le Pen in the 1990s and 2000s. Despite some occasional successes, the FNb was led by the erratic Daniel Féret who was unable to organise the party in a coherent way (Art 2008; Coffé 2005). As a consequence, the party is no longer represented in the national parliament. The VB reached its electoral peak in 2004. Only a few months after several VB organisations were condemned by the Court of Appeal of Ghent for violating the anti-racism law, the party polled 24 per cent of the vote in the 2004 regional and European elections, and became the second largest party in Flanders. In 2007 another populist party, *Lijst Dedecker* (LDD), emerged in Flanders and obtained its best result at the regional and European elections of 2009, namely 8 per cent (Pauwels 2010). Similar to the FNb, however, LDD could not consolidate because of a lack of organisational leadership and grave internal tensions. The recent national, regional and European elections of 2014 led to a serious electoral downfall of the Flemish populists with the VB obtaining only 6 per cent of the vote and LDD not able to pass the electoral threshold. In contrast to the decline in Flanders, some new populist actors have come to the surface in Wallonia: the radical left-wing populist party *Parti du Travail de Belgique* (PTB) and the right-wing populist *Parti Populaire* (PP) gained parliamentary representation after the 2014 elections.

This chapter will focus on how the Great Recession has impacted on populist discourse and the electoral performance of populist parties. With regard to the first question, however, we will limit our analysis to the only enduring and electorally significant populist party in Belgium: VB. Other parties such as LDD, PP, FNb and PTB have never obtained more than 10 per cent of the vote at national elections and are too unstable to allow for a fine grained longitudinal analysis of party ideology. The VB's ideology, on the other hand, has been studied extensively and multiple studies concluded that the party is populist (Jagers and Walgrave 2007; Pauwels 2014). The central argument of its populist message is that the established parties impose political correctness upon the VB and the man in the street in an attempt to silence the problems of multicultural society. This is considered 'part of a conspiracy by the traditional parties against the VB, the only party that defends the silent majority, the popular will and democracy' (Jagers 2006: 252). To restore the voice of the people, the VB favours the introduction of direct democracy. Combined with its ethnic nationalism (striving for a homogeneous Flemish republic), xenophobia, and concern for law and order, the VB qualifies as a text-book example of a populist radical right party (Mudde 2007).

After years of electoral success, the VB is recently in decline, while another nationalist party – the *Nieuw-Vlaamse Alliantie* (N-VA) – is currently dominating the Flemish party system. The N-VA is a nationalist and conservative party which also draws on anti-establishment appeals. As such, the N-VA has increasingly become a functional equivalent for the VB. Without being populist – the party does not emphasise the 'power to the people' principle and its party leader (De Wever) is rather elitist – the N-VA has been able to depict itself as an alternative for the established parties, which, contrary to the VB, has a realistic chance of actually realising its policy proposals. Given its borderline status with regard to populism and the fact that the party is a moderate functional equivalent for the VB, the N-VA will also be discussed in this chapter.

The remainder of this chapter is structured as follows. In the next section we explore how the economic crisis and the political crisis might have had an impact on the manifestations of populism. It is argued that Belgium is a country where the impact of the economic crisis was moderate, yet a political crisis has occurred which was largely unrelated to the Great Recession. Next, we present the data and our measurement of populism. A content analysis of party literature was carried out in an attempt to shed light on the impact of the crises on the populist discourse of the VB. The subsequent section presents the results while the focus will then shift from populist discourse to the electoral strength of populist parties in Belgium. Finally, we will present our main conclusions.

The economic and political crisis in Belgium

In the introduction to this volume, Kriesi and Pappas have argued that the Great Recession as well as a political crisis, provided a fertile breeding ground for populism. When the two go hand in hand, populist actors acquire even more ammunition to denounce the establishment. A lack of measures by political elites to fight the economic crisis opens the door for populist discourse and mobilisation. One trigger in particular might be when the political elite is confronted with corruption scandals. The idea that elites are corrupt and self-serving, while large groups of ordinary citizens suffer severely from impoverishment and unemployment, provides a window of opportunity for populism (Hanley and Sikk 2013).

According to the indicators of economic and political crisis presented in the introduction, we might conclude that Belgium is among the group of countries which have been relatively unaffected by the economic and political crises. However, as already noted by the editors, these indicators do not capture every aspect of the crisis and it remains important to assess the situation in more detail for each individual country. As we will argue below, we agree that Belgium has been relatively untouched by the Great Recession. However, we claim that the country did go through a deep political crisis. Although the political crisis predominantly took place at the level of the political elite and was less important to citizens, this event provided an opportunity for populist discourse and mobilisation.

Like other countries, Belgium was affected by the financial crisis that emerged in the US in 2008. One of Belgium's largest banks, Fortis, got into trouble and had to be saved by the Dutch, Belgian and Luxembourg governments, which decided to take 49 per cent interest in the Fortis holding. While the Dutch government decided to buy the Dutch parts of Fortis and ABN Amro, the Belgian government sold its parts to the French BNP Paribas without much consultation with the shareholders. As a result, a group of disappointed shareholders decided to go to court to annul the acquisition of Fortis by BNP Paribas. The Court of Appeal endorsed the claims of the shareholders and suspended the sale of Fortis group. Moreover, an investigation brought to the surface the fact that Prime Minister Yves Leterme had tried to influence the court, resulting in the resignation of his cabinet in December 2008. In January 2009 a new cabinet was formed with the same party composition as Leterme I, yet with some personnel changes such as the replacement of Leterme by Herman van Rompuy as the new Prime Minister. In the meantime, another Belgian bank, Dexia, was forced to apply for a bailout by the Belgian government and received more than six billion euros. The bank renamed itself as Belfius and was forced to restructure its organisation.

Despite the difficulties of these Belgian financial institutions and the resignation of Leterme as Prime Minister, the broader economic consequences of the Great

Recession were limited. As shown in the introductory chapter, the unemployment rate in Belgium hardly changed at all between 2007 and 2012, while the EU 27 average increased remarkably. It should also be noted that unemployment rates were considerably higher in Wallonia compared to Flanders, which is not entirely evident from the data for Belgium as a whole. Similarly, the figures presented in the introduction show that in terms of public debt and GDP growth, the situation for Belgium did not turn problematic.[1] In sum, while the Great Recession has had an effect on some financial institutions, these effects should not be overstated. In fact, macro-economic indicators suggest that Belgium has weathered the global economic crisis better than most European countries.

While the consequences of the economic crisis were moderate, the country has faced a severe political crisis that started even before 2008. Belgium is a federal country that consists of different regions and regions, with the division between Francophones and Dutch speakers as the main cleavage. Despite a process of federalisation, providing the Flemish and Walloon communities with increasing autonomy in matters like education, culture, and parts of economic policy, the linguistic cleavage remains salient and has recently led to political conflicts and difficult government formations (Van Aelst and Louwerse 2013).

The recent political crisis started in the months after the national elections of June 2007. An electoral alliance of the Christian Democratic CD&V and the Flemish Nationalist N-VA campaigned with a promise for more autonomy for the regions and for the split of the electoral district Brussels-Halle-Vilvoorde (BHV, comprising Brussels and parts of its periphery allowing Francophone candidates in Brussels to attract votes from Francophone voters living in Flanders).[2] The CD&V/ N-VA cartel won the elections with almost 30 per cent of the votes in Flanders, but the negotiations with the Francophone parties over constitutional reform were extremely heated and it took 194 days to form a government. Moreover, it was actually an 'interim' government led by former Prime Minister Verhofstadt to ensure the stability of the country. In March 2008, a 'full' government was finally formed, headed by Yves Leterme. Even this government, however, left salient issues such as constitutional reform to be decided. As mentioned above, Leterme was forced to resign in December 2008 (due to the Fortis scandal) and was succeeded by Van Rompuy. After a period of fragile stability in 2009, Van Rompuy was appointed as the President of the European Council. Although this enabled Leterme to make a comeback, the Leterme II cabinet fell a few months later, in April 2010, because the liberal party *Open VLD* decided to leave the negotiations on institutional reform and withdrew its government support. 'With no alternative to hand, Prime Minister Yves Leterme was forced to submit the

---

1. Belgium has a high public debt coming close to 100 per cent of its GDP. This high public debt dates back from the 1980s, however.

2. 'The existence of BHV is not in line with the linguistic territoriality principle defended by most Flemish political parties. Historically driven by the fight against 'Frenchification' of the Flemish region, they consider that the borders of electoral districts should match those of the language regions and that Francophones living in the Flemish Region should integrate by speaking Dutch' (Sinardet 2010: 356).

cabinet's resignation to the King, who accepted it four days later, thereby launching the formal process for organising new elections' (Rihoux *et al.* 2011).

The national elections held in June 2010, made the N-VA the largest Belgian party. This did not solve Belgium's political crisis, however, as it was the beginning of the longest period of government formation in history. 'The reasons for the crisis were the same as in 2007: the persisting and profound divergences on institutional issues between the French-speaking parties, on the one hand, and the Flemish ones – mainly the N-VA – on the other' (Rihoux *et al.* 2011: 917). It was only in October 2011 that the Christian Democrats, Socialists, Liberals and Green parties (both Flemish and Francophone) agreed on a split of the electoral district BHV and institutional reforms providing the regions with more fiscal autonomy. In the meantime, a caretaking government under the lead of Leterme was still in power. After a record breaking 543 days, a new government was formed, led by the French speaking socialist Elio Di Rupo. The long periods without a government led to a general feeling of crisis and undermined the credibility of the Belgian state. Some (international) commentators even spoke about the possible split of the country.

Although the impact of the economic crisis was relatively limited in Belgium, it might still be expected that the Great Recession has had some impact on populism. After all, also the economic crisis has been a widely debated topic in Belgium. We therefore expect that the VB has become more populist after the start of the economic crisis (H1a), and that populist parties in Belgium became more electorally successful after the start of the economic crisis (H1b).

Belgium's political crisis also provided an opportunity for populist discourse and mobilisation. This is even more so because the political crisis revolved around institutional reform which belongs to the core business of the VB. Research suggests that both in its party literature and in the eyes of voters, the VB is much more concerned about Flemish nationalism and state reform compared to economic issues (Mudde 2000; Walgrave *et al.* 2012). We therefore hypothesise that the VB has become more populist after the start of the political crisis (H2a), and that populist parties in Belgium have become more electorally successful after the start of the political crisis (H2b).

As the political crisis started one year before the economic crisis manifested itself, we have the opportunity to disentangle the two crises during the early years. However, we should be very careful with our inferences, because the two crises cannot be understood completely separately from each other. We should also take into account that it will probably take some time before any crisis (political or economic) will have an impact on populism (if at all). We assume that it will take at least a few months before such events generate any effects. Therefore, in order to test the first hypothesis, we will compare the time frame January–June 2008 (before the start of the economic crisis in the autumn of 2008) with January–June 2009 (a few months after the start of the economic crisis). To test the second hypothesis, we compare the time frame January–June 2007 (before the start of the political crisis in the autumn of 2007) with January–June 2008 (a few months after the start of the political crisis).

As the impact of the economic crisis in Belgium has been relatively limited we expect that the effect of the political crisis is stronger than the effect of the economic crisis, with regards to both the degree of populism of the VB (H3a) and the success of populist parties in Belgium (H3b). For the same reason we also expect that the form of populism expressed by the VB will predominantly be political, and not economic (H4).

In the introduction to this volume it has been hypothesised that populists in power tend to tone down their populism and behave more like mainstream parties. As the VB has never participated in a government coalition, this hypothesis cannot be tested here.

Definition, data and measurement

In this study we will draw on the conceptualisation of populism, as explained in the introductory chapter. Accordingly, we employ Mudde's (2004: 543) definition of populism as 'an ideology that considers society to be ultimately separated into two homogeneous and antagonistic groups, "the pure people" versus "the corrupt elite", and which argues that politics should be an expression of the *volonté générale* (general will) of the people'. We do not conceive of populism as a full ideology such as liberalism, conservatism or socialism, but as a 'thin-centred' ideology, focusing only on the relationship between the people and the elite (Canovan 2002; Freeden 1998).

According to this definition, populism consists of two main elements and one additional characteristic. The first element is 'people-centrism'. Populism is people-centrist because it emphasises that the general will of the people should be the point of departure for political decision-making. The concept of 'the people' is conceived as a homogeneous entity that can have different meanings in different circumstances. Populism could refer, for instance, to 'the man in the street', the nation, or 'hardworking men' (Canovan 1999). Populism is anti-elitist because it accuses the elite of being selfish, arrogant and incompetent. Although anti-elitism often concerns political elites, it could also refer to economic, cultural, legal or media elites.

In this chapter we focus on the degree of populism and on the form of populism. Because political parties (and other political actors) can endorse the populist message to a lesser or larger extent, parties can be more or less populist. Moreover, the same party can become more or less populist over the years (Rooduijn and Pauwels 2011). Also, populism can be expressed in different forms. Populism can take on a political hue, but it can also be 'coloured' economically or culturally.

To test our hypotheses, we have analysed all forty-four membership magazines of the VB that appeared between January 2007 and December 2010. These monthly membership magazines are titled *Vlaams Belang Magazine* (VBM). Analysing these magazines has a number of advantages. First, in contrast with party manifestos, they appear more frequently, allowing for a more fine-grained analysis of the populist message. Second, the VBM is made predominantly for members of the party (even though they can be downloaded by anyone from the party's website). The advantage is that internally orientated party literature will reveal the 'true nature' of a party to a greater extent compared to externally orientated literature (Mudde 2000). Research has demonstrated that populism can be found more often in internally orientated party literature than in party manifestos (Pauwels 2011b).

Our data is analysed by means of a quantitative content analysis, i.e. a systematic, objective, quantitative analysis of message characteristics (Neuendorf 2002). Each article (with a maximum of ten per issue) of the VBM was coded along two categories, in line with our definition of populism; 'people-centrism', and 'anti-elitism' (Rooduijn and Pauwels 2011; Rooduijn et al. 2014; see also Bernhard et al. in this volume). People-centrism is present if the people are depicted in a positive manner (e.g. 'the hard-working people'), and/or as a collective entity (e.g. 'all Flemings'). When the party writes about deceiving the electorate (e.g. 'broken promises'), this is also coded as people-centrism because it implies that 'the people' is one single entity. Anti-elitism is present when the elite is depicted in a negative manner and as a collective entity. Critique on individual politicians or the executive is not general enough and is therefore not coded as anti-elitism. Criticisms regarding the Belgian political system in its entirety have been coded as anti-elitism. The same holds true for references to conspiracy theories (e.g. suggesting that the elite is silencing the people and/or the VB).

The VBM issues of 2007 were coded by the first author, the issues of 2009 and 2010 were coded by the second author, and the issues of 2008 were coded by both authors to test the reliability of the coding. The test indicated that the reliability statistics are satisfactory. The Krippendorff's Alpha's are 0.74 for people-centrism and 0.66 for anti-elitism. Some of the articles were also analysed in a qualitative way. This allows for more in depth information on the VB's populism and for exploration of how the economic and political crises were referred to in the party literature.

In the next section, we will firstly analyse the results of the quantitative content analysis. Secondly, by means of a more qualitative analysis of the VB's discourse, we assess which form of populism manifests itself in the texts of the party.

Results

Quantitative analysis

Figure 6.1 summarises our findings. The grey, dashed lines represent the percentages of articles with people-centrism and anti-elitism. However, we are mostly interested in the black, solid line, which represents the percentages of articles in which both people-centrism and anti-elitism are present. After all, populism is a combination of people-centrism and anti-elitism. The figure demonstrates that the percentage of articles with populism did not really change between the first half of 2007 and the second half of that year. However, we see a steep increase in the first six months of 2008. This suggests an effect of the political crisis which, after all, started in the autumn of 2007. There was not much populism before the crisis, and not much populism during the crisis and

Figure 6.1: Percentage of articles containing people-centrism, anti-elitism and people-centrism and anti-elitism combined (populism) in Vlaams Belang Magazine (2007–10)

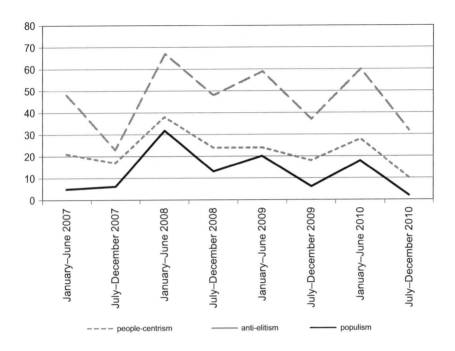

people-centrism ——— anti-elitism ——— populism

in the first few months directly after the crisis manifested itself. However, in the first six months of 2008 – in the middle of the crisis – the populism-score was multiplied by a factor of five: it increased from 6–32. Of course, we cannot know for sure whether it was indeed the political crisis that fuelled VB's populism. After all, many other variables might have had an effect. Yet the actual content of the manifestations of populism (for populist critique regarding the established political parties which are not handling the political crisis very well, see the next section) suggests that the two variables are related to one another. H2a might therefore be considered to be confirmed.

After this peak of populism in the first half of 2008, the populism score plummeted again in the second half of that year (from 32–13), to increase again in the first six months of 2009 (from 13–20). This development suggests that the economic crisis has also had an effect on the degree of populism of the VB. After all, during the time frame January–June 2008 (the months before the outbreak of the crisis) the populism score was very high. The degree of populism abated in the months during and directly after the outbreak of the crisis, and increased again in the first months of 2009. The rise of the populism score in the first months of 2009 might be due to the financial crisis, as the political situation during these months was relatively stable. However, the degree of populism was not nearly as high as during the months directly preceding the crisis. Moreover, looking at the form of populism expressed by the VB we do not see a link between the economic crisis and the populist manifestations. The populist discourse of the VB concerns the political establishment while economic elites hardly get any attention. The party also does not often link the political elite to the outburst of the economic crisis. We would therefore argue that there is only tentative support for H1a.

Our findings suggest that the effects of the political crisis have been much stronger than the effects of the economic crisis (if there was an effect at all). Further developments, after the first months of 2009, also suggest that it was mainly the political crisis that had an effect on VB's degree of populism. The populism scores basically followed the political situation. Between July and December 2009 the political situation was relatively stable and the populism score also decreased to a level comparable to the pre-political-crisis period. During the first six months of 2010 the cabinet fell again, and this coincided with a more populist discourse of the VB. After the subsequent elections, the political situation was again in relatively smooth waters, and also the populism score decreased. Hypothesis three can therefore be confirmed.

Note that in general, all these developments can also be seen when focusing on people-centrism and anti-elitism separately.

Qualitative analysis

Our qualitative analysis shows that economic populism, and a direct link between the economic crisis and populism is practically absent in the discourse of the VB. Yet the party's discourse is replete with political populism: the VB argues that the political crisis was brought about by the established political parties that have no idea what ordinary people find important.

Anti-elitism is the populist feature that the reader encounters most in the VB's party literature. The party regularly refers to political parties in a collectivist and negative way such as 'a political caste', 'the establishment', 'rusted system parties', 'the traditional parties' or 'Leterme & Co'. The front page of one VBM depicts the three main parties (Christian Democrats, Socialists and Liberals) as three monkeys who are blind, deaf and silent with regard to the 'real problems', which are according to the party 'Walloon theft, immigration and crime' (*see* Figure 6.2).

In 2009 the party argued: (*Vlaams Belang Magazine* April 2009, p. 2)

Whether it concerns the institutional debate, security policies, the democratic deficit, multicultural society or Islam: the most pressing problems are being suffocated under a blanket of political correctness. Only the VB has always been a challenger of traditional politics. That is exactly what we are good at: being a taboo breaker in the palace of lies which is called Belgium.

Commenting on riots with Turkish youngsters in Brussels, the VB argues that the local political elite is made up of a majority of immigrants and therefore does

Figure 6.2: Traditional party families depicted as deaf, blind and silent

Source: *Vlaams Belang Magazine* Dec. 2007: 8.

little to stop the violence. The party calls the elite a 'fifth column', a term that originates from the Spanish civil war to refer to a group of people that undermines the nation from within.

> In the council of the mayor and aldermen, there are only three Europeans compared to five of non-European origin. What can you expect from a *political caste* in which the fifth column has all the say?

Sometimes the VB also targets other elites such as the 'regime press' or 'phony artists'. In one article they criticise a (rare) demonstration that was held to support Belgian unity and solidarity during the lengthy government formation.

This demonstration was supported by some artists, which the VB explains by the fact that artists get subsidised by the Belgian government.

> And then there is a *group of phony artists* and people from the cultural world who suddenly have become Belgian nationalists. Their support for Belgium can be easily explained: mostly they make awful things with rusty bikes, mussel pots, or ham attached to pillars. No citizen would voluntarily buy such junk. Nobody likes these things or finds them artistic. Nobody wants to spend money on that[…] except the government. They are crazy enough to buy that phony art, *at the expense of the taxpayer* of course. They would not spend a Euro themselves on that either. Those *charlatans from the cultural world* can only survive thanks to subsidies. And now they have to provide certain services in exchange. (*ibid.*)

Other instances of anti-elitism appear when they criticise the entire political regime. In one article VB president compares Belgium with a rollercoaster with 'metal fatigue'.

> Sooner or later it will end in a wrong way. But I admit: squeaky carts, even from the most rusty rollercoaster, ride the longest. Belgium is tough and the independence of Flanders will not materialize unless we, as Flemish nationalists, polish the sledgehammer. That *rusty Belgian rollercoaster* must come down. (*ibid.*)

People-centrism appears far less often in the literature of the VBM. Most articles coded as people-centrist were articles where the people were portrayed as victims because they were said to be betrayed by the establishment (note that we coded the breaking of electoral promises as people-centrism). However, the party does emphasise the central position of 'the hardworking Fleming' or 'the ordinary man in the street'. One of the campaign slogans in 2010 was 'We Flemings first!'. In the following example, the VB made an overly clear combination of anti-elitism and people-centrism: 'We choose the side of the *ordinary man and woman. We are, and will remain, a rebellious anti-establishment party!*' In one article the VB makes clear that breaking electoral promises comes down to a 'punch in the face' of the Flemish voter:

> That the N-VA president is even prepared to make concessions on the issue of BHV and actively collaborates with the delaying manoeuvres of the Chamber commission comes down to the denial of the chief electoral promise and is without doubt a *punch in the face of the Flemish voter*. (*ibid.*)

Another example is an article in which the VB denounces the expensive flights of the Francophone Minister of Defense Flahout, which was accompanied with the sarcastic argument that 'the Flemings will pay for everything'.

These qualitative findings lead to a confirmation of our fourth hypothesis: the form of populism expressed by the VB is predominantly political.

From discourse to electoral support

We have seen that Belgium has gone through a difficult political period since 2007. This was partly caused by the economic crisis, but even more so by long periods of gridlock on the issue of state reform. So far we have focused on the question whether the discourse of the VB changed as a result of the outbreak of the economic and political crises. Another important question is whether populist parties have gained electorally during this period. Figure 6.3 shows the electoral strength of the populist parties in Belgium over time, while simultaneously depicting the 'timeline of crisis'. For the years in which elections took place (2007, 2009, 2010, 2014), we presented the electoral score that these parties obtained. For the other years we took average results in the polls. As Flemish parties can gain votes in Flanders but not in Wallonia and *vice versa*, we present the electoral scores of populist parties in their party system.

Whereas the VB obtained more than 24 per cent of the votes in 2004, its vote share declined considerably in 2009 and 2010 to 15 and 12 per cent respectively. Roughly the same happened with LDD but with some delay. Initially, LDD seemed to fare well during the economic and political crisis. However, in 2010 it gained less than 4 per cent of the vote. The latest national, regional and European elections of 2014 were even more disastrous for both Flemish populist parties with a vote share of 5.9 per cent for the VB and 0.7 per cent for LDD. So, while the populist discourse of VB increased, existing populist parties lost many votes, and no new populist actors emerged in Flanders.

The decline of the VB can be largely explained by the increased competition on the right from the N-VA combined with its permanent opposition which makes the party less relevant over time. In earlier years the VB 'has flourished behind its *cordons sanitaire*' (Van Spanje and Van der Brug 2009: 376) as its opposition status kept the party united while enabling mobilisation on the 'undemocratic exclusion' by the established parties. As the party continued to win elections, most voters hoped that it could no longer be ignored in the future. As time went by and the growth of the VB came to an end it seems that this hope faded away. Permanent opposition has made the VB less relevant, since '[m]any voters consider government power to be the real prize in a parliamentary election, and most want their vote to count in this contest' (Van der Eijk and Franklin 2009: 103). This leads to strategic voting behaviour. Van der Brug *et al.* (2005: 548) explain that 'if the second-most preferred party has more likelihood of affecting public policy, a pragmatic voter may decide that this party is actually his or her best option'. This seems to be what happened in Belgium as pragmatic voters started leaving the VB and switched to N-VA, a party that already has governed at the regional (Flemish) and local level (Pauwels 2011a).

In many ways the N-VA serves as a more moderate functional equivalent for the VB. The N-VA is a Flemish nationalist and conservative party that recently positioned itself clearly on the right on the socio-economic cleavage. Furthermore, the N-VA draws on anti-establishment appeals. Some commentators have even argued that the N-VA is also a populist party. It might be tempting to label the party

Figure 6.3: Timeline of the crisis and support for populist parties in Belgium

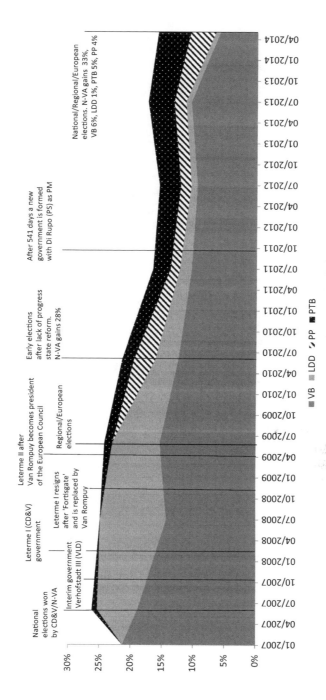

Note: Electoral support are election results (2007, 2009, 2010, 2014) or yearly averages of opinion poll results (Jan–May 2007, 2008, 2011, 2012, 2013). Polls for Flanders were carried out by DS/VRT and for Wallonia (we do not use the results for Brussels) by RTBF/La Libre. The vote share is always presented in relation to the total number of votes in Flanders and Wallonia. Theoretically, this means that populists could obtain a score of 200 per cent (100 per cent in Flanders and 100 per cent in Wallonia).

populist as it often denounces the Belgian establishment (e.g. the monarchy and trade unions) and argues to defend the interests of the Flemings. At the same time, the N-VA does not position itself entirely as an outsider either, illustrated by its electoral alliance with the mainstream party CD&V. More importantly, the N-VA does not adhere to the 'power to the people' principle. Its party leader De Wever could be characterised as elitist: he often depicts himself as an intellectual, uses Latin proverbs in his speeches and has claimed to be inspired by conservative and elitist thinkers such as Burke. Consequently, no reference to the referendum can be found in the N-VA party literature. The 2014 manifesto provides some insight here:

> Structuring and guiding society: that is the important and noble task of politics. This requires competent and honest policymakers who allocate the resources they receive as economically and effectively as possible. Trust in political institutions [...] is low [...] [and] to maintain and strengthen its legitimacy, politics should restore its credibility and increase the quality of its personnel. [...] It depends largely on the behaviour of every individual politician whether the credibility can be restored and trust can be increased. Additionally, collective measures are required.   (N-VA 2014: 77)

The party thus argues that political elites should structure and guide society. To restore political trust, the N-VA refers to 'collective measures' such as the abolishment of compulsory voting, the Senate (upper house) and the monarchy. No references to democratic innovation can be found in the manifesto. Given the lack of people-centrism in the ideology of the N-VA it seems unwarranted to classify the party as populist. At the same time it is questionable whether voters can make the subtle differences between anti-establishment appeals and populism. Moreover, since the VB has been permanently isolated as a consequence of a *cordon sanitaire*, part of the electorate has increasingly started voting strategically. Under the lead of the very popular Bart De Wever, it seems the N-VA increasingly has become a functional equivalent for the VB. Without being populist, the N-VA has been able to depict itself as an alternative for the established parties while having a realistic chance of actually realising its policy proposals.

Post electoral results indicated that in 2009 about 15 per cent of the former VB electorate defected to the N-VA (Pauwels 2011a). It can be assumed that this transfer from VB voters to N-VA continued in later elections. Other studies show that the N-VA attracted disproportionate support from those who are politically distrusting (although not to the same extent as LDD, VB, or non-voters) (Hooghe *et al.* 2011; Reeskens 2014). Some prominent VB politicians also exchanged their party card for one of the N-VA. Therefore, it seems that, unlike its populist alternatives VB and LDD, the N-VA has been able to profit from the political crisis in Flanders.

As explained in the introduction, the political power relations in Wallonia are very different from those in Flanders. Despite some occasional successes, the FNb has never been a stable populist party in Wallonia and is no longer represented in parliament. However, in recent years two new parties have known limited success in Wallonia. The PP was established in 2009 and combines neoliberal principles with a call to weaken the power of political parties and the use of more referenda. Recently, the party leader Modrikamen claimed to see the French FN under the leadership of Marine Le Pen as a guiding example and called for an immigration stop. Both in 2010 and 2014 the PP obtained one seat and hence remains a marginal actor in party politics. This can be explained by the lack of party organisation and the many conflicts inside the PP. Both the co-founder, Rudy Aernoudt and its only national representative, the controversial Laurent Louis, were expelled from the party in 2010.

More promising is the breakthrough of the PTB which is a national party that is also active in Flanders (*Partij van de Arbeid van België*). The party is currently led by the Flemish Peter Mertens and resembles other parties which have been labelled as social populist such as the Dutch *Socialistische Partij* and the German *Die Linke* (March 2011; Pauwels 2014). These parties adhere to democratic socialism as they left the revolutionary path of communism, while at the same time calling for a radical transformation of the capitalist system. The PTB is perhaps still a bit more radical compared to the SP and DL as it does not shun the term 'Marxist party'. The party strives for more equality, social justice, peace and less discrimination (Delwit 2014). The party also has populist tendencies as it depicts the current political system as no longer representative for the people (and certainly not blue collar workers) while striving for more direct democracy. In 2009 the PTB/PVDA campaigned with the slogan 'stop this political circus' (referring to the political crisis) depicting prominent politicians with clown noses. The 2014 party manifesto argues that 'those who govern us have deprived us from our right to decide on our budget and our social and economic policies' (PTB 2014: 92). Therefore, parliamentarians should consult citizens more frequently and important decisions should be decided by means of referendums (PTB 2014: 95).

At the 2014 elections, the PVDA/PTB scored 2.8 per cent of the votes in Flanders and 5.2 per cent of the votes in Wallonia. Consequently, the party only reached the electoral threshold in two Walloon provinces and obtained two seats in national parliament. This corroborates the expectation formulated in the introduction of this volume that left-wing populism might be particularly successful in countries (here a region) that have been hit hard by the crisis. The party also scored well in the local elections of 2012 and gained a significant number of seats in cities with relatively high unemployment rates such as Antwerp, Genk and Liege.

Conclusion

We explored how populist communication and mobilisation has evolved in times of crisis in Belgium. Economic indicators suggest that Belgium has suffered from the global economic crisis but has weathered the crisis better than most other European countries did. At the same time, the country suffered from a severe political crisis marked by long periods without a government. A systematic content analysis of the monthly membership magazine of the VB shows that the political crisis has had a larger effect on the degree of populism of the party than the economic crisis. The form of populism expressed in the party literature is almost completely political. Not the economic but the political elite is accused of badly messing up things. Moreover, the VB focuses on problems caused by the political crisis in much greater depth than on difficulties brought about by the economic crisis.

While the populist discourse has intensified as a consequence of the political crisis in Belgium, we found that Flemish populist parties did not profit in electoral terms. The VB faced a serious decline after a period of continuous growth, while the neoliberal populist LDD is no longer represented in parliament. This can be explained by the rise of the Flemish nationalist N-VA, which serves as a functional equivalent for the VB. This Flemish nationalist party also addresses some of the issues of the VB such as Flemish nationalism and conservatism while also drawing on anti-establishment appeals. In Wallonia populist parties have been traditionally unsuccessful. The FNb is not represented in parliament anymore. However, recently two populist parties have gained parliamentary representation: the PP and the PTB.

Our findings show how complex it is to investigate the impact of crises on populism. For Flanders we have seen a modest intensification of populist discourse yet a decline of electoral support. In Wallonia, the social populist PTB has gained a respectable 5 per cent of electoral support in times of crisis. The link between crisis and electoral support for populists is thus not evident as it is dependent not only on 'demand-side' variables such as economic conditions or political trust but also on a host of different 'supply-side' factors such as party leadership, policy positioning, the available ideological space, party unity, and being in government or opposition (Mudde 2007; Van Kessel 2013).

It needs to be emphasised that the results of the Belgian case by no means indicate that the economic crisis has no or only little effect on populism. The findings presented in this chapter only suggest that the effect of the economic crisis on populism is limited when the financial crisis has had only a moderate economic impact. Most importantly, however, this chapter indicates that populists respond to political crises. However, this increase in populist discourse will not necessarily be rewarded by voters, our results suggest. For a party to profit from a political crisis, it seems important that it can be seen as potentially relevant to deal with this crisis. It appears that the N-VA has been able to present itself as such much more than the VB has been able to.

Appendix: Codebook

People centrism

The people are depicted in a positive manner (e.g. the noble people/Flemings, the people are always right) and/or as a collective entity (the homogeneous people, all Flemings, Flemish majority). Just referring to the people/the Flemings is not sufficient to be coded as people centrism. When one talks about deception of the electorate or the people (e.g. broken promises) this is coded as people centrism since it implies that the electorate/people is wise and right but is being deceived by the elite.

Anti-elitism

The elite is depicted in a negative manner and as a collective entity. Criticism on individual politicians or the executive is not sufficient to be coded as anti-elitism. Criticism on the political regime (e.g. the Belgian political system) and conspiracy theories (e.g. suggesting that the elite is silencing the VB or the people) are also coded as anti-elitism.

Sovereignty

The author adheres to direct democracy or plebiscites or calls for the sovereignty of the Flemish state. A call for Flemish independence is hence coded as sovereignty.

Chapter Seven

Dutch Populism During the Crisis

Stijn van Kessel

Introduction

Although The Netherlands remains one of the more prosperous European countries, it did face the consequences of the Great Recession. Being a country with a very open economy, The Netherlands is sensitive to economic shocks at the international level. Negative GDP growth figures were not only recorded in 2009, but also in 2012 and 2013, consumer demand remained low, unemployment level rose, and it became increasingly difficult for the Dutch government to stick to the European 3 per cent deficit rule. Compared with harder hit Eurozone countries, such as Greece, Portugal and Ireland, the economic malaise in The Netherlands has evidently been modest, and the Dutch economy was projected to grow again with 0.75 per cent in 2014, and further (with 1.25 per cent) in 2015 (CPB 2014). Yet in comparison with surrounding Western European countries, economic recovery has been sluggish, and the crisis has clearly left its mark on the political debate.

Irrespective of slightly declining levels of trust in parliament and satisfaction with democracy a trend visible in many European countries (*see* Chapter One), it would go too far to claim that the economic crisis has also spurred a political crisis in The Netherlands. Recent Dutch governments may have been short-lived, but political trust and satisfaction levels have remained relatively high in comparison with other (Western) European countries (*see* also Bovens and Wille 2001). At the same time, the high levels of electoral volatility between Dutch parliamentary elections date back to well before the crisis (Mair 2008). Moreover, one should not be too quick to interpret these volatility levels as a sign of a footloose electorate, as most voters tend to switch between more or less like-minded parties (Van der Meer *et al.* 2012).

As this chapter will argue, the crisis also did not have apparent consequences for the electoral fortunes of populist parties. The first significant breakthrough of a (right-wing) populist party came before the Great Recession, when the List Pim Fortuyn (*Lijst Pim Fortuyn*, LPF) experienced success in the parliamentary election of 2002, and entered a short-lived coalition government. The main populist party that emerged after the quick demise of the LPF was the radical right Freedom Party (*Partij voor de Vrijheid*, PVV) of Geert Wilders, that entered parliament in 2006. In addition to the populist parties of the right, the Socialist Party (*Socialistische Partij*, SP) has frequently been identified as a case of left-wing populism. This party entered the Dutch parliament in 1994 already, but became a more notable electoral force in the 2000s after it moderated its ideological appeal, as well as its populist rhetoric.

This chapter mainly focuses on the developments of the two latter parties during the years of the economic recession. It relies primarily on election manifestos and an analysis of the party leaders' Twitter messages in order to demonstrate the effects of the economic crisis on the discourse and positions of the PVV and SP. The chapter will argue that the crisis did have an impact on the discourse of the two parties. The PVV adapted its ideological profile after the dawn of the crisis and took a clearer welfare protectionist and anti-European stance. The SP, on the other hand, temporarily bolstered its populist rhetoric at the time of the 2010 parliamentary election. It is much less evident, however, that the crisis has influenced the electoral fortunes of populist parties in The Netherlands. Before turning to these arguments in more detail, the following section will touch on the rise and characteristics of Dutch populist parties before the crisis.

Dutch populist parties in the twenty-first century

Several new political parties in the Dutch post-war period have been associated with populism; examples include the Farmer's Party, in parliament between 1963 and 1981, and the Centrum Party and Centre Democrats which were represented in parliament in the 1980s and 1990s (Lucardie and Voerman 2012). Yet only three alleged populist parties have managed to make a real electoral impact, and to threaten the position of the traditionally dominant party families (the Christian Democrats, Social Democrats and Liberals). These were the LPF and the PVV, positioned on the (radical) right, and the radical left-wing SP.

The three large established parties received a first blow after the rise of the flamboyant maverick Pim Fortuyn. Fortuyn, a columnist and former sociology professor, caused a stir with his harsh criticism of the ruling coalition and, most notably, his critical stance on immigration and cultural integration of ethnic minorities. His party LPF won 17 per cent of the vote in the parliamentary election of 15th May 2002, despite the fact that Fortuyn had been murdered nine days before by an environmental activist (*see* Table 7.1). The LPF joined a coalition government, which fell after 87 days, following a period of continuous LPF-infighting (*see* De Lange and Art 2011). The party had lost its electoral appeal and disappeared from parliament in 2006 altogether.

At the 2006 parliamentary election a new populist party entered the Dutch legislature with 5.9 per cent of the vote: the PVV. The party was founded and ever since controlled by Geert Wilders, who was a former MP for the mainstream Liberal Party (*Volkspartij voor Vrijheid en Democratie*, VVD).[1] Wilders shared Fortuyn's criticism of the political establishment, his hostility towards immigration and multiculturalism, and warned against the threats of 'Islamisation'

---

1.   Another ex-Liberal politician voicing a populist discourse, Rita Verdonk, failed to cross the electoral threshold with her party 'Proud of The Netherlands' (*Trots op Nederland*, TON).

Table 7.1: Dutch parliamentary election results (1998–2012) (in per cent)

	1998	2002	2003	2006	2010	2012
Labour (PvdA)	29.0	15.1	27.3	21.2	19.6	24.9
Liberals (VVD)	24.7	15.4	17.9	14.6	20.5	26.6
Chr. Democrats (CDA)	18.4	27.9	28.6	26.5	13.6	8.5
Democrats 66 (D66)	9.0	5.1	4.1	2.0	7.0	8.0
Green Left (GL)	7.3	7.0	5.1	4.6	6.7	2.3
Socialist Party (SP)	3.5	5.9	6.3	16.6	9.9	9.7
Christian Union (CU)	3.2	2.5	2.1	4.0	3.2	3.1
List Pim Fortuyn (LPF)		17.0	5.7	0.2		
Liveable NL (LN)		1.6	0.4			
Freedom Party (PVV)				5.9	15.5	10.1
Others	4.9	2.5	2.5	4.4	4.0	6.8
Total	100%	100%	100%	100%	100%	100%

Note: The percentage for the Christian Union (CU) in 1998 is the combined percentage of the GPV and RPF, the parties that later merged into the CU. Data: Nordsieck (2013).

of society in particular. By 2010 the Freedom Party had almost tripled its support, winning 15.5 per cent of the vote in the parliamentary election of that year. The PVV subsequently provided parliamentary support for the governing minority coalition between the Christian Democrats (CDA) and the VVD in exchange for the implementation of some of its key policies (including stricter policies on immigration). The government would not last longer than April 2012, when Wilders, refusing to sign up to newly drafted austerity measures, withdrew his support. In the early election that followed in September 2012, the PVV suffered a substantial loss. The party received 10.1 per cent of the vote, but still remained the third largest party in parliament (together with the radical left-wing SP).

Besides the surge of populist right newcomers, also the radical left-wing SP achieved remarkable success. The party was founded in 1971, when it associated itself with Maoism, but only entered parliament in 1994 with 1.3 per cent of the vote. By this time, the party had gradually moved away from its communist roots and could better be described as a left-wing populist party (*see* Lucardie and Voerman 2012). The party's greatest electoral victory was recorded in 2006, when it received 16.6 per cent of the vote. By this time, as this chapter will discuss in more detail below, the party had toned down its populist rhetoric to a large extent. Four years later – after the departure of its telegenic leader Jan Marijnissen – the party won 9.9 per cent. Although opinion polls prior to the election of 2012 indicated that the SP's popularity had soared – the party even appeared to be in the race to become the largest party in parliament – the SP was not able to increase its vote share in the actual election. The party stagnated at 9.7 per cent of the vote.

The characteristics of Dutch populism before the crisis

Populists on the 'right'

The ideological features of the populist parties on the right (the LPF and PVV) are, to a considerable extent, comparable to populist radical right parties in other countries (*see* Mudde 2007).[2] Both Fortuyn and Wilders have expressed populist anti-establishment rhetoric. Fortuyn particularly targeted the incumbent governing coalition – which was dubbed 'Purple', since it included both 'red' Labour and the 'blue' Liberals, in addition to the smaller social liberal Democrats 66. Fortuyn had previously become leader of the party 'Liveable Netherlands' (*Leefbaar Nederland*, LN) in November 2001. Although this party lacked a very detailed policy programme, it declared 'old politics' bankrupt and called for the democratisation of the political order (LN 2002). After LN had ousted Fortuyn in February 2012, due to his controversial statements about Islam and freedom of speech in a newspaper interview, he founded his own party and continued to express fierce anti-establishment rhetoric. In his book's appendix on his political programme '*The Shambles of Eight Years Purple*', Fortuyn stated that '[t]he Netherlands should become a real lively democracy of and for the ordinary people, and depart from the elite party democracy with which we are currently acquainted' (Fortuyn 2002: 186). According to Fortuyn, power had to be returned to the 'people in the country' (Lucardie 2008: 159). The number of managers and bureaucrats was to be reduced and responsibility would have to be returned to the 'real' experts: the nurses, teachers and police officers (LPF 2002).

Quite similar to Pim Fortuyn's critique of the 'left-wing church', Geert Wilders' Freedom Party later railed against the 'left-wing' elites, their culture relativism and support for multiculturalism, and their 'left-wing hobbies' such as development aid and high-brow art. The Freedom Party arguably had a more outspoken populist character; Wilders appealed to the 'ordinary people' more explicitly than Fortuyn. In Wilders' 'Declaration of Independence', written in March 2005 after his departure from the Liberals, the politician spoke of a 'range of interlinked crises which flow from the incompetence of the political elite in Brussels and [Dutch political capital] The Hague' (Wilders 2005: 1). Wilders (2005: 2) further declared: 'I do not want this country to be hijacked by an elite of cowardly and frightened people (from whichever party) any longer. [...] I therefore intend to challenge this elite on all fronts. I want to return this country to its citizens'. Wilders claimed to despise the self-sustaining political system which stood isolated from society; 'politicians should no longer be deaf to the problems troubling ordinary people in every-day life' (Wilders 2005: 16). Populist proclamations like these would remain a lasting and recurring feature in Wilders' rhetoric and his party's documents.

As far as concrete policy proposals of the right-wing populists are concerned, Fortuyn promoted a free-market economy, took a tough line on law and order

---

2. Cas Mudde (2007: 47) actually categorises the *List Pim Fortuyn* as a 'neo-liberal' populist party, not a populist radical right party.

issues and stressed the need to cut red tape in the healthcare and education sectors (*see* Lucardie 2008). The initial ideology of Geert Wilders was also characterised by economic liberalism; he criticised the overly generous welfare state, and favoured less economic state intervention and a more flexible labour market (Vossen 2011). But the populist parties on the right were, above all, associated with their critical stance towards immigration and Islam, as well as their strict line on cultural integration of ethnic minorities. Fortuyn's breakthrough can also largely be ascribed to his position on these latter issues. None of the mainstream parties placed much emphasis on immigration and multiculturalism in 2002, while a substantial share of the electorate had become concerned about these issues since the 1990s (*see* e.g. Van Holsteyn *et al.* 2003; Pellikaan *et al.* 2007; Aarts and Thomassen 2008; Van Heerden *et al.* 2013).

After Fortuyn's posthumous breakthrough and the entrance of his party into the governing coalition, the continuous LPF infighting not only instigated the early fall of the coalition, but also the party's electoral demise (*see* De Lange and Art 2011; Van Kessel 2011). When the LPF disappeared from parliament in 2006, the Freedom Party filled the space that was left vacant. In his 'declaration of independence' of 2005, Wilders primarily criticised the political elites for the oversized public sector, overly generous subsidies and welfare entitlements, and smothering bureaucracy. Yet in the following years, Wilders would reach attention primarily with his outspoken views on Islam, which were for instance conveyed in his controversial seventeen-minute film *Fitna* from early 2008 (*see* Vossen 2011; Lucardie and Voerman 2012). The 2010 PVV manifesto nevertheless argued that the PVV was not a single-issue party, and Islamisation was linked to a range of other social issues:

> [e]conomically it is a disaster, it damages the quality of our education, it increases insecurity on the streets, causes an exodus out of our cities, drives out Jews and gay people, and flushes the century-long emancipation of women down the toilet. (PVV 2010: 6)

While anti-immigration and Islamophobia are part and parcel of Western European populist radical right parties, the former quote reveals what is quite special about the Dutch populist right: its liberal attitude towards certain cultural issues such as the emancipation of women and homosexuals. Pim Fortuyn – himself openly gay – saw The Netherlands as a country of liberal enlightenment values, and was concerned about those being undermined (*see* Akkerman 2005). Wilders, too, emphasised the alleged threats of Islamisation to liberal values. At the same time, the protectiveness of the liberal elements of Dutch culture could also be interpreted as a form of cultural conservatism. What is more, in particular Wilders blamed the progressive (left-wing) elites for undermining traditional norms and values, and even though the PVV leader presented himself as a defender of women and gay rights, these themes were mainly discussed as part of Wilders' anti-Islam discourse. In its manifestos, the PVV actually remained silent about moral-cultural issues such as euthanasia and abortion.

Populists on the 'left'

The SP, which has become an important electoral force on the radical left, is regularly considered to be a populist party as well (e.g. March 2011; Rooduijn *et al.* 2014). Following Gerrit Voerman (2009: 26–7), up until the 1980s the SP combined populism with Maoism, effectively treating 'the people' and the 'working class' as one, and basing its actions and positions on the perceived opinion of the 'common man'. The party combined this discourse with a criticism of the existing political order, showed distaste for intermediary political institutions and established parties, and favoured democratisation of the decision-making process.

By the time the party entered parliament in 1994, when it won two out of the 150 seats, the SP had departed from its more radical socialist policies and dropped references to its communist heritage (Voerman and Lucardie 2007; Voerman and Lucardie 2012). It now presented itself explicitly as a protest party, exemplified by its slogan 'vote against, vote SP', and in its 1994 election manifesto the party declared that 'the SP brings back the opposition in the Chamber [i.e. parliament]' (SP 1994: 16). The SP clearly remained a party on the radical left, and argued that 'neo-liberal thinking has engulfed Western-Europe and severely infected parliamentary parties from left to right, also in our country' (SP 1994: 3). According to the SP, furthermore, economic power was concentrated in the hands of a small, unelected and unaccountable, capitalist elite. Once represented in parliament, party leader Jan Marijnissen actively tried to preserve the party's outsider image, for instance by contrasting the supposed privileged background of most other politicians with his own humble career path that started out in a scruffy factory (Voerman 2009: 29–30).

In 1999, a year after the SP increased its number of parliamentary seats to five, the party adopted a less radical constitution. After the turn of the century the SP also increasingly made clear its ambition to enter government, and the party lost its disdain for representative parliamentary democracy and party politics (Voerman and Lucardie 2012: 61–4). The SP simultaneously downplayed its anti-establishment image, and in 2002 its slogan had remarkably changed to 'Vote *for*, vote SP'. De Lange and Rooduijn (2011: 324) further showed that the anti-elitist rhetoric in SP manifestos evaporated gradually. In 1994 anti-elite references were found in 17 per cent of the paragraphs, while this percentage dropped to a mere 1.5 per cent in 2006 – the year in which the party secured its largest national election victory to date.

There is thus a case for classifying the current SP as an 'ordinary' social-democratic party, even though the party and its politicians have occasionally continued to voice populist rhetoric (Lucardie and Voerman 2012). The parliamentary election manifesto of 2006, for instance, still criticised the incumbent government for its arrogance and observed the lack of faith citizens had in political institutions. The SP claimed to take people genuinely serious and was confident that many voters would dismiss the parties who were responsible for the 'thoughtless sell-out and futile bureaucratisation of

The Netherlands' (SP 2006: 4). Yet the document did not refer explicitly to 'elites' anymore, and whether the SP programme truly conveyed a 'Manichean outlook', opposing the positive valorisation of 'the people' to the denigration of 'the elite', is questionable. It is thus problematic to view the SP as a 'full' case of populism in the years in the run up to the economic crisis, certainly in comparison with the LPF and PVV (*see* Van Kessel 2014).

The SP also differed from these latter two parties in the sense that issues of immigration and integration have played a much smaller role in the present day discourse of the SP. The party was critical of multiculturalism in the early 1980s, when it published a brochure urging immigrants (*gastarbeiders*, 'guest workers') to choose between adopting the Dutch nationality or returning to their country of origin (Van der Steen 1995). Yet the party moderated its position afterwards and has shown little concern about the alleged threat of Islam to Dutch society in more recent years. That said, the SP has remained critical of labour migration from Central and Eastern Europe, fearing the depression of wages and other negative consequences of a more competitive labour market.

The SP's signature policies have always related to socio-economic issues. After the party shed its more radical communist policies, the SP continued to advocate higher minimum wages and oppose welfare state reforms, such as raising the pension age, restricting the eligibility for unemployment benefits, and privatising healthcare provision. The party clearly did not adopt the pro-business position of the populist right parties. The SP did share the PVV's critical stance on European integration, which was, in turn, more pronounced than Fortuyn's. This became evident in the campaign for the referendum on the European Constitutional Treaty in 2005, when both the SP and PVV urged citizens to vote against – which a majority of those turning out (61.5 per cent) eventually did. While the SP criticised the neo-liberal character of European integration more explicitly than Wilders, both parties campaigned against the 'race to the bottom' in terms of working conditions and social policies.

Populism during the crisis

The first great electoral success for a populist party occurred when economic circumstances were hardly dire. The *List Pim Fortuyn* broke through at a time of economic prosperity, and the incumbent government was not in the first place blamed for economic mismanagement (Van Holsteyn and Irwin 2003). The first success of the right-wing populist parties in The Netherlands should primarily be related to their stance on cultural issues and immigration, rather than their positions on socio-economic issues.

Due to the crisis, however, socio-economic issues have gained prominence in Dutch election campaigns. Like most European countries, The Netherlands has suffered the consequences of the crisis since 2008. As discussed in the previous chapter, the Dutch government saw itself forced to buy the Dutch parts of the Fortis Bank in October 2008, when the financial institution was on the verge of collapse. In February 2013, the smaller SNS Bank was nationalised to rescue it from bankruptcy. As far as macro-economic indicators are concerned, the economy shrank not only in 2009, but also in 2012 and 2013 (with 1.2 and 0.8 per cent, respectively) (Eurostat 2014b). At the same time, yearly unemployment rates rose steadily from 3.1 per cent in 2008 to 6.7 in 2013. During the crisis years, the Dutch governments also failed to stick to the European 3 per cent deficit rule. In 2008 the budget was still balanced (with a surplus of 0.2 of GDP), but the following year a deficit of 5.5 per cent was recorded. The figures improved slightly but steadily in the years after, and in 2013 the deficit was, with 2.3 per cent, below the 3 per cent threshold again. While The Netherlands thus certainly experienced an economic setback, the effects of the crisis were relatively modest in comparison with other European countries. The unemployment level in 2013 was well below the EU-28 average figure (10.8 per cent). Furthermore, despite a significant rise in government gross debt (from 42.7 to 68.8 per cent of GDP between 2007 and 2013), the Dutch figure in the latter year was also considerably lower than the European average (85.4 per cent).

Nonetheless, in the run up to the 2010 parliamentary election, the state of the economy and the proposals to deal with it dominated the campaign. Important issues at stake were the tax relief on mortgage interest payments – one key factor behind the high levels of household debt in The Netherlands – the pension age, the eligibility to unemployment benefits, and the rising costs of healthcare provision (Van Kessel 2010). This section will discuss the developments in the discourse of the PVV and the SP in the context of these changed economic and political circumstances.

Developments in the PVV's discourse

The PVV evidently adapted to the new political reality. Even though Wilders' anti-Islam rhetoric did not wane, he was forced to place more emphasis on socio-economic issues when these started to play a more prominent role. The PVV also altered its position on several socio-economic issues, and adopted a more 'welfare protectionist' stance. Wilders had always been against raising the pension age, but previously favoured a small state and a flexible labour market (Wilders 2005). In 2010, however, the PVV called for the preservation of certain welfare entitlements and opposed easing the rules for laying off employees, amending unemployment benefits, and a 'marketisation' of the healthcare sector. Wilders had thus shifted significantly to the socio-economic left with regard to certain policy domains. At the same time, the PVV still favoured typical *laissez faire* policies such as tax cuts and deregulation, and continued to support the mortgage interest relief. The PVV's socio-economic programme had thus become a rather eclectic mix of right-wing and left-wing policies.

After the successful election of June 2010, the PVV supported a minority coalition between the VVD and CDA (installed in October) that imposed several austerity measures in response to the economic crisis. Many of those measures were in line with the PVV manifesto, and included reducing the size of the public sector, lowering subsidies for the arts, and cutting development aid. At the same time, Wilders continued to criticise the government's willingness to contribute to the bailout packages for Greece, as this concerned an area not covered by the support agreement. Since the budget deficit continued to grow in the period after the formation of the minority coalition, the VVD, CDA and PVV started negotiations on 5th March 2012 about new austerity measures. After seven weeks Wilders left the table. The PVV leader declared his unwillingness to support measures hurting the financial position of pensioners and to abide by the Brussels 3 per cent deficit rule at all cost. After the breakdown of the negotiations, Wilders vowed that 'Europe' was going to be the central theme of the campaign for the new election that would follow.

In the run up to this new parliamentary election of September 2012, the PVV would indeed pay attention to the EU issue as never before, both in its manifesto and in election debates (Van Kessel and Hollander 2012). The manifesto, tellingly titled '*Their* Brussels, *our* Netherlands', spoke derogatively of 'the blind inhabitants of the ivory towers in Brussels', 'unelected multi-culti Eurocrats', and the 'holy Great-European project' (PVV 2012: 11–12). National-level politicians, in turn, were blamed for their submissive compliance with the 'dictates from Brussels', for surrendering national sovereignty to 'Europe', and for wasting tax-payers money on supporting corrupt countries such as Greece and Romania at a time of economic hardship at home.

Although the PVV had always been Eurosceptic, Wilders' anti-EU rhetoric intensified, and he now went so far as to support a Dutch withdrawal from the EU. 'Europe' had become a much more prominent theme in both the PVV's manifesto, as well as in the personal Twitter messages ('tweets') of Wilders. Table 7.2 shows data from a content analysis of the PVV leader's 'critical tweets'; that is, those tweets in which he criticised political or non-political actors in relationship to policy proposals and social developments in general (Van Kessel and Castelein 2014). What is clear is that European integration became a much more prominent theme in Wilders' tweets in the run-up to the 2012 national election (*see* 'Election 2012' column). In this period, almost two-thirds of Wilders' critical tweets related to this issue. After the election, Wilders' tweets were less EU-dominated, yet the PVV stuck to its Euroreject position, as again became evident in the campaign for the European Parliament election in May 2014.

It is not the case that Wilders altered his views on immigration and Islam, or ignored the themes altogether. It must also be noted that Wilders spent more attention in his tweets to immigration and culture than the percentages in Table 7.2 suggest – examples of specific issues being crime levels among Moroccans and the 'Islamisation' of neighbourhoods. The PVV leader did not always relate these issues explicitly to the failure of political actors, which is a reason why the themes of immigration and culture – and law and order for that matter – were not more prominent in Wilders' critical tweets. Yet it is clear that the PVV shifted its focus more explicitly towards 'Europe' in the run up to the 2012 parliamentary election, and in particular on the social and financial costs of European integration and the loss of national sovereignty.

Table 7.2: Issues related to critical tweets of Wilders, (in per cent)

	Rutte I (N=95)	Election 2012 (N=52)	Rutte II (N=107)	All (N=254)
Social and financial issues	30.5	51.9	55.1	45.3
Immigration and culture	23.2	7.7	19.6	18.5
Law and order	8.4	1.9	7.5	6.7
European integration	32.6	63.5	29.9	37.8
Democracy	9.5	1.9	1.9	4.7
Counter-criticism	25.3	9.6	0.9	11.8
Other/Idiosyncratic	14.7	5.8	17.8	14.2

Source: Van Kessel and Castelein (2014). The 'Rutte I' column covers the period of the formation and tenure of the CDA-VVD Cabinet Rutte I (10 June 2010–22 April 2012); the 'Election 2012' column the period in between the fall of Rutte I and new parliamentary elections (23 April 2012–12 September 2012); the 'Rutte II' column the period of the formation and first seven months of the VVD-PvdA Cabinet Rutte II (13 September 2012–30 June 2013). The categories are non-exclusive; a single tweet could relate to more than one issue category, and values do therefore not add up to 100 per cent.

While the issues central to the discourse of the PVV have thus changed over the years, the thin core of the PVV's populism remained intact. All PVV manifestos have blamed the 'elites' for many of the societal ills, although the emphasis changed somewhat. Since 2010, the PVV referred more explicitly than before to the 'left-wing elites'. Wilders targeted in particular the dominant progressive 'left-wing' ideas, which were alleged to pose a threat to Dutch identity and culture. In the 2012 parliamentary campaign, in turn, the PVV intensified its criticism of unresponsive European Union (EU) elites. The degree to which Wilders applied populist anti-establishment rhetoric has also varied somewhat over the years. This is again visible in Wilders' tweets (*see* Figure 7.1). When Wilders provided parliamentary support for the VVD-CDA minority coalition between October 2010 and April 2012, the percentage of critical tweets was relatively low, while we can observe a clear surge after the government's break-up. Although the graph does not display a measure of Wilders' populism – but rather the intensity of his criticism of (political) actors – it suggests that government support may (temporarily) soften the anti-establishment character of populist parties.

Figure 7.1 also shows the percentage of SP leader Emile Roemer's tweets that contained criticism of other actors. We can observe that Roemer's critical tweets actually slumped during the 2012 election campaign, which suggests that, unlike Wilders, the SP leader did not use Twitter to wage an aggressive campaign. The following section discusses the discourse of the SP and its leader in more detail.

Figure 7.1: Percentage of critical tweets per quarter (PVV leader Wilders and SP leader Roemer)

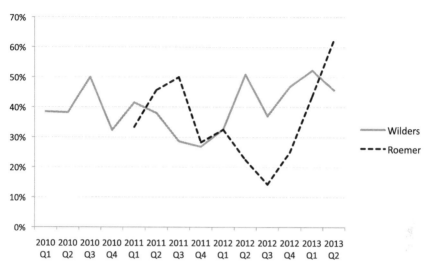

Source: Van Kessel and Castelein (2014).

Developments in the SP's discourse

At the time of the 2010 parliamentary election, it was no surprise that the radical left SP held greedy bankers, speculators and managers responsible for the economic problems; 'there can be no doubt about it: the crisis came from the right', the SP stated in its manifesto (SP 2010: 7). Instead of imposing harsh austerity measures on innocent citizens, the SP proposed to pass the bill to those it held responsible for the crisis (i.e. bankers, large companies and shareholders). It is thus clear that the economic crisis also left its mark on the SP's discourse. Yet in comparison with the PVV, the SP's programme has been characterised by more continuity: socio-economic issues remained at the core of the party's appeal. This is also evident from the critical tweets of Emile Roemer, of which almost 80 per cent were related to socio-economic and financial issues (*see* Table 7.3).

With regard to European integration, the second-most important theme in Roemer's tweets, the SP took a less radical approach than in the past. In 1994 the SP manifesto was very clear about its position on Europe: 'The interests of the people in The Netherlands and abroad are not served by the devaluation of our country to a powerless province of an undemocratic European super state. That is why The Netherlands must say 'no' to the European Union' (SP 1994: 15). European integration was perceived to serve merely the interests of big companies. In more recent years, the SP has remained critical of the EU and surrendering national sovereignty – its active role in the campaign against the Constitutional Treaty in 2005 being a case in point. In its 2006 manifesto, the SP claimed that 'the

Table 7.3: Issues related to critical tweets of Roemer (in per cent)

	Rutte I (N=81)	Election 2012 (N=9)	Rutte II (N=74)	All (N=164)
Social and financial issues	70.4	88.9	86.5	78.7
Immigration and culture	2.5	0.0	1.4	1.8
Law and order	2.5	0.0	2.7	2.4
European integration	9.9	11.1	10.8	10.4
Democracy	4.9	0.0	0.0	2.4
Counter-criticism	1.2	0.0	0.0	0.6
Other/Idiosyncratic	19.8	11.1	9.5	14.6

Source: Van Kessel and Castelein (2014). *See* notes Table 7.2.

megalomania of Brussels has estranged many citizens of the European Union', and the party criticised the proliferation of European regulations (SP 2006: 10). By this time, however, the party did not oppose membership of the EU anymore.

While the Freedom Party radicalised in its position on Europe prior to the 2012 election, and now called for a Dutch 'exit', the SP did not directly blame 'Brussels' for the economic malaise. The SP's position on European integration was actually somewhat ambiguous during the campaign (Van Kessel and Hollander 2012: 4). The SP was critical of the supposed neo-liberal character of the EU, and in an interview party leader Roemer stated that he would not accept financial sanctions if The Netherlands would fail to meet the EU's budgetary rules – 'over my dead body', Roemer declared. After criticism from political opponents, however, Roemer half-heartedly qualified this statement. At the same time, the SP supported stricter control over national budgets and the financial sector by the European Central Bank (ECB), and intended to give the ECB a role in stimulating the growth of jobs. Despite its many critical notes about the EU, then, the SP saw European integration also as a means to solve the crisis. The Freedom Party, on the other hand, identified European integration merely as the cause of the (economic) problems.

Despite the overall moderation of the SP's policy positions, the economic crisis did appear to serve as a temporary catalyst for the SP's use of populist rhetoric. In its manifesto for 2010, the party argued that most political parties in The Netherlands had betrayed their ideals in exchange for the adoption of a certain kind of neo-liberal, pro-market philosophy (SP 2010: 5). 'Politicians have failed, now the choice is yours', the document opened, adding that 'we have never seen such a painful exposure of the political and economic elite' (SP 2010: 5). The powerful language in the manifesto was not matched by a smooth election campaign. After the resignation of Jan Marijnissen, new party leader Agnes Kant failed to leave a good impression in early election debates (Lucardie and Voerman 2012: 63). With just three months to go to the general election, Emile Roemer, a relatively unknown SP parliamentarian, replaced Kant as party leader. Roemer did surprisingly well in the TV debates, but he did not share Wilders' confrontational style and abrasive populist anti-establishment rhetoric, and instead conveyed a friendly 'ideal neighbour' type of image. This ostensibly distinguished Roemer from the typical, more rhetorically aggressive, populist leader.

Roemer remained the undisputed leader of the SP in the years after the election and, judging from the opinion polls, the party appeared to gain popularity. The SP published a new election manifesto prior to the early 2012 parliamentary election, in which the economic situation again played an important role. Once more, bankers, shareholders and managers were blamed for the crisis, whilst the incumbent government was criticised for its austerity measures. These measures were alleged to have led to further economic polarisation and to have hampered economic recovery (SP 2012: 5). In comparison with the previous manifesto, however, the populist rhetoric was toned down again. A content analysis of Matthijs Rooduijn (2014) confirmed that the degree of populist statements in SP programmes declined in 2012, after a surge in 2010. What is more, the SP had not lost its ambition to take part in government, and party leader Roemer ostensibly aimed to behave in a prime-ministerial, rather than confrontational, manner during the 2012 parliamentary election campaign.

All in all, where populism has consistently been a defining core attribute of Geert Wilders' PVV, this cannot truly be said for the SP, as it had developed itself since the late 1990s. The contemporary SP is a party which likes to portray itself as an 'ordinary people's party', but for which populism is more an auxiliary rhetorical devise than an ideological core attribute.

Electoral implications

At first sight, the economic crisis cannot be said to have stimulated populist success in national elections. The PVV experienced a striking victory in 2010, but lost badly in 2012. The SP lost in 2010, and its vote share stagnated in 2012. In the European Parliament elections of May 2014, the two parties also failed to make a great impact. The PVV finished third with 13.2 of the vote – a loss of 3.8 per cent compared with the previous 2010 EP election – while the SP secured a not more than reasonable 9.6 per cent.

It is thus apparent that worsening economic circumstances do not guarantee the success of radical left-wing parties such as the SP, even if these are seemingly provided with a good opportunity to blame the crisis on unbridled capitalism and widely-loathed bankers. The Dutch case shows that populist right-wing parties do not necessarily fare better under poor economic conditions either. This is not entirely surprising, as previous studies have indicated that radical right parties mobilise primarily on the basis of cultural, instead of economic, grievances (e.g. Oesch 2008; Ivarsflaten 2008; see also Mudde 2007). It is, furthermore, questionable whether Wilders' explicit focus on leaving the EU has been an effective vote-winning strategy. Even though the Standard Eurobarometer from Spring 2013 showed that the EU was distrusted by most (58 per cent) of the Dutch, a clear majority (71 per cent) disagreed with the statement that The Netherlands could better face the future outside the EU (European Commission 2013b: 70; 102).

Besides the fact that support for leaving the EU has remained limited, it is questionable whether European integration has become a genuinely salient issue for populist voters. Table 7.4, based on data from the Dutch Parliamentary Election Studies (DPES) of 2006, 2010 and 2012, shows the motivation of PVV and SP supporters. Most of these respondents indicated they voted for the parties because of their ideology or programme. Of the ideologically-driven voters who gave a more concrete answer, the plurality of PVV voters expressed their hostility towards immigration or felt that Dutch culture was threatened (by Islam). Social policies became more prominent among the PVV respondents' motivations in 2010, and answers specifically referring to the EU became more numerous in 2012. These developments are consistent with the developments in the ideological profile of the PVV and suggest that Wilders has been able to attract support from voters who were driven by their negative views on European integration. Yet cultural issues, such as immigration and cultural integration, clearly remained the most prominent themes in the motivations of PVV voters, despite the fact that these issues played a modest role during the campaign of 2012.

For the SP, on the other hand, its position on social policies clearly remained the most important reason for voters to support the party.[3] The party also attracted a limited number of voters who were driven by an urge to protest against the existing parties, or a desire for 'change', although the PVV clearly relied on a greater number of 'protest votes'. The party leader was important for a substantial number of PVV and SP voters as well.[4]

The main finding from Table 7.4 which is of interest here is that Geert Wilders' PVV has primarily mobilised support on the basis of cultural issues related to immigration and integration, and that this did not change in the most recent parliamentary election of 2012. Wilders' explicit focus on European integration in the electoral campaign may thus not have been the best strategy, as relatively few of his supporters appeared to cast their vote on the basis of this issue. The fact that the focus of the campaign was on solutions to deal with the economic crisis, and not on the PVV's cultural signature issues, may also have disadvantaged Wilders' party in 2012. Finally, the recent losses of the PVV can also be related to organisational problems. The image of the party was damaged at least to a certain extent when Wilders was unable to prevent defections from the party in the run-up to both the 2012 national, as well as the 2014 European Parliament elections.

The prospects for the SP seemed more promising in the months before the 2012 parliamentary election; the party was expected to become one of the largest, if not

---

3. This category included voters who referred to the 'left-wing' identity of the SP as well.

4. Several other categories could also be created on the basis of an inductive assessment of the data, including voters who cast a strategic or negative ('the party was the least bad') vote, those who followed the outcome of an online Voting Advice Application (VAA), and voters with a vague or an idiosyncratic motivation.

Table 7.4: Motivations of PVV and SP vote (response to open-ended question; in per cent of respondents)

	PVV			SP		
	2006 (N=110)	**2010 (N=231)**	**2012 (N=95)**	**2006 (N=379)**	**2010 (N=219)**	**2012 (N=147)**
Ideology general	52.7	68.0	76.8	62.8	69.9	68.0
Social policies	*1.8*	*16.9*	*9.5*	*30.1*	*40.2*	*41.5*
Immig/ culture	*23.6*	*29.0*	*31.6*	*1.1*	*1.4*	*0.0*
Law and order	*2.7*	*10.8*	*2.1*	*0.0*	*0.9*	*0.0*
European Union	*0.0*	*0.4*	*16.8*	*0.0*	*0.0*	*2.7*
Protest/ change	16.4	21.2	8.4	7.7	2.7	2.7
Party leader	25.5	16.9	17.9	13.7	10.0	17.0
Strategic/ negative	4.5	6.5	2.1	14.8	7.3	8.8
Voting advice application	10.0	9.5	9.5	4.5	8.2	4.1
Vague/ other	13.6	2.6	6.3	13.4	11.4	18.4

Note: Own coding and calculations on the basis of DPES 2006 (CBS *et al.* 2007); 2010 (SKON *et al.* 2012) and 2012 (SKON *et al.* 2013). The categories are non-exclusive; a respondent's answer could relate to more than one issue category, and values do therefore not add up to 100 per cent. Categories in italics are subcategories of the 'Ideology general' category.

the largest, party in Dutch parliament. Yet when the election campaign reached its crucial stage, a few alleged slip-ups of party leader Roemer in the TV debates prompted a downward trend in the SP's opinion poll standings, and the party's campaign turned into an uphill battle (Van Kessel and Hollander 2012). In the end, the Labour Party (PvdA) became the most important contestant on the political left, and the SP suffered from the 'horse race' that materialised between the PvdA and the centre-right VVD – which may also have affected negatively the PVV's performance. While the SP thus seemingly had a good chance to win the election in times of economic crisis, the Dutch election of 2012 illustrates that voters may still prefer established mainstream parties if these are able to present themselves as more credible actors during the campaign.

Conclusions

Comparing the two alleged populist parties in The Netherlands (PVV and SP) throughout the years of the economic downturn, we can observe some notable differences. The economic crisis did not truly affect the populist nature of Geert Wilders and his PVV. Hence, the case of the PVV does not substantiate the hypothesis that the economic crisis caused an intensification of populist discourse (H1 in this volume). There have been fluctuations in the intensity of Wilders' anti-establishment rhetoric during the years of the crisis, but these can better be explained by considering party political conditions. Notably, when the PVV supported the minority government (between October 2010 and April 2012), Wilders was more 'docile' compared with the years before and after the tenure of this coalition. This is consistent with the fourth hypothesis of this volume, which stated that populist parties in office, or supporting governments, tone down their populism.

We can also observe changes concerning the policies the PVV placed at the centre of its programme. In 2010 the PVV emphasised its welfare chauvinist character to a greater extent, and the party became more protectionist of existing welfare arrangements. With the national election of 2012 in sight, Wilders' party prioritised the issue of European integration, and for the first time supported a Dutch withdrawal from the EU. It is safe to assume that the euro crisis and the economic situation at home inspired Wilders to alter his ideological course and focus.

The SP, on the other hand, did not truly emphasise different issues than before the crisis. The party merely stepped up its criticism of bankers and large companies, holding them responsible for the crisis, and blaming politicians for letting them get away with it. In its 2010 manifesto the party also increased its populist rhetoric, and directly related its anti-establishment criticism to crisis-related themes. At first sight, therefore, the case of the SP does confirm the first hypothesis. In 2012, however, the party appeared to tone down its populism again. Moreover, SP leader Roemer did not match the confrontational rhetoric and style of PVV leader Wilders in the 2010 and 2012 election campaigns. On the whole, the party was not the pure populist anti-establishment party it used to be during the 1990s, and the last national election campaign demonstrated the party's overall ideological moderation.

Although both the PVV and the SP have altered their discourse in one way or another in the face of the economic crisis, the Great Recession has not automatically improved their electoral fortunes. Although the SP appeared to head for a large victory in 2012, many left-wing voters opted for the mainstream PvdA after a disappointing SP campaign. At the same time, the decision of Geert Wilders to campaign mainly on the basis of a welfare chauvinist anti-EU platform did not appear incredibly successful, as PVV voters seemingly still cared most about cultural issues. Defections of dissatisfied PVV politicians further did little to improve the party's credibility. Both the PVV and the SP remain important challengers to the established parties, but the crisis did not seem to have fundamentally altered the two radical parties' electoral scope, or the more general structure of party competition in The Netherlands. Even if the crisis provided electoral opportunities for the two radical challengers, the Dutch case shows that voters do not automatically turn their backs on established parties if the challengers fail to present themselves as credible alternatives.

Chapter Eight

The Populist Discourse of the Swiss People's Party

Laurent Bernhard, Hanspeter Kriesi and Edward Weber

Introduction

This chapter will focus on the case of the Swiss People's Party (*Schweizerische Volkspartei*, SVP), which is considered the country's strongest populist party (Albertazzi 2008; Kriesi *et al.* 2005). Other populist success stories include the *Lega dei Ticinesi* in the Canton of Ticino (Italian-speaking part of the country), as well as the *Mouvement Citoyens Genevois* (MCG) in Geneva. These two parties notably owe their recent electoral gains to the mobilisation against cross-border commuters from Italy and France, respectively. Given their very limited influence on the federal level of Swiss politics[1], we will restrict our analysis to the SVP. We will analyse the SVP's discourse from 2003 to 2013 by content-analysing a series of public-oriented documents produced by the party itself. The examination of the party's press releases, the oral presentations at its press conferences, its party newspapers, and the yearly programmatic speeches of its leader covering the last ten years reveals that the party did not increase its populist communication as a reaction to the emergence of the financial and economic crisis. This result turns out to be in line with our theoretical expectation. We will argue that both Switzerland's astonishing resistance to the economic crisis and the fact that the SVP has acquired issue ownership on the cultural issues (as opposed to economic issues) prevented the party from reinforcing its populist discourse since autumn 2008. Our analysis further shows that the party resorts to populist figures of speech above all in the cultural policy domain in general and when it comes to the issues of European integration, immigration, and related institutional issues in particular. The SVP's populist discourse also proves to be a function of its representation in government. The party's unexpected ousting from government in December 2007 induced it to adopt a more populist strategy until it was again represented in the federal government one year later. Finally, the populism of the party's discourse tends to be particularly pronounced during direct-democratic and electoral campaigns at the federal level.

---

1. Currently, the Lega has two MPs, while there is just one representative of the MCG in Berne. By contrast, the SVP occupies 54 out of the 200 seats of the lower house (National Council) and five out of the 46 seats of the upper house (Council of States).

The SVP's ideology

The rise of the SVP has probably been the most striking feature of the Swiss party system since World War II (Kriesi *et al.* 2005). The roots of this success can be traced back to the late 1970s when Christoph Blocher took over the leadership of the party's branch of the Canton of Zurich. At that time, the SVP was a conservative mainstream party, which primarily represented the interests of small business owners and famers in the protestant areas of the German speaking part of Switzerland. The party had been losing votes at the federal level and risked losing its seat in the federal government. Blocher built on local resentment of what was then seen as the dominance of the gentleman farmers of Berne who led the party (Church 2000). Despite strong resistance by the traditional leadership of the party, the Zurich wing gradually imposed itself and subsequently set out to consolidate its position throughout the whole country.

Under the *de facto* leadership of Blocher, the federal party underwent a process of radicalisation in the beginning of the 1990s. The SVP took a profile that has turned out to be paradigmatic of populist radical right parties across Western Europe (Betz 1993; Kitschelt 1995). The party's agenda focused on exclusionist beliefs by primarily putting emphasis on issues related to the transformed cultural dimension of the two-dimensional political space (Kriesi *et al.* 2008, 2012). In particular, the party focused on two core issues – immigration and European integration. Indeed, the SVP can be credited to have acquired issue ownership over these two policy domains in the recent past. By constantly campaigning on these issues, the party has been able to build a reputation of issue competence that provided it with a decisive electoral advantage (Budge and Farlie 1983; Petrocik 1996). In line with this interpretation, the SVP's electoral success has been shown to be the result of its tough stance on immigration and its opposition to European integration (Kriesi and Sciarini 2004). Capitalising on widespread popular xenophobia and Euroscepticism, the party has been able to tap into the people's resentment by attacking the government over immigration and European integration. As has been the case in other Western European countries, the strong mobilisation of the SVP on the cultural dimension has led to a realignment of the Swiss party system by the early 2000s, characterised by a three-polar configuration consisting of the left, the moderate mainstream right, and the radical populist right (Bornschier 2010; Kriesi *et al.* 2008).

The early phase of the SVP's rise has been primarily due to its Euroscepticism (Kriesi *et al.* 2005). The immigration issue has become important only since the mid 1990s. The party's position on immigration does not necessarily involve ethnic racism, but rather what Betz and Johnson (2004), call 'differentialist nativism' or 'cultural differentialism', which entails a sharp rejection of the multicultural society more generally. As far as the European integration process is concerned, it is its cultural dimension that the SVP has placed at the center of its party platform. The SVP considers the European Union (EU) as a threat to the political institutions of Switzerland (i.e. neutrality, federalism, and direct democracy), which constitute the core of the national identity (Kriesi 2007). In the SVP's attempt to create an adversarial climate on the cultural dimension, the institutions of direct democracy played a crucial role (Berhard 2012).

The narrow rejection of Swiss membership in the European Economic Area (EEA) by 50.3 per cent in the referendum vote in December 1992 constituted the stepping stone in the party's electoral ascent. This vote is generally considered the most important popular decision of the Swiss post-war period. The campaign was both of exceptional intensity and duration, giving rise to a huge public debate. As a consequence, turnout attained, at least by Swiss standards, a vertiginous level of 78.7 per cent. The rejection marked a glorious victory for the SVP as it was the only major party to oppose the treaty.

Since the mid-1990s, prominent figures of the SVP have launched several popular initiatives that all aimed at the tightening of immigration policy (Bernhard 2012: 44ff.). These reform proposals resonated well among citizens. With the exception of a vote on naturalisation held in 2008, the SVP managed to attract remarkably high levels of support for its ballot propositions. Recently, three of its initiatives have even obtained popular majorities – a ban of minarets in 2009, mandatory deportation of criminal foreigners in 2010, and a proposal 'against mass immigration' imposing immigration quotas in 2014.

In addition to European integration and immigration, the SVP has also increasingly raised institutional issues. On the one hand, these issues concern questions of international law, which are closely related to its nationalist and anti-integrationist stance. Thus, the party has sought to increase the scope of direct democratic instruments for the ratification of international treaties, and it has set out to defend Swiss sovereignty against 'foreign judges' and 'foreign bailiffs' – ideas that strongly resonate with the Swiss public since they hark back to the mythology surrounding Wilhelm Tell, the mythical Swiss national hero who is said to have killed Hermann Gessler, the 'foreign bailiff' in the service of the Habsburg overlords, against whom the original four Swiss cantons revolted and signed their initial pact in 1291. On the other hand, these institutional issues concern the electoral rules for the Federal Council, the Swiss executive. Thus, after the leader of the SVP had been ousted from the government (*see* following section), the party launched an initiative for the popular election of the Federal Council (which is currently elected by parliament).

While the SVP clearly detached itself from its competitors on the cultural dimension, the party basically remained a mainstream party with respect to the economic dimension. This is why it is appropriate to characterise the SVP as a conservative-liberal party. It is striking, however, that economic issues have turned out to be far less salient than the cultural ones for the SVP in recent years.

The party's experiences in government

In electoral terms, the SVP's radicalisation strategy on cultural issues has largely paid off over the last twenty years. Indeed, its rise has been very impressive by Swiss standards. The party more than doubled its vote share from 1991 (11.9 per cent) to 2007 (28.9 per cent) to become the largest Swiss party. This rise enabled the SVP to increase its representation in the Swiss government, which had been characterised by an extraordinarily stable composition. Since 1959, the seven seats of the Federal Council were distributed among the four major parties according to the so-called 'magic formula': two Liberals, two Christian Democrats, two Social Democrats, and one representative of the Swiss People's Party. As a result of repeated electoral gains, parliament decided to modify this informal arrangement in 2003 by granting the SVP a second seat in government at the expense of Christian Democrats. The SVP imposed its charismatic leader Christoph Blocher for this position, as the party threatened to go into opposition otherwise (Church 2004).

However, in spite of the fact that the party won the federal elections four years later, Blocher was ejected from government in December 2007. It was essentially a coalition forged by the left and Christian Democrats that replaced him by Eveline Widmer-Schlumpf, herself a moderate member of the SVP, who was not endorsed by the party. While Blocher claimed that parliament had no viable reasons to oust him, a narrow majority of MPs held the view that the leader of the SVP could not be domesticated by holding office (Church 2008). As a reaction to the ousting of its leader, the SVP decided to adopt a systematic oppositional stance by excluding its two moderate members in the Federal Council – Eveline Widmer-Schlumpf and Samuel Schmid – from party membership. As a reaction to this measure, members of the moderate wing split from the party and formed a new party, the Conservative Democratic Party (BDP), in support of the two ousted members of the government. However, the SVP's time in formal opposition lasted only one year. In December 2008, parliament elected Ueli Maurer, a former party president, to the Federal Council, where he replaced Samuel Schmid, who had resigned for health reasons. The 2011 elections did not cause any change in the governmental composition, as parliament re-elected all sitting federal councils. Thus, despite the fact that the SVP remains by far the largest Swiss party (its vote share slightly declined to 26.6 per cent in the 2011 elections), it is currently represented by only one member in the federal government.

A comparatively sound macroeconomic situation

Compared to most Western European countries, the Swiss economy did not experience hard times in the aftermath of the 2008 financial and economic crisis. As a small open economy that is highly dependent on the business cycle of the global economy in general and of its European neighbouring countries in particular, the gross domestic product (GDP) rapidly began to contract in the fourth quarter of 2008. Growth rates remained strongly negative in the three following quarters. However, the recession lasted only for one year, as the country found its path back to prosperity in fall 2009. This limited impact of the crisis was less due to the three rather modest stimulus packages the federal authorities launched between November 2008 and September 2009 (*Swiss Political Yearbook 2008, 2009*) than to the remarkable competiveness of the export-oriented sector and the sound macroeconomic situation of the German economy, which is by far the most important customer of Swiss products and services. The Swiss economy grew by remarkable 3 per cent in 2010. Although it continuously decelerated in 2011 and 2012 under the influence of a general slowdown observed in Europe, GDP growth rates are still considerably above OECD average, while unemployment rates and levels of public debt have remained well below average (*see* Figures 1.1–1.3).

In spite of this rather smooth economic trajectory, Swiss political decision-makers have been confronted with two major challenges since the outburst of the financial and economic crisis. In October 2008, the federal authorities felt compelled to rescue UBS, the biggest bank of the country, which found itself in a precarious situation as a result of its huge exposure toward the US subprime market. In a deal coordinated by members of the Federal Council, the Swiss National Bank, and the Federal Banking Commission, sixty billion dollars was pumped into UBS in order to separate the toxic assets from the remaining bank's activities. The second major challenge proved to be the strength of the Swiss franc. Somewhat ironically, the Swiss economy ran the risk of becoming a victim of its own success. The debt crises from which many other countries suffered, increased the attractiveness of the Swiss franc as a 'safe haven'. The Swiss currency continuously gained in value, a development that alarmed Swiss exporters. The Swiss National Bank (SNB) repeatedly tried to curb the appreciation of the franc by massively buying euros on the currency market. However, the SNB had to abandon its interventions, as it turned out to be impossible to defend the targeted exchange rates of respectively 1.40 and 1.30 Swiss franc/euro. As the Swiss franc continued to soar, the SNB was obliged to impose a 1.20 exchange rate floor against the euro in September 2011, a minimum limit it successfully defended for more than three years. The SNB justified this radical and unorthodox measure that essentially pegged the Swiss franc to the euro on the grounds that it would help keeping the economy on track.

Hypotheses

Having laid out the SVP's ideological profile, its recent electoral and direct-democratic successes, and its formal representation in government as well as the comparably benign macroeconomic situation of Switzerland, we are now equipped to formulate our hypotheses. To begin with, we do not expect to find any significant increase of the SVP's populist discourse as a reaction to the economic crisis (hypothesis one). As we have outlined above, the economic crisis has been comparatively short-lived and of low magnitude in Switzerland. Hence, an increased populist mobilisation of resentment seems to be difficult in the absence of obvious crisis manifestations. However, we expect the SVP's discourse to reveal the party's 'thin' populist ideology when it comes to the cultural dimension in general and to the issues of immigration, European integration and related institutional reforms in particular (hypothesis two). This hypothesis is based on the fact that the party of Christoph Blocher has acquired issue ownership over the first two policy domains and that the third one is closely related to the SVP's stance on European integration in particular and foreign policy in general. In addition, we expect the SVP's populist discourse to be a function of its representation in the federal government. Hypothesis three states that the level of populism has been particularly high when the SVP was in formal opposition, i.e. from mid-December 2007 to mid-December 2008. As a reaction to the ousting of its leader from government, which constituted the closest equivalent of a political crisis in Switzerland, we expect the party to have been particularly resentful against the established political elite. Finally, we generally expect the SVP to exhibit a higher degree of populism when the party is involved in campaigning. More specifically, populist figures of speech should be more frequent during federal elections and in direct-democratic votes launched by the party itself (hypothesis four).

Measuring populism

To measure the populist discourse of the SVP, we rely on the three concepts proposed by March (2012) – people-centrism, anti-elitism, and popular sovereignty. We will use two dichotomous indicators for each one of the three concepts. Our first indicator for people-centrism takes the value of 'one' if the SVP appeals to the people as a homogeneous entity. Our coding of the indicator is based on an interpretative assessment of the selected texts. On the one hand, the mere occurrence of the word 'people' is not sufficient for people-centrism. The code 'one' applies only if the SVP utilises a homogeneous representation of the people. On the other hand, terms which are functionally equivalent to the people (such as 'population', 'the sovereign', or 'the Swiss') are also taken into account as criteria for the coding decision. The second indicator of people-centrism refers to the 'absolute supremacy of the people'. More specifically, we consider a claim as populist if the people (including its functional equivalents) are portrayed in a fundamentally positive way (such as in statements claiming that 'the people are always right'). With respect to anti-elitism, we first measure whether the elites in their entirety are characterised in negative terms. To identify such denigrative statements, we not only look for explicit claims (such as 'parliament simply represents the interests of lobbyists') but also for certain depreciative terms which implicitly put elite actors in a negative light (examples involve 'EU bureaucrats', or the 'classe politique'). Our second indicator of anti-elitism accounts for the antagonist relationship between the people and the elite. Claims that highlight the clash of interests between these two groups are coded as 'one'. The statement according to which 'the government flouts the people's will' may serve as an example here. As far as popular sovereignty is concerned, we shall separately consider two opposite claims. Thus, we propose to distinguish demands that ask for giving more power to the people from demands that caution against the threats to the people's power. Prominent examples of the first type of statements are requests for the extension of direct-democratic rights. Regarding the second component, international law or the EU may be painted as threats to the expression of popular sovereignty.

As populist political communication may be context dependent, we propose to examine different channels of communication (Cranmer 2011). The corpus of the SVP for the empirical analysis at hand consists of five different types of documents: 1) press releases, 2) texts presented at the party's press conferences, 3) the monthly party newspapers (*Klartext*), 4) political advertisements that were published in the party newspaper, and 5) the programmatic speeches of Christoph Blocher (the so-called '*Albisgüetli Speeches*') which he regularly holds in early January of each year in front of a crowd of about 1,500 devoted followers. This corpus covers ten years (from January 2003 to June 2013). We have used the first four types of documents for a quantitative content analysis, while Blocher's speeches serve as qualitative illustrations of our quantitative findings. For the quantitative analysis, the unit of analysis is an issue-specific claim. Given that we are dealing with a large amount of text, we decided to draw samples for the quantitative analysis. We included one in ten chronologically ordered documents regarding both press releases and press conference texts. With respect to the party newspaper, we selected the first substantive article of every third edition. In addition, we included all political advertisements that the party published in this newspaper sample. We coded the resulting roughly 200 documents according to our coding scheme. The number of observations is slightly higher (N=245) than the number of documents, given that only a few documents addressed more than one issue. The speeches by Christoph Blocher are excluded from the quantitative content analysis, because they are much longer and less focused with regard to their political contents.

When applying our coding scheme of populist communication strategies, populism no longer is an all-or-nothing phenomenon, but becomes a matter of degree (Rooduijn and Pauwels 2011). Political actors can be more or less people-centrist, anti-elitist and appealing to popular sovereignty in the sense indicated. All sorts of combinations could be possible. The Belgian example studied by Jagers and Walgrave (2007) suggests, however, that these different elements of populist communication strategies tend to go together, i.e. populist ideology constitutes a coherent set of political ideas which is expressed by a quite specific combination of communication styles. To address this dimensionality issue, we make use of Mokken scale analysis. As a nonparametric stochastic version of Guttman scale analysis, the Mokken model provides a useful starting point in scale construction, since it does not impose severe restrictions on the functional form of the item trace lines. We find that five out of our six populism items form a strong hierarchical scale (Loevinger's H coefficient for these five items is 0.68). The only exception concerns the first indicator of popular sovereignty ('more power to the people'). The type of statement that is used most frequently corresponds to 'the appeal to the people as a homogenous entity'. This component is used in roughly a third of the texts (30 per cent). Next in line are the two types of anti-elitist claims (present in 25 and 19 per cent of the texts respectively), the threat to the people's power (present in 14 per cent of the texts) and, finally, references to the absolute supremacy of the people, which occur only very rarely (in 2 per cent of the texts). The fact that these five indicators form a hierarchical scale means that the claims that are more rarely made do not occur individually in a given text, but tend to occur only together with the more frequent populist components. Claims asking for more power to the people do not conform to this hierarchy, but occur more randomly. To construct our dependent variable, we can build an additive index based on the five items of the scale, which ranges from zero (lowest level of populism) to five (highest level of populism). It turns out that populist figures of speech are generally not pervasive in the SVP's public-oriented communication. Indeed, a majority of 61 per cent of our documents do not contain any element of populist rhetoric (index score = zero). On average, we find less than one element of populism in our texts. The mean level of our populism scale is of 0.89. There is more than one populist element in only one text out of four.

Empirical results

Let us now turn to the presentation of our results. We shall investigate each of the four hypotheses by using simple descriptive statistics and relying on qualitative impressions from the texts we incorporated in our sample.

The dog that did not bark

As expected, the economic and financial crisis clearly did not lead the SVP to increase its populist discourse. According to the indicator used here, its populism even slightly declined from 0.96 before September 2008 to 0.82 afterwards. When reviewing the selected documents, it is striking to note how little attention the SVP paid to the crisis. The reader almost gets the impression that the SVP altogether tried to avoid putting any emphasis on the economic crisis. Tellingly, the first press release on this topic occurred on 16th October 2008 as a reaction to the unexpected rescue of the UBS by the Swiss authorities. The party considered the coordinated action as inevitable in order to keep the Swiss banking sector alive. Sticking to its neoliberal economic ideology, the SVP nevertheless made it clear that this kind of state intervention into the private sector had to remain an exception. One day later, the parliamentary group of the SVP presented its priorities with respect to welfare state issues before the media. In light of the difficult situation on the international financial markets and the looming recession, the party simply declared that both future extensions and abuses of the welfare state had to be stopped. The UBS episode illustrates the defensive stance taken by the SVP towards the economic crisis. Most importantly, the SVP refrained from populist references in the economic domain. The only exception concerns a statement made by Ueli Maurer, the party's president, at a press conference held on 23rd October 2008. Maurer criticised the 'unlimited greed' of managers, which had damaged the people's confidence. In order to restore the people's trust in the business community, he pleaded for more shareholder rights.

Beyond that, on various occasions, the SVP instrumentalised the economic crisis for the pursuit of its own agenda (i.e. its preferred neoliberal solutions). This happened above all at the beginning of the crisis, notably with respect to the welfare state, Swiss banking, and the energy sector. Subsequently, the SVP repeatedly made use of this strategy as is documented by a series of press releases on the issues of aviation, opening hours of shops, healthcare insurances, free movement of persons, ecology, and unemployment. Perhaps most evocatively, the SVP also used the economic crisis to promote the candidacy of Christoph Blocher, its charismatic leader, for the Swiss federal government in winter 2008. In a press release issued on 18th November, the Zurich branch of the SVP posited that in view of the probably biggest world economic and financial crisis since World War II, it had designated its 'most capable man' to fill the open position.

The crucial role of issues

In line with hypothesis two, the populist discourse of the SVP seems to strongly depend on the issues at stake. As expected, the SVP is more likely to adopt populist communication strategies when it comes to cultural issues. With respect to cultural policies, the party's level of populism attains 1.29, a level that is significantly higher than for the economic domain (0.49) and other issues (0.83). The residual category contains issues that cannot be clearly assigned to the economic or cultural domains (i.e. issues referring to ecology, infrastructure as well as party internal affairs and communications which are explicitly related to elections). Table 8.1 takes a closer look at the level of populism of various issue categories. It shows that the three issues that we have singled out – European integration, immigration and institutional reforms – are all characterised by above average levels of populism. Consistent with our expectations, the two domains on which the SVP has acquired issue ownership over recent decades (European integration and immigration) display high levels of populism. Populism on European integration is higher (1.80) than on immigration issues (1.18). The level of populism is even slightly higher for institutional reform issues (1.84). In fact, if we go into more detail on the latter, the by far highest level (2.70) is attained by the six texts on international law. In the documents related to this issue, the SVP most heavily relied on a populist rhetoric, claiming that international law is increasingly undermining the people's democratic rights.

For the SVP, the issues of European integration and international law are closely related. It is convinced that the 'political class' betrays the people and the cantons by allowing European and international law to limit popular sovereignty. This is most clearly illustrated by Blocher's 2013 programmatic speech, where he comes back to the vote of 1992 and denounces the 'political class' for not having accepted that singularly important verdict:

> [...] it ('the political class', LB *et al.*) keeps on and on and still wants to lead Switzerland onto the meander ('*Irrweg*') EU. Our elites destroy the popular rights and expand the state, politics, and public administration. In Federal Berne one undermines free Switzerland, centralizes the country, and puts the citizens and taxpayers under tutelage.

Blocher denounces the weakness of the '*classe politique*' in Berne, i.e. 'our parliament, our government and our administration', when faced with pressure

Table 8.1: Level of populism according to issues

Issue (policy domain)	Mean	N
Institutional issues (cultural)	1.84	19
Europe (cultural)	1.80	25
Animal rights (cultural)	1.50	2
Elections (others)	1.25	28
Immigration (cultural)	1.18	38
Mean	0.89	245
Social policy (economic)	0.68	28
Infrastructure (others)	0.67	9
Security (cultural)	0.57	7
Fiscal policy (economic)	0.53	19
Party internal affairs (others)	0.50	8
Economic policy (economic)	0.31	32
Defence (cultural)	0.18	11
Cultural policy (cultural)	0.00	11
Ecology (others)	0.00	8

from abroad: 'In the financial and economic war which the highly indebted states in Europe or the US lead against Switzerland, our authorities constantly buckle. Alignment ('*Anpassung*') is their recipe'. Foreign states have, of course, noticed the weakness of the Swiss government and use it to their advantage in the 'economic war'. 'Yes, ladies and gentlemen', he adds, 'you have heard correctly, we have to do with an economic war'. The contrast between 'alignment' and 'resistance' is a constant theme in Blocher's speeches. The contrast, significantly, harks back to World War II, when the issue was whether Switzerland should 'align' with the Axis-powers or 'resist' their pressure.

'Alignment' and 'resistance' was already the title of Blocher's 2009 programmatic speech. In that year, in the shadow of the Lehman Brothers disaster, and, even more significantly, in the shadow of the Madoff scandal, Blocher talked about the hypocrisy of the 'decent people' (the label which, as he claims, the 'leftists' and the 'nice guys' in parliament appropriate for themselves):

> [...] they praise cooperation ('*Konkordanz*'), speak of human rights, decency and correctness, in order to do the exact opposite. They praise the appearance, in order to pursue their scheming all the more undisturbed behind the scene [...] the louder the moralistic hypocrites talk about transparency, the more they operate in the dark.

Just as Madoff knew it, the politicians know that 'more light would x-ray the *façade* of wrong decency, the masks would fall, and the indecency would become apparent'. The SVP has to stand up where the 'goody-goodies' go in the wrong direction. It has to show what goes wrong. It has to correct the wrong. To offer resistance, resistance against the wrong, against the neglect, against the lack of principles, against hypocrisy, against the 'political correctness' ('*Gutmenschentum*') and it has to see to it that the good is done for people and country, independently of one's own reputation.

Focusing on the period in formal opposition

Table 8.2 lists the level of populism during the four distinctive periods of SVP representation in government between 2003 and 2013. The highest score (1.25) is found for the period of formal opposition (between December 2007 and December 2008). This figure lends support to hypothesis three. Moreover, the SVP's use of populism seems to be inversely related to its perceived representation in the Federal Council. The representation weights of its own peculiar counting rule are given between brackets in Table 8.2. The second highest populism score (0.94) is reported for the period from January 2003 to December 2003 when the party considered to have only 'half a Federal Councillor' in the person of its (too) moderate minister Samuel Schmid. This period is followed by the last and still ongoing period with the SVP being represented in government by its former president and representative of the dominating radical wing, Ueli Maurer (0.83). The lowest average (0.81) can be detected for the period when both Christoph Blocher and Samuel Schmid sat in government. This period of so to say '1.5 Federal Councillors' lasted from December 2003 to December 2007.

While the differences between the period-specific averages are not large, they still indicate that the ousting of Christoph Blocher from the Federal Council led the SVP to accentuate its populist discourse. This is visible in the first three press releases the party published as a reaction to the historical event in December 2007. In these documents, the decision made by parliament is called a 'flagrant disregard of the voters' preferences'. The SVP heavily criticises the 'dirty tricks' of the 'power-loving system parties', which are said to disregard the peoples' voice. The accentuation of the populist rhetoric is also visible in Blocher's programmatic speech held in January 2008 in which the ousted magistrate sides with the people

Table 8.2: Level of populism according to time periods of government representation

Government representation	Mean	N
Formal opposition (0)	1.25	32
Schmid (0.5)	0.94	17
Maurer (1)	0.83	115
Blocher and Schmid (1.5)	0.81	81
Total	0.89	245

against the elite. In the hour of bitterness, he concludes his speech by embracing the new role of opposition:

> You see, ladies and gentlemen, as opposition we are not tempted to represent the interests of the 'political class'. They are not our interests. We side without any doubt with the citizens. As opposition party, it is also easier to resist these temptations. We continue. The same politics. Simply at a different location. And by other means. But our political goals remain the same. The contract with the people remains valid.

And, even more pointedly:

> Speaking about the opposition: what has kept Switzerland alive ('*frisch*') is opposition and not cooperation ('*Konkordanz*'). What has kept Switzerland alive is direct democracy. The control of the 'political class' by the people. The vigilance of the citizen. This has kept alive the politicians' fear of the resistance by the population. What has saved Switzerland is the oppositional power of the citizen – and the fact that even a minimal rise in the value added tax of a tenth of a percentage point has to be submitted to the people. We shall give this people a voice, while others increasingly crowd out this voice! Wherever a gap opens up between the interests of the citizens and the 'political class', we shall be the party of the citizen (in the singular, LB *et al.*)! When in doubt, always on the side of the people!

Surprisingly enough however, the SVP began to contain itself in the aftermath of Blocher's ousting from government. As a matter of fact, the press releases were suddenly written in sober language. The party also consistently avoided engaging in populism. Only the frequent usage of the term 'government parties' in order to qualify the other big formations reminds the reader of the fact that the SVP found itself in formal opposition at that time. Until the election of Ueli Maurer in December 2008, there are only a few party statements that make use of the opposition status in order to disapprove of the government and its policies. In a nutshell, our fine-grained analysis of the SVP's documents reveals that its truly populist approach lasted for a short period of time – a matter if weeks. Afterwards, the party managed to contain itself.

Campaigns matter

As expected by hypothesis four, the level of the SVP's populist discourse seems to increase during campaigns. As is shown by Table 8.3, the populist discourse turned out to be most intense when the party launched optional referendums or initiatives of its own or when it deposited the signatures for such measures (1.39). Populist discourse is also intense during federal election campaigns (defined as the two month-period before such elections): during election campaigns it reaches an average of 1.26, compared to an average of 1.00 during (the one month period of) direct-democratic campaigns before the vote on SVP-proposals and of 0.54 during the remaining periods. Among the documents referring to the period when the SVP actively launched or deposited federal referendums or initiatives, most texts referring to initiatives deal with immigration (tougher naturalisation rules, tightening of asylum law, and extradition of criminal foreigners), while most texts on referendums refer to European integration (Schengen and Dublin Agreements, cohesion payments).

The impact of election campaigns is also illustrated by Blocher's programmatic speeches, three of which (2003, 2007 and 2011) fell into election years. Thus, during early 2003, before the elections which allowed Blocher to accede to the Federal Council, he attacked the three other major parties as 'the united left' that, according to him, had 'just one burning desire – the untroubled continuation of its ruinous deep sleep'. The SVP, by contrast, was 'the only force ready to fight against this ruinous disorientation'. He claimed that 'we will not join this sad coalition of people hushing up and concealing'. And he saw hope for those (like himself) 'who do not happen to look at the lowlands of high politics, but look out into the country and to the people, those who look up to the sovereign are fulfilled with confidence'. In 2007, now a member of government, he forcefully throws himself into the campaign and argues against the strange Swiss custom which forces members of government to abstain from participation in electoral campaigns. But he now identifies the opponents clearly with the left (Social Democrats and Greens) and spares the centre-right parties on whom he has to rely on in government. In 2011, now a former Federal Councillor, he delivered a speech that was mainly a variation on the 'alignment-resistance' theme in an extended historical perspective (the speech is longer and more ambitious than usual). After having pointed out once again the international pressure to intimidate the country, he addresses the weakness from within:

Just as the pressure from abroad is a constant in the history, there has always been and, unfortunately, there still is another constant, namely that there have always been and there are people in our country who want to give in to this pressure. Among them we have unfortunately today also the Federal Council, all other parties, the federal administration, many academics, persons engaged in the cultural sector, and so-called scientists. But also in the course of history,

Table 8.3: Level of populism by campaign

Campaign	Mean	N
No campaign	0.60	139
Direct-democratic campaign	1.00	12
Election campaign	1.26	61
Launching/depositing ref-initiative	1.39	33
Total	0.89	245

Switzerland has not always immediately and heroically opted for freedom. There have always been – above all in the ruling circles – people who have been blinded, who wanted to abandon the freedom in the interest of European big powers. The freedom did not only have to be defended against foreign enemies, but also against the internal enemies of freedom.

In this very long speech, the upcoming elections are not primarily addressed and clearly take second place compared to the broad historical overview that serves, however, to clearly distinguish between the evil forces of all the other parties and the resistance of the SVP.

Conclusion

As Margaret Canovan (1999) has observed, the phenomenon of populism reflects a tension that is at the heart of democracy – the tension between the ideal of democracy and its 'redemptive face' on one hand, and its actual functioning or its 'pragmatic face' on the other hand. When the functioning of democracy is not able to deliver on its idealistic promises, political actors of either stripe may be tempted to use the populist toolbox. The present analysis has focused on Switzerland by studying the populist discourse adopted by the SVP, which is commonly referred to as the most powerful populist party of the country. We have content-analysed the populist discourse of the SVP by using a corpus consisting of the party's press releases, the oral presentations at its press conferences, its party newspapers and the yearly programmatic speeches of its leader covering the last ten years. We have established that the SVP did not embark on a more pronounced populism after the emergence of the global economic and financial crisis.

Two main considerations can be advanced as to why the SVP did not face a strong incentive to increase its populist strategic communication. First, the crisis took place against a relatively benign economic background, as the recession was mild and lasted for only one year in Switzerland. Admittedly, mobilising resentment in the economic domain turned out to be difficult in the absence of an enduring crisis. Second and perhaps more conclusively, the SVP did not have much to gain from exhibiting a populist rhetoric in connection with the economic crisis. This is due to the fact that, as a consequence of its transformation into a radical right party and its relentless mobilisation against European integration and against immigration, the party enjoys 'issue ownership' over the cultural policy domain, as opposed to economic policy. Indeed, the main finding of our analysis is that the populist discourse of the SVP heavily depends on the issues at stake. The level of populist communication has been shown to quite pronounced when it comes to immigration, European integration, and related institutional issues. Independently of the business cycle, the SVP expresses its populism on the issues it owns. The party's populism manifests itself in particular during direct democratic campaigns dealing with these cultural issues and in its federal election campaigns.

Finally, this empirical investigation has also established the importance of government representation. The populist rhetoric has proved to be highest in the absence from government. When represented in government (especially by a member of its dominant radical wing), the SVP has been found to be slightly less inclined to use populist figures of speech. This result prompts the question of whether an increased representation of the party in the federal government would lead to a marked moderation of the SVP in the future. In light of the peculiar Swiss government system, this cannot be taken for granted, since government parties are not obliged to support the bills adopted by the Federal Council and by parliament. In the absence of clear government responsibility, even coalition parties can, depending on the issue at stake, easily engage in case-by-case opposition. More specifically, by making use of direct-democratic instruments (by either launching popular initiatives or by challenging laws voted by parliament by means of referendums), the discourse of the populist parties cannot be expected to become more responsible. This kind of hybrid strategy (i.e. being in government and in opposition at the same time), has been repeatedly pursued by both the left (Social Democrats) and the radical right (SVP) over the last years. This possibility constitutes a major reason for why the Swiss party system displays the highest degree of polarisation in Europe (Ladner *et al.* 2010).

Chapter Nine

The Primacy of Politics: Austria and the Not-so-Great Recession

Kurt Richard Luther

Populism until 2008

Until the late 1980s, Austria's party system contained no populist parties, but was dominated by the Social Democratic Party of Austria (SPÖ) and Austrian People's Party (ÖVP), which together regularly won over 90 per cent of votes and seats (*see* Figure 9.1). Even when not governing together in 'grand coalitions', they shared significant control of key policy areas via Austria's extra-constitutional neo-corporatist arena and their political reach was further enhanced by extensive patronage networks (Ennser-Jedenastik 2014) closely associated with the principles of *Proporz* (the proportional division of spoils between their subcultures) and segmental autonomy, which permeated Austria's consociational democracy (Luther 1999). Yet by the September 2008 general election, they could together muster only 55.3 per cent of the vote and 59 per cent of seats. This decline was due, above all, to a steep albeit not unbroken increase in support for the Freedom Party of Austria (FPÖ), from which the Alliance for the Future of Austria (BZÖ) had split off in 2005.

Prior to September 1986, when Jörg Haider successfully contested its leadership, the FPÖ was not populist. It did not have personalistic leadership and its ideology and discourse neither split society into two antagonistic camps, nor articulated a monolithic view of the people. Instead, it was an often weakly-led party that conceived itself as representing Austria's 'Third Lager', a German-national, anti-Habsburg and anti-clerical subculture dating back to the nineteenth century and containing significant *petit-bourgeois* elements. The FPÖ's elitist anti-establishment discourse rejected *Proporz*, neo-corporatism and clientelism. At least in this respect, the FPÖ's ideology was not democratically illiberal, but portrayed the party as the defender of liberal constitutionalism against Austria's corrupt party state and extra-constitutional corporatist decision-making. To be sure, the FPÖ's ideology also contained strong 'old-right' elements (Ignazi and Ysmal 1992), including a revisionist view of Austria's past and reactionary conservative values. It also rejected many of the Second Republic's founding myths, including Austria's portrayal as the 'first victim' of Nazism and the proposition that Austria's 1955 Act of Neutrality was voluntary. Alone amongst Austria's parties, it disdained neutrality and favoured European integration (albeit allegedly for Pan-Germanic reasons).

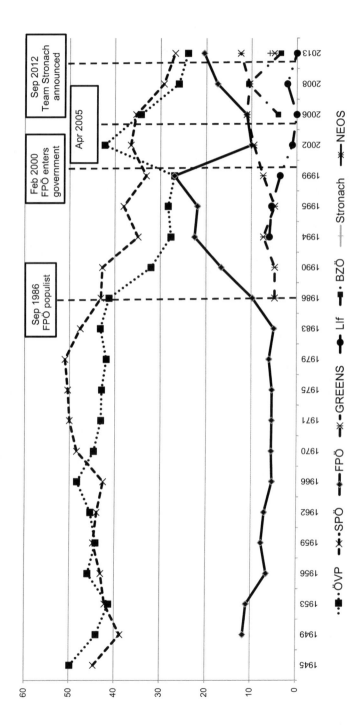

Figure 9.1: Party general election vote shares 1945–2013 and populist party development

For many years after its 1956 foundation, the FPÖ was a 'ghetto party', but periods of 'normalisation' and tentative liberalisation eventually facilitated its 1983 entry into government as the SPÖ's junior partner.

From 1986 to 1999, Haider's now oppositional FPÖ pursued a strategy of relentless populist vote maximisation, whose long-term goal was regaining office with a much larger share of seats. Haider was unable to exercise the degree of intra-party control many observers alleged, yet undoubtedly became 'the personification' (Eatwell 2006) of the party. To that extent, the FPÖ was characterised by personalistic leadership. Its anti-establishment discourse initially remained targeted on *Proporz*, neo-corporatism and clientelism, but to maximise the party's electoral reach, became increasingly opportunistic. Support for European integration was replaced by Euroscepticism. Pan-Germanism and the denial of the existence of an Austrian national identity gradually gave way to the notion that the FPÖ's prime role was to defend a monolithically-conceived virtuous Austrian nation against a self-serving party-political elite, but also against groups such as immigrants and welfare state scroungers. The FPÖ's revised conception of democracy was visible in its demands for a 'Third Republic'; these reflected its long-standing preference for significantly reduced roles for parties and other intermediary actors, but now also emphasised direct democratic structures. To enhance its potential to coalesce with the ÖVP, the FPÖ's 'thin' populist ideology was increasingly promiscuous. In 1997, for example, the FPÖ's new programme described the party as the 'best defender of Christian values'. Notwithstanding their incompatibility with existing FPÖ economic policy focused on defending of the 'little guy', the FPÖ adopted positions reflecting ÖVP-leader Wolfgang Schüssel's neo-liberal orientation. In sum, from 1986–99, the FPÖ demonstrated all the characteristics of right-wing populism.

The FPÖ's populism ensured a virtually unbroken string of electoral victories, culminating in its 26.9 per cent vote at the 1999 general election, and fundamentally transformed the party's electoral profile. Previously, older, *petit-bourgeois* and educated voters had been overrepresented. Now, FPÖ support by age exhibited a U-shaped distribution, with a distinct bias to those under thirty. Support had grown significantly more amongst men. The aggressive, anti-intellectual and anti-statist discourse helped account for the FPÖ's underperformance amongst white-collar voters, civil servants, public sector workers and those with higher levels of education. Meanwhile, support amongst blue-collar voters had risen from 10 to 48 per cent. This signalled a realignment of Austria's working class; in 1986, 57 per cent had voted for the SPÖ, but by 1999 only 35 per cent did so (Luther 2008: 112–116; Kritzinger *et al.* 2013).

The FPÖ's entry into government (4 February 2000) marked the realisation of the goal behind Haider's strategy of populist vote maximisation. Yet it also highlighted significant contradictions between the various policies to which the party had committed itself whilst maximising votes. Above all, incumbency underscored the yawning gap between the habituated anti-establishment and zero-sum orientation of FPÖ functionaries and the more office-seeking and pragmatic values of the party in public office (Luther 2011). One example was the clash over

EU Eastern Enlargement, which the FPÖ government team tacitly supported and the grass-roots vehemently opposed, albeit unsuccessfully. Such self-destructive infighting prompted its government team's resignation in September 2002 and at the premature election of 24 November, resulted in the party's vote share collapsing to 10 per cent. Schüssel recreated the ÖVP-FPÖ coalition on 28 February 2003 with a much-weakened FPÖ leadership. It had capitulated on all the policies demanded by the FPÖ functionaries, giving free rein to Schüssel's neoliberal policies. Intra-FPÖ conflict thus continued, including over the government's pension reform proposals, which in spring 2003 triggered the greatest industrial unrest Austria had witnessed in decades.

Haider had himself long vacillated between supporting and opposing the FPÖ's government team. On 4 April 2005, he finally rejected the FPÖ as irredeemably irresponsible and launched the BZÖ, which he promised would be responsible and government-oriented. As the BZÖ included the whole of the FPÖ's government team and most of its MPs, the FPÖ had been involuntarily ejected from office. Haider believed most FPÖ members and functionaries would join the BZÖ, leaving a rump FPÖ comprising incorrigible naysayers, but the overwhelming majority remained loyal. The strategy of the FPÖ's new leadership under Heinz Christian Strache was to counter its collapse to 6 per cent in the opinion polls by reverting to aggressive right-wing populist vote maximisation. It targeted above all blue-collar voters alienated by the neo-liberal discourse and policies of an ÖVP-dominated government accused of 'social coldness'. So in addition to emphasising EU-scepticism, welfare chauvinism and anti-immigration via slogans such as 'Austria first', 'We are for you' and 'Welfare not immigration', Strache's FPÖ henceforth referred to itself as the 'social homeland party' (*soziale Heimatpartei*) and advanced socio-economic policies that competed with those of the SPÖ. This strategy was communicated graphically by supplementing the FPÖ's traditionally blue marketing with socialist red and helped mitigate widely-expected losses at Vienna's October 2005 provincial election. At the October 2006 general election, the FPÖ's 11 per cent of the vote saw it regain its parliamentary caucus. The BZÖ had initially stuck to its strategy of retaining office by stressing responsibility and policies favouring small business and a limited state, but its general election campaign largely reverted to right-wing populist discourse. The election was thus contested by two parties claiming to embody the 1986–99 period of successful populist mobilisation. Indeed, 'the BZÖ's original campaign material dropped the party's official colour (orange) in favour of the FPÖ's traditional blue and included the designation "*Die Freiheitlichen*", together with the epithet "the original" […] which a court ruled […] was a deliberate attempt to deceive voters' (Luther 2008:1008).

With the BZÖ just crossing the 4 per cent electoral threshold, Austria's parliament now contained two mutually-hostile populist parties. Continuing to defend the monolithically-conceived Austrian nation against the corrupt national and European elite (as well as against undeserving 'others'), the FPÖ remained firmly right-wing on the socio-cultural dimension and committed to moving leftwards on the socio-economic dimension. Using techniques copied from Haider, Strache soon succeeded in becoming its new personification.

The BZÖ was also characterised by personalistic leadership, but took time to determine its key messages and the profile of the 'people' it purported to defend. By 2008, it was tentatively attaching its populist discourse to a more market-liberal ideology juxtaposing the hard-working Austrian middle classes (and especially small businesses) against the allegedly parasitical and incompetent national and EU (party) elite. To underscore its claim to be a responsible party of government and further differentiate it from the FPÖ, whose electoral strategy placed greater emphasis on protest voters, the BZÖ pointed to Haider's Governorship of Carinthia.[1] Indeed, the BZÖ's 2008 general election campaign focused predominantly on presenting Haider as a reformed and mature statesman. The BZÖ's vote nearly tripled (10.7 per cent). The aggressively populist 2008 campaign of Strache's *soziale Heimatpartei* appealed disproportionately to blue-collar voters and helped ensure that the FPÖ's overall vote also increased, albeit less dramatically (+3 points to 20.5 per cent) (Luther 2009; Figure 9.1).

In sum, the BZÖ's emergence had triggered not the marginalisation of Austrian populism, but its bifurcation. At the September 2008 general election immediately following but unaffected by the outbreak of the Great Recession, Austrian voters could thus choose between two populist parties, whose combined vote was to exceed that ever obtained by the FPÖ. Yet these parties were incapable of working together and appealed to rather different constituencies. At the risk of over-simplification, the FPÖ remained a right-wing populist party, focused exclusively on responsiveness, whilst the BZÖ set itself the challenging task of tempering the responsiveness of its middle-class populism with responsibility (Mair 2009).

Economic and political crisis 2008 onwards

Austria's economy has long outperformed those of most European countries. Yet as Figure 9.2 shows, during the first ÖVP-FPÖ coalition (Schüssel I; 4 February 2000–28 March 2003), growth plummeted and although recovering towards the end of that government's truncated term, remained below the EU-27 average. During Schüssel II (28 March 2007), growth rose in absolute terms and relative to the EU-27. By international standards, Austrian unemployment has traditionally been low and remained so, but in 2005 had reached the Second Republic's highest-ever rate (5.2 per cent). Benefiting from reforms undertaken during Schüssel II, the short-lived SPÖ-ÖVP coalition (11 January 2007–2 December 2008) presided over a fall in unemployment. Growth remained healthy (3.7 per cent) in 2007 and still stood at over 2 per cent in the second quarter of 2008, just before the premature election of 28 September was announced. At least in one respect, the timing was politically fortuitous for the governing parties. Since the full significance of the Lehmann Brothers collapse of 15 September was not yet apparent, they were spared a campaign conducted in the immediate shadow of the Great Recession. Moreover, as the first beneficiary of the government term's extension to five years,

---

1. Haider had opted for the Governorship over membership of Austria's Parliament, with which it is constitutionally incompatible.

Figure 9.2: Austrian macro-economic indicators (1999–2014) (annual averages)

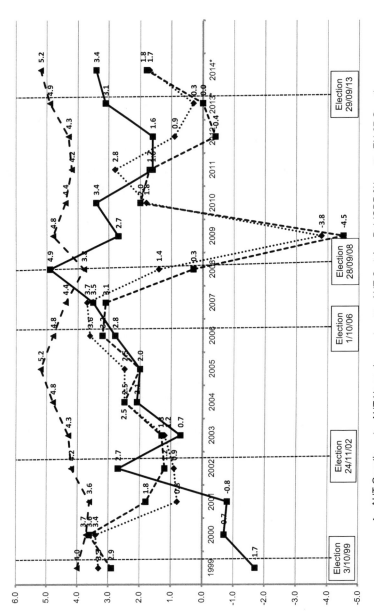

Chancellor Werner Faymann's incoming SPÖ/ÖVP coalition was not required to face a general election until September 2013, when Austria had seemingly largely weathered the economic storm. Thus neither the 2008 nor 2013 general elections were characterised by economic crisis (Kritzinger, Müller and Schönbach 2014).

However, Austria's economy was not impervious to the Great Recession's competitiveness crisis. Central to the government programme approved in late-November were measures to counter the looming economic downturn. They included a fiscal stimulus of 2.2 billion euros via tax reductions for middle-income earners, measures to stimulate growth and a commitment to keeping the budget deficit below 3 per cent of GDP. Yet as the scale of the crisis became apparent, the outlook rapidly worsened. Unemployment remained amongst the lowest in the EU, but rose by nearly a third in 2009. Eventually, Austria's economy performed better than many had feared. The 2009 contraction was 'only' 3.8 per cent and initially, the economy also recovered quite well. Growth rose to 1.8 per cent in 2010 and 2.8 per cent in 2011. By 2011, unemployment was down to 4.2 per cent. The public deficit rose to 3.4 per cent of GDP in 2010, but fell back to 1.6 per cent in 2011 and 2012. Yet in the first two quarters of 2013, it appeared that growth had dropped back (to ca. 0.2 per cent) and unemployment was again on the rise. Austria was also affected by the banking liquidity crisis. On 3rd November 2008, the Kommunalkredit Austria AG, Austria's eighth largest bank, was saved from collapse by nationalisation at an estimated cost of two billion euros. In December 2009, the government had to nationalise the Hypo Alpe Adria (Austria's sixth largest banking group), which was on the brink of collapse. On 10th October 2010, Austria's biggest listed bank, the Erste Group Bank, announced a major write-down as a result mainly of its Eastern European exposure and within days, the ÖsterreichischeVolksbanken AG followed suit. Although the Nationalbank remained concerned about continued growth in public debt, the Great Recession did not cause an Austrian sovereign debt crisis. Yet in January 2012, Standard and Poor's withdrew Austria's triple-A credit rating. It justified this mainly by Austria's exposure to the Eurozone sovereign debt crisis.

The limited economic impact of the competitiveness crisis was mirrored in the absence of an enduring subjective economic crisis. Eurobarometer surveys show that pessimism regarding the likely short-term future of the national economy spiked in October 2008, but a year later had declined to nearly pre-crisis levels. Indeed, in November 2010, Austrians were amongst the most likely in the EU to believe that the economic crisis' impact on the job market had already peaked and although optimism declined over the ensuing two years, it remained significantly above the EU-27 average (http://ec.europa.eu/public_opinion/index_en.htm).

The absence of a deep competitiveness crisis and limited extent of the banking crisis might lead one to expect the course of post-2008 Austrian populism to have not been shaped by the Great Recession. Alternatively, it could be argued that the long-running Eurozone sovereign debt crisis offered an intrinsically more promising opportunity for populist mobilisation. For one, as has been demonstrated regarding unemployment (e.g. Knigge 1998; Arzheimer and Carter 2006), poor economic performance may incline voters to opt not for anti-establishment parties, but for those to which they ascribe competence in key policy areas.[2] In a nutshell, when economic times are tough, we might expect 'responsibility' to trump 'responsiveness'. Second, the Eurozone sovereign debt crisis repeatedly saw national and European-level elites making key decisions in the glare of the international media. The 'discursive opportunity' (Koopmans and Muis 2009) of such political drama arguably offers greater potential for populist anti-elite mobilisation than a competitiveness crisis. Populists can more easily associate key decisions made at the national and/or EU level with specific (political) elites whom voters might reasonably believe should be accountable to them. Third, as argued in the introductory chapter, it is plausible to expect the Eurozone sovereign debt crisis to heighten right-wing populist discourse opportunity in 'creditor' Eurozone countries. Finally, the sovereign debt crisis might also offer a discursive opportunity for parties whose populism is attached to a market-liberal and small-state 'thick' ideology contrasting the hard-working middle classes against European and national elites of an over-bloated state. We should thus expect the populist mood of 'creditor' Eurozone states to be highest during the most contested phase of the sovereign debt crises, i.e. from about May 2010 to July 2012.[3] In the Austrian case, this implies that the sovereign debt crisis would be reflected in the discourse both of the right-wing populist FPÖ and of the middle-class populist BZÖ. *Ceteris paribus*, we might also expect that discourse to contribute to greater populist party electoral success.

A second hypothesised facilitator of populism is a major political crisis. For much of the post-2008 period, Austria's public debate was permeated by a seemingly ever-expanding number of political scandals. They pertained to at least five large, partly interconnected clusters of issues.[4] One concerned longstanding allegations of corruption by persons in or close to the ÖVP-FPÖ/BZÖ governments, often in connection with privatisations, or contract allocations. These became increasingly subjected to media and judicial investigation. A second involved seemingly routinised corruption in BZÖ-governed Carinthia and came to be disparagingly designated the 'Haider system'. Part of this centred on the Carinthia-based Hypo Alpe Adria, on which Governor Haider exerted considerable influence, and whose incompetence and recklessness[5] are widely held to have left taxpayers footing an outstanding loans bill in the region of fifteen billion euros. There were also allegations of the bank's involvement in large-scale illegal party funding. In July 2012, Carinthian ÖVP leader Josef Martinz eventually

---

2. In Austria, economic competence has traditionally been ascribed to the ÖVP and welfare competence to the SPÖ.

3. These include May 2010 (Greece bailout 1); November 2010 (Ireland bailout); May 2011 (Portugal bailout); March 2012 (Greece bailout 2 and Treaty on Stability, Co-ordination and Governance [TSCG] – ratified on 5 July against FPÖ and BZÖ votes).

4. See the Austrian Parliament's website (http://www.parlament.gv.at/PERK/KONTR/POL/UAAKTUELL/index.shtml) and Greens' parliamentary caucus report (http://www.gruene.at/themen/justiz/korruption-hat-680-seiten).

5. This included funding (loss-making) political projects and a provincial government guarantee of ca. twenty-five billion euros, about eight times Carinthia's annual budget.

confessed to having in 2007 conspired with Haider to divert twelve million euros into their parties' coffers. The casual approach to corruption was epitomised by BZÖ Deputy Governor Uwe Scheuch, who had in 2009 been secretly recorded telling a potential Russian investor it was 'part of the game' for 5–10 per cent of the planned investment to be paid to the party. The recording was published in January 2010 and judicial proceedings dragged on until December 2012, when Scheuch was definitively convicted. A third cluster involved the partially state-owned Telekom Austria AG and the lobbyist Peter Hochegger. In July 2011, it was alleged senior managers had in 2004 siphoned off cash to pay a broker to inflate the company's share price, thus guaranteeing themselves substantial bonuses. A former executive then detailed a widespread system of corrupt payments to politicians and organisations, linked particularly to the ÖVP, FPÖ and BZÖ. Two alleged recipients were former FPÖ or BZÖ ministers, both subsequently placed under investigation. Fourth, there were many claims of improper use of public money by government ministers and state-owned enterprises in connection with advertising in print media, including by then Infrastructure Minister Faymann. Finally, there were allegations of corruption in connection with the granting of Austrian citizenship. On 20 October 2011, the Austrian parliament unanimously approved a parliamentary Committee of Investigation into corruption. Its many dramatic revelations ensured that by the time it was prematurely wound up (October 2012), Austrian politics had for over two years been infused with political scandals, many concerning politicians from populist parties that had been in national or provincial government.

The scandals had a demonstrable impact on popular attitudes. Measured in terms of Transparency International's corruption perception index, between 2008 and 2013, subjective corruption rose markedly and Austria's international corruption ranking dropped from 12/180 to 26/177 (www.transparency.org). Moreover, the significant rise in the proportion of those indicating they tend not to trust political parties (from 53 per cent in summer 2009 to 64 per cent in winter 2011) corresponds to the major increase in media coverage of corruption in the 16 months prior to the Committee's formation. Pre-crisis levels did not reappear until well into 2013. Figure 9.3 shows that during the early stages of intense discussion of the sovereign debt crisis (from May 2010) FPÖ support rose significantly in the polls and during the first half of 2011, the party even headed them. Its rise was reversed, however, during the peak of the political crisis. By the start of 2009, support for the BZÖ, which had lost Haider to a fatal car crash in October, was already vastly reduced. Under the leadership of Josef Bucher (elected 26 April 2009), it dropped further, as revelations regarding the 'Haider system' took hold. It thus appears plausible that the central involvement of BZÖ and FPÖ actors in the scandals underpinning the political crisis mitigated the success these parties might otherwise have reaped from the sovereign debt crisis.[6]

6. We are speaking counterfactually, so cannot be sure these parties would have been electorally more successful in the absence of the political crisis. A further factor was Team Stronach's emergence (see next section).

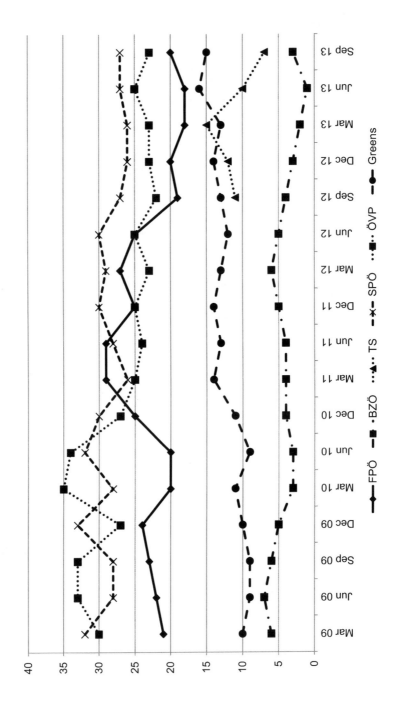

Figure 9.3: Austrians' voting intentions (2009–13)

Post-crisis populism: Populist parties' discursive response

Following the logic outlined above, this section's qualitative analysis focuses primarily on three partially overlapping events related to the banking and sovereign debt crises, which offered excellent discursive opportunities to raise the 'populist barometer': the 2010 and 2012 Greek bailouts and the EU-level and Austrian Parliament decisions on the ESM and Fiscal Compact (March and July 2012 respectively). The interrogated sources include all FPÖ (2010 and 2012) and BZÖ (2010 and 2012) parliamentary press releases, parliamentary transcripts (Parlament 2010 and 2012, or 'NRP') of party leader contributions to relevant debates and leader interviews in national television news programmes of Austrian Broadcasting (ORF) during a two-month window around each event. In addition, we examined the hour-long interviews the ORF conducted with Strache and Bucher from 2009–12 as part of its regular summertime leader interviews (ORF 2009–12 *Sommergespräche*, or 'SG'), as well as leader interviews on ORF television news from August 2012 to August 2013.[7] These latter sources help capture the parties' broader discourse development, underscoring not only the minimal attention paid to the competitiveness crisis, but also that from 2010 onward, Strache and Bucher faced interlocutors keen to focus on their (former) politicians' alleged involvement in corruption.

As the BZÖ only broke away from the FPÖ in 2005, these parties' post-2008 discourse exhibited numerous similarities. Yet there were interesting differences. In keeping with the FPÖ's long-established right-wing populist identity, Strache's people-centrism consistently focused on presenting him and his party as the tribune of above all the sovereign Austrian 'Volk' and 'true Austrians'.[8] He also presented himself as the advocate of taxpayers and small business,[9] but these groups were at the core of Bucher's people-centrism, especially after October 2009, when the BZÖ's executive approved of re-positioning the party as 'right-liberal', a branding underpinning its new programme of May 2010. Bucher thus maintained that the BZÖ was above all an 'anti-tax party' defending small business and 'the citizens […] who are willing to perform and who do so, who get up early, go to work […] work hard […] pay their taxes […] and from whom the state demands a lot of taxes'.[10] In both Strache and Bucher's discourse, the main enemy of the virtuous people remained the corrupt and self-serving Austrian 'red-black' establishment and European political elites. Yet given the BZÖ's self-proclaimed role as the voice of hard-working taxpayers and small business, Bucher's anti-elitism placed somewhat greater emphasis on attacking elites' consistent failure to address growing public debt. Moreover, to emphasise his party's moderation,

---

7. The last-named source was also used to assess the populist discourse of Team Stronach (*see* next section).

8. NRP140 and 164; SG 2011 and SG 2009 respectively.

9. FPÖ 2010; NRP66; NRP164.

10. SG 2011; *see also* BZÖ 2010, NRP64; NRP66; NRP164.

but also since nationalism was not central to its populism, Bucher condemned as excessive the FPÖ's focus on immigration and accepted the need for skilled immigration (e.g. SG 2010).[11]

Both parties pursued emotive campaigns against using Austrian taxpayers' money for bailouts. Unsurprisingly, their post-2008 discourse elevated (bank) speculators to the status of a key category of 'other' and attributed to them a major share of responsibility for the economic crises (e.g. SG 2012). This did not lessen the blame attributed to national and European political elites, however. For Bucher, taking money for bailouts 'from taxpayers' pockets' compounded their failure to manage public debt[12] and along with Strache, he argued that bailouts benefited above all the banks, with whom they suggested the elites had far too cosy a relationship.[13] Blame was also attributed to European political and economic elites (e.g. EU member states, the European Commission and the ECB), *inter alia* for false reporting (e.g. Greece, which Bucher said had achieved entry into the euro 'with a forged ticket' [NRP64] and Strache accused of 'budgetary tricks' [NRP57]), and for failing to ensure compliance with the Maastricht criteria.[14] In a nutshell, the FPÖ's largely protectionist discourse blamed the Austrian and EU political class, international capital/globalisation, as well as feckless southern Europeans. Whilst the BZÖ's founder had claimed it wished to re-establish the social market economy in place of 'globalisation mania', it now 'accepted the reality of a globalised, integrated word' (2010 Programme: 26) and its recipe was geared more towards deregulation and promoting small and medium-sized enterprises via low taxes. Indeed, in early 2011, it used the sovereign debt crisis to highlight its anti-tax position via a popular initiative entitled 'Paid Enough'.

The populists' discourse contained frequent references to alleged failings of democracy. For example, in March 2010, Strache announced the FPÖ would appeal to the Constitutional Court against the 'undemocratic' Lisbon Treaty and on 14th June 2012, both Strache and Bucher accused the other parliamentary parties of manipulation designed to avoid a proper ESM debate.[15] In July 2012's main ESM debate (NRP164), both populist leaders not only argued that the ESM was itself an unconstitutional breach of the Lisbon Treaty, but repeated Bucher's claim (NRP161) that it constituted 'high treason'. Strache characterised it as an 'unforgivable betrayal' of the Austrian people, a calculated constitutional *coup d'état* and authoritarian construct transferring Austria's sovereign rights towards a dictatorial power, a move that would ultimately abolish the Second Republic (NRP 164). He had previously claimed it would ultimately alter basic constitutional rights and result in forcible expropriation of Austrian citizens and taxpayers (NRP161) and in typically colourful language, he labelled the ESM as the 'European

---

11. Yet he continued to echo FPÖ demands for restricted immigrant access to welfare benefits.

12. SG 2010; *see also* NRP64; NRP140.

13. E.g. BZÖ 2010; NRP64; NRP66; BZÖ 2012a; NRP164; BZPÖ 2012b.

14. BZÖ and FPÖ 2010; NRP64; NRP57.

15. NRP57 and NRP161 respectively.

Sado-Masochism', or 'Gagging Treaty' (NRP143; SG 2012). The tonality of Bucher's discourse tended to be more measured and technical, or business-like, as one would expect from someone who insisted (e.g. SG 2009) that unlike Strache's FPÖ, the BZÖ was a constructive, non-aggressive and government-oriented party. Yet in respect of the ESM, he also resorted to hyperbole, describing the ESM as 'devil's work', a collective betrayal of the country and treason *vis-à-vis* democracy and Austrian parliamentarism (NRP161). Finally, defence of popular sovereignty and calls for referenda were a feature of both parties' populist discourse.[16] They were more pronounced in that of Strache, who argued for the sovereign to have the final word on all subjects (NRP140). Both he and Bucher demanded that the ESM and Fiscal Compact be submitted to a binding popular referendum (NRP164). Strache attacked Faymann for reneging on a 2008 pledge to submit future EU treaty changes to a popular referendum and accused the 'red-black referendum deniers' of permanently frustrating the people's democratic legitimate right of initiative and decision-making power and argued this was because they were not serving the Austrian people, but instead were serving their bank speculators (NRP164). The government's assertion that the ESM and Fiscal Compact did not require treaty change cut little ice.

Whilst the ESM debate was raging, an addition to the populist 'supply' came in the form of the octogenarian Austro-Canadian billionaire Frank Stronach. On 2nd July, he wrote to all MPs, urging them to reject the Treaty, and argued in the following day's television news (*ZeitimBild 2* [ZiB2] 3 July 2012) '[...] it makes no sense to pump in money which the banks skim off and which then leaves nothing for the Austrian citizens'. Indicative of his anti-establishment and anti-party orientation were his statements that 'the politicians want to serve themselves. I want to serve Austria'. The growing likelihood that Stronach would form his own populist party posed a significant threat to the FPÖ and BZÖ, as repeatedly stressed by those interviewing the parties' leaders (e.g. SG 2012). A week before he formally launched 'Team Stronach' (TS) (on 27 September, 2012), polls suggested 10 per cent of Austrians would vote for a Stronach-led party and by March 2013, that figure had risen to 15 per cent. The timing of the party's emergence had little to do with the economic crisis. Stronach had been unable to persuade existing and newly-forming parties to accept his considerable financial support in return for him effectively determining its policy and strategy and at eighty years of age, 2013 would be Stronach's last opportunity to realise his long-held ambition to head a party during a general election.

TS traded on Stronach's self-made billionaire status; claiming he was one of the world's most successful businessmen, had invested billions in Austria, created 13,000 jobs, built numerous factories and made enormous contributions to social benefits.[17] It also profited from his being regarded (at least initially) as a genuine political outsider. Indeed, he was at pains to stress he was not a politician and had

---

16. E.g. SG 2012; NR140 and 164.
17. E.g. ZiB2 27.09.2012 and 29.11.2012.

no intention of becoming one, but wanted to serve Austria by being the guardian of the values of 'truth, transparency and fairness', which were to be implemented on behalf of Austrian citizens by non-political experts.[18] TS's anti-party sentiment was succinctly encapsulated in its programme's preface: 'The government is a country's management team. Unfortunately, this management team consists of politicians. The mandate of a politician is to be elected, or re-elected. The country is thus governed by political rather than socio-economic principles' (Team Stronach 2013: 4). From the outset, the main target of TS's wrath was Austria's allegedly self-serving and incompetent SPÖ-ÖVP duopolistic 'system' that included neo-corporatist actors such as the trade unions and Chambers of Labour and of Commerce and had for fifty years allegedly not only made many Austrians fearful, but also increased public debt to unsustainable levels.[19] That system was, Stronach maintained, aided and abetted by a politicised Austrian Broadcasting and compliant journalism.[20] TS shared the BZÖ's desire for a small state, reducing public debt and policies geared to help small and medium businesses, but also defended larger enterprises and argued in favour of worker co-ownership.[21] The banking and Eurozone sovereign debt crises figured prominently in TS discourse. Like the BZÖ and FPÖ, it attributed blame above all to the banks and to the allegedly complicit politicians.[22] Its recipes lacked clarity and consistency, however. At times, Stronach argued for Austria's return to the Schilling, but at other times, TS favoured the BZÖ's call for the formation of an alternative hard-currency Eurozone.[23]

Post-2008 populist party vote: A 'new electoral politics'?

Between the general elections of 2008 and 2013, Austrians elected eleven provincial parliaments and their Members of the European Parliament. Figure 9.4 indicates the populist parties' (cumulative) vote at those elections. For parties tainted by the corruption crisis that broke in mid-2010, it was fortunate that no elections were held between October 2010 and March 2013 and it is widely believed the parliamentary vote by all but the Greens to prematurely terminate the Parliamentary Committee of Enquiry was motivated by the determination to prevent this crisis from dominating the 2013 general election.

Be that as it may, Figure 9.4 shows that within months of its emergence, TS successfully contested three elections (Carinthia 11.2, Lower Austria 9.8 and Salzburg 8.3 per cent), obtaining sufficient votes to enter both parliament and government. Carinthian and Lower Austrian exit polls (http://www.sora.at) suggest that TS support disproportionately came from BZÖ, FPÖ and protest voters.

18. E.g. ORF current affairs programme *'ImZentrum'* 30.09.2012 and Team Stronach (2013: 39).
19. E.g. *ImZentrum* 30.09.2012; ZiB2 09.04.2013; Team Stronach (2013: 17f, 21 and 26).
20. E.g. *ImZentrum* 30.09.2012; Team Stronach (2013: 61).
21. E.g. ZiB2 27.09.2012; *Öl Mittagsjournal* 14.02.2013 and 29.09.2012; Team Stronach 2013.
22. E.g. ZiB2 27.09.2012; Team Stronach (2013: 28–32).
23. E.g. ZiB2 03.07.2012 and 09.4.2013; *Puls 4 Herbstgespräch* 24.09.2012; *Öl Mittagsjournal* 14.02.2013.

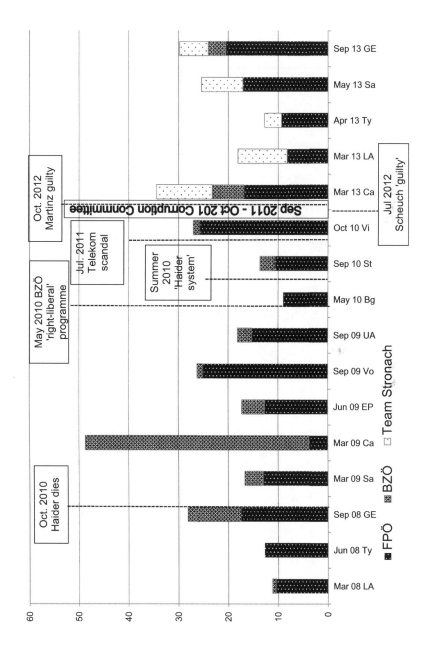

Figure 9.4: Austrian populist parties' vote and key political events (2008–13)

TS's discourse frequently referred to the sovereign debt crisis, but its successes were due more to Stronach's initial popular appeal and the financial resources he placed at the disposal of his party's populist message. Despite its achievements in spring 2013, TS's general election performance (5.7 per cent and eleven seats) was at best half of what Stronach had hoped for. This is largely attributable to his erratic media appearances, often characterised by bad-tempered exchanges, his tendency to ramble and his seeming inability to provide cogent answers to questions. Personalistic leadership had become a liability. Within days of the election, Stronach purged numerous individuals he had placed in key positions, including the caucus chair and leaders of provincial party groups. Commentators attributed this to his inability to countenance dissent and his demand that the party repay ten million euros of the twenty-five million euros he had invested in it. His autocratic actions triggered considerable intra-party criticism. Stronach was an MP for merely three months and then withdrew from Austrian politics. So the populist nature and overall fate of TS remain unclear.

Figure 9.4 highlights enormous variation in the populist parties' cumulative vote share at the various elections: from under 10 per cent in Burgenland, which has always lacked a strong organisation, to nearly 50 per cent in Carinthia, where populists have long been exceptionally densely organised and held the governorship from 1989 to 1991 and then for the entire period from 1999 to 2013. Yet Carinthia is also where their electoral fortunes have been most volatile. The change in 2009 is an artefact of altered supply. In 2005, the Haider-led Carinthian FPÖ overwhelmingly switched to the BZÖ. If the 2009 BZÖ vote is compared to the FPÖ's in 2004, there was a small increase (from 42.4 to 44.9 per cent), the consequence of an emotive campaign focused on Haider, who had died five months earlier. Meanwhile, the rump FPÖ could muster merely 3.8 per cent. Further supply-side change came in December 2009, when the Carinthian BZÖ now led by Scheuch seceded from the Federal Party. Though Scheuch blamed this on the economic liberalism of Bucher's 'right-wing liberal' strategy, it was primarily due to Scheuch's conviction that with Haider dead, the BZÖ was doomed. Re-named the *'Freiheitlichen in Kärnten'* (FPK), the party allied with Strache's FPÖ. Scheuch's subsequent conviction led to his brother assuming the FPK leadership in August 2012 and was one of many manifestations of the corrupt 'Haider system' that triggered the premature election of March 2013. The FPK collapsed to 16.9 per cent, lost eleven of its seventeen seats and was ejected from government, whilst a hurriedly-formed BZÖ led by Bucher obtained 6.4 per cent and two seats.

The secession of the BZÖ's Carinthian stronghold was a further blow to the national leadership, which had in October 2008 lost its most emblematic figure. At elections held between then and the formation of the Corruption Committee, its vote share ranged from 4.6 to 1.2 per cent (European Parliament and Vorarlberg elections respectively) and it failed to win a single seat.[24] Thereafter, it was

---

24. Subsequent to the Lisbon Treaty's ratification, it received one MEP. It polled a derisory 1.3 per cent at Vienna's October 2010 election.

increasingly damaged by the Corruption Committee's revelations regarding its former politicians and by Bucher's refusal to condemn Haider, his former mentor. From the summer of 2012, it was also squeezed by TS, which was not so tainted and whose leader had greater economic credibility. TS not only attracted BZÖ voters, but also persuaded four of its twenty-one MPs to defect and form the nucleus of a new TS parliamentary caucus. The BZÖ felt unable to contest any 2013 provincial election. So notwithstanding its instrumentalisation of the discursive opportunity provided by the banking and sovereign debt crisis, it could boast only two provincial and seventeen national MPs on the eve of the 2013 general election, when it obtained merely 3.5 per cent of the vote and was ejected from parliament.

During 2009 and 2010, the FPÖ increased its vote share at every election except the one in Carinthia, sometimes dramatically.[25] The party's instrumentalisation of the banking and Eurozone sovereign debt crises was but one contributing factor. At the 2009 EP election, for example, the FPÖ's discourse was perceived by many to have been unusually aggressively xenophobic and Eurosceptic. One FPÖ poster had the slogan 'The West in Christian Hands' (*Abendland in Christenhand*), a theme that was underscored by Strache wielding a cross at party rallies. Another called on voters to support its true people's representatives rather than EU traitors (*Volksvertreter statt EU-Verräter*). At Vienna's 2010 election, a similarly emotive and xenophobic campaign, again exploiting the discursive opportunity of the sovereign debt crisis, saw the FPÖ vote soar to 25.8 per cent (+14.8), its seats increase from 13 to 27 and the party obtain three city councillors. With the FPÖ continuing to climb in the polls (Figure 9.3), observers started to take seriously its claim that it could become the strongest party at 2013's general election. Yet from late 2011, its rating started to decline and by March 2013 was below 20 per cent. At that month's Carinthian election, the greatest absolute vote decline (-28) of any post-war Austrian party was suffered by the FPK, which Strache had brought back into the FPÖ fold in 2010. This was attributable in large measure to Carinthian exceptionality, but the same day, the FPÖ lost a fifth of its former vote share in Lower Austria and in April experienced a similar loss in Tyrol.[26] Within the FPÖ, questions were raised about Strache's leadership and strategy. Criticism subsided somewhat after May's election in Salzburg, where the city had lost hundreds of millions of euro due to unauthorised speculation and derivatives trading. As in Carinthia and nationally, the Greens were the most credible anti-corruption party. In Carinthia, they had more than doubled their vote (5.2 to 12.1 per cent) and in Salzburg achieved their best-ever Austrian result (20.2 per cent, + 13). To Strache's relief, the FPÖ vote also increased (13 to 17 per cent) and it gained one seat. The party was much weaker, however, than it had been even

---

25. March 2009: Salzburg 13 per cent (+4.3); June 2009: European Parliament 12.7 per cent (+6.4); September 2009: Vorarlberg 25.2 per cent (+12.8) and Upper Austria 15.3 per cent (+6.9); May 2010: Burgenland 9 per cent (+3.2); September 2010: Styria 10.7 per cent (+6.1).

26. Lower Austria: 8.2 per cent and four seats (-2.3 and 1 respectively); Tyrol: 9.3 per cent and four seats (-3.1 and no seat change).

eighteen months previously. It had been significantly damaged by the Corruption Committee's revelations and remained politically very exposed on this front, not least since the FPK alliance undermined its attempts to distance itself from the 'Haider system'. That vulnerability was exacerbated by the emergence of TS.

The FPÖ's Strache-centred general election campaign continued to instrumentalise the banking and sovereign debt crises. Its overarching slogan was '*Nächstenliebe*' (neighbourly charity), which provided a softer narrative for the FPÖ's anti-immigrant message and was also used to re-package its economic and social policy proposals. Strache also adopted a less confrontational style in his television appearances, arguably because the FPÖ wished to present him as a more palatable coalition partner. In light of the FPÖ's 2011 poll ratings and expectations for 2013, its result (20.5 per cent (+3.0) and 40 seats (+6)) was a disappointment. The combined vote of Austria's populist parties (FPÖ, TS and BZÖ) was 29.8 per cent, a record high. With the BZÖ failing to pass the representation hurdle and TS lacking direction, the FPÖ was again Austria's pre-eminent populist party.

The first book-length analysis of the 2013 general election (Kritzinger, Müller and Schönbach 2014) underscores the extent to which political rather than economic motivations determined voter behaviour. Having said this, populist parties have played an important role in transforming Austria's party system. They have for nearly thirty years fostered the declining loyalty of Austria's previously hyper-stable electorate and increased the personalisation of politics (Luther 2008; Kritzinger *et al.* 2013). In part, this has been achieved by the ruthless exploitation of every discursive opportunity, including the ones provided by the 'Great Recession'. The resulting increased voter volatility and party system fragmentation have made the building and maintenance of national and provincial coalitions more difficult. The populists have further destabilised the party systems by the many supply-side changes they initiated, but also by altering the 'structure of competition' (Mair 1998). Examples of populists-related party system 'innovation' include Austria's 2000–2007 ÖVP-FPÖ/BZÖ coalition, as well as the various FPÖ/BZÖ/FPK-led coalitions in Carinthia, the innovative 2013 formulae in Carinthia (SPÖ/ÖVP/TS), Lower Austria (ÖVP/SPÖ/TS) and Salzburg (ÖVP/Greens/TS). For now, the erstwhile 'grand coalition' parties together still have a national-level parliamentary and electoral majority, but it has become wafer-thin. Austria may thus be approaching a tipping-point, at which it might resume the bipolar logic exhibited in the Schüssel coalitions.

Concluding remarks

In Austria, the 'Great Recession' did not engender a deep competitiveness crisis enhancing antagonism between 'the people' and political or economic elites, or cause the established populist parties' discourse to undergo a qualitative shift. Although we have examined only a fraction of the potential examples of that discourse, we have shown that both established populist parties added (bank) speculators to their list of despised 'others', but their prime enemies remained domestic and European political elites and the discursive opportunity afforded by the banking and Eurozone sovereign debt crises was merely used to re-articulate their EU-scepticism and opposition to those elites. The FPÖ continued to mobilise mainly on the cultural dimension, utilising nationalistic and welfare chauvinist rhetoric; but having moved left on the socio-economic dimension, its rhetoric was also protectionist and anti-globalisation. The BZÖ's discourse gradually attached itself to the defence of the middle classes and argued for more market and less state. The BZÖ's electoral failure suggests this was not a 'winning formula' (Kitschelt), but this failure (and the FPÖ's poor post-2010 results) was due mainly to political factors.[27] Prominent amongst these were the entry of another populist actor, but above all Austria's corruption crisis. One would normally expect such political crises to favour anti-establishment parties and to intensify populism. Yet since former and current FPÖ and BZÖ politicians figured prominently amongst those accused (and found guilty) of corruption, it reduced the credibility of established populist parties' anti-elite platform and arguably significantly mitigated the electoral benefit they might have expected to enjoy as a result of their utilisation of the banking and sovereign debt crises.

The volume's fourth hypothesis suggests that when in power, populists tend to tone down populist discourse and behave more like mainstream parties. As we have shown in much greater detail elsewhere (Luther 2011), when the FPÖ moved from populist vote-maximisation to incumbency (in 2000), its office-holding leadership attempted to moderate the party's populist discourse and behave more like a mainstream party, a move massively resisted by the grass roots. Once the FPÖ was jettisoned from government, it wholeheartedly reverted to populist discourse. The BZÖ emerged from the FPÖ in public office and drew on those who prioritised office-seeking. Even when out of (national) office, it never decisively abandoned responsibility in favour of responsiveness. This may well have contributed to its failure to re-enter parliament at the 2013 election, where it was squeezed between the neo-liberal competition of the newly-founded NEOS and the non-xenophobic populist competition of Team Stronach.

Overall, the Austrian case suggests that although demand-side factors (such as economic crises) help explain the behaviour and success of populist parties, at least as important are political factors. These include on the one hand, the persistence (at least for now) of grand coalition government, the embodiment of Austria's cartelised establishment, and on the other, the politics of populist 'supply' and 'agency', including in particular populists' capacity to mobilise and to refrain from damaging their own prospects.

---

27. It is also worth noting that whilst the FPÖ met all three of the criteria of populism specified in the opening chapter of this volume (a thin ideology juxtaposing the homogenous 'people' against the elite and excluding 'others'; a discourse characterised by people-centrism, anti-elitism and popular sovereignty and a strategy based on personalistic leadership), after Haider's death, the BZÖ lacked the latter.

PART III

THE SOUTHERN REGION

Chapter Ten

Italy – A Strong and Enduring Market for Populism

Giuliano Bobba and Duncan McDonnell

Introduction

Over the past two decades, Italy has been one of the strongest and most enduring markets for populist parties in Western Europe. The characteristics of this market derive, firstly, from the favourable structural conditions which have presented on different occasions for the emergence and success of populist parties and, secondly, from the astute agency of these parties in exploiting those structural conditions. The political and economic crises of the late 1980s and early 1990s saw the rise of *Forza Italia* (FI) and the *Lega Nord* (LN – Northern League), while the political and economic crises since 2008 have facilitated the ascent of the *Movimento Cinque Stelle* (M5S – Five-Star Movement). This latter addition to the market resulted in the combined total vote for populist parties in Italy exceeding 50 per cent for the first time at the 2013 general election, after having oscillated between a low of 28.3 per cent (2006) and a high of 45.7 per cent (2008) in the previous five elections (*see* Figure 10.1). Italy thus presents a case of strong and multifaceted populism. Moreover, since the two main parties in the Italian government from May 2008 to November 2011 were populist – FI's successor party, the *Popolo della Libertà* (PDL – People of Freedom) and LN – Italy also provides a case of populist resilience in office (from this perspective it offers an interesting comparison with Greece – *see* the chapter by Takis Pappas and Paris Aslanidis).

Our chapter is organised as follows: in the first section, we discuss the two main populist parties in Italy before 2008 – FI/PDL and the LN – and note how the idea of 'crisis' has always been central to their message (whether in or out of power). In section two, we consider a series of economic and political indicators in order to assess how and when the recent economic and political crises affected Italy. As we explain, the economic crisis in Italy is best thought of as having occurred in two waves – the first being that which struck globally in September 2008 and the second being the more specific financial crisis which hit the country in mid-2011. This latter wave in turn fuelled – and interacted with – a fast-growing political crisis. In the third section, we look at how the PDL and LN discussed the economic crisis while in power. For the former, the reaction strategy was largely one of denial while the latter sought simply to not talk about the economy and to focus instead on its key issues of federal reform and immigration. We also note that both parties continued to use strongly populist messages while in power.

Figure 10.1: Total populist vote in Italian general elections (1994–2013)

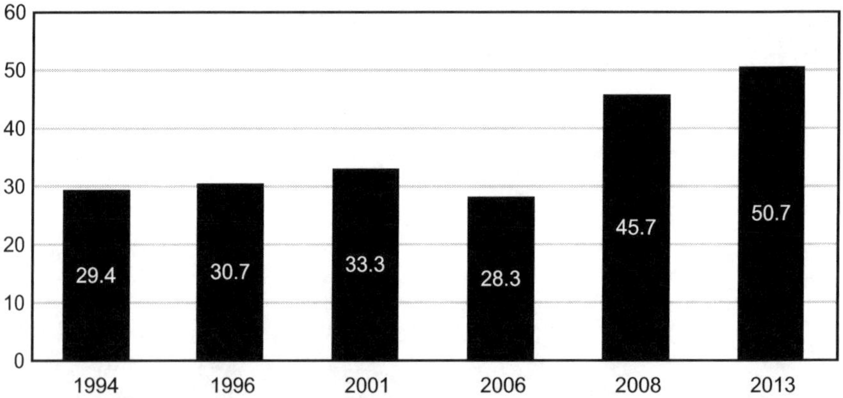

Note: General election results refer to the proportional part of the elections for the lower house of parliament, the *Camera dei deputati* (Chamber of Deputies). For the elections between 1994 and 2006, the totals are the sum of the FI and LN vote shares. For the 2008 election, the sum of the PDL and LN vote shares is used. For 2013, the sum of the PDL, LN and M5S vote shares is used. *Source:* Electoral archive of the Italian Interior Ministry, http://www.elezionistorico.interno.it.

Section four discusses how the post-2011 period also saw the emergence of a new populist actor, the M5S, which blamed the crisis on Italian and European elites (including the pre-existing populist parties, the PDL and the LN). Indeed, as we show in section five, the M5S rise culminated in the most spectacular debut election result in recent decades in Europe, with the movement taking just over a quarter of the vote – a result which meant that over half of Italians now supported populist parties (*see* Figure 10.1).

Populism in Italy before 2008: From one crisis to another

As Figure 10.1 shows, populism was already very strong in Italy before the 2008 crisis thanks to the rise of FI and the LN amidst the political and economic crises which struck the country in the early 1990s and the sustained electoral success of both parties thereafter. Although different in terms of their specific ideologies, FI (along with its successor, the PDL) and the LN have long been treated by scholars as populist (e.g. Taggart 2000; Mudde 2007). We consider the LN to be best understood as an 'ethnoregionalist' populist party (Spektorowski 2003; McDonnell 2006). While it switched between federalist and secessionist positions in the 1990s, and back to a federalist one after 2000, the party has remained constant in appealing to a specific territorial area and northern 'people', along with opposing immigration and strongly criticising national and supranational elites. In terms of its election results and institutional roles occupied, the LN has been one of Europe's most successful regionalist parties, serving in several governing coalitions led by FI/PDL's Silvio Berlusconi – briefly and acrimoniously in 1994, and then far more harmoniously from 2001–06 (Albertazzi and McDonnell 2005) and from 2008–11 (Albertazzi and McDonnell 2010). Berlusconi's personal parties (McDonnell 2013) – first FI and, after 2008, the PDL – have generally been Italy's most electorally successful during the two decades since the beginning of the 'Second Republic' and have been the largest members of coalition governments in 1994, 2001–06 and 2008–11. FI has been viewed within the literature on populism as more moderate than the LN, with the party termed 'liberal-populist' (Taguieff 2003: 104) and 'neoliberal populist' (Mudde 2007: 47). Although the lack of a strongly emphasised anti-immigrant and nativist stance means that we are certainly not dealing with a radical right populist party, the 'liberal' label is also problematic given that both FI and the PDL have often adopted strongly illiberal positions regarding the checks and balances of Italian democracy (such as media freedom, the judiciary, the Constitution, and the President of the Republic). For our purposes in this chapter, however, it is sufficient to say that FI and the PDL are safely classifiable as populist parties which have been broadly located ideologically on the centre-right/right.

Crisis and populism tend to go together – at least rhetorically – and both the LN and FI/PDL provide good examples of this. As Benjamin Moffitt (2014: 2–3) argues, we should see crisis as 'an internal feature of populism' rather than something which is 'purely external'. In other words, crisis – whether real, alleged, or perceived – is an ever-present element of populist mobilisation given that 'populist actors actively perform and perpetuate a sense of crisis, rather than simply reacting to external crisis' (Moffitt 2014: 7). FI/PDL and the LN have each presented themselves as saviours on a mission to restore sovereignty and prosperity to a 'people' cast as victims of a series of elites and faced with a multi-faceted and ongoing situation of crisis. The presence of crisis has been a fixed component of these parties' appeals. In the early 1990s, the (objective) crisis in Italy was both economic and political – the country was under enormous pressure due to its large public debt and the pressures created by the need to fulfil the Maastricht criteria for eventual entry into the euro. At the same time, the exposure of widespread corruption among the main parties which had governed Italy for decades (in particular, the Christian Democrats and the Socialists), along with the collapse of the former Communist Party, created a political crisis and a vacuum of representation which both FI and the LN sought to fill.

Born out of political and economic crisis, the two parties continued to base their key messages for the following fifteen years on the idea of persistent, unresolved crises (and the warning that these were set to get much worse). In LN discourse, the democratic rights and economic wellbeing of its 'people' (hard-working northern Italians attached to their local traditions) were said to be menaced, from above, by corrupt elites in Rome and Brussels and, from below, by southern Italians (although this was toned down after 2000) and immigrants (with Islamic immigrants in particular being the focus of LN attention after 9/11). For FI/PDL, its people (decent, ordinary, family-oriented Italians) were depicted as under threat from the undemocratic and immoral elites of the left, the *intelligentsia*, the judiciary, and those parts of the media not owned by Berlusconi, all of whom were also said to have combined to impede economic growth due to their supposed continuing attachment to communist and 'anti-Italian' values. For both populist parties, the solutions proposed were simple: FI/PDL promised in successive campaigns to usher in a new Italian 'economic miracle' (harking back to the boom years of the late 1950s) by reducing taxes, cutting bureaucracy and promoting public works, while the LN urged the introduction of regional autonomy and a clamping-down on immigration. Even during their years in power, the presence of 'crisis' and its alleged effects continued to play a key role in the discourse of both parties. In particular, external crises were used as explanations both in the 2001–06 and 2008–11 periods for why they were unable to achieve their aims in government and why the promised economic boom had failed to materialise. Hence, after taking office in 2001, Berlusconi regularly referred to 9/11, the wars in Afghanistan and Iraq, the effects of the allegedly mismanaged introduction of the euro and the unfair competition deriving from India and China's entry into the World Trade Organization (WTO) as unforeseen events which had created crises preventing his government from delivering on its campaign pledges and forcing it into a 'fire-fighting' role.[1] Consequently, in FI's 2006 election manifesto, readers were told that the government had presided over 'five extremely difficult years due to the continual crises that emerged', both due to internal factors (the legacy of the left's time in office between 1996 and 2001) and external ones such as those mentioned above (FI, 2006). Faced with such adverse circumstances, so the argument of both FI and the LN ran, they had in fact done a very good job of 'crisis management'.

Although the centre-right alliance narrowly failed to remain in government at the 2006 election, a slimmed-down version of it (consisting almost entirely of the newly-created PDL and the LN, alongside a couple of miniscule parties) returned to office just two years later after the fall of Romano Prodi's centre-left administration. The April 2008 election was a successful one for both populist parties. As we see in Figure 10.2, the LN increased its share from 4.6 per cent in 2006 to 8.3 per cent, while the PDL took 37.4 per cent of the vote – the highest general election result to date for any Berlusconi-led party.

Economic and political crisis in Italy after 2008

As we have noted already, it is best to think of the crisis as having hit Italy in two waves, the first in September 2008 and the second in mid-2011 (Jones 2012). While the first did have discernible effects on the Italian economy, it was the second which had by far the greater political impact, with the events of 2011 increasing the pressure on an already-beleaguered Berlusconi government that had seen its

---

1.   *See*, for instance, the comments by Berlusconi about India and China's entry into the WTO and the effects of globalisation on the Italian economy in his 2006 general election campaign speech in Genoa on 21 March. Available at: http://www.radioradicale.it/scheda/254146/politiche-2006-comizio-di-silvio-berlusconi.

Figure 10.2: FI/PDL and LN in general elections (1994–2008)

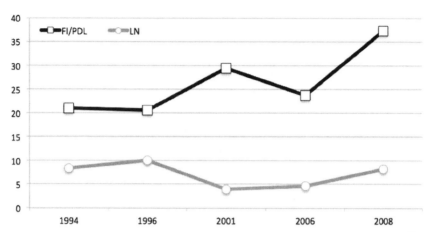

Note: General election results refer to the proportional part of the elections for the *Camera dei deputati* (Chamber of Deputies). In all elections except 1996, the two parties ran together as part of the same coalition. The PDL was created by a merger between FI and other parties in 2008 – hence the apparent sudden rise in the FI line at the 2008 general election.
Source: Electoral archive of the Italian Interior Ministry, http://www.elezionistorico.interno.it.

parliamentary majority dwindle since mid-2010 due to a series of expulsions and defections from the PDL.

When we look at the data regarding the Italian economy over the last decade, we can clearly see that Berlusconi's eight years in power neither ushered in the promised era of prosperity nor improved Italy's position compared to its European partners. As Figure 1.3 in the introductory chapter to this volume shows and Figure 10.3 presents in further detail, Italian GDP per capita went from above the European average in 2002 to just below it in 2012. At just 12.5 per cent, Italy also had by far the lowest growth over these ten years of any EU-27 member state – far less than Germany's 39.7 per cent, France's 25.6 per cent and even Greece's 20 per cent.

As shown by the data on the trend of GDP and public debt presented in the introductory chapter (Figures 1.1 and 1.3), Italian GDP noticeably declined after 2008, while the level of public debt went up in the same period by almost twenty-one points (reaching 127 per cent of GDP in 2012). The available data on changes in the workforce also highlights the effects of the crisis. Unemployment in Italy increased from 7.8 per cent in 2009 to 12.2 per cent in 2013 – an increase of 4.4 percentage points (well above the average EU-27 rise of 1.9 points).[2] Even more revealing, however, is the data from Italy's 'wage guarantee fund' which subsidises workers on permanent contracts (particularly in medium-large

---

2.   All Eurostat data is taken from epp.eurostat.ec.europa.eu.

Figure 10.3: Gross domestic product per capita in EU-27 (2002–12)

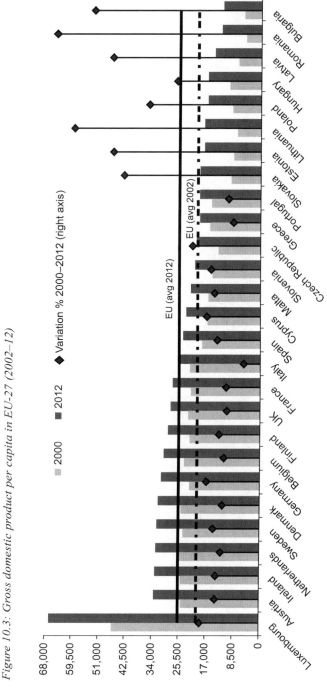

Source: Eurostat, http://epp.eurostat.ec.europa.eu.

Figure 10.4: Wage Guarantee Fund (2005–13) (thousands of hours)

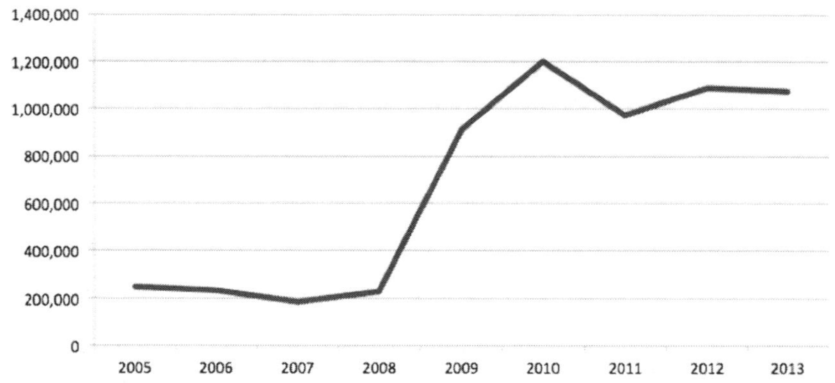

Source: INPS (http://www.inps.it).

companies), when their employment hours are cut. It is therefore a very good indicator of how such companies are faring generally.[3] As we can see clearly from Figure 10.4, the number of hours for which payments were made rose extremely sharply from around 227,660,000 hours in 2008 to circa 914,035,000 hours in 2009 and 1,197,816 hours in 2010. Although these numbers declined slightly in the years thereafter, they nonetheless remained at levels far higher than prior to 2008.

While the Italian economy therefore clearly felt the effects of the Great Recession in the post-2008 period, it was also hit by a second 'wave of crisis' in the summer of 2011 when the markets began to lose confidence in the ability of the PDL/LN government to introduce key reforms and bring down Italy's large public debt. In the space of just a few weeks, the stock market in Milan suffered a series of heavy losses and, most worryingly for Italy's prospects of managing its debt obligations, the spread between Italian and German ten year government bonds widened rapidly from 268 points on 17 August 2011 to 575 on 9 November. Although faced with repeated (and very specific) requests from its European partners, the European Central Bank (ECB) and business leaders within Italy, the Berlusconi government only passed weak measures. Whether through inability or unwillingness, this failure to respond convincingly to the crisis in turn fuelled a growing lack of faith in the country's economic outlook, with several rating agencies downgrading Italian debt in the early autumn and successive emergency European Council summits in late October calling on Italy

---

3. The Wages Guarantee Fund (*Cassa Integrazione Guadagni*) is 'a special public fund used to protect workers' income, financed by companies and the state and administered by the National Institute of Social Insurance (INPS). In cases laid down by law, the Wages Guarantee Fund makes up the pay of employees affected by lay-offs or short-time working, up to 80 per cent of the lost pay'. (http://www.eurofound.europa.eu/emire/italy/wagesguaranteefundcig-it.htm)

to provide formal assurances that it would indeed pass tough measures to bring down the debt and promote growth (Bosco and McDonnell 2013: 41–43). With his parliamentary majority slipping away, his party plummeting in the polls and his government unable to tackle the crisis, Berlusconi resigned on 12th November 2011 and was replaced by President Giorgio Napolitano's nominee, Mario Monti, who led a technocratic executive (containing no MPs or party representatives) which swiftly set about introducing the austerity measures desired by Europe and the markets.

The year 2011 also saw the deepening of a political crisis in Italy. Of course, there has usually been some degree of real or potential political crisis bubbling away in Italy since the early 1990s.[4] Nonetheless, we can clearly see the escalation of political crisis following the economic crisis – and the 2011 financial crisis – if we look at indicators such as electoral volatility, and public trust in parliament and in the functioning of democracy (*see* Figure 1.4 in the introductory chapter). As far as electoral volatility is concerned – Italy is second only to Greece – but this is largely explained by the spectacular success of the M5S at the 2013 general election. The growing distrust of citizens in politics is more evident, however, if we look at the data regarding dissatisfaction with democracy and public trust in political institutions. In addition to the failures of the parties to provide solutions to the problems facing Italian society, the numerous scandals during this period involving elected representatives at all levels (both local and national), along with the effects of the economic crisis, produced an unprecedented distance between the political elites and the public in Italy.[5] Trust in political institutions, taken as a whole, fell from 41 per cent in 2005 to 24 per cent in 2013, while for parliament alone it dropped dramatically from 22.5 to just 7.1 per cent.[6] Similarly, after a period of relative stability, dissatisfaction with democracy as expressed in Eurobarometer surveys also began to grow noticeably from 2009 onwards, rising to 69 per cent in 2013.[7]

The data discussed here confirm that a strong economic crisis in 2011 was accompanied by a strong political crisis. Of course, this combination was also the product of long-term trends: the frequent governmental crises of previous years along with the persistently high levels of public debt were clear indicators that all was not well either economically or politically in Italy. However, what we can safely say is that both types of crisis – economic and political – degenerated severely in 2011, with one feeding off the other.

---

4. For example, no single government has lasted for an entire legislature since 1994 and only in one case (2001–06) has the same Prime Minister (Berlusconi) remained in power for a full five years.

5. Since the outbreak of the economic crisis in 2008, the major political scandals in Italy have been: the sexual scandals involving Berlusconi, the misappropriation of public funding for parties involving Bossi, corruption scandals involving several high-profile members of the PDL, along with a series of expenses scandals involving politicians at regional and local levels.

6. *See Gli Italiani e lo Stato – Rapporto 2013*, available at: http://www.demos.it/a00935.php.

7. *See* Eurobarometer 63, 72, and 79: http://ec.europa.eu/public_opinion/archives/eb_arch_en.htm

Governing in crisis, by crisis

In this section, we consider how the PDL/LN government reacted rhetorically to the economic crisis after September 2008. Here we find a division of roles between the two populist parties: while Berlusconi's party, as in the 2001–06 period, stressed the presence of external crises or internal ones (created by others) and emphasised its success in managing these crises, LN for most of the period spoke little about the economic crisis, focusing instead on its key issues of federal reform and immigration/law and order (on which it achieved several significant results during its first two years in office).

Berlusconi's strategy when discussing his government's handling of the crisis was to claim that Italy was in fact doing better than other EU member states thanks to the PDL-LN administration's careful management of a crisis which it had found itself forced to deal with. In a speech to the Chamber of Deputies on 29 September 2010, he said:

> We did not get caught unprepared as the crisis escalated. Although nobody could have envisaged it would be so serious and so profound. I have said many times and I repeat it again today: even though Italy was in a difficult starting position due to its enormous public debt, it has tackled this crisis with measures judged effective by all international organizations. In fact, I could even say that Italy has tackled the crisis better than other countries.

In November of the same year, at the PDL's national executive meeting, Berlusconi returned to this theme, again lauding the ability of his government since 2008 and blaming internal factors (the economic mismanagement of the left) and external ones (the global economic downturn) for not having been able to deliver on all his pre-electoral pledges. Beginning by rejecting criticism from the left and the media, he said:

> They falsely accuse us of not doing anything so that they can play down our achievements in government. It is a battle with no quarter given, which we are fighting from a position of strength and confidence in what we have done, against their poison and their indefatigable factories of lies and smear. What we have done is indisputable. First of all we faced numerous crises inherited from the previous Left government and solved them quickly. We also faced a global crisis, the worst since 1929. We have faced this and overcome it thanks also to the work ethic and capacity for savings of the Italians[...]in the whole history of the Republic, our government has done more than any other, and we have done so in objectively difficult circumstances given the international economic crisis.

Even during its last year in office, the PDL stuck to its claim that 'the worst is over' and repeatedly stressed that – despite the crisis – it had been able to combine responsibility with responsiveness by keeping its 2008 election promise of 'not putting our hands in the pockets of Italians' (i.e. raising taxes). Once again pointing to Italy as having fared comparatively well, Berlusconi announced in December 2010 that 'Italy is no longer part of the economic problems in Europe, but has become part of the solution' and then, in February 2011, asserted that 'we have tackled the economic crisis well and have avoided the worst consequences'.

As mentioned, for most of the 2008–11 period, the LN avoided discussing the economy, preferring to delegate this to the PDL. Instead, it focused on those areas over which it held issue ownership and could claim to have achieved important results – notably, federal reform and immigration/law and order (Albertazzi and McDonnell 2010). On those occasions when the party did talk about the crisis, this occurred almost exclusively within the frame of a critique of globalisation and unfair competition from countries such as China or those in Eastern Europe. For example, in its manifesto for the 2009 European Parliament (EP) elections, the LN committed itself to 'combating the passage of measures – based on the pretext of the free market – which lead to unfair competition, thus hurting production and employment'. When the second wave of the crisis in 2011 made it impossible for the Lega to avoid the subject, the party focused on its role within government of opposing the reforms requested by Europe, such as those on pensions. For example, in a speech in September 2011, Bossi said that 'it was unjust and so we opposed it and there was no stopping us. They tried to get it through by all means possible, we had everyone against us: the powers-that-be and *Confindustria* [the employers' association]. But in the end we won the battle'. In this way, the party sought to differentiate itself from the PDL and present itself as the sole defender of 'the people' against the elites of Rome, Brussels and the financial markets amidst a situation of crisis.

The 2008–11 period in Italy is also interesting because it gives us a chance to see how populists communicate when in power. While answering such a question definitively would require a type and breadth of analysis beyond the scope of this chapter, we can say that both the PDL and the LN continued to issue strongly populist messages (and in similar tones) to those they used in opposition. Hence, we find that Berlusconi and those close to him persisted in attributing blame for Italy's problems to 'the communists' and railed against bureaucrats, the state and 'undemocratic' judicial elites. For example, in his *'Forza Silvio'* newsletter on 24 June 2010, Berlusconi complained about the difficulties facing businesses because 'Italian politics has been dominated by a certain culture (communist and catholic-communist), according to which someone who takes on the responsibility and risk of setting up a business is a potential exploiter, tax dodger and swindler'. He added that business people were also faced by a bureaucratic culture that expressed itself in 'the language of a totalitarian state which conceives of its citizens as subjects'. Such claims were by no means exceptional: in another *'Forza Silvio'* newsletter on 16 January 2011, he focused his ire on the country's judges and claimed that 'a country is not free when there is a caste of privileged and unaccountable people who can commit all sorts of abuses against other citizens'.

Likewise, the LN did not tone down its anti-elite or anti-immigrant populist rhetoric after entering government. For example, in a speech in Padua on 20 July

2008,[8] Umberto Bossi announced 'Either we obtain reforms, or else there will be a battle and we will attain our liberty. We have to fight against this fascist state. The moment has arrived, brothers, to put an end to things'.

New crisis, new populists

As pointed out earlier, trust in political institutions hit a new low in 2011 and Italy found itself in a situation of both economic and political crisis – with the latter reinforced by the presence of a technocratic government, put in place to do what the parties could not (or would not) do themselves. By early 2012, almost half of respondents in different opinion polls were saying that they were either undecided or not planning to vote.[9] An ISPO/*Corriere della Sera* survey at the beginning of February 2012 produced similar results to the public trust figures cited above, with 91 per cent of respondents saying they had 'little' or 'very little' faith in political parties.[10] In the ensuing months, however, many Italians began to turn towards a new political actor and, as had happened in 1994, the presence of objective economic and political crisis again led to an increase of populism in the system. This occurred in the shape of the M5S, which began a startling rise in opinion polls from 5.6 per cent in April 2012 to 18.6 per cent by June 2012.[11]

The M5S is hard to classify ideologically due to its short history, its eclectic mix of policies and its unique organisational characteristics. The movement was founded in October 2009, building on the success of Beppe Grillo's political blog and the 'Beppe Grillo meet-up' groups which came into existence in 2005 and 2006 respectively (Bartlett, Froio and McDonnell 2013: 21–22). Nonetheless, there has already been broad agreement among scholars that the M5S discourse – and particularly the statements of its founder, Beppe Grillo, both before and after the movement's foundation – is classifiable as populist (Bordignon and Ceccarini 2013; Corbetta and Gualmini 2013; Fabbrini and Lazar 2013). Certainly, Grillo's exaltation of 'good' citizens (i.e. 'the people') whose wellbeing and democratic rights are oppressed by all political elites – along with his framing of this as a perilous crisis – fits the key elements for the definition of populism as discussed in the introductory chapter. The M5S is not, however, a case of right-wing populism: in its policies it combines a range of themes from different ideologies (left, right,

---

8. Northern League online post, 20 July 2008. Available at: http://www.leganord.org/notizie2/6992-Bossi-_mai_più_schiavi_di_Roma._Gobbo_ricletto_alla_guida_della_Liga.html

9. *See*, for example, the surveys by ISPO/Corriere della Sera, '*Liberalizzazioni, d'accordo 6 italiani su 10*', http://www.sondaggipoliticoelettorali.it/asp/visualizza_sondaggio.asp?idsondaggio=5159, and by Ipsos/RAI–Ballarò, '*I cento giorni di cura Monti*,' http://www.sondaggipoliticoelettorali. it/asp/visualizza_sondaggio.asp?idsondaggio=5221.

10. *See* the ISPO/Corriere della Sera survey, '*Fiducia nei partiti, dopo il caso Lusi giù all'8% e il 56% degli elettori vuole cambiamenti radicali*,' http://www.sondaggipoliticoelettorali.it/asp/ visualizza_sondaggio.asp?idsondaggio=5193.

11. These figures are based on the averages of pooled monthly opinion poll data. *See* Figure 10.6 later in the chapter.

environmental) and there is no clear identification – and denigration – of 'the other' in its discourse (Bartlett, Froio and McDonnell 2013: 25–27).

As regards the M5S response to the crisis, Grillo laid the blame for this firmly on the shoulders of Italy's entire ruling class (comprising all existing parties, the media, business leaders, President Napolitano and the technocrats of Monti's government) and European elites, which were said to have caused democracy to malfunction and the economy to decline. As he explained in a statement on his blog in September 2012:

> The media, the parties, *Confindustria* and the banks are all one. They support each other in defence of their economic interests. Meanwhile, unemployment grows to levels never seen before, small and medium enterprises (the only ones keeping this country going) have to close, lay off staff or move abroad. Tax revenues will plummet [...] and Italy will find itself bankrupt, having saved the banking system and propped up an absurdly-organized state.

The M5S thus spares none of the other Italian political actors – whether partisan or not – from blame. In its 'political *communiqué* no. 51' on 28 June 2012, the movement says that 'Monti's remedy has made the public debt increase and the spread continue to rise. As a consequence, the interest we pay has also risen'. However, 'the debt was created by the parties, the PDL and the PD first and foremost, and now the citizens are being made to pay with tax increases, unemployment and cuts to services'. Of course, in the M5S view of Italian politics, elites misbehaving and usurping the sovereignty that ought to belong to the citizens is nothing new. As the 'political *communiqué* no. 50' on 6 May 2012 says: 'we have never had democracy in Italy. We went from a monarchy to fascism to partyocracy'. For the M5S, citizens in Italy are therefore 'servants of an extended group which holds power'.

As we shall discuss in the next section, this new populist force would prove to be more than a mere blip in mid-2012, as some commentators had predicted. Rather, not only would it sustain its support levels in the polls up until the February 2013 general election, but it would produce a stunning general election result which went beyond all expectations.

The populist majority

The 2013 election campaign saw the PDL, LN and M5S all blaming external forces for the crisis and promising to return sovereignty and prosperity to the people. As noted earlier, the M5S cast the citizens of Italy as the victims of a system dominated by corrupt and incapable elites at national and supranational levels. The solutions it proposed were rather vague in terms of policy specifics, but involved overturning the system entirely, removing the current elites and restoring power to the Italian citizen by online direct democracy. The PDL copied the M5S to some extent, in particular by adopting a Eurosceptic stance and blaming Germany for Italy's economic condition. For example, in its election manifesto,

Figure 10.5: PDL, LN, PD and M5S results in the 2008 and 2013 Italian general elections

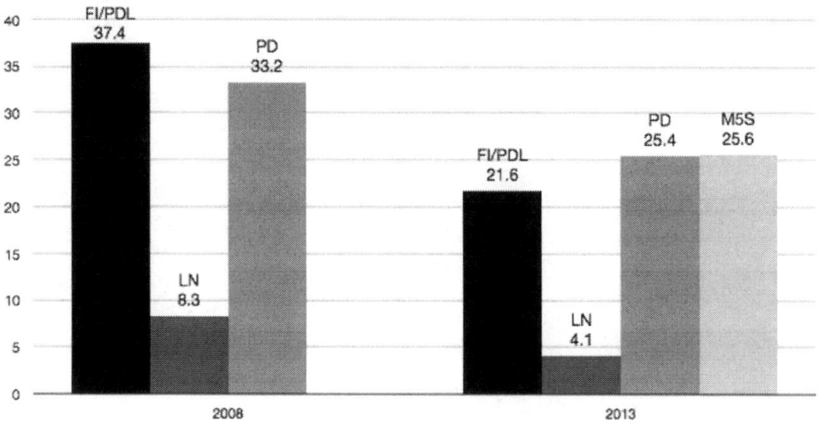

Source: Electoral service of the Italian Interior Ministry (http://elezioni.interno.it/).

the party claimed that the technocratic government had wrongly 'chosen to follow the politics of austerity imposed by a Germanocentric Europe and the depressing results are there for everyone to see'. Again distancing itself from measures taken by Monti, the PDL also promised to abolish the property tax which Monti had introduced (and the party had voted for in parliament). Finally, the LN repeated its denunciation of elites and said it would strive to free northerners from the tyranny of Rome and Brussels by allowing regions to retain 75 per cent of the taxes collected within their territory.

The election on 24–25 February 2013 was the second-most volatile general election of recent decades in Western Europe.[12] According to Pederson's index of electoral volatility, there was an increase from 9.5 and 9.7 at the 2006 and 2008 Italian general elections to 41.3 in 2013 (Chiaramonte and Emanuele 2013; Pedersen 1979). As Figure 10.5 shows, the PDL dropped 15.8 percentage points compared to 2008, slumping to 21.6 per cent, while its main centre-left opponent, the *Partito Democratico* (PD – Democratic Party) declined by almost eight points from 33.2 to 25.4 per cent (although the centre-left coalition as a whole obtained 29.6 per cent and so received the majority bonus of seats in the lower house of parliament, awarded to the largest coalition). The LN also did very poorly, slipping from 8.3 to 4.1 per cent. By contrast, the M5S performed extraordinarily well, taking 25.6 per cent. As noted in the introduction, this meant that – although the PDL and LN both declined – the total populist vote in Italy exceeded 50 per cent for the first time.

---

12. The analysis of the 2013 election is based in part on a fuller account of the LN and PDL's performances in the general election, available in Albertazzi and McDonnell (2015).

Figure 10.6: PDL, LN and M5S voting intentions and consumer confidence monthly trends (July 2006–February 2013) (variation on April 2006)

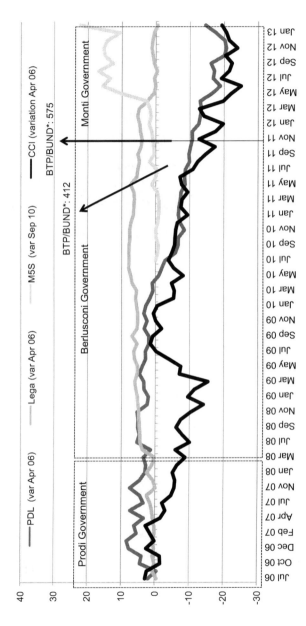

Note: All points in the graph display the averages of voting intention surveys for particular months, with the exception of February 2013, when the general election was held (we use the actual election data for this month). All points regarding party support display the variation from the April 2006 general election results. The CCI line shows the variation from its value in April 2006. * stands for Italian-German Long-Term Interest Rate Differentials.

Source: Data concerning the parties are calculated using the averages of voting intention surveys conducted by the main Italian polling houses (Cfi, Crespi, Datamonitor, Demopolis, Demos, Digis, Emg, Euromedia, Fullresearch, Ipr, Ipsos, Ispo, Lorien, Piepoli, Swg, Tecne). These can be accessed at sondaggipoliticoelettorali.it. The data for the Consumer Confidence Indicator (seasonally adjusted data) are taken from Eurostat: epp.eurostat.ec.europa.eu.

While, at first glance, it might seem that the LN had been punished for its performance in government (*see* Figure 10.5), in fact the roots of this result can be traced back to the news in April 2012 that the party's founder and leader, Umberto Bossi, was under investigation for misappropriation of party funds. Although he duly resigned and was replaced as leader in July 2012 by Roberto Maroni (who had previously been an extremely popular Minister of the Interior in the PDL-LN government), the party never recovered from this blow. We can see this quite clearly in Figure 10.6, which presents the variation from April 2006 onwards of our three Italian populist parties in pooled monthly opinion poll data – as the data shows, the LN in fact improved slightly during its first months back in opposition after November 2011. Once the scandal about Bossi became public, however, the party quickly dropped in the polls over the course of just a few months and did not recover in time for the general election.

Given FI-PDL's focus on the economy, we also investigated the relationship between the parties' average poll figures and monthly consumer confidence trends. As Figure 10.6 again shows, after the end of a long 'honeymoon period' in 2010, the PDL's poll results mirrored the drop in consumer confidence fairly closely. By contrast – and in line with that party's 'delegation' of the economy to the PDL and concentration on its key issues – the LN's results seem to be much less affected by consumer confidence trends. While it is impossible to demonstrate conclusively, we believe it very likely that the PDL decline is linked to the fact that it had stuck its colours so strongly to the flag of economic revival. As Van der Brug, *et al.* (2007) have shown, bad economic conditions tend to hurt larger parties in coalitions more than junior ones, especially when responsibility for economic policy is clear – something which was most certainly the case in the PDL-LN government.

As regards the M5S result: the movement took votes from both left and right at the 2013 election. ITANES data shows that 29.8 per cent of its voters had supported the PD in 2008, but 30.4 per cent of them had backed the PDL and 6 per cent had cast their ballots for the LN.[13] Grillo was able to exploit the combination of economic and political crisis – along with the discontent these produced – better than the other populist actors present in the Italian party system. Or, to put it another way, he was able to exploit the same structural conditions as the PDL and LN had done in the past, but using fresh contents.

Finally, although they fall beyond the formal remit of this chapter, it is worth briefly noting the results of the May 2014 EP elections. These were a triumph for Matteo Renzi who, in his first major test at the ballot box as party leader and Prime Minister, led the PD to an unexpected 40.8 per cent – the largest vote share achieved by any Italian party in a national election in the past fifty years.[14] While these elections also saw a decline in the M5S vote to 21.2 per cent, we believe this

---

13. *See* ITANES Rolling Cross Section Survey 2013. Available at: www.itanes.org/en/data/.

14. Renzi was elected leader of the PD in primaries held in December 2013. He then replaced Enrico Letta of the PD as Prime Minister in February 2014.

was still a good result which showed that the movement – at least so far – is not a 'flash-in-the-pan'. As for Berlusconi's party, the 16.8 per cent it received was down on its already very poor 21.6 per cent at the general election. However, this needs to be put into context: the PDL suffered a split in late 2013 when the more moderate wing chose to form a new party led by Angelino Alfano called *Nuovo Centrodestra* (NCD – New Centre-right) and remained in coalition government with the PD while Berlusconi led the majority of the PDL into opposition and changed the party's name back to FI. That caveat aside, the EP result was still below expectations. Indeed, perhaps only in a personal party like Berlusconi's could a leader stay on after losing so many votes at two consecutive elections (McDonnell 2013). Meanwhile, the LN in its first election under new leader Matteo Salvini obtained 6.2 per cent and thus began to reverse the steep drop in its vote suffered at the 2013 general election.

Conclusion

As occurred in the early 1990s, the combined presence of economic and political crisis in recent years has again seen an increase of populism within the Italian party system. While two decades ago, those crises led to the emergence and success of FI and the LN, this time the M5S rose swiftly from under five per cent in the polls in February 2012 to over 25 per cent in the general election just a year later. The M5S did so both by exploiting the economic and political crisis present in Italy from 2011 onwards and by casting itself as the only force willing and able to act responsively for the people and against the corrupt elites. In this sense, they gave the existing populist parties – the PDL and the LN – a taste of their own medicine. However, the experience of Italy since 2008 not only points to the importance of crisis (and especially the combination of economic and political crises) for the initial success of new populist parties. It also offers us a rare case of how populist parties in government fare during situations of objective crisis. To put it in the terms used by Peter Mair (2009), the PDL was unable to be either responsive (it failed to deliver the economic growth it had promised in 2008) or responsible (it also failed to introduce the measures requested by Europe and others at the height of the 2011 crisis). Hence, despite quite a long honeymoon in the polls, its support declined steadily after the first quarter in 2010 and the party's attempt to re-cast itself as 'responsive' in the 2013 election campaign failed to generate a recovery. While the case of the LN seems similar to the PDL if one looks just at general election results, in fact – as Figure 10.6 showed – the party was able to serve in government during the crisis without seeing its support levels slip at all. It thus offers us an important example of how populist parties can indeed serve in government without losing support, even during a crisis which has seen incumbent parties across the continent haemorrhage votes (Albertazzi and McDonnell 2015).

So, overall, how has populism interacted with economic and political crisis in Italy? As we have explained, the timing of events is crucial: the key moment in Italy for economic and political crisis and, by consequence, for an increase in populism, is from 2011 onwards, not September 2008. While the first two years in office were generally good for the PDL and LN, the country's long-standing debt problem triggered – with the help of jittery markets – a financial crisis in 2011 that in turn fuelled an already-growing political crisis. This latter political crisis, for its part, mushroomed and manifested most notably in a crisis of representation through which neither the leading populist party of the time (the PDL) nor the principal mainstream party (the PD) was willing to take on the responsibility of government in November 2011 and so Italy found itself with a technocratic administration consisting solely of non-elected, non-party ministers. And it was on the back of this period of combined economic and political crisis that we saw the subsequent rise of the most electorally successful new populist actor in Western Europe: the M5S. Whether that party is able to overcome the many organisational (and ideological) difficulties its sudden success has aggravated and laid bare remains an open question. However, what we can say is that, despite the media attention on the country's new – and so far, electorally successful – Prime Minister, Matteo Renzi of the PD, Italy continues to offer excellent market conditions for populism.

Chapter Eleven

Greek Populism: A Political Drama in Five Acts

Takis S. Pappas and Paris Aslanidis*

Contemporary Greece presents arguably the most intriguing case of populist development among all European nations. Emerging strong shortly after the country's 1974 transition into democracy, populism was initially represented by the Panhellenic Socialist Movement (PASOK), a nominally radical socialist party founded by rabble-rouser Andreas Papandreou. So successful was the new party that, already by 1981, it was able to win power by landslide, and thus become postwar Europe's first populist party in office. That however was only the beginning of Greece's populist saga, since PASOK, through a paradigmatic use of populist tactics, held power firmly throughout the 1980s, during which time it undertook to forge a solid electoral majority allegedly representing the authentic Greek 'people'. PASOK's successes made a large impression on New Democracy (ND), the other large party in Greece's two-party system, so that, in the early 1990s, it also decided to imitate its rival's vote-catching populist methods. Eventually, populism permeated the entire political system as it became the main parties' only rational strategy for winning 'the people' in a race of polarisation and overpromising at the expense of liberal institutions, political moderation, and social compromise. For many years thereafter, and as long as the international political and economic environment was favourable, Greece's populist democracy seemed to work relatively well. But in the late 2000s, when the global economic and financial crisis hit Europe, with Greece its earliest and most prominent victim, the old government parties, now under tight international control, realised that they could no longer serve their electoral constituencies. Then something remarkable occurred: 'the people' largely abandoned the old populist parties, PASOK and ND, fleeing to the support of any contender promising to continue serving them as if nothing had changed. Populism rebounded magnificently on both the left and the right of the political spectrum. With the populist constituency having dispensed with its old loyalties and already up for grabs, new parties took advantage of the situation by both revamping the discursive-symbolic groundwork laid by populism's early pioneers and arousing the biased beliefs it had created in society. Theirs, as this chapter is going to show, was an almost instant and remarkably impressive feat with long-term consequences for the country.

---

*   The second author gratefully acknowledges the support he received for this research from a
      scholarship granted by the Alexander S. Onassis Public Benefit Foundation.

Evidently, then, contemporary Greek politics offers perfect, near-laboratory conditions for the study of populist development over a considerably long time span, which moreover culminated in major polity failure. The chapter sections that follow correspond to what we identify as the main five 'Acts' in Greece's populist drama.[1] 'Act I' describes how in post-authoritarian Greece, PASOK, through the oratory of its leader, forged 'the people' as a distinct community sharing similar emotional and ideological beliefs, and turned it into a powerful electoral constituency. 'Act II' is about PASOK in power during the 1980s and how that party used the state for serving its own constituency while at the same time crowding out the opposition. 'Act III' covers the 1990s and 2000s and shows how populism became entrenched in Greek politics after the erstwhile liberal ND also began tapping into the constituency of 'the people' thus effectively turning into another populist contender. 'Act IV' is about populism during the Great Recession and explains the stampede of the populist constituency from the traditional government parties and their transfer of loyalties to newly emergent populist actors. 'Act V' focuses specifically on the narratives of the new populist contenders who emerged strong during the crisis, examines similarities with old populist themes, and explains their success in capturing the disenchanted 'people'. In a last section, the chapter concludes by addressing the hypotheses put forward in the introduction of this volume.

Act I. Populism in opposition, 1974–81: Forging 'the people'

Contemporary Greek populism evolved directly out of Andreas Papandreou's specific narrative about the country, its history and its politics. As his own son describes him, PASOK's leader was a storyteller *par excellence*, a *virtuoso* of simile and metaphor full of powerful emotional undertones, a great inventor of compelling slogans. 'He has a knack for words', writes the son about the father, 'he re-defines the out-of-daily-usage word "establishment" [*katestimeno*] to mean just that, […]calls government changes a "re-structuring" [*anadomisi*], a new relationship with Turkey acquires the status of "no-war". He draws his metaphors from the WWII [Greek] liberation movement and labels his political enemy a "collaborator" or "national betrayer"' (Papandreou 2014: 20). This is a splendid case study of how 'the people' is built.

As effectively explained by Rogers Smith (2003), building 'the people' hinges on narratives that promise citizens a better and more prosperous future while also seeking to define their identities and worth. In examining the creation, maintenance, and transformations of such community-building, Smith argues that 'political leaders engage in such "people-forming" or "people-building" endeavours to a greater or lesser degree all the time' (*ibid.*: 4) but, of course, few of them succeed. In the context of post-authoritarian Greek politics, Papandreou managed to build a

---

1. Given both space constraints and this volume's time-specific focus, Acts I-III are herein presented in brief while Acts IV and V will receive a more thorough treatment. For a comprehensive analysis of populism in Greece *see* Pappas (2014b), from which the present chapter freely draws.

resonant and timely narrative, the symbolisms of which operated as a mechanism for achieving several ends: a novel interpretation of the world as being divided by binary oppositions; the amalgamation of disparate social demands into a single collective unit, 'the people', with a communal consciousness; and the urge for radical political action on a promise of a better and fairer society which relies on national sovereignty. Papandreou claimed to represent many classes of people, 'particularly the "wronged" and non-privileged, the ones who have the right to come to power but who have been left out so far' (Nick Papandreou 2014: 21). He continues:

> Leaving aside generalities, [Andreas Papandreou] addressed the specific problems affecting small craftspeople, pensioners, and farmers – problems like irrigation, the lack of local government autonomy, the hydra-headed central administration. Yet everything was encompassed in the broader vision of a new Greece – a vision summarised in a manner accessible in the mid-1970s to every voter by PASOK's key slogans: national independence, popular sovereignty, social liberation, and democratic processes. (*ibid.*: 21)

Papandreou presented reality as a dense historical drama which revolves around the endless battle between good and evil, weak and strong, moral and corrupt, fair and unjust. In the end, firmly siding with and assuming the representation of the weak and moral, the narrator promised the final victory of the righteous people over the immoral and degenerate foes. His narrative was built around two main pillars. A self-proclaimed Marxist, having been greatly influenced by dependency theory in the early 1970s, he proceeded to build the first pillar as dividing the world between countries of a dominant imperialist 'centre' and those of a dependent underdeveloped 'periphery', presenting Greece as having undergone a process similar to colonisation by the Great Powers. The second pillar represented the alleged conflict between an exploiting 'establishment', both foreign and domestic, and the so-termed 'underprivileged' Greeks. This story was based on the theoretical construction of a grossly unfair system of exploitation that extended from the global centres of capitalism down to the smallest Greek village.[2] PASOK was a strongly anti-European party those days, presenting the imminent accession of the country to the European Community as an abolition of national sovereignty, and promising to cancel any such actions upon its coming to power (Verney 2011).

In sum, Papandreou's narrative was the following: Greece's continuing dependence on foreign powers had caused the inevitable conflict between two irreconcilable camps – one wishing to preserve dependence and another set to fight for its abolition. If the second camp wanted to win over the first, there was only one available option: the establishment of popular sovereignty in Greece. Through the symbolic articulation of diverse social categories, which had been marginalised in the years of the repressive reign of 'the right', Andreas Papandreou

---

2.   On the construction of 'enemies' through the symbolic discourse of political leaders, *see* Edelman (1988: esp. 66–89); for the construction of 'the people' through a similar process, *see* Laclau (2005a: esp. 65–172).

was thus able to forge a single and seemingly unified political entity, 'the people'. What remained was to capture state power by effectively turning the people into an electoral majority.

Act II. Populism in power, 1981–89: Serving 'the people'

Papandreou fought the 1981 electoral campaign on the promise of *'allage'* (change), a rather neutral word, which however encapsulated PASOK's all other main slogans about national independence and popular sovereignty. When the ballots were counted, PASOK was found to have won a stunning 48.2 per cent of the national vote and be in control of 172 out of 300 seats in parliament. Papandreou's populist strategy had triumphed and his other campaign motto 'PASOK in office – the people in power' was realised. The two would now rule in tandem.

Once installed in the premiership, Papandreou had to face an altogether different task – from forging the people, he now had to serve them. This practically amounted to satisfying the multitude of demands and claims raised by PASOK's electoral constituency, let alone providing them with material and other rewards. But in 1981, PASOK had no clear programme for reforming the country. Instead, enjoying tight and unrestrained control over the state, it fell back to traditional patronage politics and, indeed, perfected it. PASOK offered its constituency two types of state-related goods. The first type included tangible benefits such as real incomes from state employment or pensions. It has been calculated that total public sector employment in Greece increased during the 1980s 'at an average annual rate of about 4 per cent – around four times as fast as in the private sector' (OECD 2001: 50). Pensions and other social expenditure increased at a similar, if not higher, pace. In addition to such tangibles, however, the Greek people also became recipients of a host of intangible benefits ranging from the selective protection by the state to several professions against market hazards to widespread impunity from violating the law (as in the cases of tax evasion, illegal construction or squatting on state property).

With regard to internal political struggles, PASOK routinely employed acute polarisation since it constituted the most efficient strategy for both crowding out the opposition from state-related benefits and retaining office. The ruling party did not realise its threats – while in opposition – to withdraw from the European economic community, and also reneged on its promise to discontinue the use of Greek territory for NATO military bases and operations. However, PASOK kept bashing the domestic enemy that was now in the opposition with the same fervor as before. The idea was that more time was needed to bring PASOK's agenda to completion and safeguard the sovereignty of the people; a return of the right would reverse this progressive course, and should thus be avoided at all costs.

No less significant from a macro-political point of view, were the repercussions produced by PASOK's populist record in power on two other major matters – liberal institutions and popular sovereignty. As Papandreou himself famously fused them in dictum form during a broadly televised party rally, 'There are no institutions – only the people rule this country'. Successive PASOK governments developed an ever-growing disrespect for political liberalism and its institutions, which, as the current logic went, could be compromised, impaired, or otherwise twisted as long as it was in favour of realising popular supremacy. Following that logic, institution building ceased to be a priority, and an understanding of institutions as means of achieving the gratification of the people was put firmly in place.

The major consequence of Papandreou's populist discourse and political tactics while in office was the creation in large parts of Greek society of biased beliefs about politics and economics, which would swiftly become systematised and, crucially, come to determine the voters' future behaviour. Such biased beliefs – based as they were on strong social biases against the market mechanism, immigrants and immigration, liberal institutions and the need for social compromise (more on this in Pappas 2014b: 33–40) – would in turn create a constant demand for populist appeals that, even after Papandreou was past and gone, no power-aspiring politician could afford to neglect.

Act III. Populism entrenched, 1990–2009: Tapping into 'the people'

In 1990, ND regained office and, under the leadership of Constantine Mitsotakis, proceeded to shift away from populism and reinstate political liberalism by introducing appropriate institutions and reinvigorating the market economy through privatisations and other reforms. As the new government was soon to find out, however, it not only had to fight against the populist PASOK opposition; it was also undermined by a populist (*and* nationalist) streak that had developed strongly inside its own party. Intraparty contention culminated in 1993 with the overthrow of ND from power, thus once again opening the way for Papandreou and his populist party to return to power.

For ND, that was a particularly shocking defeat and the major lesson it drew was that, given the circumstances, when it comes to vote-decision, populism trumps liberal reformism. As the electorate had largely become accustomed to identifying itself with the category of 'the people', and was already driven by the irrational biases cultivated during the previous decade, interest groups used their power to divert the flow of state spoils towards their way while resisting reforms. Thus, following its instinct for survival in a world that had changed for good, ND decided to take the well-trodden populist path. It discarded Mitsotakis from the party helm in favour of populist Miltiades Evert, who promptly rebranded ND as a 'people's party' and set out to outbid PASOK's already excessive promises. From there on, populism contaminated Greece's two-party system as both of the country's major political forces had understood that it consisted of the best strategy to win 'the people' and achieve electoral majority. In the next two decades, Greece's political system (herein dubbed 'populist democracy') reached a comfortable balance, during which PASOK and ND would alternate in power with a combined performance averaging well over 80 per cent of the total vote (and over 90 per cent of parliamentary seats).

Nowhere was the predominance of populism more evident than in the crucial area of reform implementation in key sectors of state policy such as health, pensions, and education. Reform-minded politicians (including reformist Prime Minister Kostas Simitis) did, of course, exist during that period, but their efforts to reinforce liberal institutions invariably failed. Greeks, now highly averse to losing benefits already received (or expected) through patronage and populist politics, stood firmly against any reform. In the context of Greece's populist democracy, then, most politicians became intent on outperforming the electoral market by giving 'the people' the policies they asked for. And on occasions where those were bold – or careless – enough to introduce a reform agenda aimed at promoting the general public welfare rather than the satisfaction of specific social interests, they were punished at the polls.

Another development that was underway during the second half of the 1990s and the 2000s was the emergence of populist spinoffs from both PASOK and ND. One such party was the leftist Democratic Social Movement (DIKKI) under former PASOK Minister of Finance, Dimitris Tsovolas, which garnered almost 9 per cent of the vote in 1999 before it went into irreversible decline.[3] Perhaps more noteworthy is the case of the radical right-wing Popular Orthodox Rally (LAOS), which was founded in 2000 by George Karatzaferis, a former ND deputy. In typical populist fashion, Karatzaferis invested in standard themes, such as anti-Americanism, anti-semitism, and various conspiracy theories, much like in the manner of Le Pen's *Front National*, with which LAOS had established close links. In a speech at his party's first convention in 2002, he elaborated on the distinction between people and elites in the following way:

> On the one side it is we, with our souls, with our hearts dedicated to Power; with our lungs with which we breathe, dedicated to the grandeur of ancient Greece. And on the other side it is all the others – those who yield, who compromise, who get sold; those who, for a pat on the back from the Americans, sell off the Greeks' [true] ideals, prospects, dreams, and visions.   (quoted in Tsiras 2012: 357)

Regarding its own concept of 'the people', LAOS employed the ethnic and religious identity of the Orthodox Christian Greek, alluding to historical themes ranging from ancient Greece to recent wars against Turkey. And, like most populists, Karatzaferis also stressed the direct link between party and people: 'We originate from you. We fight like you [...] We are one with you. You are one with us' (*ibid.*: 375). But in this version of populism, 'the people' identify with the nation: 'Societies move forward – they do not retreat; they do not bend. They must move forward as an indivisible force: one People, one Nation – without divisions and abstractions' (*ibid.*: 412).

Although at the time both DIKKI and LAOS remained small and politically insignificant, those parties were a portent of the new populist forces that were to

---

3.   DIKKI lingers on to this day as a component of SYRIZA.

rise during the Great Recession. Irrespective of their different brands of populism, both were based on the idea of 'the people' and echoed themes that had already been developed by PASOK and ND, and which, as we are going to see next, would be reiterated by the new populist forces to emerge during the Great Recession.

Act IV. Populism in the wake of crisis, 2009–12: Revolt of 'the people'

After our brief analysis in Acts I–III of the evolution of populism in the Greek political system until the Great Recession, and having already identified its main agents as well as discursive and symbolic tenets, we are now ready to examine how the crisis influenced the populist framework that had been erected until then.

When the global financial and economic downturn hit Europe in 2008, Greece still seemed to enjoy relative political stability and, according to official statistics, even some economic fitness. And, despite a bout of intense social unrest between December 2008 and January 2009,[4] the old populist behemoths of PASOK and ND could still control together about 80 per cent of the national vote. In October 2009, PASOK's leader George Papandreou, son of the party founder, won by a landslide after a bitter campaign dominated by his slogan 'The money exists; it is only that [the ND government] prefers to give it to the few and powerful'. After that, everything in Greece went downhill. In November, as the European Commission had started an investigation over the reliability of Greek statistical figures, the state's new Minister of Finance publicly revealed that the books had been 'cooked' by the ND administration and deficit actually stood as high as 12.7 per cent of GDP (Eurostat later updated this figure to 15.7 per cent). In early December, Fitch downgraded Greek debt. The risk premium of Greek bonds soared to more than 500 basis points over the German ten-year bund, and the country was effectively locked out of the global financial markets. In May 2010, the Greek government signed with the foreign creditors of the Troika (EU, ECB and the IMF) its first bailout agreement for 110 billion euros in exchange for strict austerity measures. The 'Greek crisis' was making headlines across the globe.

The economic crisis evolved into a full-fledged social and political crisis once it became evident that the state coffers were empty and that governments could no longer serve society. The majority of voters, having resisted partial reforms in the past, were anything but prepared to bear the weight of the more general and more onerous reforms now demanded by the Troika. Indignant and guided by already dyed-in-the-wool biased beliefs, various social groups began manifesting their opposition to the austerity bills, withdrawing their loyalty to the government, and, above all, severing their allegiance with the old populist democratic system. During the period beginning with the first bailout (May 2010) and ending with the general elections of June 2012, Greece experienced mass social unrest that

---

4. In December 2008 an insurrection against the state was prompted by the shooting of a teenager student by a policeman and featured riots that soon spread throughout most Greek cities, with massive participation and unprecedented violence.

involved strikes, demonstrations, sit-ins, arson attacks against public buildings and widespread destruction of private properties, verbal and physical attacks against MPs and parliament, and terrorist attacks, many of which were directed towards immigrants. The radicalisation of the Greek electorate culminated with the advent of the Greek *indignados* who, for many weeks during the tumultuous summer of 2011, filled the country's city squares.[5] The element that united the revolting society was a common desire to punish both the old government parties and political class for having let them down and, by means of newly emergent populist forces, reclaim the sovereignty of 'the people'.

Meanwhile, under the combined pressure of social protest and his European peers, but also due to his own inability to provide solutions, Prime Minister Papandreou resigned in November 2011, thus allowing the formation of a caretaker coalition government headed by technocrat economist Lukas Papademos, consisting of the two mainstream parties, PASOK and ND, and the smaller rightist populist LAOS. The new government would ratify 80 per cent of privately held debt, as well as a new loan agreement of 130 billion euros. It was not enough. Amid rumours of an imminent default and the exit of Greece from the euro a real probability, Greeks hastened to withdraw their life savings, either to send them over to foreign banks or to keep them safe 'under the mattress' in the hope of better days. A huge bank run had already unfolded since 2010, forcing the Greek central bank to fly more than five billion euros in new bills into the country from the central banks of Italy and Austria, in order to cover outstanding demand (Bank of Greece 2014: 177). Greek banks effectively went bust in early 2012, once the haircut on their sovereign bonds took place and their books lost most of their value.

The Greek crisis was the most severe in Europe in both economic and political terms. From the general election in crisis-free 2007 to the contest of nearing-crisis 2009 elections and from there to the dramatic election in crisis-thick 2012, all indicators had worsened (*see* Figure 11.1). Annual growth rates began declining sharply in 2008 and since then have remained negative. In fact, between 2008 and 2013 Greece lost more than 25 per cent of its GDP. Unemployment rose from about 8 per cent in 2007 to a stunning 25 per cent by the third quarter of 2012 with increasing tendency. Gross public debt skyrocketed from 107.4 per cent of GDP in 2007 to 156.9 per cent of GDP in 2012. Political indicators were no less dispiriting. The Greeks' satisfaction with democracy dived from an already gloomy 46 per cent in 2007 to a menacing 14 per cent in 2012 – the lowest in Europe. Distrust in parliament increased during the same period from 45 per cent to 86 per cent and distrust in government increased from 59 per cent to no less than 91 per cent. Within this picture, the two elections of May and June 2012 election were the

---

5. It is worth noting that the initial reaction of ND to the crisis of legitimation that followed the first bailout programme in early 2010 was a hands-on critique of it as a 'mistake' and a 'wrong approach' that would not achieve growth. Using typical populist language, ND leader Antonis Samaras invested in polarisation, accused the PASOK government of political timidity against its creditors, and demanded immediate elections and a renegotiation of the loan agreement. For those tactics, there was a high price that ND would soon pay.

Figure 11.1: The fortunes of electoral populism amid Greece's economic crisis

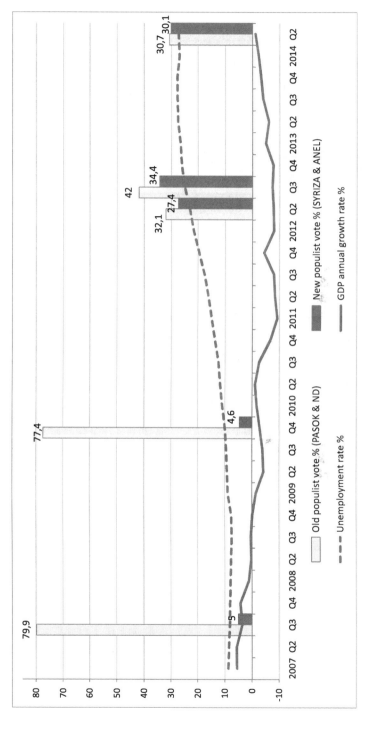

Sources: Eurostat (GDP growth); National Statistical Service of Greece (unemployment); Greek Ministry of Interior (electoral results).

Table 11.1: Greek national election results (2009 and 2012)

	7 October 2009		6 May 2012		17 June 2012	
	% of votes	N of seats	% of votes	N of seats	% of votes	N of seats
ND	33.5	91	18.9	108	29.7	129
PASOK	43.9	160	13.2	41	12.3	33
SYRIZA	4.6	13	16.8	52	26.9	71
ANEL	–	–	10.6	33	7.5	20
GD	–	–	7.0	21	6.9	18
DIMAR	–	–	6.1	19	6.3	17
KKE	7.5	21	8.5	26	4.5	12
LAOS	5.6	15	2.9	–	1.6	–
Others	4.9	0	16.0	0	4.3	0
Total	100	300	100	300	100	300

Source: Greek Ministry of Interior.

most volatile in Europe's postwar electoral history (*see* Figure 1.4 in this volume's introductory chapter). They had important political consequences, as well.

First and foremost, the elections of 2012 caused the collapse of the country's time-honored two-party system (Pappas 2003) (*see* Table 11.1). By the second of those contests (June 2012), formerly formidable PASOK plummeted more than 30 per cent compared to 2009, now standing at a paltry 12.3 per cent, having lost more than 2.25 million voters. ND scored below 30 per cent, having at least recovered from a shameful 18.9 per cent in May, its worst performance ever. ND had invested in the polarisation of the electoral constituency in the heydays of the *indignados* in order to win over the disgruntled PASOK voters, fuelling the anti-bailout zeitgeist, only to perform a U-turn in face of imminent financial disaster, and support the technocratic Papademos cabinet. The constant pressure that the party leader, Antonis Samaras, had to endure from his peers in the European People's Party towards supporting a coalition government seems to have been crucial to persuade him to perform this U-turn. However, ND's 'betrayed' constituents did not follow along, turning their backs on their party in search of something more radical.

Two new populist parties, one on the left the other on the right, emerged particularly strong as a consequence.[6] On the left, the new champion of populism

---

6.   Besides the populist parties of SYRIZA and ANEL, which are the main focus of this chapter, the other great winner during the crisis in Greece was the neo-Nazi Golden Dawn (GD). This party also made wide use of several populist themes that resonated with the constituency of 'the people' but, unlike its other populist competitors, it is openly *not* democratic. In consequence, and in contrast to populist parties that are distinct species of the democratic-party genus, GD belongs to an altogether different genus – that of the nondemocratic parties. This is not an innocent remark. It urgently calls for setting more clear boundaries for the concept of populism, thus allowing distinguishing it, not only against non-populism, but also against nondemocratic populism.

was the coalition of the Radical Left (SYRIZA), a merger of a dozen organisations ranging from the radical-reformist to the communist left, under the leadership of young Alexis Tsipras. Support for SYRIZA, which had first appeared in this configuration just before the national elections of 2004, when it garnered a paltry 3.3 per cent of the vote, now, having won the lion's share of the populist constituency that used to side with PASOK, jumped to almost 27 per cent, making it the major opposition force. According to one source (Metron Analysis 2012), from the one million of its May 2012 voters, an impressive 39 per cent originated from PASOK, 12 per cent came over from ND, and 26 per cent from other sources. On the right, the Independent Greeks (ANEL), led by Panos Kammenos, a recent defector from ND, rose as another potent representative of new populism. With 7.5 per cent of votes in June 2012, somewhat lower than the 10.6 per cent his party had gathered in May, and with fiery speeches in the parliament that became viral on YouTube, Kammenos retained a strong grip on that part of the former ND conservative electorate that did not drift so far to the right as to land in the ranks of the neo-Nazi Golden Dawn. According to the exit polls of the May election, 15 per cent of former ND voters chose to cast their ballot for ANEL, with the party being overrepresented among young voters, women, and private sector wage earners (Metron Analysis 2012).

What was moreover remarkable about the 2012 elections in Greece was the fact that, with the exception of the Democratic Left (DIMAR), a moderate social-democratic force sitting uneasily between PASOK and SYRIZA, no self-professing liberal party (as had been the Democratic Alliance; Creation Again; Action; and the Green Ecologists) succeeded to enter parliament. As in the pre-crisis past, populism still trumped liberalism.

In sum, during a long political crisis centred upon the failure of the traditional Greek political class to deliver as in the past, a sizeable part of 'the people' decided to sever their old political attachments and became free-floating voters. And while the former paragons of populism were now forced by the Troika to reluctantly turn reformist, strengthen liberal institutions, and pursue further European integration, a new breed of radical populists emerged, forcefully represented by SYRIZA on the left and ANEL on the right, both standing firmly for a large, protecting and over-spending state, as well as the distancing from the EU and growing nationalism. In the next section, we examine the populist discourse articulated by these two parties, which to a large extent explains their continuing electoral success, as verified by more recent results of the May 2014 elections for the European parliament (*see* Figure 11.1).

Act V: Populist discourse during crisis: 'The peoples' turnabout

Why did the new populist parties, whether on the left or on the right, become so successful during the Great Recession at the expense of both the old populists, who were now forced to turn into reluctant reformers, and a host of purely liberal parties, which in the 2012 elections invariably failed to pass the electoral threshold and enter parliament? The answer, as we shall try to show, lies in the adroit use of old themes and the exploitation of biased beliefs that were first developed in the 1970s, became hegemonic in the 1980s, and eventually became diffuse in Greece's party and political systems. We begin with the rightist ANEL and then move on to leftist SYRIZA.

The electoral success of ANEL was a severe defeat for ND, driving another nail in the coffin of the two-party system. Panos Kammenos skillfully managed to produce a populist party from scratch and present himself as an outsider even though he had been serving as a loyal MP of ND since 1993. Obviously, Kammenos rode upon the populist anti-bailout wave that was partly produced by Samaras's own actions in the early days of the crisis, yet, in order to see how populist tactics enabled his spectacular emergence into the political scene, we need to analyse his discourse.

ANEL is a typical case of a populist radical right-wing party (Mudde 2007), which, however, far from being a voice of moderation, is not characterised by extremist violent tendencies. The people are constructed mainly in ethnic terms, a language familiar to the average conservative right-wing voter, while at the same time racist oratory is avoided, and Golden Dawn is considered a purely fascist party. Apart from the ethnic definition of the people, ANEL stresses other traditional themes of the conservative right agenda, such as the role of the family and Greek Orthodox religion. On the organisational side, Kammenos never misses a chance to claim that ANEL is a movement, rather than a party, born from within the popular mobilisations of 2011 and organised via Facebook and Twitter. Yet, the party remains strongly personalistic. ANEL's leader employs a rhetoric which is broadly based on two mail pillars: anticorruption, and the conspiracy of the New World Order. As an MP of ND, he had always been famous for conducting research and producing documents that allegedly pointed to conspiracies or severe cases of mishandling of public finances, and had a habit of appearing in court to either defend himself in litigations against his person, or to accuse others as sycophants. With the onset of the crisis, this aggressive rhetoric became highly resonant with the public, since it provided an explanatory narrative for the troubles of the country, produced as they were by a small minority of corrupt elites who burdened the country with excessive debt and enslaved the people.

While corruption is a recurrent theme, evidence of a purported decades-old sinister pact among members of the political caste, Kammenos manages to link this theme with the onset of the Troika and the current financial toils of the country. He holds that foreign powers and their domestic lackeys artificially induced the crisis by bringing Greece to her knees and take advantage of her riches. 'The story of the introduction of our country into the Stability Mechanism, the memorandums, and the surrender of national sovereignty', he further explains, 'is a rigged game, set up by specific bankers in order to acquire profit' (Kammenos 2014). According to Kammenos, Prime Minister Papandreou, acting as a conscious broker for international banking interests, signed Greece into the bailouts while there was no real need for such an action; the deficit figures had after all been mischievously bloated by his cabinet upon assuming power.

For ANEL, behind all the toiling and suffering of the Greek people lie the forces of the New World Order and their scheme for global domination. Even though the members of this evil network are not always named, all the governing coalitions after 2011 are accused of being collaborators. This plot has three stages: first, to deprive Greeks from their private property, then to do the same with public property, and finally, to undermine and disband the armed forces, thus dissolving the Greek state into a European federation which acknowledges no nations, and no flags, all under German rule. Since current rulers are nothing but collaborators in this scheme, Kammenos declares the government as a product of German occupation, a mere 'regime', refusing to acknowledge its democratic legitimacy. This modern occupation is termed 'the 4th Reich', a continuation and a reminiscence of the Nazi assault and subsequent occupation of Greece during the Second World War, a legacy which still rings strongly in the collective consciousness of contemporary Greeks. 'We are not dealing with a democratic process', he claimed right before the 2012 election, 'we are dealing with occupation troops which violate democracy, which violate the Constitution, which violate the laws' (Kammenos 2012).

The discourse of the ANEL is typically anchored in the traditional themes of the populist radical right. The attack by foreign forces aims at the Greek nation and Christian Orthodox traditions, while immigrants are seen as a weapon in the hands of the New World Order. For this reason, the programme of the ANEL supplies a quota for immigrants, up to a maximum of 2.5 per cent of the total population. When it comes to economic issues, the picture is mixed: on the one hand, corporate taxes as low as 8 per cent, and VAT up to 10 per cent are favoured in order to kick-start the economy and focus on export-oriented growth. And yet, layoffs in the public sector are abhorred since a large protective state is considered as the indispensable provider of welfare and security to the Greek citizenry. Additionally, the maintenance of a strong, populous military mechanism is also a central component in the ANEL programme.

Turning from ANEL to SYRIZA, its populist counterpart on the political left, one cannot but be stricken by the essential similarity of the two parties' discourses. For instance, the populist themes of the 'Nazi occupation' and the '4th Reich' were anything but an exclusive ANEL trademark. Indeed, on the trail to the 2012 elections, many SYRIZA candidates, now lawmakers, chose to campaign along those lines.

SYRIZA has a long history in Greek politics, ranging back to a 1968 split in the Greek Communist Party. Its current brand, a blend of old communists and radical leftists, was mainly assembled during the days of the alter-globalisation mobilisation (Tsakatika and Eleftheriou 2013). SYRIZA's programmatic aim is 'twenty-first century socialism' (*à la* Chávez), a withdrawal from NATO, the socialisation of the means of production, direct democratic interventions, and participatory democracy. Their interpretation of reality is still based on the classical Marxist framework of class struggle, however, this monotonous prose has been significantly altered in the hands of its young leader, Alexis Tsipras. While until the crisis the main themes of the party were economic inequality, immigrant rights and ecological issues, all within an 'anti-neoliberal' framework, populist elements now chiefly populate its discourse (Stavrakakis and Katsambekis 2014).

As with ANEL, the rhetoric of SYRIZA is also couched in battle terms. The party identifies itself at the forefront of a struggle against the German order in Europe. There is also a messianic flavour inherent in this war. Tsipras alerts his comrades that it is their obligation to win; victory is a duty for the party, not an ambition. The citizens face only two options: either to side with SYRIZA, or to choose the reactionary neoliberal establishment of Mrs. Merkel and her domestic lackeys, the governing coalition. While SYRIZA also refers heavily to issues of corruption, they do not present the investigative fervor of Kammenos, preferring to talk more broadly about the 'corrupt establishment', and the *diaploki*, a graphic byword for interlocking interests between politicians and business agents.

In all, the populist conceptualisation of 'the people' in SYRIZA's discourse is very akin to that of early PASOK, except for a few quirks. A major difference is the lack of explicit nationalist overtones, since the party's origins in the radical, internationalist left, prevents it from putting forward such kind of images. 'The people' is not defined in ethnic terms; it is rather class-based, anti-capitalist values that provide the substrate upon which SYRIZA builds its brand of populism. Clearly, however, Tsipras actively tried to win over the 'underprivileged people' that Andreas Papandreou created and solidified. In his main speech in Athens, just before the first 2012 elections, he attacked PASOK on its own grounds, proclaiming that:

> PASOK nowadays has replaced the wide social coalition that used to support it for decades with a new one, one of wealth and oligarchy. With the few who become rich when the many become poor. Mr. Venizelos's party [PASOK] chose the few privileged, who increase their wealth and privileges through the Memorandum, and abandoned the many and underprivileged. (Tsipras 2012)

Tsipras does not indeed use the mantra of the 'underprivileged' without citing its creator, however, he clearly depicts the current PASOK leadership as traitors of their own roots, and himself us the rightful successor. For SYRIZA, the 'we' is constructed in terms of 'the Greece of the many', or 'the determined people'. On the other hand, the dark side has many faces: the enemies are exploiters of the people, 'an almighty authority of the triangle of sin, which has the corrupt bipartisan political system on its top corner, the bankers on the other, and the interweaving media on the third' (Tsipras 2012). This rotten political personnel and its patrons, be it Chancellor Merkel and her vision of 'Germanic Europe', or the 'state-fed bankers', see the government as a tool to pursue their own interests. According to party leader Tsipras, the 'pro-bailout bloc' is part of a capitalist financial establishment which has formed a sacred alliance to pursue its own ends.

In his attempt to encroach towards the right, Tsipras does not appeal solely to the left. He also appeals to the average conservative voters, who suffer because of austerity. He speaks to them in a condescending language:

[W]e are now on the same side of the river. Whatever held us apart until yesterday is a lot less than what today brings us together. For, as always in history, when the people are faced with the perils of hunger and poverty, they can only overcome in unity. (Tsipras 2012)

The main motto of SYRIZA since the 2012 elections is also straight out of the populist toolkit: 'It's either Them or Us' was all across billboards and stickers. 'Together we can overturn them', was the byline. 'SYRIZA is *you*' wrote another party poster in bold type, its background laden with a series of words one next to another, as a laundry list of who 'you' is: teacher, student, doctor, newly fired, unemployed, pensioner, farmer, etc. Yet another motto was 'They decided without us: we move on without them'. Clearly, SYRIZA heavily invested in populist discourse during the crisis; judging by its current performance, this change of course has proven to be more than valuable.

Conclusions

Unlike most other countries in Europe, the case of Greece with respect to the impact of the crisis on populist manifestations is quite unique due to the predominance of political populism in domestic politics long before the economic crisis. As has been shown, populism grew strong in opposition immediately after Greece's transition to democracy and, by the early 1980s, had established itself in power. It thereafter contaminated all major political forces, thus transforming Greece into a 'populist democracy' with specific characteristics. When the crisis hit, and the Greek state became insolvent, the old populist actors were forced to moderate their discourse and play by the tune of Greece's foreign creditors. Then, a sizeable part of the formerly solid populist constituency ('the people') abandoned their old party moorings and offered their vote (and hearts, and minds) to newly emergent populist actors. That being the case, the crisis served as a broad window of opportunity to new populist forces on both left and right, which emerged to claim the defecting populist voters. A kind of *dejá-vu* populism was then born, built upon an appropriate repackaging of the old populist toolkit and, especially, exploiting society's biased beliefs as they have become systematised during the long period of populist hegemony. At the moment, as fears about the future of contemporary Greek democracy seem to grow, no one can be certain about the next act in this country's still unfolding populist drama.

The Greek case provides ample confirmatory evidence for all the hypotheses put forward in the introduction to this volume, and, perhaps because of the enormity of the crises that have afflicted it, also suggests interesting new venues for future research. Greece's economic crisis was the deepest in Europe and, indeed, it facilitated the re-construction of new categories of 'the people' and their 'foes'. It greatly intensified populism-*qua*-discourse both in popular mobilisation and in the party system, and produced a brand new divide in Greek society between voters who understood the necessity of bold reformism at any cost and those who insisted being served by a spendthrift state. Populist discourse became particularly intense in Greece because the economic crisis was intimately coupled with a major crisis of political legitimacy, which was already underway when the Greek state went bankrupt. As the twin crisis unfolded, the anti-American zeitgeist of the first populist wave in the 1980s was substituted by strong anti-German feelings, keeping the original narrative of the small, recalcitrant and threatened nation intact. The established Greek political elite failed miserably to provide a sustainable future to the citizens of the country, and paid a heavy price for this failure. In this respect, Greece has revealed the interesting – and as yet not-theorised – phenomenon of ruling populists (the ND-PASOK coalition government) who, when compelled by an external enforcer (the Troika) to promote necessary reforms rather than falling back on old populist practice, lost most of their electoral constituency. Finally, the Greek case has revealed that populism may easily override traditional ideological boundaries. As shown by the cases of ANEL and SYRIZA, there seems to be an osmosis between right-wing and left-wing populisms, each of them bidding for the same electoral constituency, now freed from old allegiances. As Greece's populist drama still evolves, we witness a strong coalition potential between rightist and leftist populist forces – another empirically and theoretically significant lesson of Greece to the comparative study of populism. For the time being, however, Greece's populist drama is still unfolding and only time will tell if and how many more acts there will be before it ends.

PART IV

THE CENTRAL-EASTERN REGION

Chapter Twelve

The Economic Crisis in the Shadow of Political Crisis: The Rise of Party Populism in the Czech Republic

Vlastimil Havlík

For a long time, the Czech Republic experienced a relative lack of viable populist political parties; moreover, the country has also had a relatively high degree of stability in the party system. From the first half of the 1990s, the party system was composed of four major parties – the Civic Democratic Party (ODS) on the right side of the political spectrum, the Czech Social Democratic Party (ČSSD) and the medium-sized Communist Party of Bohemia and Moravia (KSČM) on the left, and a small Christian Democratic party (KDU-ČSL) in the centre. These four parties were supplemented by smaller formations of a predominantly liberal orientation. In 2010, however, the electoral support of the established parties started to become increasingly unstable, as a result of the surge of support for new parties including the right-centre TOP 09 and three populist challengers – Public Affairs (*Věci veřejné*, VV), ANO 2011 (Action of Dissatisfied Citizens, i.e. *Akce nespokojených občanů*, acronym ANO means 'yes' in Czech,) and Tomio Okamura's Dawn of Direct Democracy (*Úsvit přímé demokracie Tomia Okamury*, henceforth as 'The Dawn') (*see* Table 12.1).

The aim of this chapter is to analyse the character and development of the discourse of these newly successful populist parties during the time of the economic crisis. Our chief argument is that the rise of populist parties in the Czech Republic was due to a political crisis, rather than any economic crisis. We understand populism as a combination of the three main components, namely (1) people-centrism; (2) anti-elitism; (3) popular sovereignty and proposals to restore popular sovereignty. The results presented here are primarily based on a qualitative analysis of various data sources from the three successful recent populist parties. The data used for analysing these parties' populist appeal is comprised of three types of sources: (1) the parties' programmes for the 2010 and 2013 elections to the Chamber of Deputies; (2) materials (articles, interviews) from the parties' websites (www.veciverejne.cz, www.anobudelip.cz, www.hnutiusvit.cz) and their leaders' blogs; and (3) interviews with party representatives in national newspapers and on TV and radio, including their

Table 12.1: Allocation of seats in the Chamber of Deputies (1996–2013)

	1996	1998	2002	2006	2010	2013
ODS	68	63	58	81	53	16
ČSSD	61	74	70	74	56	50
KSČM	22	24	41	26	26	33
KDU-ČSL	18	20	31*	13	0	14
TOP 09					41	26
VV					24	
ANO						47
Dawn						14
Others	31	19	0	6	0	0
Total	200	200	200	200	200	200

Source: volby.cz.

participation in TV debates.[1] Moreover, for a quantitative assessment of the evolution of the intensity of populist discourse of Public Affairs before and after the party entered the government, the party's journal, *Věci veřejné* (*Public Affairs*) was used.[2]

This chapter is divided as follows: the first section focuses on a very short description of relevant populist parties prior to the eruption of the economic crisis in 2008. This is followed by an overview of effects of the economic crisis in the Czech Republic, and a section analysing the political crisis and the discourse of Czech populist parties.

Populist parties until 2008

The Czech Republic has not always been a country with successful populist parties (*see* Figure 12.1). The only exception was The Association for the Republic – Republican Party of Czechoslovakia (*Sdružení pro republiku – Republikánská strana Československa*, SPR-RSČ), which has been classified as a radical-right wing populist party (Hanley 2012; Mareš 2003; Mudde 2007). SPR-RSČ combined anti-communism and anti-establishment positions with xenophobia and even outright racism in its communication (Sládek 1992; Sládek

---

1. These materials were obtained from the Anopress database.

2. Similar analyses of ANO 2011 and The Dawn have not been carried out for two reasons. Firstly, there are no data available comparable to those that were used in case of VV's discourse analysis (neither ANO 2011, nor The Dawn publish their own journal). Secondly, even if a different data source had been used (e.g. posts on Facebook profiles of the two parties), the analysis would not have been able to prove any long term change in the discourse of the parties since this text was finalised less than a year after the 2013 general election (and less than nine months after ANO 2011 entered the Cabinet).

Figure 12.1:Combined electoral results of populist political parties*

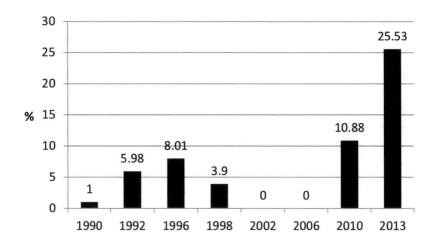

Source: http://www.volby.cz *1990–98: SPR – RSČ, 2010: VV. 2013: ANO + The Dawn.

1996; *see* also Mareš 2005). However, in 1998, the party failed to win enough votes to stay in parliament and despite several attempts to 'resuscitate' it, SPR-RSČ has not won enough votes to enter the Chamber of Deputies since then. For many years thereafter, populist parties in the Czech Republic were largely marginalised. However, changes could be seen in the elections in 2010, in which VV successfully entered the parliament, followed by the successes in 2013 by ANO and The Dawn. The increase in party populism took place in the context of the crisis in the economy but was – as will be shown – facilitated especially by the crisis on the political scene.

Economic crisis

The economic crisis certainly had an impact on the Czech Republic, but in comparison to other European nations as Greece, Ireland or Spain, these effects have been rather mild. The Czech Republic largely avoided the problems associated with the mortgage and housing bubble as well as its accompanying artificial boom in the construction industry (in contrast to Spain or Ireland), as well as the fact that even though the Czech budget deficit is relatively high, its overall debt is low in comparison to that of other European nations.

Even so, we should point out that mainly due to its high level of economic openness and its dependence exports, after several years of growth, the Czech economy slowed down markedly in 2008, and entered into quite a sharp recession in the fourth quarter of 2008. More detailed information on the economic situation is illustrated by selected macroeconomic indicators defined in Chapter One.

The economic situation at the end of 2008 brought about a significant decrease in GDP (*see* Figure 1.1, Chapter One). This was followed by sputtering short-term growth that nevertheless failed to reach pre-crisis levels, and once again collapsed. One immediate result of the GDP decrease was the increase in unemployment. Even if average quarterly unemployment figures were in fact somewhat lower in the aftermath of the crisis than before the crisis, it is important to emphasise the change in the trend of unemployment. While unemployment had followed a downward trend before the crisis, from a rather high rate of about 9 per cent in 2004, to 4 per cent in the first half of 2008, it increased steeply after 2008 and reached a peak at the beginning of 2010 (*see* Figure 1.2, Chapter One). The fall in GDP also resulted in a reduction in tax revenue (and as a consequence, an increase in the state budget deficit), which in turn led to a significant increase in the debt-to-GDP ratio (*see* Figure 1.3, Chapter One). The average level of debt to GDP has been considerably higher since the second half of 2008.

In sum, significant negative changes occurred across all three economic indicators after autumn 2008, and the Czech economy has not fully recovered in subsequent years. Up to the electoral campaign of 2013, the Czech Republic experienced a continuation of stagnant GDP growth, relatively high unemployment, and growing public debt. On the other hand, the impact of economic crisis did not reach the intensity experienced by some other European countries (for comparison *see* Chapter One).

All-in-all, economic issues became important topics during the election campaigns in 2010 and – to a lesser extent – in 2013. The parties of the right tended to focus on the need for austerity measures and warned against excessive debt, the parties of the left argued for solutions to the economic problems of the Czech Republic in the form of a more active role for the state and the support of investment (Eibl 2010, 2014; Gregor and Macková 2014). Nevertheless, as I will argue bellow, economic matters were not the only and not the most important issues of the elections in 2010 and 2013 in relation to the rise of populist parties.

The rise of populist parties after 2008 – The result of a serious political crisis

What is most important to understanding when considering the rise of the populist parties in the Czech Republic, is that it took place in the context of a deepening political crisis, the roots of which can be traced back to the times before the economic crisis. The core element of this crisis was the widespread loss of trust in political institutions and political parties. The following three indicators of political crisis, defined in the theoretical portion of this book, demonstrate this souring of attitudes towards political subjects (*see* Figure 1.4, Chapter One).

The years between 2007 and 2012 witnessed a substantial drop in the satisfaction of citizens with the functioning of democracy in the Czech Republic (the share of satisfied citizens dropped from one half to less than one-third), as well as trust in the Chamber of Deputies (which fell from 17 per cent to barely 10 per cent in the year 2012 – Kunštát 2012). Over the same period, from 2006 to 2010, electoral volatility nearly doubled. Since then it has levelled off and was somewhat lower in 2013 (Havlík 2014). The political crisis thus was embodied in a long and gradual decline in satisfaction with politics and political institutions that began more than a year (Linek 2010) before any economic decline, and indeed in a time of economic prosperity. In relation to the timing of the rise of the populist parties, it is necessary to emphasise a sharp decline of the political trust in the period after the 2006 general election, which was related to the complicated process of government formation followed by weakness and instability of the government, and extensive (and often well-founded) allegations of corruption (Havlík 2011).

After the 2006 general election, a coalition government headed by Mirek Topolánek (ODS) finally took office a full seven months (!) after the elections which ended with a deadlock between the left and the right. The government could only be formed thanks to the support of two MPs from ČSSD, who for unclear reasons changed sides and chose to support the government of their long-time ideological and political rivals (Foltýn and Havlík 2006). While in previous years public satisfaction with the political situation and trust in political institutions increased after elections (Linek 2010)[3], in 2006, the immediate reaction after the elections led to record lows in both indicators and did not return to a higher number before the 2010 election. According to the data provided by the Centre for Public Opinion Research, just after the 2006 elections, in the middle of the unsuccessful talks on the formation of the new government, the satisfaction with the political situation dropped from 17 per cent in May 2006 to 9 per cent in October 2006. Similarly, trust the Chamber of Deputies halved from 44 per cent to 21 per cent (Čadová 2006).

The weak position of the government *vis-à-vis* the Chamber of Deputies was supplemented by friction among the coalition parties, which led to the fall of the government in spring 2009 (Havlík 2011), contributing significantly to the crisis of trust in political institutions and in politics in general. The political parties in the Chamber agreed to the formation of a caretaker government composed of non-partisans (but nominated by ČSSD, ODS and SZ), as well as announcing early elections (Hloušek and Kopeček 2012). However, due to the alleged unconstitutionality of the move,[4] the Czech Constitutional

---

3. The only exception was the drop of political trust after the 1996 general election (Linek 2010). However, the context and consequences were very different in comparison to the period after the 2006 election. The Czech Republic was experiencing a severe economic crisis and dissatisfaction with the political situation targeted mainly at the centre-right government which had been in office since the beginning of the 1990s. Consequently, the main winner of the 1998 election was not the populist SPR-RSČ (on the contrary, the party lost its parliamentary representation that year) but the Czech Social Democratic Party presenting itself as a leftist alternative to the previous right-centre governments.

4. Dissolution of the Chamber of Deputies was quite difficult at that time. To make the process faster and following the procedure applied in 1998, the Chamber of Deputies passed a special constitutional act which was supposed to shorten the term and call for early elections.

Court overruled the Chamber's call for early elections. This led to a *de facto* extension of the caretaker government's term (up to thirteen months), which continued in spite of its low level of legitimacy and no clear support in the Chamber of Deputies (Balík 2010). The paradoxical position of MPs after the decision of the Constitutional Court was expressed by Petr Fiala: 'the political representation already decided to leave voluntarily but they were forced to stay' (Fiala 2010).

The lack of public support for the Chamber of Deputies (and dissatisfaction with the political situation in general) was also fuelled by media suspicion of corruption by various members of the government (as well as politicians from the opposition) increasingly reported in the media. Systematic links between big business and politics increasingly came into the open right after the 2006 election. Klíma (2013) has described the symbiosis between political parties on one hand, and 'well-connected' private businesses on the other, and defined 'clientelist parties' as a best way of capturing the functioning of the established parties in the Czech Republic. Paradoxically, it was Mirek Topolánek, the Prime Minister and chairman of ODS, who introduced the term '*kmotr*' (godfather) describing people (usually regional businessmen or politicians) considered responsible for corruption, especially in public tenders. The term started to be widely used in media and the fact that the chairman of the biggest party had used it for describing the situation in his own party contributed significantly to public allegations of the established parties of being corrupt. In other words, even though the level of political trust in the Czech Republic was comparatively low at least since the second half of the 1990s, the events in the period after the 2006 election including the weak government, the postponed elections and corruption allegations led to a further and, more importantly, substantial drop of political trust to unprecedented low numbers.

The results of the 2010 elections demonstrated continued voter frustration with the established parties as is illustrated by the high level of electoral volatility (Havlík 2014). In particular, the two longtime anchors of the Czech right and the Czech left, ODS and ČSSD respectively, bore the brunt of the voters' anger. In 2006, the two parties had received two-thirds of all votes. By 2010, their combined share of votes barely amounted to 40 per cent (Haughton *et al.* 2011). Conversely, Public Affairs (VV) won enough votes to enter the Chamber, running primarily on a platform of criticising the established political parties and fight with corruption.

Hunting the 'political dinosaurs' – The discourse of the Public Affairs Party

VV was established in 2001 as a local civic association in Prague focused on issues concerning local city politics. In June 2009, the party announced that it would compete in the early election of the Chamber of Deputies with Radek John, a popular former writer and investigative journalist, as leader of the party's election campaign. However, the real chairman of the party was the well-connected businessman Vít Bárta, whose corruption allegation would later prove to be disastrous for the party

(Hloušek 2012; Kmenta 2011). In the end, the party enjoyed relative success in the election, winning 10.9 per cent of the vote and twenty-four seats in the Chamber, eventually becoming a coalition partner in the centre-right government.

The party's election campaign was based on a combination of a strong anti-establishment appeal, calls for more direct democracy (including within the VV party itself), and anti-corruption slogans, but without targeting any particular social group (Matušková 2010). Its main election slogan called for 'the end of the political dinosaurs'. Chairman John defined such a dinosaur as:

[...] someone who has been in politics for more than ten years, can't do anything other than politics, understands it as his trade and starts to make deals [...] It's someone who's lost touch with reality and ceases to be useful.   (Právo 2009)

'Dinosaurs' were also a central theme of one of the party's TV spots, in which John drew a dinosaur, while the accompanying voice explained how the 'dinosaurs' were responsible for the deteriorating state of affairs, both in the economy and elsewhere: 'They're everywhere. They invade the space of every one of us. Corruption. National debts. Parasitism. Low-quality education. Shameful pensions. The dinosaurs of years past' (VV 2010b).

In this way, VV lumped all of the established parties together, their representatives were seen as a homogeneous entity of incompetent politicians responsible for the decline of the Czech Republic. One key element was VV's rallying of voters with anti-establishment demands to fight corruption. VV dedicated more space in its party platform to the topic of fighting corruption than any other party that received seats in the Chamber. Above all, politicians of the established parties were said to be guilty of abusing their positions when dealing with public tenders:

And then there is all this palm-greasing around, for the Gripens [fighter jets], for the Pandurs [armored personnel carriers]. And the army contracts for other weapons, overpriced over the last three years to the tune of fourteen billion [...] So we've lost an enormous amount of money here and it's the parliamentary parties who are to blame. Let the gentlemen work out which one of them is specifically responsible for this.   (Frekvence 1 2010)

Members of VV were particularly critical of the two large parties, who were accused of being guilty of corruption as well as of incompetence when governing the country, and were unable to change. As one party vice-chairman, Vít Bárta, stated:

The large parties are either irredeemable or could be reformed only with difficulty. A democracy of robber barons has taken upper hand within their internal functioning. [The robber barons] hold some regions of the country under their control and influence the functioning of several political parties at the same time.   (Mladá fronta Dnes, 7 May 2010)

VV rejected any possible participation with 'political dinosaurs' in the government (Česká televisation 2010a). Nevertheless, in light of the election results, hoping to participate in the formation of the new government and after the government was formed in particular, VV softened its expressions concerning the established parties, and claimed that it was the voters who had the decisive say over who is (and who is not) a 'political dinosaur' (Český rozhlas 2010b). In other words, VV sought to leave the door open for cooperation with parliamentary political parties (*see* next section).

VV's representatives regularly presented the decision-making of political parties as being against the voters' will. As a consequence of the emphasis on people-centrism in the party's discourse, VV proposed greater emphasis on direct democracy and a greater number of direct elections as its chief recipe to remedy the allegedly bleak state of Czech politics. The party proposed a law on general referenda, and argued that the pool of directly elected public offices should include the president, regional governors, and mayors (VV 2010a: 5). The emphasis put on direct democracy is apparent from the very first sentence of the party's programme for the 2010 election of the Chamber of Deputies: 'The Public Affairs political party intends to transform the present political (non-) culture through a greater involvement of citizens in decision-making [...]' (VV 2010a: 5).

The party called itself a 'party of direct democracy', and the chairman – Radek John – described the principles of direct democracy as a 'common-sense model' (Český rozhlas 2009b). Moreover, the party sought to differentiate itself from others in terms of intra-party governance: 'We are for the direct election of party chairmen, as this will clean things up [...] Let people decide and let's make this grow from the bottom up. People are not stupid' (Prima TV 2009).

Thereafter, principles of direct democracy were implemented concerning decision-making within VV itself. In addition to its members, the party also recognised its registered supporters, the so-called *Véčkaři* (the 'Vs'), who could register on the party's website. Party regulations adopted in June 2009 granted a key position to these supporters, in terms of deciding on party leadership and its election candidates (VV 2009b). Registered supporters could also decide, by means of intra-party referenda, on the party's stance on selected issues. Referring to the results of certain referenda within his party, John opined: 'It seems to me that voters are brilliant and this is how I imagine a cultivated nation. In my view they're more cultured than MPs' (VV 2009a).

To a large degree, populist appeals functioned as a substitute for any 'full ideology' in the party's profile. Although the party initially presented itself as a centre-right challenger to the established political parties, the rhetoric related to its own ideological orientation changed and representatives of the party either attempted to position the party in the 'centre' or resisted positioning the party on the left-right spectrum. As John said: '...[T]he ideology is totally empty. The right-left perception is so last century. And we say: we are a centrist party with clever solutions' (Česká televisation 2010). 'We don't want to move left or right, we want to move forward' (Pokorný 2010).

Vít Bárta spoke in similar terms and connected the refusal to view politics in terms of the left and right with the party's anti-establishment appeal: 'The classic sign of a political dinosaur is a strict right-left view of society [...] There is also a centrist ideology, the ideology of correct solutions. That's what I believe in' (Mladá fronta Dnes, 7 May 2010).

Instead of clear ideological arguments, party representatives emphasised common sense as the leading principle behind the party's programme. John repeatedly described a vote for the party's candidates to the Chamber of Deputies as 'votes for common sense' (Frekvence 1 2010). He rejected the idea that his party's promotion of direct democracy was somehow leftist; instead he described direct democracy as 'centrist common sense' (Český rozhlas 2009b).

While the dominant themes of VV's political communication concerned the political crisis, VV also naturally discussed the economic crisis. In its programme and in statements by party officials it warned of the Czech Republic's rising debt, and made capping it a priority (Česká televisation 2010; Instinkt 2010; VV 2009a). Indeed, capping the debt was even a condition for VV's potential participation in a coalition government (Český rozhlas 2010a). The VV repeatedly demanded austerity measures, and pointed to the alleged threat of state bankruptcy:

[W]e demand an end to the money squandering. During the good times, when there was money, unfortunately nothing was set aside; and at this moment every citizen of the Czech Republic has a debt of 108,000 crowns [...] Each one of our grandchildren will eventually owe 500,000 crowns.   (Český rozhlas 2009b)

Nevertheless, economic topics were not vital components of party communication; of all parties that entered the Chamber of Deputies, VV dedicated the least space of its party platform to economic questions (Eibl 2010). Even more importantly, the VV's references to the economic crisis were subordinated to anti-establishment rhetoric, in which the party linked the economic crisis and rising public debt to the issue of corruption. By curtailing corruption in public tenders, savings could be made in the budget, the party argued. As Radek John said:

At this moment we need to solve a very practical issue, namely the fact that there's an awful lot of stealing going on here; a third of it is stolen money, a third of the state budget.   (Český rozhlas 2009a)

As such, the economic crisis was not a theme around which the discourse of VV consolidated. While economic topics indeed were occasionally present, they chiefly were relegated to a secondary role and were often utilised in the context of VV's anti-establishment demands and in relation to the need to battle corruption.

The populist discourse of the party underwent significant changes after the party had entered government. In order to demonstrate this trend quantitatively, the content of the journal *Věci veřejné*, which was published by the party between January 2009 and February 2012, was analysed. Each article published in the journal (including the main headline on the cover page) were included in the analysis (N = 287). Based on a qualitative interpretative assessment, three elements of populism (people centrism, referring to representation of the people as homogeneous entity and/or supremacy of the people; anti-establishment appeal as denigration of political elites in general; and calls for the strengthening of popular sovereignty) were observed in the articles and their presence coded as '1'. Therefore, each article could reach a maximum value of '3' if all three elements were identified in the text, and a value of '0' in case the article was 'populism-free'. In order to assess the development of the role of populism in the discourse of the party over the time, we analysed the level of populism in each issue of the journal (N = 20) – *see* Figure 12.2.

The two peaks indicating the highest levels of populism refer to the period preceding the planned (and then cancelled) early election in 2009 and the election which actually took place in May 2010. The populist rhetoric of the party almost disappeared from the VV discourse after it had entered the government in July 2010. This difference in the intensity of populism rhetoric (almost five times lower while in office) is clearly demonstrated in Table 12.2. The steepest decline could be indentified in the anti-establishment component of the discourse. Therefore, the hypothesis on decline of populism in relation to government participation set in the theoretical chapter of the book can be verified in the case of VV.

Figure 12.2: Overall level of populism in the discourse of VV

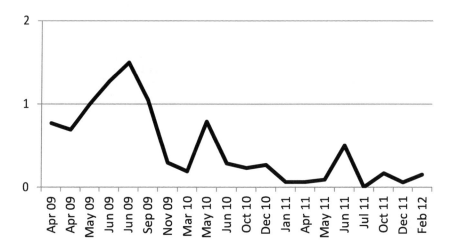

Table 12.2: Populist appeals in the discourse of the VV before and after entering the government (N = 287)

	Pre-government period	In office
Overall	0.72	0.15
People-centrism	0.15	0.04
Anti-establishment appeal	0.35	0.04
Sovereignty of the people	0.22	0.08

Political crisis – Version 2.0

The period after the 2010 election failed to bring about a significant shift in the perception of politics by the public. The starting position of the Nečas centre-right government was better (118 deputies out of 200) than that of the Topolánek government. However, the government was seriously weakened by ongoing conflicts within the governing coalition (Hloušek 2012), and by several corruption scandals.

Trust in politics slumped notably after an internal VV document was made public which clearly indicated that the party's election campaign against corruption was chiefly designed as a way to increase business opportunities for vice-chairman Bárta's private security firms through public procurement. Moreover, Bárta allegedly paid off deputies from his own party for their allegiance (Kmenta 2011). Subsequent speculation about a suspected intra-party putsch of 'compromised' VV deputies collaborating with ODS and TOP 09 (the other parties in the government) led to a split in the party, with some members of VV leaving the government altogether. In addition, internal ODS conflicts about party policy and whether or not the government was sufficiently 'on the right' meant that eventually the government as a whole found itself without a secure majority in the Chamber of Deputies (Hloušek 2012).

The government's weakened position was seen most clearly in a vote on changing the tax code, which for the first time failed to pass because of opposition by 'rebels' from the ODS. Before a repeat of the vote two months later the 'rebels' resigned their seats and were replaced by more loyal party colleagues. Later, it came out that the resigning deputies would be nominated for the board of directors of state-run companies. This became one of the reasons for a police raid on the Office of the Government in spring 2013, and, for charging Prime Minister Nečas and the rebel deputies with corruption. The Prime Minister was forced to resign under pressure, which brought down the entire government. The political crisis was prolonged by President Miloš Zeman, who refused to appoint a representative of ODS as the new prime minister, even though the new government had the declared support of a majority in the Chamber of Deputies. Instead, the President appointed Jiří Rusnok, a former minister of finance from his government in the early 2000s, as Prime Minister. However, the government did not win a vote of confidence. As a consequence, the Chamber of Deputies voted to dissolve itself. Elections were then scheduled for the end of October 2013, which meant the longest period in the Czech history with a cabinet without a clear legitimacy, as well as the longest period with a dissolved parliament.

Even more often than during the previous election term, the media reported about various alleged corruption scandals involving almost all the parliamentary parties. Among the most visible, one can mention so-called ProMoPro affair (overpriced purchase of various equipment used during the Czech presidency over the EU), purchase of CASA airplanes for the Czech army, non-transparent public tenders at the Ministry for Environment or several instances of misappropriation of the money from EU operational programmes at the regional level (one of the MPs was even arrested for alleged bribery). As in 2006–10, repeated corruption scandals and government instability led to another drop of trust in the parliament and satisfaction with the political situation fell to another historical low. In the weeks after a part of VV had left the government, average satisfaction with the political situation collapsed to just 5 per cent of the population, while trust in the Chamber of Deputies crumbled to 12 per cent (Kunštát 2012; Kunštát 2013b). General satisfaction with political situation was further weakened by a controversial amnesty decision made by the President Václav Klaus in January 2013 after it had been revealed that several people imprisoned for serious financial crimes and corruption (only 3 per cent were satisfied with the political situation in January 2013, while trust in the President dropped drastically from 53 per cent in December 2012 to 26 per cent in January 2013 – Kunštát 2013a).

Consequently, with a deepening of the crisis of political trust before the 2013 general elections conditions for the rise of populist parties were even more favorable than three years earlier. As a result, two populist parties recorded impressive successes in the elections.

'We're not like the politicians – we work!' – The discourse of ANO 2011

In November 2011, a billionaire of Slovak origin and the owner of the biggest agro-chemical company in the Czech Republic, Andrej Babiš, released a document entitled 'Action of Dissatisfied Citizens', in which he criticised the existing situation in Czech politics and the politicians, calling on citizens to take part in an initiative towards 'a more just society, and a functional state with the rule of law' (ANO 2011). The initiative became the basis for ANO 2011, which rolled out a very intensive election campaign before the 2013 election and finished with 18.65 per cent of the vote and forty-seven out of 200 seats. ANO eventually became part of the new government alongside ČSSD and KDU-ČSL.

The discourse of the party combined a very strong anti-establishment appeal but differed to some extent from the discourse VV had applied before the 2010 election. The cornerstone of ANO's anti-establishment rhetoric was a contrast constructed between practices typical for running companies – symbolised by the successful businessman Andrej Babiš – and a supposedly dysfunctional, spendthrift, and corruption-ridden state (run by the current set of politicians):

My name is Andrej Babiš. In the Czech Republic I employ thousands of people in my companies, I pay hundreds of millions of crowns in taxes, and I'm angry, just like you. I'm angry because since the revolution, politicians of our country not only have failed to lead, but they have watched over the embezzlement of the country. I'm angry that we live in a dysfunctional state.   (ANO 2011)

None of the current parties, none of the politicians who stated that they would solve the most burning problems facing the Czech Republic have been successful. We're voting for the same people who because of their own interests only make promises and lie […]. Isn't it about time that someone goes into Czech politics whom you can trust? Isn't it time that people enter politics who have some experience behind them and know what real work looks like? Isn't it time that we all have it a little better?   (ANO 2013a)

Creating an efficient, private-sector style approach as the main solution for politics and public administration was reflected in the slogan 'I will run the state like a business', which ANO took into the election campaign. The election slogan, 'We're not like the politicians – we work!' also clearly illustrates the dichotomy constructed in the ANO discourse between the 'incompetent' politicians of the established parties and the representatives of ANO (Babiš in particular), successful in 'real' life. As an alternative to the politics of intrigue and pointless conflict, ANO promised to 'run the state simply, effectively – using common sense' (ANO 2012a). The movement spoke of the 'corrupt system of political parties' (ANO 2013b), which it framed by economic argumentation and set against Babiš's own ability and experience managing a large corporation. ANO presented politicians and politics, as compared to the 'real world', as something negative, a realm serving only the personal interests of politicians and the interest groups connected to them: 'Politicians do not work to make things better for everybody, but for their own hunger for power, and the interests of the influential groups that placed them into office and at the top of their candidate lists' (ANO 2013b).

What is important is that the movement's anti-establishment appeal was not focused on one or more specific parties, but against practically every relevant political party which was blamed for the bad situation of the Czech Republic:

And the politicians bicker [while the situation in the Czech Republic worsens]. [The Chairmen of the governing parties] Nečas and Kalousek between one another in the coalition; and Bárta with all of them. Sobotka [the Social Democrat chairman] battles with party colleague Hašek [the Social Democrats' vice-chairman], while [President] Zeman and [former Social Democrat chairman] Paroubek try to get their parties into parliament on a single motivation: to get revenge on the ČSSD. Mrs. Bobošíková with Mach and Bátora [representatives of small parties] advance the further political career of Mr. President [Klaus], while the lobbyists chuckle. […] And President Klaus reigns over all of this and says the corruption is no worse than in the countries around us, and demands hard data.   (ANO 2011)

Similarly to the VV case, anti-establishment rhetoric dominated ANO's communications with the public in reference to the economic crisis as well. The worsening economic situation in the Czech Republic thus served as yet another opportunity for criticism of the established political parties and governments (the prescription for the relatively high unemployment rate was 'to do the opposite of what the previous governments have done' [APRI 2014]), especially in the context of the expanding national debt:

> Our country wasn't always in debt; on the contrary, others were in debt to us. It was not always systematically robbed by nameless 'godfather' groups and people whose names nobody knows and who hide behind the faces of inept politicians. (ANO 2013b)

The discourse of ANO nevertheless differed from that of the rhetoric from VV and The Dawn (as will be shown in the next section) in that the strong anti-establishment message of ANO never extended to arguments with a strong emphasis on the need to restore popular sovereignty despite the fact that Babiš, referring to the broad movements that emerged at the time communism fell, said that he had founded ANO as a 'Civic Forum for the future' (Česká television, 2013a). But later, the role of 'the people' faded into the background, and was limited to occasional mentions of elements of direct democracy. For ANO, the problems of the Czech Republic were not to be solved by broadening the spaces for elements of direct democracy, but by competent professionals on the ANO ballot, with Andrej Babiš at the top of the list.

Populist claims effectively substituted a clearer profile of the movement in terms of party families or left-right division. This corresponds to the high proportion of valence issues (as opposed to positional issues) in ANO's election platform, which exceeded all other parties' space in their respective platforms (Eibl 2014). With respect to ideological vagueness, ANO was to a marked extent similar to VV or The Dawn. Chairman Babiš's words on this are illustrative: 'There is no such thing as right and left. In the Czech Republic we have completely different categories. On one side are the current parties and current politicians, and on the other side are the voters' (Babiš, 2013).

In sum, ANO in its discourse before the 2013 elections skillfully took advantage of the deepening of the political crisis and laid its populism in a strong anti-establishment setting. The dichotomy between the ineffective and compromised arena of Czech politics represented by the established political parties and the efficient world of private enterprise symbolised by the successful businessman Andrej Babiš became a key rhetorical point of the movement. In this way, the economic crisis was barely a rhetorical rallying point for the movement, but it became part of the anti-establishment dimension of ANO's discourse. In contrast to VV and The Dawn, the broadening of the use of direct democracy or more active input of citizens in decision-making processes was not particularly important for ANO.

The end of demo-democracy – The discourse of Tomio Okamura's Dawn of Direct Democracy

The Dawn was founded by Czech-Japanese businessman Tomio Okamura, owner of a firm that imported Japanese food as well as a travel agency. In 2012, Okamura was elected to the Senate (the upper house) and wanted to run in the historic first direct presidential elections in January 2013, but the interior ministry barred his candidacy for having an insufficient number of valid petition signatures. Despite the fact that his Dawn movement was registered just a few months before the 2013 general election, it was able to gain 6.9 per cent of votes and fourteen seats out of 200. Strong anti-establishment rhetoric and Okamura's adamant refusal to participate in any governing coalition left the movement in opposition.

The key element of The Dawn's discourse was an unending emphasis on direct democracy as the most important element of any proposed reforms of the political system. The current setup of the political system of the Czech Republic – a representative parliamentary democracy with a proportional voting system – was understood by Okamura as the main culprit of the political crisis. Direct democracy would be further supplemented by a reform of the voting system, the option of recalling politicians in office, material responsibility, and the introduction of a presidential system. Only a model of direct democracy was understood as 'actual' democracy, in contrast to what Okamura characterised as 'demo-democracy ruled by godfather-like party mafias' (Úsvit 2013c):

> The system as it stands is not real democracy – political scientists call it oligarchy – the rule of the powerful. In our case it's a government of the big mega-firms, the godfathers, and as their tools they have the individual parties. (Okamura 2013a)

In advocating direct democracy, The Dawn emphasised the element of accountability and the necessary checks on politicians, and presented a contrasting image of incompetent elites versus the sensible people. As The Dawn's leader said:

> We not going to trust the elites who tell us we are too stupid to govern ourselves. I don't know anyone so stupid who would let so much public property be stolen as our elected have managed to do. (Okamura 2013b)

> It [direct democracy] is the complete opposite of the current situation, in which people know that nothing changes, and so they are either resigned to public problems or they complain. (Okamura 2013c)

The key role of direct democracy and greater citizen involvement in decision-making for the movement was confirmed during negotiations over support for the new coalition's vote of confidence in parliament. The Dawn's leader repeatedly declared that: 'I support and will allow to function any government that helps us pass a law on a general referendum without exception, so that the voices of the Czech Republic's citizens become the ultimate voice' (Lidové noviny 2013).

An important part of The Dawn's discourse was antiestablishment appeals (often combined with people-centrism) that made no difference between representatives of the governmental and opposition parties, but which generally criticised the political representation at the time. In one pre-election interview, Okamura explained The Dawn's candidacy by saying he wanted to curb 'thievery, fraudsters, and the political-economic mafia' (Česká televisation 2013b). On another occasion he labeled politicians from the established parties as 'do-nothings and mouth-runners' (Úsvit 2013b). As expressed by future Deputy Radim Fiala: 'After twenty years we see a plundered country led by a select elite of godfathers who run the country without regard to who its real masters are – without regard to its citizens' (Úsvit 2013a).

As in the cases of VV or ANO, the topic of economic crisis was rather subjugated to populist rhetoric, in which The Dawn blamed the other political parties on both the right and left whose 'false games have led our republic into a vicious circle of economic crises, deep indebtedness, and high taxes' (Úsvit 2013c) and the bad economic situation was seen as 'the result of a failure of the political system created in the Czech Republic after the era of totalitarianism' (Úsvit 2013d). In his book *The Art of Governing*, Okamura blamed the Czech Republic's growing indebtedness on 'robbery under the governments of the right [and] wasteful management under the left' (Okamura 2011: 64). Okamura repeatedly focused on the moral dimension of politics, which he understood as the most important; as the source of these negative phenomena, including corruption, everything else was somewhat tangential:

> It is mainly the missing morals, the missing politeness, the honesty, and responsibility to others. It's senseless to pretend that what we need is GDP growth, production growth, growth of whatever else. What we need is to be happy. We need to feel secure – each of us need to feel secure from poverty, from hunger, from cold, from violence, from injustice change to [...] These things are absolutely independent of the gross domestic product numbers. (Okamura 2013b)

The discourse of The Dawn was similar to that of VV in the sense of the emphasis put on direct democracy as the chief prescription for all the problems in the Czech Republic. However, The Dawn differs by its anti-Roma stances, which was not an issue either for VV or for ANO at all:

> In the Czech Republic the biggest 'multicultural' problem is obviously Roma. For those to whom this doesn't apply, forgive me, but a large portion of them are simply a huge burden on society [...] The number of Roma in society is increasing, but their proportional contribution to the common wealth does not. Quite the opposite. (Okamura 2013d)

The negative attitude to the Roma minority pushes The Dawn toward Sládek's Republican Party of the 1990s, and toward the family of radical right populist parties (Mudde 2007). On the other hand, leading up to the 2013 general election this attitude did not play a decisive role in the discourse of The Dawn.

To conclude, the central element of The Dawn's discourse in reaction to the political crisis in the Czech Republic was a critique of the establishment at the time. In contrast to ANO, but like VV (even more intensively), The Dawn emphasised the need to reform the political system with direct democracy serving in a key role. Indeed, for The Dawn, direct democracy was a panacea for all societal problems. Portions of the populist appeals of the movement were also indictments of the political elite on the poor state of the Czech economy; nevertheless, economic topics were not particularly important for Okamura's movement. Finally, anti-Roma stances in the discourse of The Dawn echoed those of the rhetoric successfully employed by the SPR-RSČ in the 1990s.

Figure 12.3: Timeline of the rise of populist parties in the Czech Republic

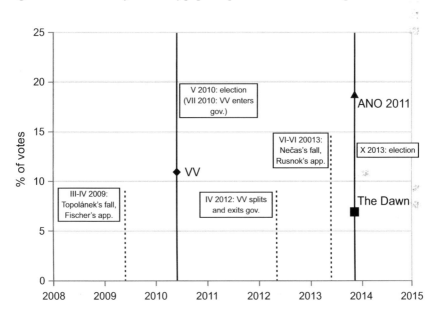

Conclusion

The Czech Republic has experienced an unprecedented rise of populist political parties in recent years. However, we cannot draw a clear connection between the impact of the economic crisis and the growing support for populist parties in the Czech Republic. Even before the economy began to slump, the Czech Republic was hit by serious political crisis reflected in plummeting satisfaction with the political situation and trust in the political institutions. Consequently, the opportunities for employing strong anti-establishment appeal opened and were successfully exploited firstly by VV in 2010 and later, after the deepening of political crisis, by ANO and The Dawn (the main events related to the political crisis are depicted in Figure 12.3).

The discourse of all the political parties which were included in this analysis took advantage of the political crisis. Its central theme was criticism of the established parties, which the populists associated with corruption and incompetence. Although all of the parties can be described as populist, there are also some significant differences in their discourse. Whereas VV and especially The Dawn promoted direct democracy as the main prescription for the cure of all social ills, ANO did not emphasise direct democracy to such an extent. Instead, the movement contrasted 'standard' politics and business practices, preferring the latter. Moreover, anti-Roma and xenophobic stances became a part – although not a key one – of the discourse of The Dawn. What was shared by all the parties under analysis, is the lack of presence of any other ideology besides populism. In other words, the discourse of ANO, The Dawn and VV was based solely on populist appeals with intentionally avoidance and criticism of traditional left-right vision of politics.

The question, however, remains whether the success of the populist parties may be due to the economic crisis. I have demonstrated that not the economic but rather the political crisis and significant changes in the perception of politics and political institutions were crucial for the discourse of populist parties. On the other hand, the established political parties were also blamed for the economic crisis. Thus, the economic crisis was used as one of the issues in the broader context of anti-establishment rhetoric. In other words, the economic crisis may have strengthened the effectiveness of the protest rhetoric used by the populist parties.

Chapter Thirteen

The Delayed Crisis and the Continuous Ebb of Populism in Slovakia's Party System

Peter Učeň

This chapter will try to address the question as to whether the economic recession of 2008 and its repercussions, namely the sovereign debt crisis that influenced a number of EU member states in 2010, had an impact on the incidence and forms of populism in Slovak politics. It also makes inquiries into the role populism may have played in the construction of grand political narratives of political actors. In other words, it aspires to learn whether populism had become attractive for an increasing number of political actors – newcomers or established ones – and if the politics informed by populism has been capable of attracting more popular support than prior to the crisis.

Given the chosen concept of populism as inspired by Mudde (2004; 2007) and Stanley (2008) and defined in the introduction to this volume, I use here 'populist parties' as a term of convenience for the parties that adopt elements of populism as a part of their ideology, appeals by which they address voters and interpret the world for political purposes in general. Therefore, 'populist parties' is in no way presented here as a (new) party type – it simply denotes the parties which use populist appeals irrespectively of their form or 'magnitude'. Populist parties may be differentiated in this text, but their populism is not quantified; there is no attempt to measure the populism of parties in question. When I assess the relative weight of populism within the party appeals it is by no means measured. Overall, in all cases I study here populism is the secondary characteristic of the party appeal and in general, practically all 'populist parties' are primarily 'something else' rather than 'primarily populist'. Therefore, it is of great interest to focus on the role that populism played in the construction of grander narratives of the parties in question. Similarly, the term 'populist politics' is used here as a handy replacement for the 'politics of populist parties', or a cumbersome but more precise expressions such as 'politics informed by populism' or 'politics including the elements of populism'.

Slovakia as a primary example of populism has been part of any discussion of the phenomenon since the 1990s. This was due to the fact that the success of the local populist politician, Prime Minister Vladimír Mečiar, caught the attention of the international community who did not save time and effort to remind Slovak people that continuing support for his politics would seriously hamper the country's chances of integration into the European Union (EU). It was the local mobilisation of youth and voters minding the bleak prospect of Western integration, preceding the 1998 elections, that enabled the formation of an anti-Mečiar coalition capable of ousting a long-time prime minister from the positions of power. The 1998 change marked the beginning of the process in which populism in Slovakia started to recede, change its character and the role it played in narratives by which political actors interpreted the political realm. It will be argued throughout this chapter that the economic depression of 2008 and its repercussions intervened with the process but did not modify it in a crucial way. The transformation of Slovak populism started before the crisis hit. It has been driven by domestic political logic and that logic retained a notable hold in spite of the politically relevant repercussions of the crisis.

Party-based populism between the emergence of party pluralism and the impact of the crisis

So far, Slovakia's party politics have witnessed three waves of the emergence of parties that challenged the liberal democratic order, often in line with the ideas of 'democratic illiberalism', including populism.

The first one was intimately linked to the process of transition from authoritarianism and its immediate aftermath, and was marked by the struggle over the definition of the rules of the emerging liberal democratic polity. This generation of populist actors – the Movement for Democratic Slovakia (HZDS) and the Slovak National Party (SNS) – combined populism with nationalism, although in different ways. The new political parties in the late 1990s and early 2000s challenged the political order in Slovakia as defined by the conflict between the Mečiar and anti-Mečiar 'liberal democratic' coalitions. This wave brought about the Party of Civic Understanding (SOP), Direction – Social Democracy (SMER-SD) and the Alliance of a New Citizen (ANO). Out of these, only SMER-SD can be characterised as a populist party while the remaining two were better defined in terms of Hanley and Sikk's (2013) concept of the 'anti-establishment reform party' with rare episodes of populism. The third wave of the new challenger parties in the second half of the 2000s roughly coincided with the beginning of the crisis, but it was equally – if not even more – a reaction to the first two years of the rule of the 'populist coalition' of SMER-SD, ĽS-HZDS and SNS formed after the 2006 elections. This wave brought two new parties with a potential to become a stable part of the party system – Freedom and Solidarity (SaS) and the Ordinary People and Independent Personalities (OĽaNO) out of which only the latter can be considered a populist (anti)party. This wave of challengers has been in one way or another influenced by the political ramifications of the crisis.

The shared characteristic of the two 'traditional' populist parties of the 1990s – HZDS (later renamed as ĽS-HZDS, People's Party – Movement for Democratic Slovakia) and SNS – was that they both in their appeals combined populism and nationalism. They did so, however, in different ways.

SNS as one of the oldest parties in Slovakia was formed in March 1990 as a general nationalist party with articulate separatist tendencies which advocated granting Slovakia national sovereignty within – but increasingly outside of – the

Czechoslovak federation. After the achievement of independent statehood in 1993 the party suffered from severe internal disagreements about the nature of the politics in the new state which led the moderate national conservative faction to leave the party. While the moderates soon formed one of the pillars of the nascent Slovak centre-right, SNS became the populist radical right party combining nativism, authoritarianism and populism roughly in line with Mudde's (2007) definition. After achieving its separatist objective in 1993, SNS came to represent the nativist and authoritarian conception of Slovak polity and society. However, the nativist nationalism of SNS suffered from a competition by another blend of nationalism and populism presented by Vladimír Mečiar.

Mečiar appeared in 1990 among the new elites of the (nominally) liberal democratic, anti-communist camp as a very capable instinctive populist with the remarkable lust for power. Given the context of the intra-elite conflict regarding the constitutional form of the state in the federal Czechoslovakia, he quickly came to dominate the 'Slovak camp' who called for a transfer of as much power prerogatives as possible to 'Slovak hands' (*see* Učeň 1999 and Deegan-Krause 2006). For this purpose, he developed a *sui generis* blend of nationalism and populism – his 'populism-fortified nationalism' (Deegan-Krause 2004: 204). In this blend, populism played a much stronger role than in the appeals of SNS. In his move from the general call to 'the people' to the appeal to the 'Slovak people', he has developed both a different kind of nationalism – compared to SNS – and a distinct set of populist arguments. Regarding his nationalism, between 1990 and 1998 Mečiar managed to get under one roof practically all forms of nationalist sentiments in Slovakia – with the exception of the hard core nativism of SNS – and to cement an affinity between the preferences among the constituency for Slovak nation(alism) with the vote for his party, HZDS (*see* Deegan-Krause 2004). Mečiar's nationalist appeal differed from the backward looking nativism of SNS in that it defined the Slovak people not only by ethnicity but also by other characteristics such as being the victim of the regime change. Mečiar's appeals touched on resentments regarding the perceived negative outcomes of the transition. Therefore, 'the Slovak people' were not only ethnic Slovaks, but also the victims of the new order – those who suffered under it and felt abandoned by its structures and actors. In an exemplary populist manner, the mechanism of such failing of the people was presented as the neglect and malice of the elite:

First, he successfully combined the social and the national aspects of the Slovaks' disillusionment with the new order in his (party's) appeal to the people making the national interpret the social. Second, he added a strong populist ingredient to the movement by both defining the people (members of the Slovak nation affected by the post-transition deprivations) and pointing out the harmful elite which, ill-serving or betraying the people was to be blamed for those deprivations. Finally, he provided a suggestion for a solution (a 'bearable transition') appealing to a noteworthy number of Slovaks, that meant taking (some) economic and political power to 'Slovak hands', those hands being the hands of people that understood the needs and would not fail the people

Vladimír Mečiar himself and his Movement for Democratic Slovakia. (Učeň 2010: 28)

The primary purpose of Mečiar's populism was to fortify the dominant nationalist argument with a moral(istic) skeleton. This was done by keeping the notion of an enemy of the people in the public's mind – anti-national elite. While ethnically Slovak, Mečiar's opponents were skilfully portrayed as elite and being outside of the national community at the same time. Deegan-Krause (2012: 190) summarised Mečiar's populism as 'an ideological appeal to re-take power now held by elites outside of the boundaries of one's own ethnic group'. This is a *précis* of the strategy in which an extremely talented populist was capable of presenting his opponents as the powerful elites that needed to be warded off – even though he himself controlled almost absolutely all institutions of state. As a three-time Prime Minister, he retained an image of an underdog whose only motivation to be in politics was to keep at bay the harmful anti-national elite plotting against the people in collusion with foreign powers. A crucial emotion that Mečiar was incessantly and successfully evoking was the necessity for the Slovak people to be constantly guarded and tended by the strong 'Slovak' government against the threat from such elites.

SNS and Mečiar differed both in their nationalism and their populism, and in the way these two were related. While the nationalism of SNS referred to the 'one thousand years of Magyar oppression', Mečiar and HZDS emphasised the suffering of the Slovak people in the aftermath of the regime change. Mečiar made a more effective blend of nationalism and populism than SNS and presented it to the nationwide audience in a much more convincing way. This enabled him to claim the necessity to stay in power in order to resolve the predicament of the Slovak people.

The essential part of Mečiar's success was his use of populism: in his ideological mix it played a much more prominent role than was the case with the appeal of SNS. While avoiding nostalgia for the past regime, Mečiar skilfully employed the appeal of 'absolution of sins of the life under communism' in which he assured people that whatever life strategies they had pursued prior to 1989, their life should be considered dignified and there was no need to be ashamed of it, as some other members of the new anti-communist elite suggested.

The populist-nationalist dominance of the 1990s was brought to an end as the consequence of the increase in authoritarianism necessary to keep Mečiar's political project alive. Along the way from the successful opposition strategy to the political programme of the new state, and finally of the 'ruling regime', *Mečiarism* after 1995 became increasingly more authoritarian. Its founding father, who started as the champion of the idea that politics should be an expression of the will of the people, ended up as a schemer trying to obscure and constrain the revelation of the very same popular will. His regime first abused the majority rule, later tried to hollow out the liberal element of the Slovak liberal democratic polity by encroachments on institutions of horizontal accountability and, finally, in one case – a referendum thwarted by the government – also attacked the popular sovereignty core of Slovak democracy. When justifying the domestic authoritarian tendencies *vis-à-vis* the international pressure became unsustainable, Mečiar had to resort to openly severing the ties with the international community, namely the EU. This meant a clash with the ambitions of many Slovaks who would still preferred Mečiar, but with the EU passport in their pocket. The obvious impossibility to square these options and the impending harm to the prospect of European integration marked the notable political mobilisation prior to the 1998 elections which yielded results that made it possible to form a government coalition without HZDS.

Mečiar's populist nationalism influenced the formation of both the contemporary Slovak left and right in a decisive way as both were created in an environment when the dominant political conflict dividing the political scene was not about socio-economic questions separating the traditional left and right but about the 'conduct of power'. Even though the dominant division between the populist-nationalist camp and the civic-democratic camp began to wane following the 2002 elections, the repercussions of the 'founding effects' are discernible until the present day: the modern Slovak centre-right was born in the conflict with populist nationalism rather than in the conflict with any form of the worldview of the left, while the modern Slovak centre-left – as witnessed by the story of SMER-SD – came out of the anti-establishment populist movement.

Finally, Mečiarism gave birth to such a deep conflict, that in the late 1990s a whole bunch of anti-establishment parties, including SMER, SOP and ANO, could appear and blame the 'obsession' of the establishment – both Mečiarist and anti-Mečiarist – with waging ideological warfare for the deplorable state of Slovak politics, economics and society. So, the legacy of Mečiar's populist nationalism had also become an indispensable part of the story of the new populist proponent, Robert Fico.

The crises and Slovak politics, economics and society

The first attack of the crisis, represented by the fall of Lehman Brothers, hit Slovakia at the peak of prosperity – certainly in terms of industrial output – when the country's economy registered double-digit growth (*see* Figure 13.1). Between 2008 and 2009, as demand for Slovak products fell, GDP dropped by roughly 10 per cent. The following year, however, GDP grew again by some 9 per cent returning to solid black figures. Since then, the Slovak economy has been registering a continuous but moderate decline in GDP growth, which remained positive. In general, the impact of the crisis on the Slovak economy can be considered moderate and indirect. While the 2008–09 drop in GDP caused problems in the area of employment, it did not bring about an immediate precipitation of social standards as, for example, in Latvia. Also, due to the character of the Slovak economy as a production and service appendage to the major West European economy, Germany, the negative repercussions of the 2008 have been shielded by the notable resistance of the German economy to the crisis. Importantly, Slovak banks, which had been financially fixed in 1999, remained solvent. They were

222 European Populism in the Shadow of the Great Recession

practically free from the exposure to 'toxic assets' that caused the crisis in the first place. The national debt, however, started to grow after 2008 and this was the aspect of the crisis that – when later politicised – had the most notable impact on Slovak party competition. While the overall impact of the economic crisis on Slovakia was moderate, indirect and delayed because of the 'German cushion' it did have an impact on Slovak politics and the crisis interacted with the processes of change that started before the recession hit in 2008.

The first set of changes took place on the anti-establishment side of the political spectrum. In 1998, SOP, a centre-left, but primarily anti-establishment party, tipped the balance to the advantage of the anti-Mečiar coalition and enabled the overthrowing of Mečiar. The party, however, disintegrated rapidly during its tenure in power. In 2002, ANO enabled the formation of the centre-right coalition by replacing the leftist SDĽ (which then collapsed, split and rapidly fell prey to the unifying efforts of SMER in 2004). While in power, ANO proved to be the power-seeking project of its leader, a sort of business party. An internal opposition against the leader's conduct produced the tension that tore the party apart. As a result of the demise of ANO along with the split within the SDKÚ-DS the ruling centre-right coalition *de facto* lost the majority and only remained in power by means of bribing individual MPs to support the coalition on *ad hoc* basis. Such practices, along with allegations of corruption, repelled a part of the centre-right electorate and undermined the centre-right's reform legacy as well as its chance for re-election in 2006. In spite of undeniable economic success, the centre-right helped to produce its nemesis: the rekindled opposition of SMER and the formation of the new anti-establishment generation on the right.

The process of transformation of the traditional populist parties (SNS, HZDS) had been under way since the period preceding the 2002 elections. HZDS became an ideologically empty political vehicle courting all major party families. It has been steadily losing the popular support as well as any political purpose other than providing leverage and impunity to its founder and leader, Vladimír Mečiar. While the nativist SNS remained electorally sound, as an organisation it suffered from crippling disunity and splits that caused its absence from the parliament between 2002 and 2006. The public image of both parties had been damaged by the rampant corruption linked to their participation in the executive after 2006. While the newly renamed ĽS-HZDS continued to refer to its 'parenthood' of Slovak statehood, it gradually ceased to be a party capable of attracting the nationalist votes. SNS, on the contrary, tamed its nativist radicalism for the sake of government acceptability and consumption of spoils of power. Had it not been for the occasional drunken anti-Magyar outbursts of the party chairman Ján Slota, the profile of Slovakia's prime radical right party might have been unnoticeable.

Finally, after 2002, Direction (SMER, *smer* means direction in Slovak), dramatically redefined the opposition against the centre-right government and came to dominate Slovak politics for a decade to come. Figure 13.1 shows that SMER became dominant not only among the populist parties of our interests but also within the Slovak party system in general.

Figure 13.1: Electoral gains of the traditional populist parties in Slovakia,
1990–2012

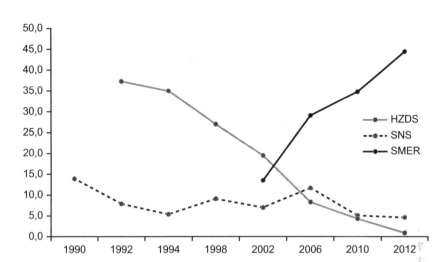

SMER appeared in 1999 as the political project of the maverick and ambitious Robert Fico. Fico was the popular, young – but politically relatively senior – deputy chairman of the (reformed Communist) Party of the Democratic Left (SDĽ) – a hesitant part of the anti-Mečiarist coalition and a partner in the first Dzurinda government. He parted with his party as well as the establishment of the early post-Mečiar era to fulfil his political ambitions and to protest against the SDĽ's participation and conduct in the centre-right government.

Fico used the wave of resentment against the establishment following the fall of Mečiar, when a growing segment of the electorate thought that the fight between Mečiar and his opponents cost the country a lot in terms of neglect of more important issues. Fico promptly joined the ranks of those who claimed that the established elites were bothering Slovaks with their ideological infighting, while neglecting their true needs and concerns. This new anti-establishment strategy was based on taking equidistant detachment from both main camps within the 1990s' establishment and called for the replacement of ideological straightjackets with common sense solutions and the substitution of the traditional politicians with 'new faces' (*see* Učeň 2003; 2004). The new party was from the beginning capable of accommodating a 'non-ideological', business wing with the 'left-wing nationalists' in its founding group and of selling the product wrapped in appeals such as the necessity to introduce new faces into Slovak politics or tough stances on law and order issues (including the tough treatment of 'the inadaptable', read the Roma).

This strategy seemed to be very successful in the 1999–2002 period when SMER was recording support, peaking at about 30 per cent. The 2002 elections however yielded only a disappointing 13 per cent for SMER's political project that was meant to bring government participation to its 'stakeholders'. Instead, a purely centre-right coalition with a slim majority had been formed with the help of the new anti-establishment, economically liberal party ANO. This experience initiated a gradual, often mocked, but ultimately politically successful process of the 'social-democratisation' of SMER. The expression stood for a deliberate ideological move from common sense, non-ideological anti-establishment ranting towards merging Fico's soft populism with the topics of the left. The party successfully moved from a niche that Fico had built in 1999 to an ample and empty space on the left side of the ideological spectrum in Slovakia.

Between 2002 and 2006 SMER managed to advance the shift ideologically as well as organisationally. After merging and devouring smaller leftist and social democratic groupings and remnants of his original party, SDĽ, SMER became Direction – Social Democracy (SMER-SD). Its ideological transformation has until these days remained incomplete when compared to the mainstream social democratic parties of Europe. Particularly, SMER-SD always paid more attention to the old left, bread and butter issues of the constituency and was very hesitant in questions of identity and lifestyle (such as ethnic or sexual minorities). And it has always remained the party that caters to the moods of the socially conservative electorate (arguing that the country was not ready for such social democratic topics as the rights of sexual minorities).

SMER has also made a notable change from its ambiguous relations with the EU to the euro-enthusiast position of tactical Eurofederalism. This clever tactical move enabled Fico to sustain the discussed strange ideological deviation from the social democratic mainstream: while being leftist in terms of its appeals on the socio-economic aspects of people's lives, the party remained socially conservative and largely particularistic in its view of societal norms and relations between the individual, state and society. While SMER-SD constantly sends out discreet promises that its convergence with the social democratic mainstream is just a matter of time, referring to the manifest immaturity of the Slovak society, it also makes sure that it will remain a socially conservative party as long as this serves its electoral purposes.

Regarding the role of populism in the appeals of SMER-SD, the main factor to consider is the personal populist inclinations of the party leader Fico. Fico's populism underwent a change from the initial drawing of a moral distinction between the people and the elite for the sake of discrediting the established politicians to making essentially the same distinction, but for purposes of becoming 'a radical social alternative to the anti-popular [centre-right] government', as was the case between 2002 and 2006. Compared to Mečiar, Fico's populism was different in the sense that it was not primarily in the service to the dominant nationalist narrative. Also, it was subtler, as the antagonism between the people and the elite was not presented in such an intense way as was the case with Mečiar. While the latter's populism was an expression of the fight about the definition of the new state and the rules for the new polity, Fico's populism served anti-establishment purposes. As I have argued elsewhere, over time Fico developed his populist package that in stark opposition to life options offered by the centre-right, merged social (generically leftist), national and populist arguments in a working mix capable of mobilising a plurality of voters in the country.

Fico's challenge to the 'SDKÚ world'[1] took the form of a 'strong social state' which integrated explicitly welfarist, but also other kind of assumptions and offers. *Prima facie*, this alternative world included a promise of a welfare state that would be equally – or more – extensive, just as available, and strong (ready to pay greater allowances). But it went further and deeper by offering the hope of a different treatment of people also on a 'non-welfarist' plane. While the concept implicitly hosted an offer that the national identity and the 'national interest' would be taken care of, it also included an appeal to the alienated via a promise of being treated in a dignified way regardless of their actual socio–economic status. The anti-establishment aspect of Fico's appeal – blaming elite conduct for the misery of the people – was supplemented by a subtler populist pledge of reuniting the people and politics. It was to take the form of a relationship in which nobody was left behind anymore and somebody interested in ordinary people's problems was always available to take care of them and lift their burden. This was cleverly juxtaposed with the 'cold', technocratic and individualistic nature of the 'SDKÚ world' in which, allegedly, it was inevitable that somebody could – or, indeed, was meant to – be left behind (Učeň 2011: 82).

Here populism served the role of morally fortifying Fico's effort to build an opposition alternative to the ruling right and his appeal to those who were – or came to be – disappointed with the order based on the neoliberal conceptions of the right. The transformation of Fico's populism – from non-ideological anti-elite ranting to generically leftist arguments in favour of the ordinary men – were a part of the 'catch-allisation' of the appeal of his movement. By doing so his party managed to monopolise the left part of the political spectrum.

Populism and radical politics in Slovakia after the crisis

There are four ways in which the crisis (may have) affected Slovak party politics: First, it contributed to the reputation of traditional populist nationalists (SNS, ĽS-HZDS) being irreparably damaged by exposing their governing incompetence and corrupt, particularistic character. Second, it interfered with the process in which SMER-SD altered its appeals, including the transformation of its populism and its role in the party appeal. Third, it facilitated the emergence of the new anti-establishment attitude of the right. Fourth, it encouraged the new type of the anti-establishment appeal on the left.

The first two previously discussed trends were linked to the fact that the outbreak of the crisis caught Slovakia when it was ruled by the 'populist coalition'

---

1. The notion is referring to the then most important centre-right party and symbol of the neoliberal reforms, Slovak Democratic and Christian Union – Democratic Party (SDKÚ-DS).

of SMER-SD, SNS and ĽS-HZDS. The crisis sealed the fate of traditional populist parties blending populism and nationalism. It happened through a merciless exposure of their inaptitude to govern and their extremely particularistic character as witnessed by the corruption of their cadres in the 2006–10 executive. While in the case of ĽS-HZDS this led to the total loss of popular support and self-dissolution, SNS – while falling below the threshold of parliamentary representation – has attempted repairing its image at home and in the international arena. It has strengthened its links to the community of populist radical right parties such as FN and FPÖ trying to replicate their path to political acceptance.

The crisis also intervened with the transformation of the way populist notions were used by Robert Fico and his SMER-SD. Here, paradoxically, the increase in the popular support for this populist party should be attributed to factors other than the increase in intensity of its populism. The necessity of directing the state and economy after 2006, and especially navigating through the troubled waters of the euro crisis, actually limited the use of populist arguments in the party's appeals. It was a combination of SMER's downplaying of its populist elements and of the colossal failure of the ruling centre-right coalition in October 2011 that made the support for SMER skyrocket after the 2010 elections.

The crisis – and its perception in Slovak society – certainly contributed to the emergence of the arguments favourable to the new anti-establishment challengers on both the left and right. A new pattern of anti-establishment politics emerged which treated Fico and his party as 'the' establishment. While on the (radical) left we have not witnessed yet the success in establishing a lasting party-political project, the anti-establishment surge on the right yielded two parties with a potential to last, namely SaS and OĽaNO. The success of the new anti-establishment right is linked to the crisis perception through the successful politicisation of the topic of the responsible handling of public finances in times of crisis.

As discussed before, Slovakia's economy had been hit by the competitiveness crisis, namely by the drop in production in 2008 and 2009. But the fall of the demand for its products has been cushioned by its role as a provider of parts and products to the German economy and did not cause any pressing social crisis. While the banks remained careful and the price of the credit increased following the market crash, a banking crisis *per se* was not an issue in Slovakia. There was an attempt to politicise the fear that some 'exposed' parent institutions of Slovak banks would use their Slovak daughters' profits to embellish their balance sheets but it did not succeed. Regarding the sovereign debt crisis, even though Slovakia's numbers remained in the safe zone, the topic of indebtedness has been politicised in a peculiar way. For the first time in Slovak history public finances and national debt became an issue after 2008. For the opposition, the government's ability to handle public finances became the synonym for its (in)ability to deal with the crisis in general. Figure 1.3 in the Introduction shows that the indebtedness (as the percentage of GDP) started to swiftly grow following the 2008 market crash. While it was not entirely possible to attribute this growth to the policies of the 'populist coalition' in power, it was absolutely clear that the government was not willing to match revenues that declined as the consequence of the recession, with cuts in expenditures. Therefore an argument appeared within the opposition relating the growing national debt with the overall incapacity of the government to counteract and withstand the crisis. It became possible to sell this position to a predisposed segment of voters by linking the government's inability to control debt – which was still far from catastrophic – with corruption and a predatory attitude to the state resources on the side of the ruling 'populist coalition'. A new anti-establishment and economically liberal SaS party emerged that mobilised such sentiments. By its energy, anti-establishment charm and intensity of campaign, SaS decisively contributed to the imposition of the issue of governing-amid-crisis competence as a competitive issue of paramount importance. The traditional centre-right also adopted the issue and helped to cement the perception of the lack of governing capacity on the part of the SMER-SD-led coalition. As I have argued previously (Učeň 2011), the successful promotion of the topic of fiscal responsibility and of the capacity to manage national finances in the crisis may have mobilised the relatively small – but at the end decisive – segment of voters who, by granting 12 per cent support to SaS – made it possible to oust the 'populist coalition' by joint efforts of the old and new, anti-establishment right following the 2010 election.

The issue of crisis management, however, backfired on the new centre-right coalition in 2011 following the outbreak of the euro crisis. The coalition failed to overcome disagreements regarding the Slovak participation in the European Fiscal Stability Facility (EFSF) with SaS opposing the participation in the direct clash with the position of the traditional, EPP-related centre-right. When Prime Minister Iveta Radičová linked the vote for joining EFSF with the confidence in her government, with SMER-SD not participating and SaS abstaining from the vote, the government fell in October 2011. As a consequence, this crisis-related topic was essential for SMER-SD's popularity boost – both in absolute and relative numbers – which resulted in 44 per cent support for SMER-SD in the 2012 snap elections.

Another manifestation of the impact of the crisis on Slovak party politics was the emergence of the radical criticism of SMER-SD from the left. Two new parties, namely the (re-founded) SDĽ and 99 Per Cent – Civic Voice ('99%') combined fervent criticism of the establishment with radical stances that could be often located quite on the far left. The novelty of such criticism – along with that of SaS – was that it considered SMER-SD as part of the establishment. Therefore, a new model of anti-establishment politics emerged. It marked the end of the era when Fico's 'subtle populism' was capable of absorbing any kind of disillusionment with 'the system' by formulating an appropriate promise of redemption of people's concerns. The new anti-establishment mood held Fico accountable for his governmental policies and the failure to deliver on the promises of his otherwise vague 'subtle populism'.

The pattern that emerged within the political discourse after 2008 could be described as 'Fico versus the rest'. This arrangement differed from previous criticism of Fico's 'populism' in that the most fervent critics originated among the newly emerging anti-establishment challengers on the left and right rather than from the mainstream right. For these actors, SMER-SD has become 'the' establishment, while the traditional centre-right still tended to see it still as the populist usurper within the Slovak democratic polity. More precisely, drawing on Mair's (2009, 2011b) distinction between the responsive and responsible government, the new radical left challengers criticised SMER-SD for being unresponsive – not responsive enough or at all – to its main principal, the Slovak people. The new anti-establishment right criticised Fico for being too responsible to certain group of principals, namely foreign and EU-related ones, at the expense of responsibility to the local principals – not necessarily the people, but rather the domestic business sector, through which the people were supposed to benefit as well. These previously unthinkable approaches became valuable political strategies for the new challengers. It was, however, denied to the traditional centre-right which was paralysed by its general commitment to the neoliberal model of economic modernisation and adherence to the mainstream of the European integration. As Fico adhered to the mainstream of the EU on handling the euro crisis as well, the traditional right could not compete in radicalism with the new anti-establishment right of SaS and OĽaNO which was free from such constraints.

SMER-SD inevitably tried to square the contradictions of the requirements of responsiveness and responsibility. Fico has been suggesting that the party was the only political force capable of being responsive to the people (and bread and butter-related interest of this principal) in the domestic arena as well as responsible to the Slovak national interest defined by the compatibility with the mainstream of the EU. This approach has been the primary communication strategy of Fico's single party government since the return to power in spring 2012. While it largely worked – namely thanks to the disinterest of the Slovak population in the European topics – it has, however, left SMER-SD uncomfortably vulnerable to the new form of the anti-establishment criticism.[2]

Figure 13.2 illustrates some arguments about the possible interference of the crisis with inherent trends within Slovak party politics discussed above.

It shows that the combined support for the populist nationalists (SNS and ĽS-HZDS) has been declining since the elections in 2006. The same, even though less pronounced, applies for the combined support of the parties of the Dzurinda II government (2002–06, SDKÚ-DS, KDH, SMK and Most – Híd). The support for SMER-SD has been fluctuating but at levels well above any other party.

The creation of the 'populist coalition' of SMER-SD, SNS and ĽS-HZDS in 2006 was enabled by the still solid support for the latter two junior partners. The return of the centre-right opposition to power in 2010 can be attributed not only to a certain decline in the support for SMER-SD but also to the fact that

---

2. The fragmentation of opposition strategies, including anti-establishment ones can be best illustrated by the results of the May 2014 elections to the European Parliament in which Slovakia sent to the European Parliament representatives from eight parties, seven of them being nominally right-of-the-centre.

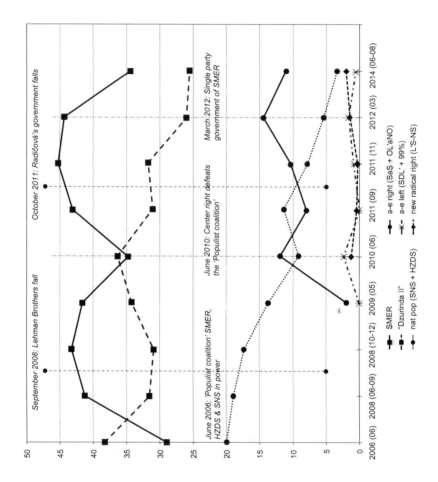

Figure 13.2: Timeline of populism during the economic crisis in Slovakia

his coalition partners became seriously marginalised. SMER-SD recorded a solid rise during the first half of its tenure, but the second half was marked by the ebb of support. After 2009, the politicisation of the topic of the crisis-related fiscal responsibility not only boosted the new anti-establishment right (SaS) but also gave new life to the traditional centre-right's call for 'reforms' that had lost some appeal after 2006 (*see* Učeň 2011). The combined effect of the increase of support for the traditional centre-right and 'coalitionable' new right made it possible to put together a new centre-right majority under Prime Minister Iveta Radičová in 2010. Support for SMER-SD returned to the low forties around the time Radičová's government fell and remained at such a high level until the snap elections in March 2012.

SMER-SD's impressive electoral victory in 2012 should not be accredited to the effect of its populism, which has been in decline for almost a decade. Instead, it was caused by consolidating their grip on the left side of the political spectrum, taking over the nationally aware constituency of SNS, and above all ĽS-HZDS, an ultimate failure of the ruling centre-right and an astute political tactics played by SMER-SD in the aftermath of the failed vote of confidence in October 2011. The intra-coalition clash over attitude to euro crisis, namely Slovakia's participation in the EFSF, constituted a fully developed political crisis in the country in which the ruling right lost the confidence of the parliament. Many of their voters considered the cause as not worthy of bringing down the government and wasting the chance to introduce reforms to politics and governance of the country. This may have caused their electoral withdrawal. More importantly, SMER-SD played it well by not demanding immediate snap elections and letting the centre-right government rule for another six months with the constitutionally restricted mandate amid the mutual recriminations as to who was responsible for the government's fall. The demoralised centre-right agreed to remain in such a humiliating position – in the name of responsibility – by voting for the constitutional changes curbing the prerogatives of the 'diminished government', and ruled under supervision of the president allied with SMER-SD.[3] Thus they enabled SMER-SD to transform an acute political crisis into the protracted, 'institutionalised' one, which was, moreover, steered by Robert Fico. The resulting malaise made it possible for SMER-SD to present itself as the only 'normal' and responsible political power in the country and helped to create a comfortable environment conducive to the unparalleled victory. Therefore, it was a masterful management of the political crisis rather than populism that lead to the unprecedented victory for SMER-SD. It took another two years of the single party rule for the party's support to decline towards the mid-thirties, as indicated by 2014 poll numbers.

While the performance of the new anti-establishment left may seem unimpressive in electoral terms, its importance lies in the fact that it introduced a

---

3. Slovakia's participation in EFSF has been approved shortly after the fall of the government with the votes of SMER-SD and the rump centre-right coalition.

new type of anti-establishment criticism of SMER-SD that can be revived in the future by more viable political entrepreneurs.[4]

Finally, the two landmark events – the hit of the Great Recession and the fall of the centre-right government – do not seem to have had an immediate effect on the popularity of parties at issue – be they 'populist' or not.

By means of conclusion: Anti-establishment politics versus populism

In order to understand the transformation of Slovak party politics under the conditions of the economic crisis – or, more precisely, crises – it is useful to introduce the distinction between two concepts that are often treated as synonymous – anti-establishment politics and populism. They both differ from the classic anti-incumbency appeal of the (loyal) opposition which criticises the governing for its actual or alleged underperformance in governing. An anti-establishment appeal consists of deprecation of the entire establishment – its ruling as well as the opposition faction, its actors, institutions and ideas – for the misconduct in governing suggesting a principal incapacity of the establishment to produce a good or desired politics without being replaced by *homini nuovi*. While populism may share a lot of resemblance with the anti-establishment appeal, it inevitably includes an unbridgeable moral distinction between the people and the elite while criticising the elite for having deprived the people of its legitimate place in politics and for having prevented the revelation of the popular will (which ought to be the essence of democratic politics). Therefore, while populist tropes are often part of the anti-establishment appeal, it is not an inevitable element of it. In short, it is possible to be anti-establishment without being populist.

This distinction leads to the basic claim of this analysis that if there is an area where the crisis significantly influenced the party politics (in Slovakia) it is exactly the emergence of ample space for various new ways of criticising the establishment. The second anti-establishment wave in Slovakia, coinciding with the crisis, attempted to mobilise the perceived losers of globalisation (anti-establishment radical left) as well as its assumed beneficiaries (new anti-establishment right, namely SaS). The former electorally dwindled because the 'losers' are still caught in the competing lures of Fico's 'subtle populism', old fashioned anti-capitalist appeal of the Communist Party of Slovakia (KSS) and the fresh appeal of the new anti-establishment left. It has, however, managed to challenge the monopoly of Fico's claim for the redemption of the socially deprived and seed some doubts about the status of SMER-SD as the political force siding with the people as opposed to being part of the establishment disinterested in it. Regarding the anti-establishment right, it was more successful in capturing the segment of 'winners' of globalisation – the middle class and young professionals

---

4.   At certain point during the 2012 election campaign the support for 99 per cent – Civic Voice reached 7 per cent just to evaporate after the dubious origins of the generous funding for the new party has been disclosed.

demanding a more honest capitalism and the transparent politics in the name of the public interest. Table 13.1 summarises the electoral gains of the populist as well as anti-establishment parties of various generations in the Slovak polity.[5]

The second important conclusion of this analysis is that while the broadening of space for anti-establishment politics was systematic during the crisis, the incidence of populism was episodic. In addition to my previous claim about the decrease of SMER-SD's populism and its unrelatedness to the party's recent record high support, the post-2008 period yielded only one relevant party that could be considered populist. The party I refer to is OĽaNO, formally a movement that emerged after the

Table 13.1: Electoral gains of populist, radical left and AERPs (1993–2012)

	1990	1992	1994	1998	2002	2006	2010	2012
'Populist parties'								
HZDS		37.3	35	27	19.5	8.3	4.3	0.9
SNS	13.9	7.9	5.4	9.1	7.0*	11.7	5.1	4.6
SMER					13.5	29.1	34.8	44.4
subtotal	13.9	45.2	40.4	36.1	33.0	49.1	44.2	49.9
Radical/ anti-establishment left – old and new								
KSS		0.8	0.7	2.8	6.3	3.9	0.8	0.7
ZRS			7.3	1.3	0.5	0.3	0.2	
SDĽ						0.1	2.4	0.2
99%								1.6
subtotal	0	0.8	8.0	4.1	6.8	4.3	3.4	2.5
Anti-establishment reform parties								
SOP				8.0				
ANO					8.0	1.4		
SaS							12.1	5.9
OĽaNO								8.6
subtotal	0	0	0	8.0	8.0	1.4	12.1	14.5
New radical right								
ĽS-NS							1.3	1.6
total	13.9	46.0	48.4	48.2	47.8	54.8	61.0	68.5

Notes: In 2002 the gains of SNS and its splinter True Slovak National Party (PSNS) were added together as the parties re-merged again in 2005.

5. For the sake of completeness it also includes the new generation of the radical right represented by the People's Party Our Slovakia (L'SNS) which exceeded the old SNS in its radicalism and toying with the extremist ideas. It has also made an extensive use of novel anti-establishment arguments in building its political base, namely in the breakthrough elections to the regional government in Banská Bystrica region in November 2013.

outbreak of crisis while its founders first participated in the parliamentary politics on the list of SaS before breaking ranks and offering a distinct way of criticising politics in Slovakia. OĽaNO is, however, primarily antiparty. Its articulated anti-establishment sentiment and frequent populist postures serve the 'higher cause' of criticism of the idea that political parties should be the principal organisational form of democracy. OĽaNO does not criticise political parties for doing their job poorly, nor does it want them to do a better job; it promotes the replacement of political parties by other mechanisms of aggregation of popular opinion and recruiting the governing personnel. These alternative mechanisms through which the popular will should be revealed include primarily procedures of direct democracy. In short, the new movement rejects party government as the dominant form of government in democracy.

This chapter's main focus included the changing role the populism in appeals of Slovak political parties. (This subject is only logical as I consider populism an ancillary appeal which plays a supportive role in formation of grand(er) political narratives and appeals.) It is perhaps appropriate to conclude that the role of populism has been changing from fortifying the nationalist mobilisation of Vladimír Mečiar in the 1990s through backing the development of Fico's rebellion against the establishment and the later construction of 'subtle' social populism in the 2000s, to the current undermining of the very idea that democracy in Slovakia should be based on political parties.

Finally, as populism provides a moral distinction between the elite and the people and therefore supplies a moral justification for the people-centric criticism of the politics as usual, it will remain an obvious opposition strategy in contemporary democracies which have grown increasingly elitist, oligarchic and depoliticised. A populist cry for the repoliticisation of government and bringing politics back to the people will remain around as a relevant and lasting sentiment and appeal. But it may well be the various forms of anti-establishment politics – randomly employing populist tropes – rather than 'pure' populism that will be driving the dynamics of change in Slovak polity, with the latter performing its supportive role in the articulation of critical or constructive ideas as to what Slovak politics should look like.

Chapter Fourteen

Plebeians, *Citoyens* and Aristocrats or Where is the Bottom of Bottom-up? The Case of Hungary

Zsolt Enyedi

During the global financial crisis a number of peripheral populist parties became major players. Hungary was, however, the only country where parties often described as populist, *Fidesz* and *Jobbik*[1], managed to receive about two thirds of the vote and where one such party, *Fidesz*, obtained the constitutional majority in two consecutive elections. This chapter investigates the ideology of *Fidesz* and *Jobbik* by referring to programmes, interviews, speeches, legislative and governmental initiatives and public gestures. Party ideologies are analysed as narratives that account for the status quo, identify the faults of the opponents, suggest ways of improvements, mobilise supporters and link political decisions to values. This chapter identifies ideological and practical responses given by these two parties to the crisis ranging from the outright rejection of liberal democracy to the advocacy of 'workfare-society'. The chapter also highlights the non-populist features of the examined parties and demonstrates the existence of factors that constrain the emergence of populism in its pure form.

Conceptual network

Populism may coexist with various ideological orientations. This chapter focuses on the combination of anti-globalism, nationalism and illiberalism as this ideological configuration defines what is often regarded as the most fundamental attitudinal cleavage of the twenty-first century (Kriesi *et al.* 2006).

As is the case throughout the volume, the term 'populism' refers to a thin ideology that regards the elite and the people as two separate, antagonistic and homogenous groups, considers the people as pure and the elite as corrupt, and evaluates the political system against the standards of popular sovereignty (Canovan 1999; Kriesi and Pappas 2015; Mudde 2007; Deegan-Krause and Haughton 2009; Stanley 2008; Učeň 2007a; Pelinka 2013; etc.). Additionally, populists are also expected to elevate the 'true interest' of the people above formal, indirect political institutions, to reject compromise-based politics and to

---

1. Anti-establishment sentiments were also central to the discourse of another minor party, the LMP. But because LMP remained a strong defender of individual and minority rights, liberal democracy and constitutionalism, the chapter does not cover it.

object to the preferential treatment of minority interests. The most obvious anti-populist orientations include elitism, technocracy, liberalism and pluralism. Anti-populists (or a-populists) disparage the common men, argue for the superiority of the elites (whether defined in intellectual, economic, traditional or moral terms), defend the interests of (unpopular) minorities, support the established decision-making procedures of liberal democracy, or have a business-like attitude to pacts and compromises. While the existing literature is often satisfied by counting the statements that can be classified as populist, the current chapter is based on the logic that one needs to take into account the presence of both populist and anti-populist aspects in a party's discourse and actions in order to arrive at a balanced assessment.

The analysis below will also consider a number of further features which may not be part of the core definition of populist ideology, but which characterise a supporting mentality. These features include a tendency towards disregarding long-term costs and feasibility concerns and ideological flexibility, meaning a lack of traditional ideological constraints. The criticism of public opinion based on values or on cost-benefit analyses is considered to signal a non-populist mentality. Populists are also expected to portray their politics as the common-sense-based representation of the self-interest of the people and to question the legitimacy of their political opponents. While nowadays multi-party competition is rarely rejected explicitly, populists are characterised by gestures of disrespect towards their opponents, towards the institutions of dialogue and towards party-based democracy. They call for unity, but this call also justifies the shunning of those who are seen to disturb social harmony.

The crises

Pre-crisis Hungary had a consensus-oriented liberal institutional framework and a relatively consolidated party system. But these features could not counterbalance the deep and increasing divisions within the country. Left and right routinely questioned the other's legitimacy. The fear of political annihilation by the other side, was, most probably, one of the main factors behind the support within the political elite for financially reckless policies during the early 2000s. These policies included the introduction of thirteenth month pensions, and at one point even a fourteenth month pension was promised to the voters. Under the socialist-led 2002–06 government the balance of the budget radically deteriorated, the government deficit went above 9 per cent, the national sovereign debt increased above 60 per cent. In order to avoid a financial catastrophe austerity measures were required, but the government postponed them until after the 2006 election. The incumbent socialists (MSZP) won the election, but as soon as the public learned about the planned austerity measures the popularity of the government collapsed. A few weeks later parts of the capital city were in flames.

Note that the Hungarian crisis differed from the 2008 world crisis not only in terms of timing, but also in terms of its origin and configuration. The trigger for the September 2006 riots was a political event: the leaked speech of the Prime Minister to socialist MPs in which he claimed that prior to the election his government lied to the people about the actual state of economy. The political authority of the government was further eroded by, first, the timidity, and then, the brutality of the police *vis-à-vis* the protesters. The freefall of the government's popularity could have been followed, in principle, by a recovery, but the 2008 financial crisis, that hit Hungary particularly hard, made such developments all but impossible. In October 2008 Hungary was the first European country to accept a guarantee package from the IMF, worth twenty-five billion dollars. The ensuing second wave of austerity measures exacerbated public discontent and did nothing to address unemployment. In 2009 the GDP fell by 6.8 per cent, public debt reached 80 per cent of the GDP, and the country's economic prospects looked worse than ever since the regime change (*see* Figure 1.1).

The ensuing alienation and anti-elite sentiments were major factors behind the fact that in 2008 Hungarians voted on referendums against the newly introduced healthcare and university tuition fees (less than one fifth of the citizens supported the government's position), that in the 2010 elections they voted two established parties, SZDSZ and MDF, out, and two new protest parties, LMP and *Jobbik*, into parliament. But contrary to many other countries in the region, the main beneficiary of this anti-establishment mood was an 'old' party, the *Fidesz*. While all Hungarian parties experimented with populist gestures, only in case of *Fidesz* did populism become central to the party's strategy. This was, however, a rather peculiar form of populism, as the next paragraphs will demonstrate.

The discourse of *Fidesz*

Fidesz was launched as an anti-communist and liberal initiative in 1988. The party's ideological repertoire even included a considerable dose of anti-populism. For example, in 1992 *Fidesz* was the only party opposed to raising pensions. But the party fared badly at the subsequent election and afterwards the resolute anti-populist stance has been abandoned once and for all.

The nationalist and anti-liberal turn of the party was sealed in 1997 by a major speech of Viktor Orbán, the party leader, in which he characterised the activities of the left-wing government with the following words:

> At the end of this road one finds an 'open society', weakened, bled, shaken in its morals, confused in its self-awareness, tormented by guilt-feeling, and deprived of self-confidence. An 'open society' where there is no country any more, only habitat, there is no homeland any more, only an investment-site. Where no nation, only population exists. Where progress equals assimilation into world-wide processes. Where progress does not serve the interests of the nation but simply satisfies the ambition of the narrow power elite to become world citizens. (Debreczeni 2009: 120)

The speaker contrasted 'open society' with the 'rising nation', attacked cosmopolitans and those who expect Hungarians to feel guilt for alleged historical crimes, and claimed that the left wing government is 'foreign-minded', not under the influence of the Hungarian nation.

While the new identity of the party contained important ingredients of right-wing populism, nationalism and conservatism prevailed over the populist aspects. The leaders of the party have actually embraced a number of rather unpopular positions. In this period the party became clerical in a largely secular country and promoted the cult of little-known conservative politicians from the turn of the century. Its rhetoric appealed explicitly to the middle classes, showing little interest in attracting working-class voters. It added to its name *Magyar Polgári Párt*, which is officially translated as Hungarian Civic Party, but the Hungarian term '*polgári*' means not only civic (citoyen) but also bourgeois. In the coming years all major *Fidesz* speeches were given on behalf of the *polgári Magyarország* (i.e. civic/bourgeois Hungary). After winning the 1998 election the party continued to elaborate further its conservative identity, exemplified by the removal of the Holy Crown from the National Museum to parliament and by a multitude of gestures towards the 'historical churches'.

After the narrowly lost 2002 election *Fidesz* again modified its strategy and discourse. It turned towards more radical forms of populism and nationalism. In the subsequently delivered speeches the nation was identified with the right, the foreigners with the left. After the lost election, on 7 May 2002, Orbán announced:

> The homeland doesn't cease to exist when it is under foreign domination, neither when it plundered by Turks or Tatars [...] It doesn't cease to exist when the responsibility of governing is not with us [...] It may well be that our parties and representatives are in opposition in the Parliament, but those of us who are present on this square are not, and cannot be, in opposition, because the homeland cannot be in opposition. (Debreczeni 2009: 196)

While many of Orbán's speeches implied that the nation is one, the context of the lost election forced him to use more elitist formulations. These references identified the right not with the entire nation but only with its core, or its avant-garde. On 23 October 2002 Orbán declared:

> [...] A larger part of Hungarians from Hungary[2] have decided to follow a different path [...] We have decided to stay on the same road [...] One cannot get on this road simply by chance. One needs to choose it with clear mind and pure heart [...] We can count on ourselves only [...] (Debreczeni 2009: 187)

During the 2002–04 period, the party's populism was more spectacular in organisational matters than in rhetoric. Orbán initiated the so called Civic Circles, a loose network of largely informal clubs, initiatives and associations. The movement provided an ideal frame for populist politics because its amorphous structure served the prevailing anti-party sentiments well and because it lacked internal formal procedures for accountability. Orbán, like

---

2. That is, not within the entire nation, which includes co-ethnics living outside of the borders.

Berlusconi in *Forza Italia*, was the initiator, the leader and the only relevant politician of the movement.

The year 2002 was also the starting year of engagement with social (i.e. left-wing) populism. On 8 April, after the first round of the election Orbán declared that the government of socialists will be a government of big business and of financial capital. In 2004 two new developments pushed *Fidesz* further on this path. First, a wealthy entrepreneur became the new socialist prime minister. A negative campaign focusing on his background promised working class defectors to *Fidesz*. Then, on 5 December 2004, the referendum initiative to extend citizenship to Hungarians living in the neighbouring countries was defeated due to low turnout, indicating that solidarity with co-ethnics across the border is not, in itself, a winning strategy. On the very same day citizens also voted on the issue of the privatisation of hospitals. The outcome revealed that the voters are more enthusiastic about preserving welfare provisions than about the right-wing version of national identity.

As a result, after 2004 the concept of '*polgár*' was dropped from the party's rhetoric and replaced by the simple '*emberek*' (people) and by the somewhat more specific '*plebejus*' (plebeian) adjective. Opponents were increasingly attacked as aristocrats. Consider the following excerpt: 'Those new aristocrats, good-for-nothing fellows, who have never worked, have never struggled for something, who feel secure only in an artificial environment, are averse from the reality, because confrontation with reality shows how weak and helpless they are'. The discourse increasingly acquired a non-political tone, the conflict between *Fidesz* and the government was increasingly cast as the opposition between strong and healthy, on the one hand, and weak and sick, on the other. The 'clique of aristocrats, opulent millionaires' was contrasted with 'the new majority':

> Those who work hard, raise children, take care of each other, try to survive with dignity get less and less, while ever more goes to loafers, the lying millionaire swindlers, conmen protected by the state. [...] everything people worked for is taken away, everything that was the common property of people is sold [...] a privileged group treats people as fools [...] the people fare ill, while those in power gather ever more fancy, ever more wealth, ever more privilege. (Debreczeni 2009: 241)

The voice of ordinary people was interpreted as a generic criticism of pluralistic political arenas. When Orbán rejected calls for electoral debates (he stayed away from campaign debates both in 2010 and in 2014) he argued:

> No policy-specific debates are needed now, the alternatives in front of us are obvious [...] I am sure you have seen what happens when a tree falls over a road and many people gather around it. There you always have two kinds of people. Those who have great ideas how to remove the tree, and share with others their wonderful theories, and give advice. Others simply realise that the best is to start pulling the tree from the road. Dear Ladies and Gentlemen,

we need to understand that for rebuilding economy not theories are needed but, let us say, thirty robust lads who start working and implement what we all know needs to be done.   (Orbán 2010)

The previous enthusiasm for conservative elite traditions was pushed into background. At the 17th June 2005 party congress Orbán said 'for politics everything is more important than the personal life of people. Liberal, social-democratic and conservative politicians are loudly arguing whose worldview is the better one. And nobody thinks of human lives, everyday difficulties, personal lives of people' (Debreczeni 2009: 240). Direct democracy was increasingly considered superior to the cumbersome mechanisms of representative democracy. The party organised a number of petition-drives and claimed that its party-programme was based on the opinions collected from more than 1.6 million people. Two years later the party initiated a set of referendums aimed, among other things, at the abolishment of tuition fees in higher education, of fees paid by patients in hospitals and fees paid when visiting state doctors. The specific issues on the ballot were secondary; as the initiators admitted, the meaning of the referendum was to demonstrate that the government does not have the support of the public. In Orbán's words:

The indirect or parliamentary democracy has deprived us from the possibility to take the fate of the country into our hands. In such situations people should turn to direct democracy [...] In a democracy people have two choices. One is to go and elect representatives and then to trust them. But in Hungary people were misled, deceived, they cannot trust indirect democracy, therefore I wouldn't recommend this to Hungarians. The other option is to turn to the tools of direct democracy, instead of indirect democracy. This is the referendum, where I, as the people, can decide for myself on a number of issues. Not through politicians.   (Debreczeni 2009: 336)

In line with the new strategy, *Fidesz* also promised to halve the political class by drastically reducing the number of MPs and local councillors.

The populist demands did not completely crowd out elitist cultural views, although the top politicians largely avoided expressing them. But for example a close associate of Orbán, who was after 2010 appointed to be the special envoy of the Prime Minister, claimed that: 'MSZP and SZDSZ are anti-Hungarian. If they win the election then we need to start a revolution. We, *the historical ruling class*, need to re-seize power' (Piros 2006).

To conclude, prior to the crisis, *Fidesz* increasingly embraced populism. But even in its most populist phase the party refrained from condemning the entire elite and elements of elitist conservativism have never completely disappeared from the party's discourse.

The discourse of *Jobbik*

Jobbik was established in 2003. Many of its leaders were activists of the then declining extreme right party, MIÉP, but some of them, including Gábor Vona, the future leader of the party, came from the Orbán-led Civic Circles. Until 2009, *Jobbik* remained a marginal force. After 2006, however, the clashes between anti-government demonstrators and the police, the corruption scandals, the economic malaise and finally the humiliating IMF agreement created a more fertile ground for radical right wing propaganda. Several highly publicised conflicts between the Roma minority and the majority population served as final triggers (Karácsony and Róna 2010). After a high-profile lynching of a teacher by a group of Roma villagers and after Vona had formed a (weaponless) paramilitary organisation, the Hungarian Guard, *Jobbik's* popularity skyrocketed, reaching 15 per cent at the 2009 EP election. Demands for tougher law-and-order measures were in the centre of the party propaganda, but the party also demanded a halt to the demographic increase of the Roma, the move of Roma children to boarding schools, and the withdrawal of welfare subsidies from the relatives of the criminals.

In line with the anti-establishment rhetoric, Vona claimed that *Jobbik* is the only 'bottom-up' organisation among the 'multinational'[3] parties (Vona 2012: 48). He called for a challenge of 'cartel-democracy, or rather cartel dictatorship' (Vona 2012: 76). The party programme (*Jobbik* 2010) devoted much larger space to economic issues (poverty, unemployment, issue of flexible employment of women, and other practical-material conditions) than MIÉP, the previous radical right-wing force, had ever done. But among the leading issues of the party one finds the exclusion of foreigners from land ownership, the rejection of the Lisbon treaty, and the punishment of corrupt politicians. The party popularised the concepts of 'politician-crime' and 'Gipsy-crime' in parallel to each other.

The world-view expressed in party magazines and in various speeches, as opposed to the one expressed in the party programmes and campaign videos, has been unmistakably extremist. The world is seen as dominated by an international, largely Jewish,[4] network, spearheaded by multinational companies. This network benefits from the decline of nation states in general, and from the decline of Hungary in particular. The local representatives of the colonisers are the liberals, who govern the country even if their party has no public support (Vona 2009). In fact the entire current, inorganic, ruling elite is in the service of foreign interests, and uses its power to consciously corrupt the nation. *Jobbik* politicians repeatedly claimed that the growth of the Roma population is part of a sinister plan: 'What is Gypsy-crime? Lets not deceive ourselves: it is a biological weapon in the hands of Zionism' (Bíber 2009). Western forces use the country as market, as source of cheap labour and as terrain for waste disposal (Vona 2012:188) and intend to bankrupt it in order to create space for future immigrants (Vona

---

3. Note the dichotomy.
4. Antisemitism is often framed as an anti-Israeli attitude. As Vona said 'Hungary is a country that Israel wants to occupy or it has already occupied'.

2012: 148). The austerity policies, the privatisation of healthcare, the downsizing of the armed forces or the state registration of same sex couples are not simply erroneous policies but conscious steps towards depriving the nation of its self-defence so that it can be freely robbed and occupied. Hungarians are second rate citizens in their own country, threatened by a demographic decline, exploitation by multinational companies, moral decay, and destroyed environment. The remedies include tougher law-and-order policies, prioritisation of Hungarian entrepreneurs, restriction of abortion, support for large (but decent) families, nationalisation of key industries, and patriotic education.

Under a *Jobbik* government liberal democracy, 'the refuse imported from abroad' (Vona 2012: 94), would be replaced by a 'value-based democracy'. The constitution would be based on the sacred, supernatural institution of the Holy Crown. Merit would come first, rights later (Vona 2013: 82). Citizens would get the right to elect the president and recall their MPs. The members of the government would be legally responsible for their decisions, the MPs' immunity would be abolished (*Jobbik* 2010). Direct democracy would be complemented with elements of corporatist order to the extent that churches and civic organisations would constitute a second chamber. *Jobbik* endorses multipartism (e.g. Vona 2012: 152), but it expects all parties to accept the fundamental national doctrines of the Holy Crown.

In spite of the anti-liberal, anti-establishment, and pro-direct democracy claims, the core of the party's ideology is dominated by elitism rather than populism. Vona lists among his favourite authors Nietzsche and Julius Evola, regards himself as 'traditionalist', and mourns the advance of renaissance, rationalism, positivism, humanism, enlightenment, and finally, of liberalism (Vona 2012: 190, 2013: 35). The party would also establish a national board with the task of scrutinising the mass media from moral standpoints. The role of the state is to show direction to the national community, and therefore it cannot be ideologically neutral (Vona 2012: 131).

Jobbik considers liberalism and liberal democracy, together with fascism, communism and national-socialism, as part of the corrupting modern mentality (Vona 2013: 64). This mentality made humans lose touch with transcendence and become similar to animals (Vona 2012: 187, 197). Somewhat surprisingly from an avowedly Christian party leader, Vona sees Islam as the last bastion of traditionalism (Vona 2012: 190). He acknowledged with disdain that the public opinion cherishes freedom and democracy above everything else. His preferred values are: 'tradition, faith, order, natural hierarchy, monarchy, universal values, honour, chivalry, the heroic ideal, harmony between community and individual' (Vona 2013: 188, 193), and 'true' freedom, based on all these. *Jobbik's* rhetoric (not unlike Orbán's) has been organised around such concepts as 'fight', 'strength', 'faith', 'will', 'order' and 'nation'.[5]

---

5. The title of the series of articles written by *Jobbik's* president in 2010 was 'Order, Welfare, Awakening', with the motto: 'I believe we need nothing else but faith, strength and will'.

The party discourse often expresses nostalgia for the rule of traditional elites. These elites were thinned down in the nineteenth and twentieth century, and destroyed between 1945 and 1956 ('the head of the nation was cut off', Vona 2012: 77). The task is to recreate the elite, at least in spiritual terms (Vona 2012: 210). In line with this spirit, consumerism and mass media are regular targets of criticism, the preferences of the median voter are often treated with indifference. The party is ready to go against the public opinion on the issues of abortion, military service or foreign policy. In the latter arena the party's positions are particularly off the mainstream: *Jobbik* is not only strongly anti-Israel, pro-Palestine and anti-American, as all radical-right Hungarian movements are, but it also supports Russia, Kazakhstan and Iran. Even the decrease of the numbers of local councillors was rejected by Vona as a populist move, one that decreases transparency (Vona 2012: 57).

The conclusion of this section must be that while *Jobbik* uses an antagonistic language directed against the corrupt establishment, on a number of dimensions it is more elitist than *Fidesz*. Its propaganda directed to voters (and subsequently its electoral success) is anchored in populist ideas and gestures, but many elements of its core ideology are in tension with populism.

Framing the crisis and developing populist policies

The results of the first post-2008 national election revealed a new balance of forces (*see* Table 14.1). The MSZP-*Fidesz* two-party system that prevailed during the 2000s was replaced by a three party system. *Fidesz* and *Jobbik* received two-thirds of the vote, the left-wing government parties collapsed. But the financial crisis was more a facilitating than a causal factor behind these outcomes as *Fidesz* was leading in the opinion polls already in the summer of 2006 and *Jobbik's* rise in 2009 had more to do with the Roma issue than with the economic conditions. The protest-atmosphere fuelled by the financial situation helped both parties, but the fact that four years later, in 2014, they achieved virtually the same results, indicates that their success was a symptom of a deeper transformation of Hungarian politics than simply an expression of protest against austerity measures.

Nevertheless the success of these parties is closely related to the fact that their ideological and discursive formula fitted the crisis very well. *Jobbik* promptly identified the US and Israel behind the difficulties of the euro (Vona 2013: 130, 168, 176). It has regarded the crisis as a perfect illustration of the fact that globalisation is increasingly uncontrollable, destroying state, constitutional order and human norms (Vona 2012: 218), and, eventually, undermining its own existence.

The angle of *Fidesz* had to be different, as the party moved from opposition to government and even managed to win more than two-thirds of the seats in parliament. The party was forced to engage with the actual management of the crisis. The next section therefore discusses mainly the ideological and policy-responses of *Fidesz*, and it will investigate whether the governmental status changed the party ideology. The following paragraphs will show that the combination between

Table 14.1: Percentage of list-votes at parliamentary elections in Hungary (2006–14)

Party	2006	2010	2014
Fidesz	42.0	52.7	44.9
Jobbik [1]	2.2	16.7	20.2
MDF	5.0	2.7	–
SZDSZ	6.5	–	–
LMP	–	7.5	5.3
MSZP [2]	43.2	19.3	25.6
others	1.1	1.1	4
Total	100	100	100

Notes: [1]2006: Joint list with MIÉP. *[2]2014:* Joint list with *Együtt*, DK, PM and MLP.

populism and governmental power is inherently unstable: Many of the populist components of the party ideology were phased out after the electoral victory. Other decisions, however, demonstrate how populist ideas can be translated into institutional solutions.

Prior to 2010, *Fidesz*, as the government-in-waiting, toned down its criticism of representative democracy. But the new tone did not imply more pluralistic views. In 2009 Orbán spoke of the eclipse of political dualism, the forthcoming rule of *Fidesz* for fifteen to twenty years, and claimed that in the coming period his party will define the national interest 'not in constant debates but in its natural way'.

While the clear bourgeois identification of the 1994–2002 period has not returned, the financial crisis and the impending victory pushed *Fidesz* towards a traditional right wing direction. It has concluded that the age of welfare-state is irrevocably over, the solution is a 'workfarist' state that provides work but also demands work from everyone and reduces welfare expenditure to the minimum. In line with this approach the government reduced the personal income tax, abolished progressive taxation and replaced social benefits to large families with tax breaks.

Yet the position of the party on economic issues has not become wholly rightist: it actually stepped up its criticism of the markets, particularly of the financial markets, and introduced a massive expansion of state regulation of almost all economic sectors. Prior to the 2014 election it reduced utility prices and the prices of communal services (energy, waste-collection, etc.). The governmental rhetoric treated this decision as the very essence of its policies as it hurt few monopolistic and mainly foreign, non-productive, business groups, while it helped ordinary Hungarians.

In line with the classical populist frame, actual physical work, the production of tangible products, has occupied a central role in Orbán's rhetoric already prior to the crisis. After 2010 this attitude was channelled into a sharp distinction between the productive and the speculative sectors of the economy. Resources from the latter were siphoned away through extraordinary taxes and hefty penalties.

The criticisms from Brussels strengthened further the image of a government of ordinary people, and the conflicts with banks, multinationals and Brussels contributed to the re-election of the government in 2014.

While the left-wing opposition also tried to capitalise on anti-elitist sentiments (pointing out, for example, that the reduction of utility prices benefits the owners of heated swimming pools more than the poor), for most of the time it presented a classical anti-populist position, claiming that the governmental solutions are not prudent, create a volatile business environment, lead to the loss of confidence of investors, etc. The government dismissed the critics as spokespersons of foreign financial circles and argued that there can be no policy realms that are beyond the orbit of democracy (i.e. majority). The debate acquired a populist versus anti-populist format.

Popular sovereignty continued to be a major *Fidesz* slogan, but it became even more clearly interpreted as the sovereignty of those with Hungarian culture and descent. This interpretation led to the extension of citizenship and voting rights to Hungarians living in the neighbouring countries and to discrimination against foreign companies, particularly in the service, financial and retail sectors. The government even bought a large share of private companies, particularly in the energy sector. The attempts to challenge the logic of globalisation went beyond economy. For example the government confronted brain-drain by demanding the return of scholarships from those who work abroad.

The 2010 victory was interpreted in the most radical terms. Orbán labelled it 'revolution' and 'regime change', comparable to the fall of communism, and announced the establishment of the Regime of National Cooperation. Within a few months a completely new constitution was adopted, without any input from the opposition parties. In less than four years the political community was extended with more than half a million new citizens. At the same time *Fidesz* also made an attempt towards narrowing the active citizenry with the help of new electoral regulations. The law, accepted by the parliament but finally rejected by the Constitutional Court, demanded citizens to pre-register to vote. This new institutional barrier would have reduced the size of the electorate, excluding primarily the least educated social strata. Interestingly this initiative followed up on a similar, but more radical initiative of *Jobbik* according to which the completion of primary school would be a precondition for voting at the parliamentary elections. The argument used by the two parties was the classical nineteenth century conservative justification: voting is a serious matter, those who lack basic cognitive abilities and who can be easily influenced should not be able to decide the fate of the government. Both initiatives would have affected the Roma disproportionately. But it is remarkable that both parties were ready to move into the direction of basing the government on significantly smaller electorates, excluding many of the ethnic Hungarian citizens too.

Under the new system of 'National Cooperation' the earlier existing convention according to which opposition could set up select committees was not tolerated any longer and most of the legal initiatives were hurried through a fast track procedure. The rights of interest groups for consultation or co-decision were either abolished or altered so that only government-supporting organisations were allowed to sit around the table. The new approach to decision-making was justified with the claim that the government must take responsibility for all major decisions, and blurring responsibility with consultations and veto rights would lead to less accountability.

In order to escape from the tutelage of international financial institutions some of the fiscal and monetary policies of *Fidesz* were rather conservative and this sense non-populist. The budget deficit was reduced below 3 per cent, and by 2014 inflation was practically eliminated. But the resources necessary for balancing the budget were partly provided by the nationalisation of private pension funds and the rigorous maintenance of financial discipline was counterbalanced by a host of popular/populist measures. The size of the local legislatures and of the parliament was cut to half, the *'cumul des mandats'* was forbidden, the severance payments given by the previous governments to state employees were taxed with a 98 per cent tax. The taxes on banks introduced in 2010, and then renewed during the subsequent years, were larger than anywhere else in Europe.

Although *Fidesz* changed its attitude towards referendums after the electoral victory, Orbán continued to communicate directly with the voters. The various waves of 'national consultation' were, however, rather one-sided, mainly involving letters sent to citizens about the achievements of the government. Before the acceptance of the new constitution Hungarians received a questionnaire. The replies (which were never made public) to this questionnaire were interpreted by the Prime Minister as indicating that people regard duties (duty to work, to care about family members, etc.) to be as important as rights and therefore the liberal constitution should be replaced with an illiberal one.

The architecture of parliamentarism remained essentially intact, but the autonomy of the judicial branch was curtailed. The legislative branch took over from the judiciary the right to decide which religious community is entitled for state support. The government forced more than 200 judges into retirement (the European Court of Justice later repelled the decision), replaced the president of the Supreme Court, increased the size of the Constitutional Court and packed it with its loyal supporters, including leading politicians. Within two years the new constitution was modified five times, and a number of legal initiatives that were rejected as unconstitutional by the Court were moved (in a somewhat modified form) into the constitution. In line with this revolutionary spirit, the coming years brought the takeover of all relevant decision-making positions. The government replaced the chief prosecutor and the members of the Election Commission with loyalists, its minister of economy became the Chairman of the Central Bank. Another new official, the head of the National Judicial Office (filled by the spouse of the *Fidesz* politician who drafted the constitution) was given the right to move cases from one court to another (due to the European pressure later the government had to compromise on the issue). According to the Bertelsmann Transformation Index by 2014 Hungary became a 'defective democracy'.[6]

---

6. http://www.bti-project.org/reports/regional-reports/ecse/.

These policies and institutional reforms were supported by a majoritarian rhetoric, fitting well the stereotypes of a populist rule that undermines checks and balances. Parallel, however, to these developments, the new constitution also placed numerous constraints on the power of future majorities and it also restricted the room for a bottom-up input into decision-making. The requirement of supermajority was extended to new policy areas, including taxes, family subsidies or the boundaries of electoral districts. The terms of the office holders of independent agencies (media board, national judicial office, public prosecutor, state audit office, etc.) were increased to eight and twelve years. The threshold for valid referendums was increased. *Actio popularis*, the right of any citizen to turn to the constitutional court for the examination of the constitutionality of laws, was abolished. The Budget Council was given the right to veto budgets, and the president acquired the right to call for a new election if the budget was not accepted in a timely fashion. While these changes benefited the current government, in the long run they have the potential to function as elitist, non-majoritarian components of the political system.

These non-majoritarian institutions can be partly explained by the fact that they protect the interests of the current governments against future governments. But it is important to point out that they are also in line with public sentiments. As Daniel Smilov (2013) argued recently, in Eastern Central Europe populism and constitutionalism do not necessarily contradict each other, as populists need to satisfy the fear and mistrust of citizens against politics and therefore they often maintain or even expand the existing constitutional constraints on governments.

The enacted reforms had both elitist and populist aspects and in some instances the two aspects manifested themselves in the very same decisions. The ban on deficit-producing budgets and the authorisation of a specific council to veto the budget proposed by the parliament expressed the suspicion of 'ordinary citizens' against politicians while at the same time they increased the power of, largely non-elected, office holders. The idea that citizens' full political rights should be based on merit (reflected by the emphasis in the new constitution on duties) has an equally paradoxical character: it is in line with the anti-liberal values of the majority but it also establishes an elite-defined standard.

In *Fidesz's* ideology the interest of the nation must prevail over particularistic interests, but the people themselves cannot be left alone to rule, they need the help of the benevolent state. As the principal ideologue of the new regime, Gyula Tellér wrote in his manifesto, social decay, exemplified primarily by the contraction of the population paying taxes and raising children, went so far that the society could no longer reverse the negative processes by itself, and therefore a strong state had to step in (Tellér 2014: 353). In this discourse even the concept of society acquires state-like attributes:

> [...] the society is a historically shaped organisation composed of people defined by culture and descent which defends its members against internal and external attacks and diversionary actions affecting their living space, personal matters, physical and intellectual properties, institutions, individual and community-based

activities and their joint obligations in the world, it organises those activities that can be done only through joint actions or it teaches the members how to organise themselves and provides them with the necessary tools.   (Tellér 2014: 356)

Obviously, such a state/society cannot behave in a neutral way towards its internal enemies.

Reflections on 'populism'

Populism is one of those terms of political science that are widely used by the politicians themselves. In 2012 Orbán explicitly addressed the populism-debate and placed it into a historical context. According to him the Western leaders after the WWII acted according to the logic of fear:

They feared not communism or fascism any more, but the masses, especially the politically active masses. Because of the fact that fascism won power democratically, today's Western European elite thinks that one should be cautious with the people, because the decisions of the people can cause big difficulties. So, democracy is regarded by them to be important but it is still better if power is not exercised by the people. This is how one can summarise the attitude of contemporary Western-European elite towards the people, towards its own people.

Then he went on tapping into the role of institutions. 'This approach gave rise to a politics – still prevailing – in which the power of principles and of institutions need to be achieved, and not the power of people'. He admitted that up to a point he also believed that:

[...] institutions and principles are more important than the actual power relations among people and that if the institutions and principles are strong then one can expect them to protect us against dictatorship. But by today we must realise that this is a false thought. The idea implanted into the public opinion that the European community should not be governed by people but by impersonal principles and institutions, leads to crisis. To condemn decisions made by people and stemming from personal will as dangerous is a dead-end for European politics.

The speech continued by pointing out that the media and the Western elite condemns populism, but in fact

the term "populist leaders" refers to politicians who simply say what people talk at home. Expressions such as populism embody the rejection of popular passions, sentiments, observations and desires. Europe should accept that historical decisions, good ones or bad ones, are made by people and persons, never by principles and institutions.   (Orbán 2007)

Not accidentally, in the cited speech the central term was not 'the people' ('*nép*'), but 'people' ('*emberek*') which can also be translated as 'individuals'.

As a result, the sentences above can be simultaneously read as endorsing bottom-up and top-down logics of decision-making: as calls for the power to the masses and/or for the power to individual leaders. Even more likely the appropriate decoding is the one that merges these two interpretations: a call for the rule of individuals who express the will of the masses.

Conclusions

Hungary is an extreme case as it was one of its major parties that engaged most deeply with populism and because this party subsequently managed to concentrate an unprecedented amount of power in its hands. It is an extreme case also because right wing critics of liberal democracy received two thirds of the votes both in 2010 and in 2014. There are few corners of Europe where democratic illiberalism represents a significant ideological alternative to the liberal status quo. In the West liberalism is too deeply entrenched, while in most Eastern European countries the social consensus behind the project of catching up with the West marginalises the explicitly illiberal ideologies. In Hungary, and to some extent in Poland, the cultural and institutional preconditions are present for challenging the prevailing norms of modern democracies. The global crisis provided an opportunity for such a challenge.

One can read the Hungarian story as an illustration of the claim that populism thrives on political crisis. But even more importantly, the case reminds us of another claim: that political crises are, by definition, constructed, and populists can have an important role in the framing-process.

Most of the answers of the analysed parties to the global crisis were ready well before 2008. The core of these answers lay in 'the recreation of national sovereignty'. In the case of *Jobbik*, this position was embedded into an outright rejection of liberal democracy. As far as *Fidesz* is concerned, the core of the response was provided by the combination of national sovereignty with the idea of a workfare-state.

This chapter also demonstrated that populism characterised the analysed parties only to a limited extent. In Hungary illiberalism and nationalism have deeper roots than populism. The former two support the latter but they can also constrain it.

The leaders of *Jobbik* had particularly many reservations about the 'empirically existing 'people', while *Fidesz's* populism was moderated by the fact that the party functioned as a government-in-waiting. Both of these parties treated formal, indirect political institutions with reservation, but they embraced direct democracy only partially, and in the case of *Fidesz*, clearly strategically. Both parties rejected compromise-based politics and questioned or attacked liberal and constitutional provisions. Both argued against legal, economic, technical or bureaucratic limitations of the scope of democratic politics and, at the same time, presented themselves as being motivated by non-political values and principles, such as family, strength, faith or will. *Fidesz* was more opportunistic, but throughout the analysed period stayed loyal to a set of traditionalist conservative values.

Remarkably, there has been no serious attempt at establishing centrist or leftist populist forces in Hungary. Both of the major populist projects were firmly anchored on the right, and the culprit of the crisis was not the undifferentiated elite but specifically the governing left. Having said that, one must emphasise that *Fidesz* displayed signs of both leftist and right-wing populism. The party's trajectory could be well interpreted a set of movements between these two faces of populism and as a series of efforts to synthesise them. While the new institutional structures set in government were designed following a majoritarian, power-concentration logic, they also incorporated a number of constraints on future majorities, satisfying both the interests of the party and the demands of the public.

The present study showed not only that parties may have both elitist and populist ideas, but also that ideas and policies exist that have an ambivalent character. While contrasting the (politically correct) world of liberal and multinational elites with the honest ambitions of ordinary people, as most populist movements do, the analysed parties also rejected the bottom of the society. Some of their initiatives simultaneously constrained the political elite and reduced the possibilities for a bottom-up input. The key to understand this ambiguity lies in the fact that the 'people' often meant a select group of people. In the references to ordinary citizens, 'ordinary' implied decent and virtuous citizens, who deserve more say than others.

The exclusionary feature of right-wing populism is of course much discussed in literature, but the phenomenon described here is slightly different. The analysed discourses and policies indicated not only that collective interests trump the rights of individuals and of minorities, but that they may even restrict the room for manoeuvre of the majority.

The interpretation of this phenomenon takes us back to the very concept of populism. A number of studies reflected on the flexibility and on the constructed nature of the category 'the people' (Laclau 2005a; Canovan 1999; etc.). Mudde and Rovira Kaltwasser (2013:151) call categories like 'people' and 'elite' empty vessels filled in different ways by different actors. But can the terms 'people' and 'elite' indeed mean anything? While this question may need to be treated in depth elsewhere, it is important to emphasise that in the reviewed cases the references to the 'people' went together with attempts at reducing the voice of the uneducated and the political underclass. Both of the analysed parties emphasised the duties of the citizens, implying that one needs to fulfil them in order to be considered as equal. Such views have strong popular backing but they link the concept of full membership in the community to something that is not 'a given', like citizenship or ethnicity, but is based on performance. One could argue that the expected performance is minimal and that in the Hungarian case the would-be-excluded overlap to some degree with the Roma population, and therefore this phenomenon can be absorbed into the standard formula of right wing populism. But conceptually what matters is that a performance-standard is applied, one that leaves the concept of the 'people' open upwards and closed downwards.

Finally, the Hungarian case revealed that the scope of populism as a governmental force can be larger than usually assumed. Prevailing conventions and international constrains, widely regarded to render populist and nationalist demands, especially within the EU, illusionary, can be, at least for a certain amount of time, circumvented. Liberal democracy can be defeated. This lesson is even more relevant as it comes from one of the ten most globalised countries of the world.

Chapter Fifteen

The Post-Populist Non-Crisis in Poland

Ben Stanley

Introduction

In May 2009, with Europe reeling from the impact of the global financial crisis, Poland's Prime Minister Donald Tusk and Finance Minister Jacek Rostowski held a press conference at the Warsaw Stock Exchange. A confident Tusk averred that Poland had 'passed the first test of the crisis better than any other country in Europe', contradicting the 'choir of economic Cassandras' who had issued bleak warnings about Poland's exposure. A colour-coded electronic map on the wall behind Tusk helped to tell the story: while a 0.8 per cent growth in GDP during the first quarter of 2009 was hardly impressive by pre-crisis standards, Poland nevertheless stood out as a 'green island' against a sea of red (Gazeta Wyborcza 2009).

This image resonated with two objectives of the coalition government, formed by Tusk's party Civic Platform (*Platforma Obywatelska*, PO) and junior partner the Polish Peasant Party (*Polskie Stronnictwo Ludowe*, PSL). Economically, Tusk aspired for Poland to become a 'second Ireland', which in pre-crisis times stood as a model of what rapid economic reform could achieve (Dudek 2013: 596). Politically, Tusk sought to reject the conflict and aggression that had become characteristic of Polish politics prior to his taking office.

While Poland continued to avoid the worst of the economic crisis, Polish politics remained characterised by the tendency for conflict to overshadow hard-won consensus. Nevertheless, the economic crisis had no significant impact on the presence and intensity of populism in Polish party politics. Poland was not affected by the economic crisis to the same extent as most other European countries, so its impact on party politics was more muted than elsewhere. Furthermore, Poland had experienced a significant and traumatic political crisis just prior to the period of the Great Recession, the resolution and aftermath of which was characterised by the rejection of populist 'crisis narratives'. Populism was not eliminated from the Polish party system after the 'populist coalition' of 2005–07, but was internalised by the system in the shape of the mainstream party Law and Justice (*Prawo i Sprawiedliwość*, PiS). This party would periodically return populist arguments to the forefront of Polish party politics, but the overall presence and intensity of populism was diminished after 2007. Furthermore, when populism returned, it tended to have a largely non-economic character, focusing on issues such as Polish identity, corruption and the overall competence of the state to govern.

Mapping Polish populism

The recent literature has settled on a broad consensus that populism denotes an antagonistic confrontation between a morally pure and authentic people and a morally impure and inauthentic elite (Stanley 2008: 102), but there is less consensus on how the concept ought to be operationalised for empirical research. On the one hand, populism is a binary category: either a party has a certain set of attributes which permits it to be designated as populist, or it does not. On the other hand, disaggregating populism into its component concepts allows us to analyse the extent to which a given party fulfils the definitional criteria of a populist party at a given moment. The latter approach is most relevant to the task of mapping the trajectory of Polish populism. If qualitative judgements about the consistency of a party's rhetoric with the core concepts of populism are coded numerically, we can arrive at a measure of the overall presence of populism within the party system. In the following analysis, populism is operationalised as a set of seven distinct conceptual opposites.

— Unit of analysis (*unit*): Conceptions of the fundamental political entity vary from circumscribed and heterogeneous to undifferentiated and homogeneous. The least populist unit of analysis is the liberal individual. Social classes imply greater homogeneity, but are nevertheless more circumscribed in character. Quasi-popular majorities such as 'the nation' or a religious majority are significantly less differentiated and more homogeneous in character, while the concept of 'the people' implies a broad, undifferentiated and homogeneous mass.

— Idiom of parties' political appeals (*idiom*): The rhetorical pitch of political parties' language ranges from technocratic to colloquial. The least populist of political actors operate within a consciously refined linguistic register and stresses the importance of specialised technocratic knowledge. The most populist of political actors uses a colloquial register and emphasise the importance of a wide-ranging popular 'common sense'. In between are those political actors who do not consistently employ either of these idioms.

— Attitude toward the elite (*elite*): Non-populists espouse a positive, laudatory attitude to the political elite, emphasise its meritocratic character, and express respect for its particular qualities, while populists depict the elite as a political, business and media cartel and criticise it as incompetent and corrupt. In between are those who criticise some elements of the elite and praise others, typically – but not necessarily – for party-political reasons.

— Diagnosis of crisis (*crisis*): Populists both exploit crises and seeking to provoke them in order to benefit from the ensuing sense of elite incompetence and loss of control. They discern an all-pervading and chronic state of crisis across all domains of public life which exists due to elite incompetence and/or conspiracy. The non-populist stance is to deny that there is a crisis (or at least make no attempt to raise the notion), and to emphasise the incremental solvability of political problems. In between are those who identify elements of crisis in one or more domains as a result of mistaken choices by other parties.

— Attitude to other parties (*parties*): Populists view other parties as politically and morally compromised due to their association with the elite, and therefore adopt a stance of enmity toward all of them. On the other hand, non-populists pursue dialogue and understanding between parties and across ideological and historical divides, limiting their criticisms of other parties to matters of policy. In between these two extremes are those parties who maintain an ideological or moral 'line in the sand' which divides acceptable allies from unacceptable ones.

— Liberal constitutionalism (*libcon*): Populists oppose the liberal system of institutions and legal proceduralism as a barrier to efficient rule and the implementation of policies that accord with the popular will. Non-populists see constitutionalism, liberal institutions, the separation of powers and the rule of law as overriding values. In between are those who essentially adhere to liberal constitutionalism, but express frustration with its often sclerotic nature.

— Democracy and representation (*demcon*): A focus on majoritarianism is a logical extension of populism's emphasis on popular sovereignty. Democracy is understood by populists as the means by which the will of the popular majority achieves representation. To this end they advocate institutional solutions that can ensure this will is expressed and acted upon in as unmediated a fashion as possible, such as direct democracy and majoritarian electoral systems. By contrast, non-populists view democracy as an instrument for restraining the tyranny of the majority, articulating the range of interests in society, and promoting the politics of consensus and compromise. In between these extremes are those who advocate increased majoritarianism within the confines of an essentially proportional system, and/or advocate the limited use of instruments of direct democracy to settle certain issues.

For each of these categories, the stances of all relevant political parties[1] are assigned a numerical code, with non-populist stances coded 0, intermediate stances coded 0.5, and populist stances coded. In the case of *unit*, the two other intermediate categories are coded 0.25 and 0.75 respectively. While the populist stances of parties may vary during parliamentary terms, elections are focal points for the ideological self-definition of parties and allow the political appeals of parties to be captured at a single time point. Three main sources of information are used to identify the stances of parties: election manifestos, speeches of the party leader during and immediately after the election campaign, and the parliamentary

1. Relevant parties are defined as those who achieved more than 5 per cent of the vote in a given election, and thus entered parliament. In 1991 the 5 per cent threshold did not apply, but for consistency's sake has been used as the cut-off point here.

debate that takes place prior to the vote of confidence for a new government. Table 15.1 shows the codings for each party, and Figure 15.1 plots the distribution of populist stances at each election from the first fully-free election of 1991 to the most recent election in 2011.[2]

The boxplots in Figure 15.1 give a visual representation of the presence and intensity of populism in the party system. The higher the median line, the more consistent the average party's political appeal with the key tenets of populism, and thus the higher the presence of populism. The greater the spread of values, the greater the deviation between parties on the populist scale, and thus the greater the intensity of populism as a source of political competition. The 'whiskers' outside the boxes show the first and third quartiles of the distribution, and the dots show outliers.

The anxieties of transition: Polish populism prior to the crisis

From the outset of Poland's transition to democracy, the new liberal political elite was concerned about the possibility of an immediate populist backlash to

Figure 15.1: Level of populism in the Polish party system (1991–2011)

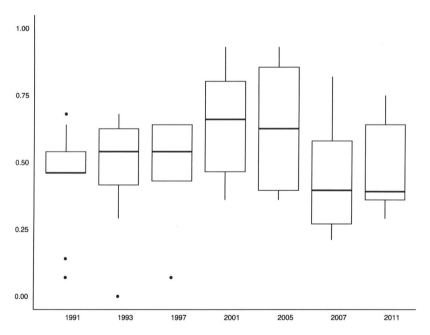

Source: Author's own analysis of party election manifestos, leaders' speeches and debates prior to votes of confidence in new governments.

---

2. Poland held an election in 1989, but it was not fully free, and has therefore been excluded from the analysis.

Table 15.1: Coding of populism present in party appeals

Party	Year	Unit	Idiom	Elite	Crisis	Parties	Libcon	Demrep	Popul
UD	1991	0	0	0	0	0.5	0	0	0.07
SLD	1991	0.25	0.5	0.5	1	0.5	0	0.5	0.46
WAK	1991	0.75	0.5	0.5	0.5	0.5	0.5	0.5	0.54
POC	1991	0.75	0.5	1	1	0.5	0.5	0.5	0.68
PSL	1991	0.25	1	0.5	0.5	0	0.5	0.5	0.46
KPN	1991	0.5	0.5	1	1	0.5	0.5	0.5	0.64
KLD	1991	0	0	0	0	0.5	0.5	0	0.14
PL	1991	0.5	0.5	0.5	0.5	0.5	0.5	0.5	0.50
NSZZ 'S'	1991	0.25	0.5	0.5	0.5	0.5	0.5	0.5	0.46
SLD	1993	0.25	0.5	1	1	0.5	0.5	0.5	0.61
PSL	1993	0.25	1	0.5	1	0.5	0	0.5	0.54
UD	1993	0	0	0	0	0	0	0	0.00
OJCZ	1993	0.75	0.5	0.5	0.5	0.5	0.5	0.5	0.54
UP	1993	0	0.5	0.5	0.5	0	0	0.5	0.29
KPN	1993	0.75	0.5	1	1	0.5	0.5	0.5	0.68
BBWR	1993	0.5	1	0.5	1	0.5	0.5	0.5	0.64
AWS	1997	0.75	0.5	0.5	0.5	0.5	0.5	0.5	0.54
SLD	1997	0.5	0.5	0.5	0.5	0.5	0	0.5	0.43
UW	1997	0	0	0	0	0.5	0	0	0.07
PSL	1997	0.5	1	0.5	1	0.5	0.5	0.5	0.64
ROP	1997	0.5	0.5	1	1	0.5	0.5	0.5	0.64
SLD-UP	2001	0.5	0.5	0.5	0.5	0.5	0	0	0.36
PSL	2001	0.5	1	0.5	0.5	0.5	0.5	0.5	0.57
PO	2001	0	0.5	0.5	0.5	0.5	0.5	0.5	0.43
SRP	2001	1	1	1	1	1	1	0.5	0.93
PiS	2001	0.75	0.5	1	1	0.5	1	0.5	0.75
LPR	2001	0.75	1	1	1	0.5	1	0.5	0.82
PiS	2005	0.5	0.5	1	1	0.5	1	0.5	0.75
PO	2005	0	0.5	0.5	1	0.5	0.5	0.5	0.50
SRP	2005	1	1	1	1	1	1	0.5	0.93
SLD	2005	0.5	0.5	0.5	0.5	0.5	0	0	0.36
LPR	2005	0.75	1	1	1	1	1	0.5	0.89
PSL	2005	0.5	1	0.5	0.5	0	0	0	0.36
PO	2007	0	0.5	0	1	0	0	0.5	0.29
PiS	2007	0.75	1	1	0.5	1	1	0.5	0.82
PSL	2007	0.5	1	0.5	0.5	0.5	0	0.5	0.50

Table 15.1 (continued)

Party	Year	Unit	Idiom	Elite	Crisis	Parties	Libcon	Demrep	Popul
LiD	2007	0	0	0	1	0.5	0	0	0.21
PO	2011	0.5	0.5	0	0	0.5	0	0.5	0.29
PiS	2011	0.75	0.5	1	1	1	0.5	0.5	0.75
RP	2011	0.5	1	0.5	0.5	1	0.5	0.5	0.64
PSL	2011	0.5	0.5	0.5	0	0.5	0	0.5	0.36
SLD	2011	0.25	0.5	0.5	0.5	0.5	0	0.5	0.39
AVERAGE	1991	0.36	0.44	0.50	0.56	0.44	0.39	0.39	0.44
AVERAGE	1993	0.33	0.50	0.58	0.67	0.33	0.25	0.42	0.44
AVERAGE	1997	0.45	0.50	0.50	0.60	0.50	0.30	0.40	0.46
AVERAGE	2001	0.58	0.75	0.75	0.75	0.58	0.67	0.42	0.64
AVERAGE	2005	0.63	0.75	0.75	0.83	0.58	0.58	0.33	0.64
AVERAGE	2007	0.31	0.63	0.38	0.75	0.50	0.25	0.38	0.46
AVERAGE	2011	0.45	0.60	0.60	0.40	0.60	0.20	0.60	0.49
AVERAGE	All	0.44	0.59	0.58	0.69	0.49	0.41	0.39	0.51

Source: Author's own analysis of party election manifestos, leaders' speeches and debates prior to votes of confidence in new governments.

painful economic reforms. In light of these uncertainties, the 'shock therapy' reform programme that came into effect at the beginning of January 1990 was rushed through parliament to capitalise on the brief window of opportunity for technocratic governance before politics again became subject to the bargaining of parties and interest groups.

The imposition of painful economic reforms by a technocratic elite in the absence of established patterns of political representation might have been expected to generate opportunities for populists. However, while the first decade of transition did not lack the kinds of unorthodox political parties and entrepreneurial demagogues who tend to attract the designation of 'populist', it was only in the second decade of transition that populism exerted a significant effect on the Polish party system.

The post-communist divide and the failure of Polish populism in the 1990s

As Figure 15.1 shows, the first decade of transition was marked by lower overall levels of populism than those which followed it, and also by a rather irregular distribution of populist sentiments. The median party in 1991, 1993 and 1995 was in an intermediate position on the scale of populism, and there were a number of outliers, mostly at the non-populist end of the distribution. Populism was thus neither particularly evident in the political appeals of relevant parties, nor was it an influential line of division between political parties.

In contrast to theories that suggested that post-communist party systems would coalesce around a divide between economic winners and losers of transition – a divide which might have been expected to be conducive to the emergence of populist parties – the main line of competition in Polish politics at first ran between the successors to the Communist Party and a multiplicity of parties which emerged from the communist-era opposition. The major parties on either side of the regime divide adhered to a general consensus about the principles of liberal democratic transition, and were not characterised by high levels of populism. The liberal Democratic Union (*Unia Demokratyczna*, UD) – which subsequently became the Freedom Union (*Unia Wolności*, UW) – was strongly anti-populist, while the successor post-communist alliance (and subsequently party) the Democratic Left Alliance (*Sojusz Lewicy Demokratycznej*, SLD) and the large post-communist umbrella coalition Solidarity Election Action (*Akcja Wyborcza Solidarność*, AWS) adopted an intermediate position. The broad and coalitional nature of political parties in this period meant that groups with a more significantly populist profile tended to be sunk within more ideologically moderate formations, while parties which could not clearly be located on either side of the regime divide were simply irrelevant to the main locus of political competition.

Poland's political earthquake and the emergence of populism: 2001–05

At the start of the second decade of transition, the presence and intensity of populism increased significantly as Poland's party system experienced an 'unexpected political earthquake' (Szczerbiak 2002). The 2001 parliamentary election saw only SLD and PSL return to parliament, with four new entrants: the liberal Civic Platform (*Platforma Obywatelska*, PO), the conservative and anti-communist Law and Justice (*Prawo i Sprawiedliwość*, PiS), the Catholic-nationalist League of Polish Families (*Liga Polskich Rodzin*, LPR) and the agrarian populist Self Defence (*Samoobrona*, SRP).

This upheaval resulted from the volatility of Polish voters, a decline in public support for the politics and political elites of transition, and the inadequacy of the regime divide as a means for the articulation of emerging political interests and differences. A growing disenchantment with the politics of transition on the part of 'transition losers' (Czapiński 2006: 184) created new opportunities for populists to gain electorally from attacks on the transition elite. SRP concentrated in particular on the economic inequities of transition, attacking parties on both sides of the regime divide for failing to make transition to capitalism work to the benefit of all and insisting that Poland should 'be ruled by the people and the representatives of their majority' (Lepper 2002: 196). LPR focused above all on the impact of transition on the Polish family, the 'elementary unit of the life of the nation' (Liga Polskich Rodzin 2006: 5–6), and gave political representation to the aims and discourse of the Catholic-fundamentalist Radio Maryja movement, which was founded both on the personal charisma of its proprietor, Redemptorist priest Father Tadeusz Rydzyk, and on a thriving 'alternative civil society' of volunteer labour and grassroots initiatives (Burdziej 2008: 28).

The post-communist SLD-PSL government that took office in 2001 struggled with recession, corruption scandals and the difficulties of European Union (EU) accession, all of which afforded SRP and LPR many opportunities to criticise the transition elite for their incompetence and venality. The increasing mood of political radicalism also benefited PiS, whose leader Jarosław Kaczyński had long argued that the process of democratic transition had been captured by a network (*układ*) of post-communists and liberals which spanned the political, administrative, business and media sectors and monopolised the real levers of political power (Gazeta Wyborcza 2006). PiS gained support as the public became increasingly conscious of the issues of corruption and decommunisation.

Poland's populist moment: 2005–07

The presence and intensity of populism persisted after the 2005 parliamentary election, and it became a central feature of the party system during the tenure of the 'populist coalition' during 2006 and 2007. After an acrimonious dual parliamentary and presidential election campaign, the expected post-Solidarity coalition did not emerge, and PiS formed a coalition with the previously uncoalitionable SRP and LPR. The coalition agreement outlined an ambitious programme of reforms to remove the transition elite from positions of power and initiate a 'genuine' transition to democracy by replacing Poland's Third Republic with a Fourth Republic (*Czwarta Rzeczpospolita*, IVRP).

The coalition's attempts to implement this programme drew it into repeated conflict with the Constitutional Court, the major opposition parties, and leading politicians and public figures associated with the Third Republic. The increasingly antagonistic relationship between the coalition and the liberal media, business, academic and administrative elite prompted the emergence of an emotional and polarising public discourse which pitted the 'Poland A' of transition winners against the 'Poland B' of transition losers. Issues of traditional values, identity and material interests engaged and animated the people, and large-scale protests and counter-protests over aspects of coalition policy became commonplace features of public life.

The opposition of state institutions – in particular the Constitutional Tribunal – to some of the coalition's flagship proposals hindered the realisation of the coalition's legislative programme, but contributed to a swift spiralling of populist rhetoric and countervailing anti-populist rhetoric among Polish political elites. The invocation of crisis, emotionalisation of differences, and the attempt to gain proprietorship over 'authenticity' are all key tropes of populism, and became increasingly characteristic of PiS's political appeal during the tenure of the populist coalition. Political discourse reached new heights of aggression and emotion, with PiS proving more proficient than its partners in the art of populist rhetoric. A particularly aggressive parliamentary speech given by Kaczyński at the beginning of his term of office attacked the 'mendacious elites' (*łże-elity*) of the Third Republic, who served as a 'front for the defence of criminals' (*front obrony przestępców*). The task of the coalition was to eliminate this 'network' (*układ*) from public life, and to do so 'in the interest of ordinary people, ordinary Poles' (Sejm Rzeczypospolitej Polskiej 2007, 12 May 2006).

Both SRP and LPR couched their claim to popular authenticity in their emergence from grassroots movements. However, on coming to power PiS was still associated primarily with the 'alternative elite' Kaczyński and his circle had begun to cultivate in the early 1990s. The polarising of public life during the coalition's tenure enabled Kaczyński – at the expense of SRP and LPR – to position his party as the representative of those social groups whose way of life was threatened by the heedless pursuit of 'imitative modernisation'. In power, PiS rapidly superseded LPR as proprietors of the Catholic-nationalist narrative of transition politics. Rydzyk's transfer of patronage from LPR to PiS was a boon for the latter, the Radio Maryja movement providing organisational resources and disciplined participants for the large public rallies and marches that were a hallmark of this period. It also helped PiS lay claim to being the representatives of an authentic popular majority.

PiS's attack on the Third Republic elite and out-manoeuvring of its coalition partners was one of the reasons why populism became so central to Polish politics during this period, but the logic of populist discourse also generated a counter-reaction on the part of transition elites which further entrenched the divide between the two political camps. Tense public debates over emotive issues such as the 'lustration'[3] of high-profile public figures and the coalition's confrontational approach to foreign policy produced coordinated responses from post-communist and liberal-solidarity politicians who shared concern at the perceived radicalism of the coalition. The short-lived 'Movement for the Defence of Democracy' (*Ruch Na Rzecz Demokracji*) sought to defend the achievements of the Third Republic against the actions of a government with 'a fundamentally different concept of the state and its role, not understanding the essence of democracy, neglecting the rule of law, and striving for the 'party-isation' (*upartyjnienia*) and ideologisation of the state' (Ruch Na Rzecz Demokracji 2007).

A green island: The absence of economic crisis and its consequences for populism

The 'populist moment' of 2005–07 had significant consequences for the subsequent course of Polish party politics. PiS's radical turn rendered SRP and LPR largely irrelevant to the political debate, and the attempts of the junior coalition partners to protect their positions in the party system destabilised the coalition to the extent that it ultimately became unsustainable. PiS was eventually forced to accede to the calling of early elections, which turned into 'a referendum on a polarising and controversial government' (Szczerbiak 2008). These elections clarified the shape of the Polish party system, although it still

---

3. 'Lustration' is the term given to the provision of information about the collaboration of public functionaries with the security services.

remained susceptible to volatility (*see* Table 15.2 for parties' vote and seat shares). The victorious PO formed a coalition with the post-communist PSL, becoming the first government to transcend the regime divide. The distinction between post-communist and post-Solidarity no longer dictated the pattern of competition between parties. Instead, attitudes toward the politics of transition became the new dividing line. With its roots in early 1990s liberalism, PO was regarded as the natural representative of the 'Poland A' of transition winners, while PiS's claim to uphold the interests of the Poland B' of transition losers was strengthened by the failure of SRP and LPR to return to parliament.

After the reckoning of 2007, populism declined in importance, but still remained a significant element of Polish party politics. As Figure 15.1 illustrates, the median party was considerably less populist than in 2001 and 2005. The decline in the overall presence of populism reflects the disappearance of SRP and LPR and the reaction of the opposition parties to the actions of the populist coalition. The economic crisis might have been expected to encourage the flourishing of economic populism, with PiS linking its critique of the politics of transition to a fundamentally different model of economic reform such as that advanced by its former coalition partner SRP. However, this did not occur, as the economic crisis had only a limited impact on Poland, which made outright criticism of the neoliberal orthodoxy – and its advocates – less powerful than it might otherwise have been. As a result, the economic policies of PO and PiS tended to converge, restricting the potential for populist agitation over economic issues.

The main theme of the 2007 election campaign was not policy differences between the parties, but their attitudes towards the political system in general. PO opened its electoral manifesto with the observation that the elections of 2007 had 'fundamental meaning' for the future of Poland; they would determine whether

Table 15.2: Parties' share of the vote and number of seats: (2001–11)

Party	2001	2005	2007	2011
SLD	41.0 (216)	11.3 (55)	13.2 (53)	8.2 (27)
PO	12.7 (65)	24.1 (133)	41.5 (209)	39.2 (207)
SRP	10.2 (53)	11.4 (56)	1.5 (0)	0.1 (0)
PiS	9.5 (44)	27.0 (155)	32.1 (166)	29.8 (157)
PSL	8.9 (42)	7.0 (25)	9.0 (31)	8.4 (28)
LPR	7.9 (38)	8.0 (34)	1.3 (0)	–
RP	–	–	–	10.0 (40)
Other	9.2 (2)	11.2 (2)	1.4 (1)	4.3 (1)
Total	100% (460)	100% (460)	100% (460)	100% (460)

Source: Państwowa Komisja Wyborcza (n.d.).
Notes: In 2001, SLD ran as an electoral coalition with UP and in 2007 as part of the electoral coalition LiD. The figures quoted are for these coalitions as a whole, rather than for SLD alone. In 2011, SO ran as *Nasz Dom Polska-Samoobrona Andrzeja Leppera*.

Poles opted for 'a Western European quality of life, efficient organisation and democratic standards, or a quarrel[some], messy, Eastern European 'democracy' (Platforma Obywatelska 2011). In a similar spirit, the Left and Democrats (*Lewica i Demokraci*, LiD) electoral coalition, which brought together the SLD and minor parties of both post-communist and post-Solidarity descent, prefaced its electoral manifesto with an appeal to protect the 'great Polish miracle' of transition to democracy from the destructive actions of populists. LiD's programme was explicitly a response to 'the conditions of deep political crisis' engendered by the rule of an 'authoritarian' and 'incompetent' government (Lewica i Demokraci 2011: 368–9). Rather than issues of economic policy, it was unresolved conflict over the nature of democratisation that drove the emergence of populism in Poland, and its periodic re-emergence after the downfall of the populist coalition.

The economic crisis and the Polish economy

Poland stood out against other OECD countries for the relatively minor impact of the economic crisis. In 2009, real gross domestic product (GDP) contracted by 4.5 per cent across the EU27. The Baltic States were particularly hard hit, with GDP declining by 14.1 per cent in Estonia, 14.8 per cent in Lithuania, and 17.7 per cent in Latvia, and even in those post-communist countries less badly affected, recession was still significant, with GDP declining by 4.5 per cent in the Czech Republic and 6.8 per cent in Hungary. By contrast, Poland's economy grew by 1.6 per cent during 2009 (Eurostat 2014b). Poland's strong performance was attributable to a number of factors. The financial sector remained robust, with a comparatively low percentage of non-performing loans and a relatively healthy loan-to-deposit ratio (Leven 2011: 185). Significant inflows of regional and structural funds from the EU led to substantial investment in the modernisation of infrastructure. Poland's relatively large domestic market, the absence of severe austerity measures and the maintenance of government spending all kept internal demand strong. Poland's lower labour costs and strategically important location made it an attractive investment opportunity for foreign capital searching for opportunities at a time when Western European economies were in crisis. The złoty's floating exchange rate allowed it to depreciate, which boosted the competitiveness of Polish exports (Leven 2011: 185).

Poland's avoidance of recession during the crisis enabled it to outperform other post-communist countries in the pursuit of convergence with the economies of Western Europe. In 2008, Poland's GDP was 56 per cent of the EU28 average; by 2012 this figure had grown to 67 per cent. By comparison, Hungary saw a more modest increase from 64 per cent to 67 per cent over this period, while there was no change in the Czech Republic at 81 per cent (Eurostat 2014b). Yet while Poland's growth outpaced that of most post-communist economies in 2010 (3.9 per cent) and 2011 (4.5 per cent), it fell back in 2012 to a modest 1.9 per cent (Eurostat 2014b). The absence of significant austerity measures contributed to a deterioration in public finances as growth slowed. With levels of public spending sustained alongside a decline in revenues, Poland's general government deficit grew from -1.9 per cent of GDP in 2007 to -7.9 per cent in 2010, falling back to -3.9 in 2012 (Eurostat 2014b). Public debt rose from 45 per cent of GDP in 2007 to 55.6 per cent in 2012, coming perilously close to the constitutional debt limit of 60 per cent (Eurostat 2014a).

The situation in the labour market also worsened. After Poland's accession to the EU in 2004, average annual unemployment declined from 19.1 per cent in that year to a low of 7.1 per cent in 2008. However, it increased during the years of the economic crisis to 10.3 per cent in 2013 (Eurostat 2014b). This remained just under the EU28 average of 10.9 per cent, but detracted from the credibility of the government's claim to have dealt successfully with the effects of the crisis. The precarious situation of Polish youth also contradicted the success story. In 2008, youth unemployment was at its lowest since EU accession, with 17.2 per cent of those aged less than twenty-five out of work. However, by 2013 this proportion had increased to 27.3 per cent, compared with an EU28 average of 23.5 per cent (Eurostat 2014b). Poland's relatively encouraging economic performance had also done little to alleviate the problem of so-called 'junk' contracts which offered little job security and often no employer social security contributions. In 2004, over a fifth (22.7 per cent) of Polish employees had contracts only of limited duration, increasing to over a quarter (26.9 per cent) in 2012, compared with an EU28 figure of only 13.7 per cent (Eurostat 2014b).

The politics of the economic crisis

At the level of economic policy, the divide between 'social' and 'liberal' Poland remained largely rhetorical. This was evident even prior to the economic crisis: the legislative activity of the 2006–07 populist coalition centred around reform of the state, a more assertive foreign policy, and the restoration of traditional values, and it did not depart in any significant way from the macroeconomic orthodoxies of transition.[4]

In 2007, the electoral appeals of the three parties which had comprised this coalition reflected the rather incoherent character of the coalition's economic policy. Rather than criticising neoliberal transition, PiS focused on taking credit for the economic growth that Poland had enjoyed during its term in office. Furthermore, it couched its rhetoric of economic success in the language of neoliberalism: the economic growth Poland was enjoying could be attributed to the lowering of taxes and decreasing of the budget deficit, which had encouraged international ratings agencies to upgrade Poland's credit rating and led to an influx of foreign investment (*Prawo i Sprawiedliwość* 2011: 136). By contrast, SRP sought to reiterate its critique of the neoliberal orthodoxy, continuing to emphasise the need for a living wage and an increase in unemployment benefits

---

4. One of the few pieces of legislation passed during the coalition's tenure which had major consequences for the economy actually contradicted its aspiration to make 'winners' pay a larger share of the costs of transition: reforms to personal income tax resulted in a *de facto* 18 per cent flat tax, with only 1.5 per cent of taxpayers falling into the higher tax bracket.

(*Samoobrona Rzecypospolitej Polskiej* 2011: 340). Meanwhile, LPR opted to run in an electoral coalition with the libertarian Union for Real Politics (*Unia Polityki Realnej*, UPR), a party which criticised the politics of economic transition as insufficiently capitalist. This led it to endorse an economic policy significantly further to the right of the mainstream parties (*Liga Prawicy Rzeczypospolitej* 2011). At the same time, PO softened its orthodox neoliberal programme with concessions to public sector workers (Szczerbiak 2008: 422). The debate over the economy assumed a valence character, with the two main parties competing over which was more competent to bring about economic growth.

The absence of polarisation on the economic dimension is evident in the expert placements of these parties by specialists on Polish politics (*see* Figures 15.2–15.4).

Figure 15.2: Party placement in issue space (2002)

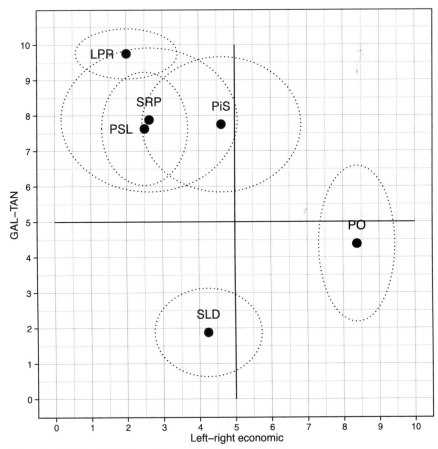

Source: 2002 Chapel Hill Expert Survey (Bakker *et al.* 2012).
Notes: The black dots denote the mean placement of all experts surveyed. The dotted line plots the standard deviation.

Figure 15.3: Party placement in issue space (2006)

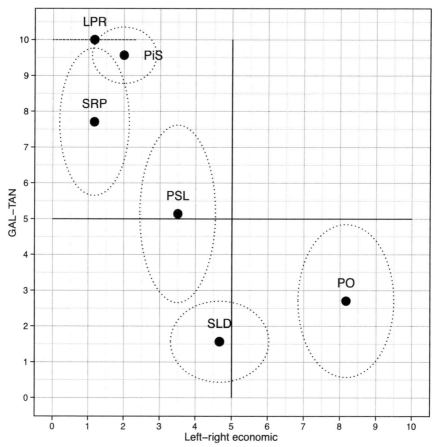

Source: 2006 Chapel Hill Expert Survey (Bakker *et al.* 2012).
Notes: The black dots denote the mean placement of all experts surveyed. The dotted line plots the standard deviation.

In 2002, PiS's overall stance on the economy was unclear; the average respondent rated it as centrist and the standard deviation was large. In 2006, during its term in office, there was greater consensus among experts that it should be placed alongside its coalition partners as a party of the economic left. By contrast, the PO was regarded as clearly right wing on the economic dimension in both 2002 and 2006. However, by 2010 both parties were seen to have moved towards the centre.

The first PO-led government of 2007–11 largely failed to implement the ambitious set of economic reforms on which PO had campaigned. This was due in part to the nature of the coalition, with junior partner PSL distinctly less enthusiastic about neoliberal policies. Cohabitation with PiS-affiliated President Lech Kaczyński also made it more difficult for PO to pass legislation in areas where

Figure 15.4: Party placement in issue space (2010)

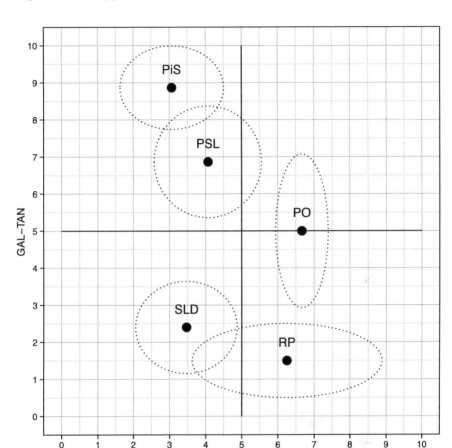

Source: 2010 Chapel Hill Expert Survey (Bakker *et al.* 2012).
Notes: The black dots denote the mean placement of all experts surveyed. The dotted line plots the standard deviation.

they lacked sufficient support to overturn a presidential veto. Allied to the rising fear of the contagion of recession, these circumstances compelled the PO-PSL government to proceed cautiously, favouring a 'government of small steps' over the 'economic miracle' PO had advocated prior to the 2007 election. This strategy drew criticism from those in the media and business sector who had expected bold liberal policy initiatives, but made it more difficult for the opposition to draw battle lines over the economy.

The increase in economic uncertainty had a clear impact on public opinion. When the Tusk government took office in November 2007, a third (33 per cent) of Poles thought that the economy was heading in a positive direction. At the end of the first quarter of 2009, generally regarded as the nadir of the global recession, this figure had fallen to only one in ten (11 per cent). Confidence in the economy fluctuated thereafter, and at the end of the second quarter of 2013 only 14 per cent of Poles had a positive opinion of the country's economic situation (CBOS 2014). However, there was little scope for PiS to exploit this discontent. As Markowski (2008, 1061; 1065) shows, in 2005 and 2007 the Polish electorate was clustered on the economic dimension of issue space, with each party's average voter holding interventionist and redistributive views. This suggests that voters' choices were not strongly motivated by ideological differences on economic issues. Furthermore, the very lack of progress PO enjoyed in realising its economic programme had the effect of making it increasingly difficult for PiS to emphasise the ideological differences between the parties, reinforcing instead the valence character of economic issues. In these circumstances, there was little scope for the economy to become the focal point of populist mobilisation.

The Fourth Republic in abeyance: Populism during the crisis

While populism did not remain a definitive characteristic of Polish politics during the Great Recession, it was nevertheless a recurring aspect of Polish party politics. With the major opposition party unyielding in its criticism of the Third Republic and unwavering in its intention to implement a Fourth, the potential for a return to the ideological warfare of 2005–07 remained latent.

The cohabitation of the PO-PSL coalition and President Lech Kaczyński afforded PiS a means to check the actions of the government and keep the radical principles of the Fourth Republic in the public eye. As well as vetoing key reform bills such as healthcare and public media and providing a strong negative incentive against further liberalising measures in areas such as state funding for *in vitro* fertilisation, President Kaczyński attempted to pursue an independent foreign policy. Increasingly, PO used the difficulties of cohabitation as an excuse to delay significant reforms until after the election of a more cooperative president.

This cautious approach was part of a strategy to widen the party's appeal from its origins in the urban middle class. If PiS had succeeded in broadening its base of support through populist mobilisation, PO sought to achieve the same outcome by appealing instead to Poles' distaste for the divisive and confrontational rhetoric of the populist coalition. This involved exploiting the fear of voters that a return of PiS to power would mean a return to the politics of the Fourth Republic, a technique which became known as 'threatening them with PiS' (*straszenie PiSem*). At the same time, PiS sought to regain the trust of moderate voters. In a new party programme, issued in 2009, PiS focused on developing its profile as the proprietors of a 'social Poland' which looked after the interests of the collectivity, in contrast to PO's heedless individualism. Some of the party's more controversial policies were pushed into the background: in the space of 216 pages, the 2009 manifesto used the word 'lustration' only twice (Prawo i Sprawiedliwość 2009).

If the period 2007–09 was characterised by a less antagonistic atmosphere than before, the Smoleńsk tragedy and its aftermath exposed just how profoundly the period of the populist coalition had affected the relationships between major political actors and sections of society. In what was widely seen as an attempt to exploit the tensions between the two halves of the Polish executive, Russian premier Vladimir Putin invited only Prime Minister Tusk to a ceremony commemorating the thousands of Polish nationals murdered by the Soviet NKVD in the Katyń forest in 1940. In response to this snub, the presidential office organised a separate ceremony at Katyń, to be attended by the presidential couple, military, political and state dignitaries, and representatives of the descendants of the victims of Katyń. On 10th April 2010 the entire delegation perished when the presidential plane crashed near to the Smolensk airbase.

In the immediate aftermath of this disaster, it seemed possible that the desire for unity in the face of tragedy would serve to bring about a fundamental change in the character of Polish politics. However, the legacy of Smoleńsk was not to be the disappearance of the antagonisms on which populism thrived, but their renewed affirmation. Among political and cultural elites, the decision to bury the presidential couple in the crypt of the Wawel Cathedral in Kraków (the resting place of national heroes) proved extremely divisive. At the level of the public, controversy raged around the erection of a large cross outside the presidential palace in the days following the crash. The attempts of the authorities to remove the cross, and the refusal of a staunch group of PiS-sympathising Catholic and nationalist mourners to permit this, stoked the resurgence of unresolved conflicts over the relationship between Church and state and the relationship of Polishness

Figure 15.5: Percentage of public with a positive opinion of the Polish parliament (2008 Q3–2013 Q2)

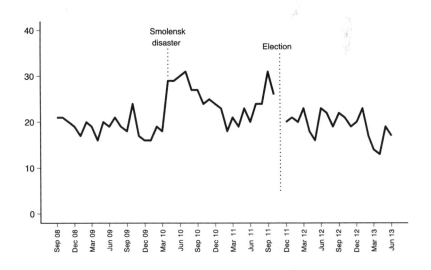

Source: CBOS (CBOS 2008; CBOS 2009; CBOS 2010; CBOS 2011; CBOS 2012; CBOS 2013).

and Catholicism. As in 2005–07, it was the politics of identity, rather than the politics of interests, which drove the re-emergence of populism. As Figure 15.5 shows, while positive public attitudes towards the Polish parliament rose in response to the Smolensk disaster, this did not last long, with Poles soon perceiving the resurgence of political enmities.

Initially, PiS's response to Smoleńsk was muted, with the party refraining from exploiting the tragedy during the presidential election campaign. However, it soon became a key feature of the party's political appeal after Jarosław Kaczyński's defeat to acting president and former parliamentary speaker Bronisław Komorowski.

The party's return to radicalism and the unwillingness of Kaczyński to countenance greater internal party democracy alienated some of the party's centrist deputies, who left to form a new and ultimately unsuccessful party, Poland Comes First (*Polska Jest Najważniejsza*, PJN). In the period prior to the 2011 parliamentary elections, the party oscillated between the aggressive rhetoric that would appeal to its core voters, and a more substantive critique of the government's legislative record. This election also saw the emergence of a new party, the Palikot Movement (*Ruch Palikota*, RP; subsequently renamed *Your Movement*), led by former PO deputy Janusz Palikot. This party's eclectic mixture of economic liberalism, cultural libertarianism and anti-clericalism, leader-centricity, and electoral campaign based on breaking apart an allegedly 'frozen' (*zabetonowany*) party system ensured that it attracted the term 'populist'. However, while it was unsparing in its criticism of the established parties, it did not articulate a clear dichotomy between the elite and the people, and lacked the aspect of moral condemnation that is a distinct characteristic of populist parties.

Conclusions

In comparison with the 2005–07 parliamentary term, populism did not have a strong and consistent impact on Polish party politics during the period of the economic crisis. In the early 2000s, the accumulation of discontent with the functioning of Polish democracy and with the dominant transition elites led to the articulation of a populist moment: a brief and intense conflagration which brought down the existing party system. Since that juncture, populism remained a feature of Polish politics, but an episodic and largely inconsequential one. In the absence of economic crisis, these brief resurgences of populism reflected instances of political crisis, but even so, those crises have proven insufficient to sustain a lasting resurgence of populism.

To return to the hypotheses which we set out at the beginning of this paper, the Polish case lends support to the expectation that economic crisis would stimulate populism (H1). Poland did not experience an economic crisis, and at the same time did not experience an increase in populism. Poland did not experience a political crisis during this period either. However, while the hypothesis that populism rises in response to political crisis (H2) is not refuted here, the Polish case draws attention to a more complex relationship between crisis and populism. The politicisation of the Smoleńsk disaster and the recurrence of identity-based populist mobilisation that occurred in its wake suggest that populists may choose to create political crises through the manipulation of the meaning and significance of events. The absence of economic crisis, and the ambiguous relationship between Polish populism and political crisis, means that the hypothesis that simultaneous economic and political crises will generate particularly intense instances of populism (H3) must also be regarded as not proven.

The Polish case challenges the conventional wisdom that populists become more 'responsible' and less populist as they become part of the government, and less responsible and more populist on rejoining the opposition (H4). The case of PiS shows exactly the opposite process: this party became more populist when in power as a result of its increasingly antagonistic conflict with the transition elite, and less populist when in opposition as a result of its attempts to gain more support among moderate voters.

Even if Poland had been more significantly affected by the economic crisis, it is by no means obvious that this would have stimulated a populist response. In 2001, Polish populist parties gained support partly as a result of growing dissatisfaction with the painful costs of economic transition. However, as the populist moment of 2006–07 demonstrated, the politics of history, culture and identity constituted the most fecund ground for populist mobilisation. It is thus by no means certain that the counterfactual of a Polish economic crisis in 2008 and after would have succeeded in stimulating a populist response. Polish populism is still very much rooted in the legacies of the past, rather than the politics of the present.

PART V

THE ANGLO-CELTIC REGION

Chapter Sixteen

The Great Recession and the Rise of Populist Euroscepticism in the United Kingdom

Matthew Goodwin

Introduction

In the comparative study of populism and radical politics in Europe, the United Kingdom (UK) has traditionally been viewed as a deviant case. Since the late 1970s, and as populist parties in many European states left the margins for the mainstream, similar parties in the UK continually failed to establish a significant and sustained presence in the party system (Eatwell 2000; Kitschelt and McGann 1995; Goodwin 2007). While at various points in history leaders from the mainstream parties have embraced populism, such as Margaret Thatcher and Tony Blair (Mair 2000, 2002; Mudde 2004), at least until 2010 populist challengers to the established political class remained a marginal force.

Since 2010, however, the arrival of the Great Recession and a period of fiscal austerity coincided with a sudden and sharp rise in public support for a populist party. Founded in 1993, and rooted in a national tradition of 'hard' Euroscepticism, the UK Independence Party (UKIP) has more recently come to exhibit the defining features of the populist radical right, namely nativism, authoritarianism and populism (Mudde 2007). Amidst the economic crisis and austerity UKIP attracted growing support from a 'left behind' electorate of older, white and working-class voters who are primarily motivated by their concerns over Europe, immigration and political elites in Brussels and Westminster, leading some to question the extent to which the UK remains an exceptional case in the study of Europe's radical right (Ford and Goodwin 2014). By 2014, UKIP had attracted sufficient support to match the performance of the Danish People's Party and the *Front National* in France by winning the European Parliament elections, with over 26 per cent of the vote.

But to what extent can the rise of this 'new' populist force be explained by the financial crisis that erupted in 2008? And how has the political and economic fallout from the Great Recession impacted on populist mobilisation in the UK more generally? This chapter begins by exploring the evolution of populism prior to the crisis and then turns to examine the economic and political effects of the economic downturn. The chapter then examines the rise of UKIP in detail, and asks whether the UK has joined other EU member states in witnessing the arrival of a sustainable populist force.

Populism before the crisis: A weak and divided milieu

In the six decades that followed the end of the Second World War, populist parties in the UK continually failed to achieve a position of electoral significance. Explanations for the absence of successful populism often stressed the institutional environment. A majoritarian electoral system posed a major hurdle to the rise of a populist party, by encouraging the development of a two-party system that has long been dominated by the Conservative and Labour parties, each of which can trace their roots back more than a century. Between 1945 and 1970, this system enabled the two main parties to consistently recruit over 85 per cent of the vote, and at least 70 per cent until 2005.[1] Furthermore, remaining space for a populist party was arguably filled by the Liberal Democrats, a third party that since the 1990s specifically appealed to voters who are dissatisfied with Labour and the Conservatives.

A second hurdle to a populist insurgency was presented by a tendency for the two main parties to adopt a populist style on social and cultural issues that have tended to benefit the radical right in other European states. On immigration, multiculturalism and the UK's traditionally 'awkward' relationship with the EU, leaders from the mainstream parties have often adopted a populist strategy, framing migrants, asylum-seekers, the EU or the euro currency as threatening the interests of native Britons (Ford and Goodwin 2014; Mair 2002). Conservative Party leaders such as Margaret Thatcher, William Hague and Michael Howard, and Labour leaders like Tony Blair and Gordon Brown have each employed populist rhetoric when addressing public anxieties over these issues. The absorption of populism into the mainstream has been especially visible on the centre-right, where academics such as Kitschelt and McGann (1995) have identified this tendency as a key barrier bulwark to a populist insurgency from outside of the mainstream.

Despite these obstacles, by the first decade of the twenty-first century studies of public opinion in the UK began to point to significant opportunities for populist mobilisation from outside of the mainstream. As elsewhere in Europe (Mudde 2010), analyses of survey data uncovered strong public sympathy for an array of nativist, authoritarian and populist policies that are advocated by the populist radical right, and which has arisen against weakening identification with established parties, heightened political distrust and increased electoral volatility. The message from this research was that while populists in the UK have faced a harder institutional environment, and strong competition from mainstream actors, there is a similar level of public demand for radical right populism as in other European democracies where these parties have been far more successful (Ford 2010; Goodwin 2011; John and Margetts 2009; McLaren and Johnson 2007).

The inability of populists to mobilise this potential brings us to a third hurdle, namely the absence of a credible and articulate populist campaigner. On the

---

1.   In 2005 the combined share of the vote for Labour and the Conservatives fell to 67.6 per cent and then in 2010 to 65.1 per cent of the vote, which I discuss in greater detail below.

supply-side of UK politics, and at least until 2010, space for populism has been dominated by two distinct cultures, which have been shaped by different traditions and forced to compete for public support.

The first and most significant of these populist cultures is rooted in the UK's long tradition of Euroscepticism, which has drawn followers from within and outside of the mainstream, enjoyed significant public support and is generally perceived as a legitimate current of political expression (Aspinwall 2000; Evans 1998; Forster 2002; Geddes 2003). After the fall of Margaret Thatcher and the Maastricht Treaty in 1993, the Eurosceptic tradition was increasingly manifested outside of the mainstream, spawning an array of populist challengers to the centre-right. The most significant was the Referendum Party, which campaigned for a national referendum on EU membership at the 1997 general election. Following the collapse of the Referendum Party due to the death of its leader, Sir James Goldsmith, UKIP dominated the populist Eurosceptic scene. Like its predecessor, UKIP was defined by its 'hard' brand of Euroscepticism – a principled objection to EU membership – which is distinct from the 'soft' Euroscepticism that broadly accepts EU membership but agitates for reform of the European Union (EU) (Szczerbiak and Taggart 2008).[2]

By the time of the financial crisis in 2008, UKIP was the main expression of the Eurosceptic tradition and its origins provided the party with a 'reputational shield' against accusations of racism and extremism (Ivarsflaten 2005).[3] Increasingly, UKIP also embraced a more populist strategy, infusing its founding Eurosceptic message with nativism and welfare chauvinism. Like other populist parties in Europe, UKIP attacked the 'metropolitan political elite', unelected Eurocrats and claimed that more than seventy million migrants from EU member states in Central and East Europe were about to settle in the UK (Ford and Goodwin 2014). These three pillars of hard Euroscepticism, opposition to immigration and populism came to form the bedrock of UKIP campaigns, or as the party told voters in 2004: 'Say no to uncontrollable EU immigration. Say no to the EU spending your money, and say no to this country being governed by Brussels'.[4] By the time of the 2004 European Parliament elections the party's embrace of a more overtly populist strategy was producing stronger political effects; UKIP finished in third place with 16.1 per cent of the vote, and ahead of the traditional third

---

2. According to Szczerbiak and Taggart (2008), hard Euroscepticism refers to 'a principled opposition to the EU and European integration and therefore can be seen in parties who think that their countries should withdraw from membership, or whose policies towards the EU are tantamount to being opposed to the whole project of European integration as it is currently conceived'. In contrast, soft Euroscepticism refers to hostility toward European integration but not a principled objection, and typically encompasses calls to reform (rather than terminate) membership of the EU.

3. This is not to say that UKIP do not face such accusations. The party was regularly accused in the media of recruiting right-wing extremists and, increasingly from 2010, advancing a xenophobic agenda. However, in contrast to the extreme right-wing, Eurosceptic parties such as UKIP have also enjoyed a greater level of access to the media and – in general terms – have not been portrayed as an anti-democratic pariah party.

4. UKIP European Parliament Election Broadcast, 2004.

party, the Liberal Democrats. However outside of second-order elections UKIP was struggling to exert an electoral impact. At the 2005 general election its support slumped to 2.2 per cent, and over the next three years UKIP made few advances. This stagnant electoral growth was not helped by the fact that UKIP devoted little effort to domestic elections, instead focusing on second-order European Parliament elections that were held under a form of proportional system.

As UKIP emerged as the dominant voice of the Eurosceptic tradition there has also been another movement on the populist landscape that is rooted in a stigmatised current of ethnic nationalism and neo-Nazism (Eatwell 2000; Goodwin 2011). In the immediate years that preceded the post-2008 crisis, the most significant populist party from outside of the mainstream was the right-wing extremist British National Party (BNP), which had emerged from the National Front (NF) and shared its predecessors' obsession with biological racism, disdain for liberal democracy and thinly-disguised conspiratorial anti-semitism. Under the leadership of Nick Griffin, from 1999 the BNP adopted a more populist style of campaigning; the party demanded that the UK withdraw from the EU, enact direct democracy through referenda and defend the 'silent majority', while attacking the established political class for colluding with corporations, bankers and conspiratorial groups to cause the global economic crisis.

While the BNP attracted some isolated local gains in economically deprived areas, and won one seat on the devolved Greater London Assembly, by the time of the financial crisis the party was struggling to achieve a wider breakthrough.[5] Like other right-wing extremist parties in Europe that were rooted in a neo-Nazi tradition, the BNP struggled to establish an image of legitimacy and seemed destined to remain on the electoral fringe (Carter 2005). Nonetheless, between 2005 and 2010 the BNP did attract more support than UKIP at domestic elections and, for a short period, seemed likely to emerge as the primary populist challenger in the UK (Ford and Goodwin 2010; Goodwin 2011).

As the crisis approached, therefore, populism in the UK was a generally weak and divided force, characterised by internecine rivalry and electoral marginality. Neither UKIP nor the BNP had been able to mobilise mass support at the ballot box. While before the crisis these two parties that regularly employed populism did attract significant support at European Parliament elections, their combined share of the vote at general elections remained at very low levels (*see* Figure 16.1).

The crisis hits: Economic effects of the Great Recession

The UK officially entered recession in January 2009 after a credit crunch that began in late 2007 and which, by 2008, had spiralled into a global financial crisis. It was the first time that the UK had been in recession since 1991. Compared to

---

5.   The BNP's core areas of strength were in Pennine Lancashire in North West England, West Yorkshire, parts of the Midlands and also outer-east London. On the geographical base of support for the party *see* Goodwin (2011) and Ford and Goodwin (2010).

Figure 16.1: Support for populists in general and European Parliament elections (1992–2014)

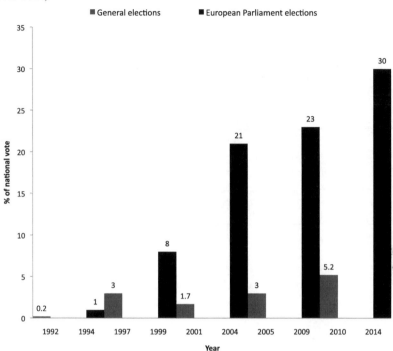

Note: The populist vote combines the total vote shares for several different parties, namely: the BNP and NF in 1992; UKIP in 1994; the Referendum Party, UKIP and BNP in 1997; UKIP and BNP in 1999, 2001 and 2004; UKIP, the BNP and a UKIP splinter party, Veritas, in 2005; UKIP, the BNP, English Democrats and NO2EU in 2009; UKIP, BNP and English Democrats in 2010; and UKIP, BNP and An Independence from Europe, English Democrats, NO2EU, We Demand a Referendum Now and Britain First.

several other states in Europe the impact of the crisis was severe. As outlined in the introduction, while these effects were not as strong as in cases such as Greece, Ireland and Spain, the UK remained among the 'hardest hit'. Analysis of data relating to GDP, unemployment and gross government debt reveals that the impact was greater in the UK than in fifteen other European states. Only in Spain, Greece and Ireland did the crisis have a greater economic impact.

We can further explore the economic effects of the crisis and how they relate to populism through a range of additional data. First, the percentage growth in the UK's gross domestic product (GDP) declined sharply, falling from 1.2 per cent in the third quarter of 2007 to -0.9 per cent in the second quarter of 2008, and to its lowest figure of -2.5 per cent in the first quarter of 2009. This was the sharpest contraction of output since 1958 (Vaitilingam 2009). While the economy began to recover it continued to enter periods of negative growth throughout 2010–12, and did not return to consecutive growth until the first quarter of 2013. Meanwhile, government debt as a percentage of GDP more than doubled, increasing from

44 per cent in 2007 to 91 per cent in 2013. Only Portugal, Italy, Greece and Ireland reached higher levels of indebtedness.[6]

Unemployment also increased significantly, though not as sharply as in other European states. In the UK the overall rate of unemployment increased from around 5 per cent in the immediate pre-crisis period to a peak of 8.4 per cent in October 2011, thus failing to emulate the peak rates of over 20 per cent seen in states like Greece and Spain. Unemployment also remained below the average rate in the EU, and did not return to levels seen during an earlier recession, when in 1984 unemployment peaked at 11.9 per cent. Yet there was still a clear impact on the number of citizens claiming welfare (Jobseekers Allowance); the number of claimants increased sharply from an average of 906,000 in 2008 to over 1.4 million for each year in the entire period 2009–13 (although the claimant count has still remained at generally lower levels than those seen in earlier years). A similar picture emerges for youth unemployment; while the percentage of unemployed youths (i.e. aged under twenty-five years old) increased from 14 per cent in 2007 to 21 per cent by 2011, this was consistent with the broader EU-level trend, while these figures remained much lower than those witnessed in Greece, Ireland, Spain, Italy and Croatia.

This is perhaps one reason why the UK did not experience major social unrest, alongside the fact that the state continued to provide basic social goods (*see* Pappas and O'Malley 2014). While there was an outbreak of rioting in several major cities in 2011, this was arguably rooted more in grievances within black British communities over policing practices than public anger over political management of the crisis. Nonetheless, the sudden downturn in macroeconomic conditions appeared to offer new opportunities for populist mobilisation, and to parties that had long been arguing that the EU, migrants and allegedly incompetent elites in Westminster posed a threat to the economic and cultural interests of native (white) Britons.

The UK amidst crisis: Exploring the political effects

What were the political effects of the crisis in the UK? As in other European states, in the immediate short-term the crisis contributed to electoral losses for the incumbent Labour government, which had been in power for eleven years (since 1997) and was already behind the opposition Conservative Party in the polls. In fact Labour had been trailing the Conservatives since 2006, before the onset of the crisis, and only enjoyed a temporary return to a position of dominance in the polls in 2007 when Tony Blair was replaced by Gordon Brown as Labour leader and Prime Minister. By the end of 2007, however, and before the eruption of the crisis, Labour had again fallen behind the Conservatives.

That the crisis exacerbated these difficulties for Labour can be seen in two sources of data. The first concerns the attitudes of voters toward the statement 'in the long-term this government's policies will improve the state of Britain's

---

6. By 2013 France had approximately the same percentage of consolidated debt as the UK.

economy'. Since 2007, voters had become increasingly unwilling to endorse this statement with regard to the Labour government; net agreement slumped from +3 at the beginning of the year to -7 per cent in September 2007, and to -35 per cent by September 2008, suggesting that many voters drew a straight line from the crisis to the policies of the incumbent Labour government. A second source of data similarly underscores the political effects of the crisis. As shown in Figure 16.2, when voters were asked to select the 'best' party for managing the economy, between 2007 and 2010 Labour's image of economic competence deteriorated sharply; the percentage of respondents who selected Labour as the best party to manage the economy dropped by more than ten percentage points, from 38 to 26 per cent, while the percentage of voters selecting the Conservatives surged three-fold from 13 to almost 40 per cent, and in only one year.

Against this backdrop, in 2009 the party system was also affected by a national political scandal that was largely unrelated to the crisis. In the same period that the salience of the economy among voters increased, a parliamentary expenses scandal erupted in the national media, revealing that Members of Parliament from all three established parties had abused the expenses system. As others observe, most voters were aware of the crisis; according to the 2010 British Election Study pre-election survey, 93 per cent of voters were aware of the scandal, over 90 per cent agreed or strongly agreed that the expenses scandal had made them angry, and over 80 per cent of voters agreed or strongly agreed that MPs who were implicated in the scandal should resign (Vivyan, Wagner and Tarlov 2012). While there is surprisingly little aggregate evidence that MPs implicated in the scandal were punished by voters at the ballot box (Curtice *et al.* 2010; Eggers and Fischer 2011;), it nonetheless appears plausible to suggest that the revelations

Figure 16.2: The 'best' party – managing the economy

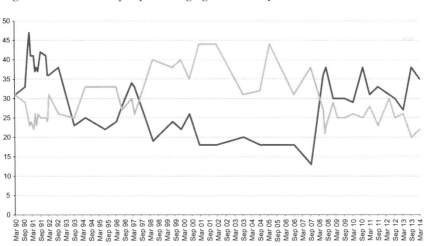

Source: Ipsos-MORI tracker poll.

contributed to a broader decline in political trust and the cultivation of a more fertile breeding ground for anti-establishment populists.[7]

The first opportunity to gauge the direct political effects of the crisis arrived with the 2009 European Parliament elections. Consistent with wider trends in Europe, and a tendency for voters to punish incumbents at second-order elections, Labour suffered a significant loss of support (-6.9 per cent). It is interesting to note, however, that despite the crisis and the parliamentary expenses scandal, neither the populist radical right nor the extreme right attracted a sharp rise in support. UKIP attracted 16.6 per cent of the vote, winning thirteen seats but saw an increase of only 0.3 per cent on its result in 2004. Meanwhile, the BNP which blamed the crisis on the neoliberal global economy, corrupt bankers and conspiratorial forces, attracted 6.3 per cent – enough to secure its first two seats in the European Parliament but an increase of only 1.3 per cent on its result in 2004. The failure by populists to more fully exploit those trends above can be explained partly by the fact that the economic crisis was not joined by a deep political crisis of the sort seen in other European states.

In contrast to cases such as Greece and Italy, the UK did not experience a sudden and dramatic collapse of public trust in politics or a major rupture in its party system. This is reflected in the data on levels of political trust in the UK, presented in Figure 16.3. A cursory glance at these data might suggest that the onset of the crisis in 2008 did correspond with a sharp fall in political trust. These data from the British Social Attitudes survey reveals how the percentage of citizens who 'trust the government to put the needs of the nation first' declined from 38 per cent in 1986 (when the question was first asked) to 17 per cent in 2013. This includes a sharp drop in trust over a two-year period that covers the economic crisis; between 2007 and 2009, the proportion of voters who trusted the government almost halved, from 30 to 16 per cent. Moreover, while levels of trust have since rebounded slightly they have not returned to the levels of trust witnessed before the crisis. However, given that this decline in levels of trust commenced before the crisis, and coincided with the parliamentary expenses scandal, it is difficult to separate out the effects of these events at the aggregate level. While it may be that the crisis contributed to this trend, it also appears likely that this was already underway and was shaped more strongly by domestic political events. Some evidence for this assertion can be found in the Introduction to this volume and data in the Eurobarometer surveys, which reveal that whilst voters in the UK have tended to be less trustful than their EU neighbours these levels remained broadly consistent with the wider trend across the EU. This undermines the suggestion that the crisis has had disproportionate political effects within the UK, and thus fuelled a more intense form of populism (as hypothesised in the introduction to this volume).

7. As Vivyan, Wagner and Tarlov (2012) note, among sitting MPs implicated in the scandal and who stood for re-election in 2010, the electoral cost is estimated to have been around 1.5 per cent.

Figure 16.3: Trust in national government in the UK (1986–2013)

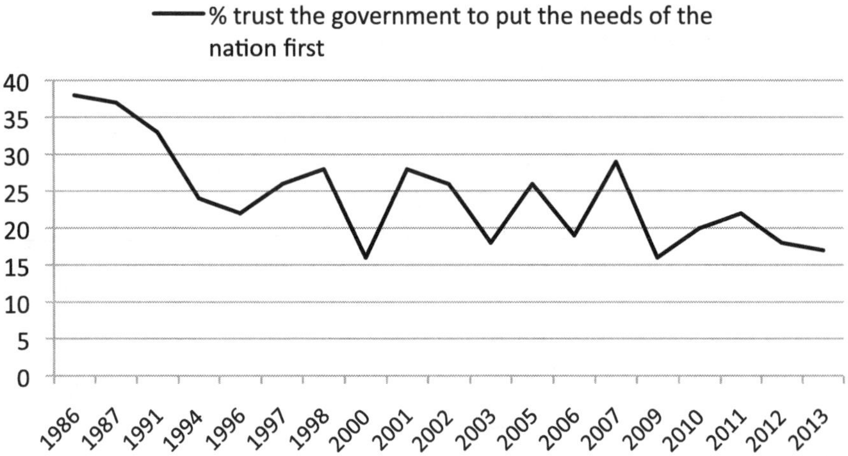

────── % trust the government to put the needs of the nation first

Source: British Social Attitudes (BSA) survey.

The emergence of new opportunities for populist parties was further underscored by the outcome of the general election in 2010. Having been out of power since 1997, the Conservatives had turned to David Cameron, who promised a more socially liberal stance on issues like equal marriage and climate change and to downplay his party's past emphasis on opposition to immigration, asylum and the EU. At the 2010 general election, Labour was removed from power after thirteen years in office and with only 29 per cent of the vote, its lowest share of the national vote since 1983 (and before that 1922). But while Cameron and the Conservatives were the largest party they had failed to win an overall majority, and increased their vote share by only 3.7 per cent. The Conservatives were subsequently forced to form a coalition government with the Liberal Democrats; the third party that had traditionally framed itself as the 'outsider' vehicle for politically dissatisfied voters was now an insider member of national government (Russell and Fieldhouse 2005).

Aside from producing the first coalition government in the UK for seventy years, the 2010 general election also revealed other pressures in the party system that are important when considering the rise of populism. The UK might not have experienced a political crisis like that seen in EU states such as Greece, but several trends were challenging the traditional two-party system, many of which were rooted in the pre-crisis era.

The first is a weakening of the two-party system and a growing inability of Labour and the Conservatives to mobilise mass support. Combined, in 2010 the two main parties won only 65.1 per cent of the vote, a figure that has been in steady decline since it peaked in the 1950s at over 96 per cent and only first dropped below 70 per cent in 2005.[8] The inability of the two main parties to mobilise the same level of support as in earlier years partly reflects another trend; rising public support for third parties. Since 1970, the combined vote share for the Liberal Democrats and other parties has risen more than three-fold, from 10.5 per cent to 30 per cent in 1983, 32 per cent in 2005 and 35 per cent in 2010. Such trends paint a picture of an increasingly fragmented party system.

While these trends created a more favourable demand-side for populists, changes in party competition also enlarged space for a populist insurgent on the radical right. In the shadow of the crisis, the extreme right-wing BNP struggled to sustain an electoral presence. In contrast to the resurgent extreme right in countries like Greece that profited from a deep political crisis, in 2010 the BNP increased its share of the vote to only 1.9 per cent (+1.2 per cent) and failed to have a serious impact in its targeted seats.[9] While there was some evidence to suggest that the party was beginning to benefit from the crisis by polling strongest in seats that had seen the largest increases in unemployment since 2005 (Curtice, Fisher and Ford 2010), the BNP subsequently collapsed due to stagnant growth and infighting (Goodwin 2014).

Alongside the wider changes in party competition discussed above, the decline of the extreme right further enlarged space for UKIP, which amidst the crisis had initially also struggled to mobilise support. At the 2010 general election UKIP averaged only 3.1 per cent (an increase of just 0.9 per cent), prompting its leader to resign and be replaced by Nigel Farage. From here on UKIP's fortunes radically improved. UKIP moved quickly to exploit the changed political environment by targeting Eurosceptic social conservatives who were disillusioned with Cameron's more socially liberal brand of conservatism, non-voters and political protestors who might otherwise have supported the Liberal Democrats, and former supporters of the extreme right BNP. UKIP's founding Eurosceptic message was widened to include a stronger emphasis on immigration and anti-establishment populism while its electoral strategy was overhauled.

Yet while UKIP modified its leadership and strategy, these changes owed little to the economic crisis. Ever since the arrival of the crisis in 2008 UKIP had moved to address public anxieties about the recession and its effects by framing the Eurozone crisis as validating its long tradition of hard Euroscepticism. As the crisis unravelled, the party responded by reiterating its older demands for the dissolution of the euro currency and a return to a Europe based on trade alliances, rather than full economic and political union. Such opportunism was also reflected in UKIP's resurrection of old themes; amidst the crisis, the party warned repeatedly

---

8. Because of the strength of the old Liberals the two main parties combined won only 68 per cent of the vote in 1922 and 1923, however after the decline of the Liberals both Labour and the Conservatives increasingly dominated the vote and did not attract less than 70 per cent combined until 2005 (when they won 67.6 per cent).

9. The BNP had promised to mount a serious challenge in the outer-east London seat of Barking and Stoke-on-Trent Central in the Midlands but finished third and fourth respectively. On the collapse of the BNP *see* Goodwin (2014).

that a failure to manage the economic fallout in the Eurozone was producing a 'German-dominated Europe', a growing divide between north and south, and risked the prospect of mass civil unrest, revolution and a return of extreme nationalism.[10] Such arguments were often infused with claims that Europe had witnessed a failure of leadership at the national and EU levels; Farage pointed to 'puppet [technocratic] governments' in Greece and Italy as evidence for how the crisis had further revealed the 'anti-democratic' credentials of the EU. The Eurozone, UKIP told voters, is 'now run by people who don't respect democracy, who don't respect the rule of law, who don't respect the basic principles upon which western civilisation is supposed to be based'.[11]

Yet rather than signalling a new innovation in its discourse, such arguments reflected an extension of UKIP's pre-existing tradition of hard Euroscepticism that can be traced back to its formation in the early 1990s. It is revealing, for example, that the Eurozone crisis was not specifically mentioned in UKIP's election manifestos for the 2009 European Parliament election or 2010 general election. Rather than push the economic downturn to the forefront of its campaign, UKIP remained heavily focused on its founding goal of withdrawing the UK from the EU, incorporating the crisis into its hard Eurosceptic narrative but not focusing specifically on the crisis as a possible driver of its support. One example arrived at the 2010 general election, and as the full effects of the crisis became clear. Rather than target specific public anxieties over the economic downturn or fiscal austerity, UKIP continued to associate its core platform with a range of benefits, arguing that '[w]ithdrawal from the EU can benefit the UK right across the spectrum, from immigration to crime, tax, jobs and the economy, pensions, public services, and even through to animal welfare and the Post Offices' (UKIP 2010: 2).

Nor did UKIP's growing embrace of anti-immigration stem from the crisis. While UKIP had long been hostile to immigration, throughout the 1990s and early 2000s it had distanced itself from an issue that was associated more closely with the stigmatised BNP (Ford and Goodwin 2014). From 2010 onward, however, with the extreme right in decline and the salience of immigration rising UKIP increasingly targeted public concern over this issue, specifically the rising number of migrant workers from Central and East European states, such as Bulgaria and Romania, similar to the strategy of Timo Soini and the True Finns (*see* Chapter Four).

As noted in the introduction, populist radical right parties often mobilise support along cultural lines, stressing the negative effects of cultural diversity and reframing economic conflicts in cultural terms. While UKIP certainly referenced the economic downturn when setting out its opposition to the free movement of labour, for example claiming 'immigration has coincided with soaring youth unemployment and stagnant wages that have not kept pace with the cost of living', foremost the party anchored its campaign in the theme of 'regaining

---

10. For example 'Farage slams 'German-dominated' EU', *Daily Express*, 16 November 2011

11. 'Euro is a house of cards waiting to topple – Nigel Farage', *Reuters* 22 March 2013; also 'Farage slams 'German-dominated EU'.

control' (UKIP 2014). As we will see in the next section, the political effects of these changes on the supply-side and a more concerted embrace of radical right populism would quickly transform UKIP into the most successful populist party in modern UK politics.

New electoral politics: UKIP and the arrival of credible populism

Amidst an economic crisis in the UK a 'new' populist radical right party was pushed to the forefront of political and media debate. From 2010 onwards UKIP would poll increasingly strongly across sixteen parliamentary by-elections, finishing in second place in seven of these contests. The party's electoral growth was also clear at the local level, where at the 2013 local elections UKIP averaged 26 per cent of the vote and gained over 140 seats in local government. At the 2014 European Parliament elections – which took place as the salience of the economy had begun to decline in the minds of voters – UKIP reached new heights by winning the contest outright and polling 26.6 per cent of the vote. It was the first time since 1929 that a new party had won a nationwide election, and the first time since 1906 that a party other than the Conservatives and Labour had won the highest share of the vote. Shortly afterward, UKIP reached a new record in domestic voting intention polls by averaging 14.9 per cent and becoming the most popular choice among white, working-class pensioners.

But to what extent has the rise of radical right populism in the UK marked a response to the post-2008 crisis, and how have economic and political factors shaped this new populist force? One useful way of addressing this question is to examine the social bases of support for UKIP and populist Euroscepticism since 2010. This provides some evidence to suggest that the crisis has to some extent contributed to the appeal of UKIP, although by itself is clearly not sufficient. Analysis of almost 6,000 self-identified UKIP supporters has revealed how, since 2010, the party's appeal has been strongest among older, white working-class pensioners who tend to be men with few qualifications and are deeply pessimistic about their economic prospects (Ford and Goodwin 2014; Ford, Goodwin and Cutts 2012). These 'left behind' voters were struggling economically before the onset of the post-2008 financial crisis, but were then hit the hardest by the economic downturn. Nor are these voters motivated by single-issue concerns over the EU. Dissatisfaction with how the main parties managed the post-2008 financial crisis emerges as a significant predictor of support for UKIP, which provides some evidence that while the crisis has facilitated the emergence of populism in the UK it is clearly not the whole story.

This is reflected in more detailed multivariate analysis of UKIP support (*see* Ford and Goodwin 2014), which reveals how a wider array of motives than solely concerns over the financial crisis or its management underpin the rise of populism. Since 2010, support for the populist radical right UKIP has been most significantly predicted by strong Euroscepticism, intense concern over immigration and its effects, and populist dissatisfaction with the established political class, all of which points to the conclusion that populism in the UK has prospered amidst broader political trends and from a national tradition of Euroscepticism. In fact, dissatisfaction with how the established parties have managed immigration emerges as a more significant driver of support for UKIP than dissatisfaction with how the established parties have managed the post-2008 economic crisis, again underscoring the centrality of social and cultural concerns. Citizens who hold strongly negative judgements of main party performance on immigration, not only the economic crisis, are far more likely to have switched to the populist Eurosceptic party since 2010.

Since 2010, therefore, and amidst the most severe economic crisis for decades, the rise of populist Euroscepticism in the UK has been rooted in a more economically disadvantaged section of the electorate but driven chiefly by concerns over the social and cultural issues of immigration, Europe and, to a lesser extent, concerns over how the crisis has been managed. To the typical supporter of this populist radical party, the established parties are perceived to have failed to competently manage some of the main challenges facing the country, of which the economic crisis is only one.

Conclusions and discussion

Unlike events in other European democracies, the economic crisis in the UK was not accompanied by a deep political crisis. Nor did the UK witness the emergence of a new political party on the radical or extreme right, or the rise of an altogether new anti-establishment party similar to the M5S in Italy or the 'Best Party' in Iceland. In fact, contrary to developments elsewhere in Europe in the UK the traditional extreme right quickly collapsed after the arrival of a sharp economic downturn.

Instead, this chapter has shown how several political and economic factors combined to facilitate the emergence of a populist radical right party that was already visible in the party system before the crisis commenced. The arrival and onset of the Great Recession in the UK was quickly followed by a national political scandal over the abuse of parliamentary expenses that negatively impacted on the entire established political class and contributed to a decline in political trust. The next year saw considerable change in party competition, with the 2010 election bringing a more socially liberal conservative leader and the traditional third party challenger into coalition government. In the shadow of these economic and political events – a protracted financial crisis from 2008, a national political scandal in 2009, and the arrival of coalition government in 2010 – there was a sharp rise in public support for a populist radical right party that had been struggling electorally since 1993.

Unlike other parties that are examined in this volume, the 'new' populist force of UKIP was rooted in a national tradition of Euroscepticism and had commenced its rise through second-order elections long before the collapse of the Lehman Brothers. Even at the height of the crisis, UKIP did not significantly overhaul its discourse to address crisis-related themes, instead preferring to focus on its core platform of hard Euroscepticism, immigration and political dissatisfaction. While we have seen some evidence to suggest that the crisis has facilitated the rise of populism in the UK, it has also been shown how foremost support for populist Euroscepticism has been driven by stronger concerns over immigration and the state of domestic politics, and with concerns over the crisis itself playing only a minor supporting role.

Chapter Seventeen

Everywhere and Nowhere: Populism and the Puzzling Non-Reaction to Ireland's Crises

Eoin O'Malley and John FitzGibbon

Introduction

Having soared heights during the so-called Celtic Tiger and basked in the praise lavished upon it, it eventually became obvious that Ireland had probably flown too close to the sun. In late 2008 the Irish economy started on a downward spiral equalled only by Greece and Iceland. Ireland presented the ideal economic circumstances for the rise of a populist party: a sudden drop in GDP, a sudden rise in unemployment, and a sudden fall in house prices plunging many in their twenties and thirties into negative equity whereby their houses were worth less than what they owed in mortgages. During the boom immigration to Ireland, concentrated among the 2004 EU enlargement states, was at levels never seen before, leading to 17 per cent of the population being foreign born. One party had been in government through almost the entire period of the Celtic Tiger from 1997 onwards, but opposition parties at the time acted more like cheerleaders of their policies, promising more of the same, rather than genuine alternatives. The governing party, *Fianna Fáil*, had strong links to the property industry and a chequered past with corruption over illegal cash payments over planning for construction projects. Thus it would appear that Ireland had the perfect economic and political conditions for the emergence of a populist party – total economic collapse brought about by a cosy, establishment elite. Yet this did not happen.

It was not a lack of supply. Many new parties were formed aiming to oust what it thought of as a corrupt elite. Parties with names such as Direct Democracy Ireland and People Before Profit Alliance (usually eschewing using the term party) announced a 'Declaration of War' in a 'righteous fight against banking corruption and injustice' or that they were the 'real alternative to the establishment'. Nor was it a lack of demand. Distrust in political parties is high in Europe and Ireland is not an exception. The European Social Survey (Wave 6 2012) shows that 85 per cent of respondents in Ireland distrusted political parties. In the aftermath of the general election in 2011 more people mentioned the political system as the most important issue or problem influencing their vote than the economic crisis (Marsh and Cunningham 2011: 187) though no doubt the economic crisis influenced their view of politics. Understanding why an ideal type populist party has not emerged in Ireland is a fascinating study in how institutional structures and political culture can shape the nature of populist development.

Our argument is that while Ireland after the crisis lacks a classic populist party, the political system is in fact resplendent with populist actors and rhetoric. In seeking to explain this apparent contradiction we firstly discuss populism in pre-crisis Ireland; secondly we explain how the substantial idiosyncrasies of the crisis in Ireland shaped the populism that emerged after the 2011 general election; finally we argue that Irish political institutions and political culture have prevented populist parties from emerging but have greatly facilitate populists and populism to become prevalent. In conclusion we discuss the five hypotheses of Kriesi and Pappas (this volume) and how the Irish case shows them to be broadly supported.

Populism before the Crash

Populists before there was populism – the dominance of Fianna Fáil

If we define populism as Albertazzi and McDonnell (2007) do, as an approach which 'pits a virtuous and homogenous people against a set of elites and dangerous 'others' who are together depicted as depriving (or attempting to deprive) the sovereign people of their rights, values, prosperity, identity and voice' then much of twentieth century Irish politics might be conceived as populist. *Fianna Fáil*, the dominant party in Ireland from the 1930s to the economic crash, spent much of its time defining Irishness in terms of Gaelic (Irish speaking, cultural) Catholicism, but especially in opposition to Britishness. That Irish nationalism has tended to being negative (not British) shows it to be populist in nature. Other features of *Fianna Fáil* are populist. The party refused to term itself in terms of a normal political party, but instead styled itself a 'national movement'. Its aims included the unification of Ireland (with Northern Ireland) and the restoration of the Irish language 'to develop a distinctive national life in accordance with Irish traditions and ideals'. It wanted to make the 'resources and wealth of Ireland subservient to the needs and welfare of all the people of Ireland' (*Fianna Fáil* constitution). This was consistent with *Fianna Fáil's* nationalist background and social base. *Fianna Fail's* early support was primarily in poor, rural Ireland and to an extent among the working classes and the petty bourgeois in the cities. Its main electoral rival, *Fine Gael*, was portrayed as a party of big farmers, Protestants and professionals.

McDonnell (2007: 210) citing Taggart points to the creation of a 'heartland' – 'an idealised version of its chosen people, and to locate them in a similarly idealised landscape'. Dowling (1997) claims Éamon de Valera, the party's founding and long-time leader, presents Ireland as an ancient, Gaelic (Irish-speaking) nation that is united – ignoring the quite disparate groups and traditions existing on the island. De Valera tells a simplistic story, Dowling observes, 'of unparalleled brutality and of deliberate cultural destruction but also of heroic and unceasing struggle in the pursuit of justice and right'. De Valera dominated the party and the country, bringing in a new properly Irish Constitution, to replace the one agreed with Britain. He governed from 1932 to 1959 with only two brief spells in opposition. The failure of the party to deliver the economic fruits of independence was countered by blaming Britain and reimagining what the true Irish people wanted: 'a people who satisfied with frugal comfort, devoted their leisure to things of the spirit' (de Valera, cited in Moynihan 1980).

In the 1960s during which time Ireland was relatively economically successful some complained that *Fianna Fáil* had moved too far to the right, or at least become too close to big business. This did not hurt the party electorally. *Fianna Fáil's* support base at this time (and later) was surprising because it lacked the social bases one observed in 'normal' party systems in Western Europe. *Fianna Fáil* was able to garner more (and more evenly distributed) support from working class and middle classes, from rural and urban Ireland than any other party (Carty 1981). Odder still might be that its main competitor party, *Fine Gael*, was not ideologically distinct from it. *Fine Gael* might reasonably be termed centre-right. *Fianna Fáil* eschewed all ideological labels, though it can be noted that it shifted from what might have been radical rhetoric in opposition to pragmatic willingness to shift when in government. This offers support for Kriesi and Pappas' H4 that parties will tone down their populist discourse once in government and focus on pragmatic policy enactment. From the 1990s parties ceased to pin the blame on Britain for every ill that befell Ireland. The country's economic success meant that *Fianna Fáil* could not, and did not need to resort to deeply populist measures. But mild populist rhetoric was still present: in 1997 *Fianna Fáil's* election slogan was 'People before Politics'. As will be discussed in the following section, H4 is given further credence by *Fianna Fáil's* regression back to populist rhetoric as the main opposition party by contesting policies they introduced while in government.

The old new populists in town: Sinn Féin *and left-wing populism*

If policy success meant that by the 2000s *Fianna Fáil* was merely dipping into the populist toolbox (McDonnell 2007: 210) with occasional forays into Euroscepticism, had populism effectively left Irish politics? O'Malley (2008) and McDonnell (2007) have both argued that *Sinn Féin* largely took up the space that we might have expected a populist party to occupy. In fact O'Malley (2008) argues that it is a populist nationalist party, but that the nature of Irish nationalism makes it difficult for such a party to engage in anti-immigrant rhetoric. He shows that some of its supporters hold views consistent with this form of nationalism.

Irish nationalism is rhetorically bound up in its oppression as an ethnic minority or a small nation within the United Kingdom (UK). Therefore the rights of small nations and minorities tend to be important in Irish politics. Ireland was also a country of emigration and many almost took a perverse pride in reported oppression of Irish migrants in other countries. As such Irish people took pride in the fact that mass immigration into Ireland was relatively uncontroversial. Partly for these reasons, and perhaps also because it recognised that immigrants would be an important voting bloc in the future (and of course *Sinn Féin* may genuinely care about immigrants' welfare) anti-immigrant policies or rhetoric were never part of *Sinn Féin's* playbook.

In other ways, however, *Sinn Féin* might be thought populist. If populism is also about providing simple (and popular) solutions to often complex problems,

Sinn Féin saw the solution to the conflict in Northern Ireland in simplistic terms. British withdrawal would solve all of Ireland's problems. There was no sense that nationalists accept any responsibility or need to analyse their own role in the conflict.

As with *Fianna Fáil*, *Sinn Féin* likes to regard itself as leading a Republican movement. Organisationally the party is tightly controlled by its long-time leader Gerry Adams. Adams' tenure as leader (especially when compared with his predecessors) would certainly indicate that *Sinn Féin* is a leader-driven party. One *Sinn Féin* representative has said of Adams that he 'has the charisma of a pop star' (Rafter 2005: 6). Adams dominated the press coverage of the party. Adams was thought of as a key electoral asset and within the movement he 'commands almost unswerving support and inspires deep loyalty [...] He is the strong leader' (Rafter 2005: 8, 10).

Sinn Féin regards itself as a radical party. Policies *per se* are not populist, rather it is how they are communicated to the public that can make them populist or not. The party frequently juxtaposes itself with the mainstream parties, *Fianna Fáil* and Labour, and promotes itself as the only uncorrupted political representatives of the Irish people. A key element of this argument is the policy of their elected officials only taking the average industrial wage as payment. This is used to show how they understand the concerns of ordinary citizens as they earn the same money and live in the same communities as them. This is then contrasted to the mainstream political elite who they portray as only being concerned with their expenses and pensions and cannot identify with ordinary citizens who are struggling on low pay.

Euroscepticism should not equate with populism. It is a legitimate position to hold, but one that tends to correlate with nationalism and Eurosceptics often complain about a European elite denying national sovereignty (a position that may also be reasonable). *Sinn Féin* has consistently opposed EU treaties, but it has moved from being in favour of leaving the EU to the self-styled 'euro-critical'. Its election literature speaks in typically populist terms:

> EU decisions are made far from ordinary people, with little scrutiny, and in a way that prevents their active participation. The gap between ordinary people and the European Commission, Council and Parliament is growing. As a result decisions taken in the EU do not reflect peoples' real concerns or needs. (*Sinn Féin* 2009)

However, its voters are no more Eurosceptic than those of other parties (Walsh and O'Malley 2013: 211). It frequently complains that the EU is a threat to Irish neutrality, but in most debates it tends to excoriate Irish governments for not standing up for Ireland in Europe rather than blaming the EU itself. For instance it claims to fight the return of the 'billions pumped by *Fine Gael*, Labour and *Fianna Fáil* into Irish banks, and a write down of the obscene debts forced on the Irish people' (*Sinn Féin* 2014). One reason it may have toned down its anti-EU rhetoric is that it is increasingly associated with British nationalism and the far-right in

Europe. This raises the possibility that the actions of populist parties on one end of the ideological spectrum make certain policies out of bounds for populists on the other end, as has been seen with the shift in Danish Euroscepticism moving from a largely left- to a now right-wing phenomenon (FitzGibbon 2013).

Beyond *Sinn Féin* and left-wing populism, some small groups have attempted to fill a space left by the absence of a clearly anti-immigrant party. In the 2000s a small number of TDs (MPs) made what were anti-immigrant statements (*see* O'Malley 2008). They were disciplined or at least criticised by their party. An anti-immigration party – Immigration Control Platform – competed in a limited number of constituencies in a number of elections in the pre-crisis 2000s but never polled well. We can conclude that there has always been a degree of populism among mainstream parties, and while it declined by the early 2000s, *Sinn Féin* offered what might be a populist alternative that sought to reject the mainstream parties as being corrupt and out of tune with the ordinary people of Ireland. However *Sinn Féin* was a small party with limited support and confined to certain areas.

The economic crisis was to lead to a dramatic expansion of this kind of left-wing populist rhetoric from *Sinn Féin* and a wave of independent TDs who were elected in the 2011 general election. The specific nature of the crisis in Ireland focused populist rhetoric on the suffering of the Irish people under an austerity regime brought about by the connivance of the mainstream political elite, their associates in the banking industry and their 'masters' in the EU. This allows for a fascinating contrast in the styles of populism in pre- and post-crisis Ireland.

Economic crisis 2008: Banks, bondholders and bailouts

The central event of the crisis in Ireland from which the economic and political fall out flowed, was the Irish government's Bank Guarantee Scheme which essentially nationalised the huge debts of private banks, and in doing so left Irish taxpayers exposed to potentially 400 billion euros of liabilities to mostly British, French and German investors (Lane 2012). There were rumours at the time, and it is still alleged, that the Bank Guarantee Scheme was forced upon the Irish state by the EU (*see* Cowen 2012) though the only evidence was a reported phone call in which Jean-Claude Trichet is said to have told Ireland to protect its banks 'at all costs'. Indeed contemporary reports show that European Commission and the European Central Bank (ECB) were surprised at the unilateral move by the Irish state (*Financial Times* 2 October 2008). As of yet, there has been no definitive account of the executive decision making process around the Bank Guarantee, feeding the widely held perception of a corrupt relationship between the banking and political elite as being the cause of the crisis in Ireland.

The scheme succeeded in the very short term (there was no run on Irish banks), but was a total failure beyond that. In January 2009 one of the main banks in the scheme, Anglo Irish Bank, was wound up with the government assuming all its liabilities. This was followed by a second smaller bank, and in time the Irish government also had to take partial ownership of the two pillar banks in the state.

Of the parties in the Dáil (lower house) at the time only the Labour Party opposed the scheme. *Fianna Fáil*, the Greens, *Sinn Féin* and *Fine Gael* supported it.

At the time the Bank Guarantee Scheme was introduced Minister for Finance, Brian Lenihan, boasted that 'this was the cheapest bailout in the world so far' (*Irish Times* 24 October 2008). It turned out to cost the state about sixty-four billion euros. The banking crisis imposed a number of different crises. Because the state had to plug the holes in the now failing banks, this imposed costs on the exchequer. This was exacerbated by the fact that the economy was now starting to decline. Tax revenues started to fall, and in order to fill the growing deficit Ireland was forced to start borrowing from an increasingly reluctant financial market and one that was sceptical of Ireland's ability to repay. For ordinary citizens the shrinking economy had an effect on employment. Rising unemployment put pressure on the system of social welfare. Many of those employed in construction or other parts of the property industry were made unemployed, causing all other aspects of the economy to slow down. Property prices also collapsed to about half their 2007 peak.

Ireland's economic position worsened and fears for the sustainability of the euro made it desperately difficult for Ireland to borrow to meet its increasing large budget deficit. The ECB in 2010 took the step of directly financing Irish banks (with the Irish state acting as a guarantor), and the Irish government was forced to stop borrowing on money markets and instead depended on nationals savings. It is reported that at the time the ECB and European Commission 'blackmailed' Ireland into applying for a bailout (Legrain 2014: 68–69). By the end of November 2010 Ireland officially applied for emergency financial assistance from the Troika.

The bailout agreed in late 2010 directly led to the fall of the *Fianna Fáil*-Green coalition, and the management of this fall and subsequent election was farcical, leading to then *Taoiseach* (Prime Minister) Cowen resigning as leader of *Fianna Fáil* less than a week after having won a confidence vote. That election saw the collapse of *Fianna Fáil's* support with its lowest ever seat share, and its coalition partner the Green Party was wiped out. This was accompanied by the sharp fall in trust in parliament and politics. The Irish parliament is as unpopular as the government – both are trusted by 17 per cent of the voting age population, down from over 40 per cent in spring 2007. Furthermore although the EU was widely blamed for forcing Ireland into a lending programme that imposed austerity, the EU is more trusted (by a third of the population) (Eurobarometer 80.1, 2014).

A new government, a coalition between *Fine Gael* and Labour, was formed in early 2011. It had the largest majority in the history of the state of 111 seats out of 166, in what it described a 'democratic revolution'. At the same time *Sinn Féin* and smaller left wing parties, and a large number of independents increased representation in parliament. While no clearly identifiable populist party emerged from the economic and political chaos, a clear populist narrative and many populist actors did. The next two sections will explain how and why post-crisis populism in Ireland has developed in a diffuse nature.

Post-crisis populism

As is clearly evident from Table 17.1, the 2011 general election and the collapse in support for *Fianna Fáil* represented one of the largest electoral shifts in post-war European politics. It was all the more interesting as the elections producing great change in the party system – Italy in 1994, the Netherlands in 2002, Greece in 2012 – resulted in the emergence of new populist parties, *Lega Nord, List Pim Fortuyn* and SYRIZA respectively (Mair 2011b). The Irish electorate it appeared did not 'do' populism despite the unprecedented conditions that theoretically should have facilitated the emergence of new parties. This failure of populism to arise was reflected in the distinct lack of protest movement mobilisation. Aside from two trade union-led demonstrations in 2009 and 2012, anti-fees marches by students in 2010 and 2011, and a successful protest by pensioners to defend their medical benefits, there was none of the sustained protest against the economic and political establishment witnessed on the streets of Athens and Reykjavik (*see* Pappas and O'Malley 2014).

Nestled in the election debates and party discourses of the 2011 general election, however, clear traces of an emergent populist political narrative can be located. The section on pre-crisis populism outlined why explicit denunciations of immigrants as being the cause of Ireland's problems has failed to develop in Ireland. But with the calamitous events surrounding the economic crisis populist rhetoric in Ireland began to focus specifically on the 'banking elite' who were perceived as the root cause of the crisis, and their facilitators in the Irish and EU political elite. Indeed the most famous statement made by a politician during the 2011 general election campaign was by then Labour leader Éamon Gilmore. When stating the party's opposition to the austerity of the Troika budgets at a

Table 17.1: Results of Irish general election in 2011 (turnout 70 per cent) and 2007 (turnout 67 per cent)

Party	% Vote 2011	Seats 2011	% Vote 2007	Seats 2007	% Change (Seats)
Fine Gael	36.1	76	27.3	51	8.8 (25)
Labour	19.4	37	10.1	20	9.3 (17)
Fianna Fáil	17.4	20	41.6	77	-24.1 (-57)
Independents	12.6	15	5.8	5	6.8 (10)
Sinn Féin	9.9	14	6.9	4	3.0 (10)
Greens	1.8	0	4.7	6	-2.9 (-6)
Progressive Democrats	0.0	0	2.7	2	-2.7 (-2)
Socialist Party	1.2	2	0.6	0	0.6 (2)
People Before Profit Alliance	1.0	2	0.0	0	1.0 (2)
Others	0.2	0	0.5	0	-0.3

Source: RTÉ (national broadcaster).

press conference he declared that it was 'Frankfurt's way or Labour's way' and that ECB President Jean-Claude Trichet was a 'civil servant' who would do what he was told (*Irish Times* 4 April 2011). *Sinn Féin* and the other left-wing parties took this similar approach of denouncing 'euro-elites' in Brussels and Berlin for forcing Irish citizens to borrow to pay for the 'gambling losses' of French and German banks in the Irish financial system (Socialist Party: 2013). The *Sinn Féin* manifesto in 2011 pointed the finger of blame at Germany and the EU and made references to 'ordinary people', 'people like you' and calls to 'put Ireland and its people first' (*Sinn Féin* 2011). This Eurosceptic discourse was not 'withdrawalist' *á la* UKIP, more specifically it was one that blamed the Irish political elite for not fighting Ireland's cause with the EU leadership and giving in to them far too easily. Their argument was that the EU needed an overall change of direction away from 'austerity' toward economic growth and job-centred policies. This could be achieved only by removing existing Irish political elite and electing *Sinn Féin* who alone served the interests of the Irish people and would negotiate a 'better deal for Ireland' (*Sinn Féin* 2014). In none of this was there an acknowledgement that Irish spending had gotten out of control and that the current account deficit too was unsustainable.

Even the solidly establishment, pro-European *Fine Gael* participated in the anti-banker narrative by promising to give 'not another cent' to the banks and to 'impose losses' if bank creditors 'come looking to us for any more money' (*Irish Examiner* 10 February 2011). These comments came from *Fine Gael* and Labour despite acknowledging that as a likely future government they would have no scope to enact any such policies. Indeed, within a few months of the new government forming it became apparent that the 'austerity' policies of the bailout programme would continue unabated providing further evidence for H4 – the populist discourse of parties becomes more responsible and less populist as they become part of government. Overall, however the Irish case is an obvious example of H1 – a deep economic crisis enhances the antagonism between 'the people' and some political or economic elites, which serves to intensify populism-*qua*-discourse – but less so of H2 – that we expect more intense populism in countries characterised by a political crisis – or H3 where an economic and political crisis combine. Populism was not that intense, and though Ireland combined both a political and economic crisis it saw none of the more visceral anti-establishment politics seen in other crisis-hit countries. The key reason is that a mainstream alternative government was available to replace the discredited one responsible for the economic chaos. As such there was distinctly less populism based on politics than there was on economics. This was due to the lack of space for criticising the entire political elite as two of its main constituents had yet to be tried out in power. This may however change at the election due in 2016 when the 'responsible' policies of the *Fine Gael* and Labour are ready to be judged by the electorate. Already the 2014 local and EP elections point to a situation where a major party system change is underway, though we should be wary of making predictions based on second-order elections.

Pre-crisis Ireland was one of the most pro-EU member states with support for membership continuously in the 70 per cent range (Eurobarometer 2010).

Even post-crisis Ireland registered support of mid-60 per cent for membership (Eurobarometer 2013). Articulating a classic 'hard' Eurosceptic line of withdrawal (Szczerbiak and Taggart 2004) or stringent criticism of European integration as a whole would not appeal to the Irish electorate. Indeed despite clearly apportioning some blame for the Irish economic disaster to the EU political elite none of the parties represented in the Dáil advocated leaving the euro let alone the EU. Rather what occurred in Ireland was a fusion of several strands of populism – unjust taxation, corruption, anti-elitism and (soft) Euroscepticism. The populist narrative began to spread out to encapsulate a range of other issues; all linked to a perception of a corrupt Irish political elite beholden to a cabal of bankers and EU politicians. While this populist discourse was identifiable in the language of the 2011 general election campaign, it probably did not gain widespread traction until after the government was firmly ensconced in office. The failure of the *Fine Gael*-Labour coalition to deliver changes to the bailout agreement, and the introduction of property taxes and water charges, was the spark that set a section of Irish politics off in a more populist direction.

Populism in an 'age of austerity': Bankers as a focus of populist mobilisation

As outlined in the economic crisis section, as part of the 'bailout' agreement with the Troika, the Irish government instituted a programme of austerity to reduce the budget deficit with a broad policy of dramatic reductions in government spending and increases in taxation. While some government services were curtailed by spending cuts and taxation rates greatly increased[1], it was the imposition of water charges that has been central to the longer-term establishment of populist discourse in Irish politics. Much of the 'heavy lifting' of the fiscal correction in the terms of the bailout agreement was already undertaken between 2008 and 2011 (OECD 2011). Part of the agreement was the imposition of water charges and a system of property tax. Ireland was the only OECD country not to charge citizens for its water while a form of property tax had been removed as part of a populist election pledge by *Fianna Fáil* in 1977. Prior to water charges and property taxes, 'austerity' had been based around the increase of existing taxes and the decrease of existing services.

In explaining the success and failure of populist parties, Mudde (2010) says populism is not about 'shifting voters to a new position' it is more focused on shifting them toward a 'new issue'. Issue salience is fundamental for such mobilisation to succeed and the protracted and problematic introduction of these two policies provided ample opportunity for left-wing political actors to utilise them. They portrayed these policies as the embodiment of austerity and symbolic

---

1. For instance the high rate of tax 41 per cent, starts at an income of 32,800 euros for a single person - widest higher rate of tax band in the OECD. Other income related deductions mean the effective marginal rate is 52 per cent.

of the attack by domestic and European political elites on ordinary people. Socialist Party MEP Paul Murphy of the GUE-NGL group changed his affiliation for the 2014 EP elections to 'Stop the Water Tax – Socialist Party' – though he still failed to gain a seat. This tactic continued across the rest of the Socialist Party as it rebranded itself the 'Anti Austerity Alliance' for the 2014 local elections. Despite the party advocating a hard left-wing policy of wealth taxation and rent controls their central campaign message was to end property taxes and water charges that represented 'an all-out assault on our livelihoods' (Anti Austerity Alliance: 2014). Similarly the Socialist Workers' Party labelled itself the People Before Profit Alliance in the 2007 general election. However these parties are tiny.

In its 2014 European Parliament election manifesto, *Sinn Féin* harnessed this discourse more successfully juxtaposing the growing anger amongst the public at the perceived imposition of new charges and taxes to the 'austerity agenda' to put 'the needs of the banks ahead of needs of the people' of the mainstream Irish parties and their 'policy consensus' with European 'political elites [...] who want to centralise more power in the EU institutions' (*Sinn Féin* 2014). Ostensibly it appears curious that the Irish sovereign debt crisis only became successful as a means of populist mobilisation several years after the advent of the crisis itself. The principal reason it would appear for this failure was the availability of an alternative government in the form of a centre-right and centre-left party who were untainted by the failures of government after fourteen years in opposition. *Fine Gael* and Labour could appeal to voters with the legitimate claim that they were different and were not part of the previous governing political elite. These two parties made explicit promises to 'burn the bondholders' and renegotiate the terms of Ireland's bailout (*Fine Gael*: 2011). The electorate might have been unsure of the veracity of these promises but they were willing to give the new government a 'honeymoon period' to achieve them. Despite the elected officials of both parties having decades long involvement in politics, their only executive experience was for short periods in the mid-1990s and 1980s. They were not considered members of the political establishment as they had been out of power for so long. This initial period quickly subsided, however, as the prospect of 'Labour's way' over that of the Troika disappeared. The government's thorough implementation of the terms of Ireland's bailout package received plaudits from the international financial markets but built up opposition amongst the electorate, making them far more receptive to the increased supply of left-wing populism after the 2011 general election.

Policies as water charges and property taxes, which applied to every household in the state, provided the means by which to sustain non-mainstream party-based populism. No longer could the previous *Fianna Fáil*-led administration be blamed for all the failings. Rather it was the political elite as a whole, linked by their support for European integration, which had imposed these patently unfair measures on the Irish people to support the banking elite. As *Sinn Féin* and the other left-wing parties argued, the only way to ensure fairness for the ordinary people was to elect those who had been vilified as political outsiders by the three largest parties – *Fine Gael*, Labour and *Fianna Fáil*.

But can such rhetoric be classified as populist? Are these parties not articulating opposition to policies to which they are genuinely ideologically opposed to? Indeed there can be little doubt that these parties are representing the anger of the Irish public to 'austerity' policies and the property tax and water charges in particular. But the recent electoral success of left-wing parties and actors in Ireland is in part due to their opposition to taxes and charges. The relabelling of several parties so as to de-emphasise their ideology and emphasise their anti-elite *bona fides* is clear evidence of their use of populism. The continued implementation of the Troika's 'austerity' policies by the *Fine Gael*/Labour government negotiated by the previous administration created the perception of an out of touch political elite who had developed an entrenched 'corrupt' relationship with a banking and EU elite to put their interests ahead of the Irish people's. The implementation of new allegedly unjust and unfair property and water taxes was the embodiment of this corruption in the Irish political elite and was utilised as a populist issue for electoral success by *Sinn Féin* and other parties.

This emergence of a populist narrative amongst the left in Ireland makes for a fascinating case study. Stanley (2008) argues that populism can emerge from 'anywhere' in the political system but there are few examples in Europe where the populism that emerges is solely on the left. As discussed in the previous section on pre-crisis populism, right-wing populism based on immigration has failed to develop due to the specific nature of Irish nationalism. The large immigrant population was not singled out for blame, it was the banking and political elite. As Jagers and Walgrave (2007) argued, 'thin populism' as a communication narrative needs to be based on a distinct reference to the people and how the political actor listens to them and represents their will. The difference with what they label 'thick populism' they believe is the focus of this narrative on an exclusive group in society. Generally this is immigrants, Jews, Muslims, Roma or other such specific ethnic/religious groups. Here we see a clear conflation between populist communication styles and classic radical left-wing policies that blame 'bourgeois' classes and their political accomplices for the problems facing the country. Before the crisis such calls had only occasional and short-term electoral success before the fall of the Berlin Wall.[2] Afterwards the radical left split into smaller parties based around individual actors. Moreover, it was crushed under the weight of the economic dynamism of the Celtic Tiger. The events of the economic crisis brought back radical-left politics to Ireland but this time with a distinctive populist voice in a diffuse pattern of mobilisation.

---

2. The radical left's high point came with the Workers' Party (Marxist-Leninist) seven seat success in the 1989 general election. They split after the fall of Berlin Wall in opposition to the Party's democratic centralism and formed part of a coalition government from 1995–97.

New electoral politics

Ireland has not however seen the dramatic breakthrough of anti-system parties, such as those seen in France, Denmark, Italy or The Netherlands. As well as being because populism has long been a significant feature of Irish politics, it is in part because Ireland's party system is a cartel party system with rules in place on party financing which make breaking into the party system increasingly difficult. There are strict limits on donations by individuals or corporations (just 2,500 euros per year). Meanwhile parties receive significant public funds based on their vote and seat shares at the previous election. The main four parties shared over 12.6 million euros last year. This makes setting up and funding a party that can be competitive with the established parties very difficult.

But the lack of success for a newly emerging party also reflects that parties *per se* are themselves increasingly unpopular. It is possible that these two factors feed each other: the difficulty new political organisations have in making an electoral break-through causes them to campaign as independents, and making a virtue of necessity, they criticise parties as elites protecting their own interests. The European Social Survey (2012 wave 6) shows parties are distrusted by 85 per cent of Irish people (compared with parliament and the government distrusted by 75 per cent and 77 per cent respectively). Ireland is not unusual in this regard; most countries show a large majority lacking trust in parties. Danes, Swedes and Austrian's are the most trustful of politics, but even in those places just about a third of respondents claim to trust parties.

This might not matter much. Parties might be easy entities to dislike and people will say so in opinion polls, but people vote for them in droves at elections. People's behaviour indicates what they really think of parties. Ireland is unusual in having a large number of independents elected to parliament (*see* Weeks 2010). This is in part because the electoral system is candidate as opposed to party-based, the low threshold for election and the fact that TDs represent as few as 20,000 people each (8,000 votes would virtually guarantee election in 2011 (Gallagher 2011: 140)). Some independents dubbed the 2014 local and European election as 'Independents' Day', and they may have worked as the results of Table 17.2 shows. This is a contradiction at the heart of electoral politics in Ireland. On the one side Ireland has one of the most open electoral systems in the world – proportional representation with single transferable vote in multi-seat constituencies – and a political culture that focuses on personality politics, which facilitate new candidates to contest and win seats in general elections. On the other side, party funding is tightly controlled and based around specific criteria that are biased towards the well-established parties and not toward encouraging new or potential entrants to the party system.

There is also a distinctly anti-party sentiment in much of public discourse. The rhetoric from independents (and one that seems to resonate with many people) tries to portray parties as somehow craven and without principle. Independents say they will put people before party, and ask to 'move democracy on' without parties. At the same time independents have started to work together. This is in

Table 17.2: Breakdown of votes and seats in the 2014 European Parliamentary election

Party	Vote share %	No. seats	Δ in % vote
Fine Gael	22.3	4	-6.8
Sinn Féin	19.5	3	8.3
Labour	5.3	0	-8.6
Fianna Fáil	22.3	1	-1.8
Independents	19.8	3	8.3
Others	10.8	0	0.6

part driven by necessity; to ensure that they are given speaking time in the Dáil. But it is also as part of an effort to market themselves as a loosely aligned group rather than a coherent party. Irish politics has a number of people who want to lead a new alliance of independents, and so documents such as 'Independent Thought – United Vision' have been produced. There has been some talk of a new party being formed by the independents, but the one certainty there is that any new party, if one were to emerge, would market itself as an anti-party party. For instance the leading members of the proposed Reform Alliance (RA) party argue it is not about the 'perpetuation of party politics'. The potential base of such a party is in the members of the *Fine Gael* party who left after the introduction of a bill to allow abortion in limited circumstances. Their complaint was the legislation was 'whipped' through by the party leadership, instead of being a free vote on a matter of such moral conscience. As a loose grouping the Reform Alliance has made an issue the question of political reform and the dominance of party elites over all aspects of Irish politics.

For both members of the Reform Alliance and those who left the Labour Party, their anti-party tenor is focused on the whip system. One group of independents claimed in 2014 'we believe the operation of the party whip system is unconstitutional because it asks representatives to represent their party rather than the constituency that elects them as the constitution requires' (*Irish Times* 6 May 2014). This focus on the sovereignty of the people is typical of populism, but the focus on the whip system also serves as a basis for attacking ruling elites. One RA TD complained of 'a slavish adherence to the government line, an unquestioning acceptance of the superiority of others by virtue of their rank or influence, and a willingness to stay silent in the face of poor policy making and vested interests' (Creighton 2014). Anti-elitism is a key component of populism of many European states – in particular Austria, Finland and The Netherlands – but none are based on quite so esoteric an issue as the party whip system. Kriesi and Pappas' H3 expected populism to be far more intense where the economic crisis combined with a political crisis. The Irish case shows little evidence of an increase in intensity. What it does show is that the economic crisis led to left-wing populist mobilisation and the political crisis has led to a (far lesser) degree of right-wing populist mobilisation.

The crisis has damaged the mainstream parties, and *Sinn Féin* and independents have capitalised on this. This diverse group of left-wing nationalists, Catholic fundamentalists, centrists and radical left activists have all played the populist game by focusing blame for Ireland's economic crash on the bankers and the political elite. The populist element of this discourse comes through in the highly specific issues they chose to focus on – the introduction of water charges, the whip system. But the populism has been mild, and most parties, when they reach government tend towards responsibility rather than responsiveness (Mair 2013). The emergence of new populist actors shows H5 – different types of populist actors to seize the opportunity of the economic and political crises to mobilise against the established political elites – to be true in the Irish case.

But politics is usually cyclical, not seismic in its motion. A new populist challenger will promise more. The people will be transfixed. Eventually they will get into government; they will disappoint, and the cycle starts again. What is different this time is that parties themselves are now a sign of elitism and corruption. For this reason independents are on the rise and new parties are anti-party. The only certainty is that the party system that emerges from this cycle will not be the one Ireland had from 1932 to 2011.

CONCLUSION

Chapter Eighteen

Populism and Crisis: A Fuzzy Relationship

by Takis S. Pappas and Hanspeter Kriesi

Following our original intuition that populism in crisis-ridden Europe may have varied by region rather than by country, this concluding chapter parts from its hitherto individual-country focus and adopts a regional comparative perspective. Based on the information presented in the previous chapters, we attempt a first comparative analysis of the development of populism during the Great Recession across Europe's different regions.

All in all, in this chapter we account for twenty-five populist parties in seventeen countries systematised by region: Nordic, Western, Southern, Central-Eastern and Anglo-Celtic. One country, Ireland, lacks populist parties, thus serving as a negative case. For each region, we provide a cumulative table with individual country and aggregate electoral results of the parties classified as populist before and after the crisis so as to detect changes in their strength at two different times and two distinct levels of analysis. In a separate column in each one of these tables, we also include the results of our populist parties at the more recent 2014 elections for the European Parliament. This is important, not only for our better understanding of the dynamics of populist growth in specific country cases (such as, for instance, Denmark, France, or the UK, where outcomes in second-order elections heavily influence domestic politics), but also for detecting broader voting trends.

For each region, we proceed in a similar fashion. Initially, we provide brief overviews of the intra-region populist parties and compare their performances before and during the Great Recession. Then, we evaluate the impact of economic and, when available, political crises at the regional level and test our original hypotheses at the same level. Finally, by comparing our findings at the regional level (which are concisely presented in one last table), we attempt to generalise about the effects of the crisis on populist development by testing our initial hypotheses at European level. We find that populism surged rather modestly during the Great Recession, although its development varies considerably from one region to the other. We also show that our first two hypotheses (claiming that both economic and political crises have a positive effect on populism) are largely supported, even if there are some exceptions that we shall account for. Our third hypothesis (which maintains that populism is most intense when a political crisis occurs in tandem with an economic crisis) also receives firm empirical support (with one exception), as does our fourth hypothesis (maintaining that populists become more responsible when they assume office or have good chances for getting into office).

The Nordic group: Incidental crises, moderate populisms

Right-wing populism is characterised by a long-lasting presence in Denmark and Norway, where it also has reached a high level of institutionalisation by the time that the Great Recession occurred. In Sweden and Finland it is of a more recent vintage. The individual chapters dealing with the countries in this region have focused in particular on the Danish People's Party (*Dansk Folkeparti*, DF); Norway's Progress Party (*Fremskrittspartiet*, FrP); the Sweden Democrats (*Sverigedemokraterna*, SD); and the Finns Party (*Perussuomalaiset*, PS). Table 18.1 shows the electoral results of these parties before and after the Great Recession made its appearance in this region. In general, populism in the Nordic region experienced a notable increase of 4.4 per cent. It declined in both Norway and Denmark, but soared in Sweden and Finland, which present two of Europe's most interesting cases of recent populist development.

In Denmark, populism is associated with the right-wing DF, a splinter from the Danish Progress Party, founded in 1972. Having in the meantime adopted an anti-immigration stance, during the 2000s pragmatic DF accepted to formally support (with no own portfolios) successive minority governments of liberals and conservatives in exchange for tighter immigration policies. It was during the 2000s that this party turned increasingly nationalist and Eurosceptic. When the Great Recession hit Denmark, the DF still supported the government and its leader, Pia Kjærsgaard, avoided populist tactics opting instead for a responsible stance. As she put it, 'this is no time for political and economic experiments – or economic fantasy solutions' (cited in Jupskås, this volume). At least in part, this probably explains the temporary drop of DF's electoral support from 13.9 per cent in 2007 to 12.3 per cent in 2011. In the aftermath of those elections, the leadership was passed on to a new party chairman, Kristian Thulesen Dahl, and DF turned more decisively against the EU elite, although not against the EU in general. It was a strategy that yielded impressive results in the 2014 European Parliament elections.

In Norway, populism evolved from an anti-tax movement in the early 1970s to the conservative, nationalist and anti-immigration FrP, which, by 1997, had already surpassed the Conservatives and become the second largest party in the

Table 18.1: Electoral results of populist parties in Nordic region (in per cent; respective countries and election years in parentheses)

	A. Pre-crisis	B. Post-crisis	Difference B/A	EU2014
DF (DK)	13.9 (2007)	12.3 (2011)	-1.6	26.6
FrP (NO)	22.1 (2005)	16.3 (2013)	-5.8	–
SD (SE)	2.9 (2006)	12.9 (2014)	10.0	9.8
Finns (FI)	4.1 (2007)	19.1 (2011)	15.0	12.9
TOTAL country average	10.8	15.2	4.4	16.4

Norwegian parliament. And yet, despite having consolidated its position as the dominant right-wing party in the country, the FrP, unlike its Danish counterpart, has always been refused formal government cooperation with other parties, although the FrP presented itself as a responsible party, behaved moderately, and avoided populist overtures. In the 2013 general elections, the populists suffered a drop of 5.8 per cent, and were relegated to third place in parliament. This time, however, the FrP was granted power and, as it had happened earlier with similar right-wing parties in Austria, Italy, The Netherlands and Switzerland, entered government as a minor coalition partner obtaining ministerial positions.

In Sweden, the chief manifestation of populism is the SD, a party founded in 1988 and originally associated with Swedish fascism. More recently, the party underwent a process of moderation, however, which has accelerated since the 2000s as the party leadership expelled its most extremist and racist elements. Today, the SD is a right-wing anti-immigration and Eurosceptic nationalist populist party, which, not untypically for Scandinavian members of this party family, also tilts to the left on the socio-economic dimension, such as welfare state expansion. Having been treated as a political pariah by the other parties in Sweden for many years, the SD entered parliament (with twenty MPs) for the first time after the 2010 general elections. As party leader Jimmy Åkesson proclaimed, 'Our aim is to grow electorally and assume a position as a political party with real blackmailing power in other to force the other parties to take us into consideration for the making of government' (cited in Jungar, this volume). In point of fact, in the recent 2014 general elections, the SD polled 12.9 per cent of the national vote (and 14 per cent of seats in the Rikstag), thus emerging as Sweden's third largest party.

Finally, in Finland, populism finds its best expression in the PS, founded as late as 1995 but with roots in the agrarian populist Finnish Rural Party. Under the leadership of Timo Soini, the PS has made considerable electoral gains since 2007. In the 2011 general elections, it won over 19 per cent of the vote and became the third largest party in the Finnish parliament. According to its programme, the PS is on the right in social policies but follows a left-wing course on economic issues. On the one hand, it promotes conservative values by supporting the traditional family model, teaching 'healthy national pride' in schools, aiding cultural activities that foster Finnish identity, and by requiring that immigrants accept Finnish cultural norms. On the other hand, the PS is a strong advocate of progressive taxation and the maintenance of the Finnish social welfare system. Above all, this party is distinguished by its nationalism and its strong defence of the sovereignty of the Finnish state and its people against immigration and EU federalism.

When it comes to the question of how much the Great Recession affected the Nordic countries, the short answer is 'not much'. For this group of countries, the crisis was rather incidental and rather unrelated to structural weaknesses of their economies or pathologies of their political and party systems. Norway fared exceptionally well as its rate of growth only suffered a temporary setback in 2009 before regaining positive marks. Sweden's experience was similar, despite a somewhat greater slump during the catastrophic year of 2009. Denmark and

Finland were more seriously hit, even if the economic crisis remained relatively benign in these countries, too, when compared to the European average. From the Danish perspective, however, as Jupskås points out, the economic crisis acquired 'historical dimensions', which indicates that the impact of the economic crisis might be better assessed in relative (to a given country's experience), rather than in internationally comparative terms. In any case, by 2010 the economies in the region had recovered and from then on followed the European average. By 2013, only Finland experienced negative economic growth (which in part explains the relatively high ranking of this country among the economically worse-hit cases in Table 1.2 in the Introduction).

At first sight, in terms of politics, too, no country in the region can be said to have undergone a domestic crisis. Trust in parliament, the government and the political parties remained much higher in all these countries than in the rest of Europe. Moreover, party systems have remained stable everywhere in the region and, in fact, formerly anti-systemic populist parties (like Norway's FrP) have turned systemic. This point needs stressing. For, unlike in most other countries in Europe, Nordic populist parties consistently pose as systemic and, while in opposition, behave responsibly. This is why, despite frequent use of anti-incumbent elite rhetoric, they have gained political respectability and broadened their electoral bases. Thus, as we have seen, the DF has been a stable mainstay for the Danish government and the Norwegian FrP has been a coalition partner since 2013. As for the SD and the PS, they both have now sufficient blackmailing potential to significantly influence politics in their respective countries.

Looking more closely at the Finnish case, we find, however, indications of a political crisis. While the general indicators presented in Chapter One do not provide any evidence for such a crisis, as shown in the chapter on Finland, the election funding scandal which implicated all major Finnish parties in 2008–11 was interpreted as a severe crisis by the media, the voters, and the PS, which used it as a campaign weapon. This evidence suggests that not only the economic, but also the political crisis should be assessed in relative and not in absolute terms.

In fact, the spectacular rise of populism in Finland was, as the authors of the chapter on Finland put it, 'a consequence of a combination of a national political crisis and the discursive opportunity generated by the economic crisis elsewhere in Europe'. As it turns out, the discursive opportunity for the True Finns was provided not by the domestic economic crisis, but by the European debt crisis, or the euro crisis. It is important to note in this context that Finland is the only Eurozone member among the Nordic countries, which may explain why the euro crisis proved to be particularly explosive in this country. In the Finnish case, we see a shift from traditional populism that opposes domestic elites to a new brand that militates against other EU nations and foreign immigration. In Finland, this shift has been accompanied by a corresponding shift in the definition of the people: from the disadvantaged rural Finns (as opposed to the rich urban ones) to the virtuous Finnish nation (as opposed to other, less virtuous European national communities). We might add that the euro crisis provided the opportunity for the Finnish radical right, to mobilise in terms of the new demarcation-integration conflict that has already been articulated by the corresponding parties in Western Europe (*see* Kriesi *et al.* 2008, 2012). A similar shift from anti-elitism at the domestic level to anti-elitism at the European level has also occurred in Denmark. Although Denmark is not part of the Eurozone, the euro crisis has also reinforced DF's soft Euroscepticism. We have encountered a similar phenomenon in the cases of The Netherlands, the UK and, to a lesser extent, Austria.

In what concerns this volume's initial hypotheses with regard to the Nordic countries, the confirmation is partial. As for the first hypothesis, both Danish and Norwegian populists suffered electorally – irrespective of the impact of the crisis, which was felt quite differently in the two countries. While the Norwegian case is as expected, the Danish populists arguably were not able to benefit from the crisis because they were closely linked to the government during this period. The sharp ascendancy of the populists in Finland and Sweden, by contrast, is not a direct result of the domestic economic slowdown caused by the Great Recession. Instead, it was the euro crisis that proved to be crucial for the case of Finland. If we accept the definition of an economic and political crisis in relative terms (i.e. in relation to the country's own experience), then the Finnish experience confirms our second and third hypotheses: In the only Nordic country, where a political crisis occurred and where it was combined with a specific interpretation of the economic crisis (the euro crisis), the populist made spectacular advances during the Great Recession. The Swedish rise is not in line with our hypotheses one to three, and can only be interpreted in terms of the long-term tendencies invoked in the introduction, which is to suggest that, belatedly, given the overall unfavorable Swedish political opportunity structure, the general demarcation-integration conflict is making itself felt even in this country.

Finally, the region provides very strong confirmation of our fourth hypothesis, which concerns the relaxation of extreme undertones from the discourse of those populist parties that either accede to power or have a good chance of doing so in the near future. As we have seen, all populist parties in the Nordic countries have toned down their populist discourse and behaved responsibly, thus trying to appear as forces in the mainstream.

The Western group: Modest crises, declining populism

This group consists of five countries, represented in this volume by the following populist parties: the French National Front (*Front National*, FN); the Belgian Flemish Interest (*Vlaams Belang*, VB); two populist parties representing The Netherlands, one on the right (Freedom Party, *Partij voor de Vrijheid*, PVV) and another one on the left (Socialist Party, *Socialistische Partij*, SP); two Austrian parties, both belonging to the radical right: the Freedom Party of Austria (*Freiheitliche Partei Österreichs*, FPÖ) and the more recent Alliance for the Future of Austria (*Bündnis Zukunft Österreich*, BZÖ); and, finally, the Swiss People's Party (*Schweizerische Volkspartei*, SVP). Together with Norway and Denmark, this group of countries has been characterised by exceptionally strong populist parties since the 1990s – a result of the long-term development of the demarcation-integration conflict (Kriesi *et al.* 2008, 2012). However, as summarised in Table 18.2, and contrary to widespread popular perceptions, populism in this region declined during the Great Recession in all countries except France, that is, we find a cumulative decrease of 1.7 per cent. The recent European elections simply confirmed this trend, as they also confirmed the dynamism of French populism.

In France, the predominant force of populism is the FN. Founded in 1972, and led for many years by Jean-Marie Le Pen, the FN seemed to have reached a very low point by the 2009 European election. However, it rebounded spectacularly in more recent years, especially since Marine Le Pen, the daughter of FN's erstwhile strongman, assumed the party leadership in early 2011. This raises the question of whether the subsequent FN successes have been an effect of the Great Recession or, more specifically, of Marine Le Pen's new style of leadership. Be that as it may, the new leader sought to reinvent the FN and reintroduce it into French politics as a respectable force. Taking advantage of the crisis, Marine Le Pen campaigned for French sovereignty against further European integration; for national and cultural integrity against immigration; and for upholding the interests of the *couches populaires* against those of the elites. Along that process, she has led the FN from one success to another. In the 2012 presidential election, Le Pen's candidacy enjoyed the support of almost 18 per cent of the voting public, and in the legislative elections of the same year, the FN received 13.6 per cent. In the 2014 local contests, the party elected several mayors across the country and, shortly thereafter, it caused a political 'earthquake' by winning almost a quarter of the French vote in the elections for the European Parliament.

In Belgium, populism appeared later than in most other countries in the region, and it has been strongly associated with Flemish nationalism. Its most important expression has been the VB party, which, besides advocating the independence of Flanders, also opposes immigration, multiculturalism and European integration. In 2007, the VB won 12 per cent of the vote, but remained effectively excluded

Table 18.2: Electoral results of populist parties in continental Europe (in per cent; respective countries and election years in parentheses)

	A. Pre-crisis	B. Post-crisis	Difference B/A	EU2014
FN (FR)	4.3 (2007)	13.6 (2012)	9.3	24.9
VB (BE)	12.0 (2007)	3.7 (2014)	−8.3	4.3
PVV (NL)	5.9 (2006)	10.1 (2012)	4.2	13.3
SP (NL)	16.6 (2006)	9.7 (2012)	−6.9	9.6
FPÖ (AT)	17.5 (2008)	20.5 (2013)	3.0	19.7
BZÖ (AT)	10.7 (2008)	3.5 (2013)	−7.2	0.5
SVP (CH)	28.9 (2007)	26.6 (2011)	−2.3	–
TOTAL				
Country average	19.2	17.5	−1.7	18.0

from power sharing since all mainstream parties had agreed never to include it in a coalition. Since then, the VB entered into a cycle of irreversible decline. In the 2010 general elections, the party's electoral strength was reduced to 7.8 per cent, and in 2014 its vote share fell to a mere 3.7 per cent.

In recent years, The Netherlands have been a hotbed for various populist parties that, apparently, find a fertile soil in this country. Following the fast decline of the *List Pim Fortuyn* after the murder of its namesake leader in 2002, another maverick politician, Geert Wilders founded the PVV and, in 2006, won almost 6 per cent of the vote and entered parliament. Rallying against the old political establishment, European integration, and Islam, the PVV emerged as the third largest party after the 2010 general elections, and promptly provided parliamentary support to a fragile coalition government of Christian Democrats and Liberals in exchange for the implementation of some of its key policies. In 2012, Wilders refused to sign up to new austerity measures, thus causing the collapse of the government and new elections – in which, unexpectedly, his party suffered substantial losses. On the other side of the Dutch political spectrum, one finds the SP, a case of left-wing populism. Anti-establishment, Eurosceptic, and pro-welfare, the SP first entered parliament in 1994 and recorded its best electoral result in 2006 (16.6 per cent of the national vote). During the Great Recession its strength declined somewhat and, at present, seems to have stabilised at about 10 per cent.

The Swiss SVP was traditionally a farmers' party that took a populist direction in the late 1980s, when Christoph Blocher assumed its leadership. It has since focused on, and campaigned against, immigration and European integration, two issues of which the SVP has long claimed near-exclusive ownership. So great was the impact of such campaigning in the Swiss context that, by the 2000s, the SVP had become the country's strongest party. Its vote share of almost 30 per cent in the 2007 Federal Council elections was the highest vote ever recorded for a single party in Switzerland in the post-war period. However, in the 2011 federal elections, for the first time since 1987 the party suffered a loss (of 2.3 per cent) in its electoral support.

Austria features two right-wing populist parties, or rather, given that they grew out of the same party branch and present many similarities in their respective discourse and political stance, a populist bifurcation. The oldest is the FPÖ, a transformed liberal-conservative party which had been founded in 1956 and became populist after 1986, when Jörg Haider had successfully contested its leadership. In the elections of 1999, the FPÖ won almost 30 per cent of the vote and became an – albeit uncomfortable – partner in the ensuing coalition government. In 2005, Haider abandoned the FPÖ and founded a new populist party, the BZÖ. The two populist parties contested the 2006 general elections each 'claiming to embody the 1986–99 period of successful populist mobilisation' (Luther, this volume). It was the FPÖ, however, that fared better and has thereafter become the main representative of Austrian populism enjoying an ever-increasing share of the vote. As for the BZÖ, in the elections of 2008 it made a remarkably strong performance, gaining over 10 per cent of the vote. Immediately after the vote, however, Haider was killed in a car accident and his party began to decline. It lost most of its electoral strength during the Great Recession, although for reasons not directly associated with the crisis conditions.

On the whole, the group of continental Western European countries was only modestly affected by the financial and economic crisis during the period under examination. Notwithstanding the fact that in 2009 all five countries in this group experienced negative growth, none of them scored worse than the EU average for that year. By 2010, their economies had recovered quite well and all countries returned to relative prosperity. The Swiss economy grew in 2010 by a remarkable 3 per cent. Unemployment, too, remained below EU average everywhere in this region (particularly in Austria, Switzerland and The Netherlands). In Belgium, unemployment was mostly visible in Wallonia, less in Flanders, where the populists had their traditional stronghold. Only in France was the situation somewhat different. Although the macroeconomic indicators do not show a deep crisis (in fact, the immediate impact of the Great Recession was rather mild), French society was characterised by a pervasive sense of malaise. Arguably, this malaise stemmed from France's lagging behind its main competitors in Europe and overseas, as indicated by the diminished competitiveness of its economy, its increasingly negative balance of trade, a shortfall in foreign investment, a growing national debt, and the rising socio-economic inequality.

Nor was there any political crisis during the Great Recession according to our indicators in the introduction. With the partial exception of France, the citizens in all the countries of this group retained relatively high levels of trust in democratic institutions and continued to be satisfied with current democracy. There were no major upheavals in the respective political systems. In relative terms, however, there are some indications of political crises. Thus, the ousting of the SVP leader from the Swiss government in 2007 constituted a major political tremor in a country that has been governed by the same grand coalition since 1959. In reaction to this event, the SVP excluded the party's members in the government, thus causing a split and the creation of a splinter centre-right party supporting the former SVP members in government. In France, as shown by repeated opinion polls throughout the crisis, the sense of malaise already described had a profoundly negative psychological effect on large segments of the French society, which consequently prompted a significant deterioration of public trust in parliament, the political parties and, in general, representative democracy. In Belgium a severe political crisis had already started in 2007 and loomed large during the crisis years. It consisted of the inability of the parties to form a government, which led to 'a general feeling of crisis and undermined the credibility of the Belgian state' (Pauwels and Rooduijn, this volume). A new government was formed only after 534 days of political impasse. In Austria, finally, for much of the post-2008 period, public debate was permeated by a seemingly ever-expanding number of political scandals. The Austrian peculiarity, however, is that the populist parties themselves were deeply implicated in these scandals due to their participation in the national (ÖVP-FPÖ/BZÖ) and regional (Carinthia's 'Haider system') governments.

Except for France, the effects of crisis in the Western European region have been rather modest. All five countries feature solid and durable populist parties, which are well entrenched in their respective party systems. During the Great Recession, these parties continued to mobilise mainly on the cultural dimension and, profiting as the True Finns from the discursive opportunity of the euro crisis, utilised explicitly anti-EU rhetoric, some of them even advocating their countries' withdrawal from the EU. To take just one example, the Dutch PVV's manifesto, tellingly titled 'Their Brussels, Our Netherlands', spoke derogatively of 'the blind inhabitants of the ivory towers in Brussels', 'unelected multi-culti Eurocrats', or 'the holy Great-European project', and called for an end to supporting Europe's troubled economies. This severe criticism of the European project proved to be less successful than in Finland, however. Most of the populist parties in the region suffered a decline in their electoral strength. Particularly noteworthy is the case of the VB, which, contrary to theoretical expectation, lost almost two-thirds of its pre-crisis strength despite the fact that Belgium underwent a protracted political crisis. Given the limited extent of the economic crisis in these countries, we would not have expected a marked increase in their electoral success. Their decline is, however, surprising at first sight, especially in the countries like Belgium and Switzerland, where the populists might have benefited from the perceptions of a political crisis. As the country chapters show, however, there are country-specific reasons for this lack of success. In Belgium, the VB was overshadowed by a party that served as a functional equivalent – the separatist N-VA, which Pauwels and Rooduijn characterise as an anti-establishment, but not a populist party. In Austria, the populist parties suffered from their implication in major scandals and from the subsequent splits in their own ranks. Similarly, the Swiss People's Party suffered from the split between Blocher loyalists and opponents. The Dutch PVV's lack of success, finally, may be attributed to the lack of resonance of its anti-European rhetoric in the Dutch public, and, as in the Danish case, to Wilders' support of the government.

The major exception to this overall picture is France – the only country in this region where populism displays an impressive surge at both national and European election levels (*see* Table 18.2). Thus, according to all evidence, it is a general sense of economic malaise and political malfunctioning that the Great Recession has helped intensify in France and that, to a large extent, explains the growth in support for the FN.

Finally, as shown by the cases of Austria, Switzerland, and The Netherlands, all having experienced populist parties taking part in coalition governments, there is a clear tendency for such parties (FPÖ, SVP and PVV respectively) to tone down their populist discourse when they move to incumbency. But when removed from office, those same parties have most commonly reverted to populist discourse and, in several cases, to political irresponsibility.

The Southern group: Strong populism fuelled by grave crises

This group includes two countries, Italy and Greece, with a prehistory of successful populism and which were hit particularly hard during the Great Recession by both economic and political crises. Contrary to the Nordic and West European group of countries, the established pre-crisis populism in these two countries was, however, not primarily related to the long-term emergence of a new demarcation-integration conflict, but rather to the hegemonic way of doing politics, which resulted from deliberate strategic decisions by the major parties in Greece (*see also* Pappas 2014b) and from the profound economic and political crisis in the early 1990s in Italy, which provided a fertile ground for the populist reconstruction of the party system. As it happened, in both countries, populist discourse surged instead of becoming more moderate during the Great Recession. New populist forces emerged which, exploiting the emergency situation, made significant electoral gains. This section offers an overview of the findings from the analysis of six populist parties that have played prominent roles in the politics of Italy and Greece before and during the Great Recession. In Italy, they include *Forza Italia* (FI), later succeeded by the People for Freedom (*Popolo Della Libertà*, PDL), *Lega Nord* (LN) and the Five-Star Movement (*Movimento Cinque Stelle*, M5S). In Greece, they are the *Panhellenic Socialist Movement* (PASOK) and *New Democracy* (ND), which however were forced by Greece's international creditors to abandon populism by 2012 and turn into reluctant liberals (Pappas and Aslanidis, this volume), the Independent Greeks (*Ανεξάρτητοι Έλληνες*, ANEL), the Popular Orthodox Rally (*Λαϊκός Ορθόδοξος Συναγερμός*, LAOS), and the Coalition of the Radical Left (*Συνασπισμός της Ριζοσπαστικής Αριστεράς*, SYRIZA).[1] Table 18.3 shows the electoral results of populist parties in Italy and Greece before and after the Great Recession. Evidently, the two countries in this region experienced the strongest upsurge of populism in all Europe (that is, an increase of 15.7 per cent over the crisis period), which correlates perfectly well with the severity of economic and political crises in both Greece and Italy.

Italy, as the title of the respective chapter puts it, presents us with an interesting case of 'strong and enduring populism'. Initially associated with Silvio Berlusconi's two conservative parties (FI and PdL) and the regionalist LN, populism won new impetus during the Great Recession. Amid the economic crisis, and its concomitant intensification of populist discourse in Italian politics, Beppe Grillo's M5S emerged as a new populist actor with no clear identification with either the left or the right, and rose swiftly to over one-quarter of the vote in the 2013 elections. The PDL and LN remained in power throughout most of the crisis (until November 2011). However, significantly, none of them toned down

---

1. Although the Greek PASOK and ND are classified as populist parties at least until Greece's 2009 national elections (*see* Pappas and Aslanidis, this volume), they both were forced to abandon their previous populist discourse and practices, thus eventually turning into reluctant liberal reformists, following Greece's bailout by the Troika in 2010. For this reason, and also because outside enforcing points to a very particular – and theoretically unexplored – case of populist constraint, we have chosen to omit these parties' electoral results from our present numerical analysis.

Table 18.3: Electoral results of populist parties in Mediterranean region (in per cent; respective countries and election years in parentheses)

	A. Pre-crisis	B. Post-crisis	Difference B/A	EU2014
FI/PDL (IT)	37.4 (2008)	21.6 (2013)	−15.8	16.8
LN (IT)	8.3 (2008)	4.1 (2013)	−4.2	6.1
M5S (IT)	n/a (2008)	25.6 (2013)	25.6	21.1
ANEL (GR)	n/a (2009)	7.5 (2012)	7.5	3.5
LAOS (GR)	5.6 (2009)	1.6 (2012)	−4.0	2.7
SYRIZA (GR)	4.6 (2009)	26.9 (2012)	22.3	26.6
TOTAL				
Country average	28.0	43.7	15.7	38.4

its populist discourse, choosing instead to blame the crisis on other domestic and foreign elites. In the 2013 national elections, the combined vote of old and new populist forces in Italy stood over 50 per cent.

Greece represents the country that features most severe economic and political crises along with enduring and vibrant populism. Here, too, populism has a long prehistory and is mainly associated with the left-of-centre party of PASOK, which rose to power in 1981 and thereafter enjoyed office for many years. Progressively, populism contaminated PASOK's main competitor, right-of-centre party of New Democracy (ND), the two of them alternating in office within a political system termed a 'populist democracy'. When the Great Recession hit, governing PASOK was forced by Greece's foreign creditors to abandon populism and initiate liberal reforms. ND insisted for a while on its old populist tactics, but, under foreign pressure, it also had to drop blatant populism and, eventually, it even had to form a coalition government with PASOK. Meanwhile, new populist forces had emerged on both the right (LAOS, ANEL) and the left of the political spectrum (SYRIZA) to claim the old populist constituency that, having turned its back on the old populist parties, was now up for grabs. Interestingly, as analysis has shown, the discourse of Greece's disparate populist parties presents important similarities, which also indicates their strong coalition potential in forthcoming elections.

The Great Recession had a major effect on both countries' economies. Italy was hit by two waves of economic crisis. The first post-2008 wave caused a sharp decline in GDP per capita simultaneously with modest rises in unemployment rates and levels of public debt. It was the second wave of crisis that hit Italy in the summer of 2011, when the markets began to lose confidence in the ability of the government to introduce bold but necessary reforms and control public debt. This proved to be decisive for the political consequences. By 2011, and amid numerous scandals, public trust in parliament and other institutions, as well as satisfaction with democracy had fallen to very low levels. Such was the situation when in November 2011, with most rating agencies downgrading Italian debt and under foreign pressure to implement unpopular reforms, Berlusconi's government resigned and was replaced by the technocratic administration of Mario Monti. Populism, however, anything but subsided. As has been shown, it continued thriving across Italy's political spectrum. And, in February 2013, it became largely responsible for Europe's second-most volatile general election in postwar Europe. For the most volatile one, we have to turn to Greece.

Greece's economic crisis was unprecedented by contemporary European standards. In May 2010, the then government signed with the Troika of foreign creditors a bailout agreement in exchange for painful austerity measures. From there on, the Greek economy went into free fall as indicated by each and every indicator available. Thus, during the Great Recession, Greece featured the sharpest decline in GDP over the entire period (it is still negative at the time of this writing – September 2014), the highest unemployment rates in all Europe (having by 2013 surpassed even those of Spain), an enormous government deficit, which necessitated higher and higher taxes, and the biggest public debt among all EU countries. As populist parties in opposition took advantage of the bad economic situation to enhance their own electoral opportunities, a political legitimacy crisis also loomed large. Social unrest grew spectacularly in the country, as becomes evident by any indicator available: distrust in parliament grew ominously (it reached 89 per cent in the Eurobarometer survey of November 2011 – comparable only to the rates in the Czech Republic), while satisfaction with democracy hit its lowest point since 1974. This explains Greece's extraordinarily volatile elections in May 2012, which, moreover, caused the breakdown of the previous two-party system and its replacement with a new one characterised by high party fragmentation and multi-polarised tendencies. It also facilitated the emergence of a party with such extremist and antidemocratic positions as the neo-Nazi Golden Dawn party.

With respect to this volume's original hypotheses, Italy and Greece provide ample confirmation for the positive relationship between crisis and rise in populism. They also compellingly point to the significance of outside enforcers (i.e. the Troika, European public opinion) in trying to tame populism at the domestic level. More specifically, in both countries the economic crisis amplified the antagonism between 'the people' and the elites, whether domestic or foreign. Of course, populism in these two countries had preceded the Great Recession and had already scored great political successes before the crisis, including long bouts of populism in power – FI/PDL in coalition with LN in Italy, and PASOK as well as ND in Greece. In addition, both countries experienced deep political crises and saw the levels of public trust to political institutions nosedive during the Great Recession. Electoral volatility was phenomenal and Greece in particular saw its party system transform fundamentally from a two-party into a polarised multiparty one. The fact that new populism emerged on both the right and the left flanks of the party system in each country, thus overriding traditional ideological boundaries, indicates the existence of a free-floating populist majority that stretches out across the entire political spectrum, and which is up for grabs by the populist party that makes the highest bid. Finally, the case of Greece offers us important lessons about when, and under what circumstances, populist parties may become responsible. For, as empirically demonstrated, it was only under outside pressure by the Troika that erstwhile populist PASOK and ND became forced to embrace again liberalism and, however 'willy-nilly', undertake reforms, thus seriously risking electoral defeat by the new populist forces. At the same time, however, the newly emergent populist parties in Italy and especially Greece have stepped up their polarising rhetoric and manifested strong anti-systemic attitudes, mobilising against the very foreign forces that pressured the former populists (in Greece) or the technocratic government (in both Greece and Italy) into responsible action.

The CEE group: Varying crises, disparate populisms

For yet other reasons, Central and Eastern European party systems have also been characterised by high levels of populism long before the Great Recession intervened. As pointed out in the introduction, in this part of Europe, the lack of institutionalisation of the party systems has provided a general opportunity for the rise of populist challengers. The chapters covering this region have primarily focused on three recently emerging Czech parties, Public Affairs (VV), ANO 2011 and the Dawn of Direct Democracy (Úsvit přímé demokracie), Slovakia's HZDS, SNS, and Direction – Social Democracy (SMER–sociálna demokracia), the Polish Law and Justice (Prawo i Sprawiedliwość, PiS), and the Hungarian Fidesz – Hungarian Civic Alliance (Fidesz – Magyar Polgári Szövetség). Table 18.4 shows the electoral results of CEE's populist parties before and after the Great Recession.

Table 18.4: Electoral results of populist parties in CEE region (in percentage; respective countries and election years in parentheses)

	A. Pre-crisis	B. Post-crisis	Difference B/A	EU2014
ANO 2011 (CZ)	n/a (2006)	18.6 (2013)	18.6	16.1
The Dawn (CZ)	n/a (2006)	6.9 (2013)	6.9	3.1
SMER-SD (SK)	29.1 (2006)	44.4 (2012)	15.3	24.11
HZDS (SK)	8.3 (2006)	0.9 (2012)	−7.4	–
SNS (SK)	11.7 (2006)	4.6 (2012)	−7.1	3.6
PiS (PL)	32.1 (2007)	29.9 (2011)	−2.2	31.8
Fidesz (HU)	42.0 (2006)	44.5 (2014)	2.5	51.52
TOTAL				
Country average	30.8	37.5	6.7	32.5

1. Notice, however, that turnout in Slovakia, at 13 per cent of registered voters, was the lowest in the EU.
2. In alliance with the the the smaller Christian Democratic People's Party (KDNP).

As becomes apparent, this region on the whole displays a remarkable increase in populism (6.7 per cent on average for the four countries). This increase is mainly due to the recent emergence of Czech populism and to the exceptionally robust performance of the Slovakian SMER during the Great Recession. It should be noted in this context that Hungary has also experienced the rise of *Jobbik*, an extremist anti-democratic force, which has received plenty of attention in the Hungarian chapter. Like Greece's Golden Dawn, however, we hesitate to classify *Jobbik* as a populist party comparable with the rest in this group.

A note of further caution about populism in CEE is in order: After the 1989 transition to pluralism, populism became diffuse in all countries in the region but – with the exception of Hungary – certainly not dominant. To the contrary, populism suffered severe electoral defeats in Poland, Slovenia, Slovakia and the Czech Republic. And yet, populist defeats have been made up by the success of a new wave of populists who have emerged in niches left vacant after the disappearance of older populist parties. Their success has most crucially been related to their projection of newness. Following Sikk (2009) and Lucardie (2000), we may consider some of the new parties as 'purifier parties', that is, political newcomers that have emerged in polities already imbued with chronic corruption and tinted by scandals, and proposing a cleaner, less ideological but distinctly moralistic approach to governing. Following Hanley and Sikk (2013), Učeň proposes to call the more technocratic ones among these newcomers 'anti-establishment parties'. Like populist parties, such parties criticise the entire establishment for its incapacity to deal with the crisis, but, contrary to populist parties, they do not insist on the gap between the people and the elite which, for populists, is not simply the result of the elite's incapacity, but of its treason.

In the Czech Republic, until the 2010 general election populist parties 'had not generally been relevant' (Havlik, this volume). The only significant party classified as populist (*see* Hanley 2012) had been the *Association for the Republic-Republican Party of Czechoslovakia* (SPR-RSČ), which enjoyed considerable political success in the 1990s before it lost parliamentary representation in the 1998 general elections, after which it disintegrated. However, during the Great Recession several political parties emerged in the Czech Republic that, to a certain extent, displayed a distinctly populist profile. In chronological order of appearance, the first such party was VV, a non-ideological formation opposing political corruption and using anti-establishment discourse. Entrusted in the 2010 elections by over one-tenth of the voters, it entered the centre-right coalition government that formed in its aftermath, and thereafter purged any elements of populism from its public discourse. In the meantime beset by internal strife, VV failed to contest the 2013 elections and disappeared. It was replaced by a party with several populist features, most notably its anti-elitism and advocacy of direct democracy, the Dawn of Direct Democracy. Founded by the Czech entrepreneur Tomio Okamura, in the 2013 general elections this party garnered 7 per cent of the national vote. By far the most significant of parties employing a certain populist style, complete with anti-elitist and anti-corruption discourse, however, is ANO 2011, a centre-right party founded by Andrej Babiš, another successful entrepreneur. After its electoral success in the 2013 polls, this party became a partner in the new coalition government and since then tries to appeal to centrist voters.

In Slovakia, Vladimír Mečiar's populist Movement for Democratic Slovakia (HZDS) became the dominant political force in the 1990s and, in coalition with the also populist Slovak National Party (SNS), ruled Slovakia between 1994 and 1998. Once this populist coalition was forced out of power in 1998, a more ideological partisan competition emerged, since most of the parties now 'defined their positions on the left-right continuum and openly declared their ideological orientations' (Mesežnikov *et al.* 2008: 109). That, however, was only a respite as Robert Fico, a former member of the Communist Party of Czechoslovakia, created SMER (Direction) as populism's new incarnation. Although SMER initially portrayed itself as a 'non-ideological' party, it gradually adopted a more leftist, particularly social democratic, profile with respect to economic policies and a conservative, and even nationalist, one with respect to socio-cultural policies. In 2006, SMER became the strongest party of the ruling 'populist coalition' (which also included SNS and the spectacularly diminished HZDS). Europe's Great Recession thus found SMER in power, and yet nothing could shake it. Instead, in the two general elections that took place during the crisis (in 2010 and 2012), SMER went from strength to strength. Eventually, in 2012, it was able to win the absolute majority of seats in the Slovak parliament and form a single-party government.

In Poland, too, populism has been a distinct feature of politics and yet 'an episodic and largely inconsequential one' (Stanley, this volume). Its presence was mostly felt during the 'populist coalition' that governed the country during the pre-crisis years 2005–07 and consisted of the conservative Law and Justice (PiS), the agrarian Self-Defense (SRP) and the radical right League of Polish Families (LPR). After two years in power that led to a deep political crisis, the populist coalition collapsed, and when new elections were held, the voters denied the populists a return to power: neither SRP nor LPR managed to cross the electoral threshold required to enter parliament. In the years to follow, populism became 'internalised by the system in the shape of the mainstream party Law and Justice (PiS)', also followed by a general 'rejection of populist narratives' (Stanley, this volume). As put by Kucharczyk and Wysocka (2008: 99–100), the Polish experiment with populism 'has been effectively resisted by political opposition, independent media and civil society[...]The systematically growing number of opponents of the populist government led to the electoral tsunami of 2007 when voters turned out *en masse* to vote against the government, which – in their view – had made Poland a laughing stock of Europe'. With its electoral strength further declining during the crisis, in the 2011 general elections PiS came in a distant second as the Polish voters chose to renew their support for the incumbent centrist Civic Platform party, which they viewed as the best guarantor of stability amidst the continuing European recession.

Hungary, finally, stands out as the region's most special case. It features a highly successful populist party, the Alliance of Young Democrats (*Fidesz*), which has enjoyed long single-handed power, while also experiencing the rise of political extremism best represented by *Jobbik*, a party openly hostile to representative pluralism. Even in its most populist phase, Enyedi (this volume) cautions, *Fidesz* 'refrained from condemning the entire elite and elements of elitist conservatism have never completely disappeared from its discourse'. What is special about the Hungarian populists is that they linked the concept of full membership in the community not to an ascriptive criterion such as citizenship or ethnicity, but to performance – an achievement-oriented standard that leaves the concept of the 'people' more open'. *Fidesz*, an originally liberal party that gradually turned populist under the leadership of charismatic Victor Orbán, won office for the first time in 1998. After a narrow electoral defeat in 2002, this party chose to engage in disloyal opposition by refusing to participate in politics through ordinary institutional channels and reaching directly out to the people through symbolic acts and polarising populist sloganeering. In 2010, *Fidesz* returned to power with an impressive 52.7 per cent of the vote (and a supermajority of seats in parliament), which gave it full control over the policy-making agenda. From there on, *Fidesz* followed a majoritarian logic and, for all intents and purposes, moved the country away from political liberalism and towards authoritarianism. In the general elections of 2014, *Fidesz* succeeded in maintaining its electoral and political supremacy, thus remaining Hungary's dominant political force.

All in all, then, despite a perception among the general public, the media, and even academics to the opposite, populism has not been uniformly strong in the CEE countries. After some early successes, especially in Slovakia in the 1990s and Poland in the 2000s, by the time economic crisis hit Europe some radical-right populist parties in CEE had already suffered grave electoral defeats and irreversibly declined. New, less virulent versions of populism did however regain strength during the Great Recession. In the Czech Republic, ANO 2011 and, albeit at a lesser extent, The Dawn have seen their electoral fortunes increase during the crisis. Both of them toned down their populist overtures once they entered into coalition government. In Slovakia, SMER increased its electoral base by 15.3 points between 2006 (when it received 29.1 per cent of the vote) and 2012 (with 44.4 per cent). While in government, this party, too, has eliminated from its discourse the most acute elements of populism. In Poland, the PiS lost 2.2 points between 2007 and 2011 and populism became internalised within an otherwise liberal democratic discourse. The only party that remained in office and, indeed, intensified its populist – and, at times, even authoritarian – discourse is Hungary's *Fidesz*. In Hungary, populism has continuously grown in strength since the early 1990s, and it has since enjoyed long terms in office (which it still controls). It is also responsible for intense political polarisation, thus offering a first-class opportunity to non-democratic *Jobbik* to also prosper.

How did the countries of Central Eastern Europe fare during the Great Recession? Poland did get comparatively well through the crisis. It is the only EU country that maintained positive rates of growth throughout the crisis, while also keeping unemployment relatively low. The other three countries we cover in this study, by contrast, suffered sharp declines in their economic growth rates. Hungary in particular was hit hard and had to turn to the IMF already in fall 2008. All three never returned to their high pre-crisis growth and, after a strong initial recovery, suffered from declining growth. In line with our first hypothesis, this contrasting experience contributes to the explanation of the differences in the populists' fate in these countries – their decline in Poland and their initial (CZ), renewed (SK) or continuous (HU) success in the other three countries.

With respect to crises more directly related to the conduct of politics, compared to Western Europe, political trust is invariably low in these countries as is satisfaction with the way democracy works. Against this general background of widespread political dissatisfaction, country-specific political crises contributed to the populists' success in the three countries that were already more or less heavily hit by the economic crisis. In the Czech Republic, the political crisis was closely linked to the long, gradual decline in satisfaction with politics and political institutions which had set in already before the economic crisis occurred. In this case, the general political dissatisfaction was amplified by the chronic weakness and instability of successive governments – a weakness that was accompanied by extensive (and often well-founded) allegations of corruption. In Hungary, the success, and increased predominance of *Fidesz* is above all explained by the political crisis that was triggered by the leaked speech of the socialist Prime Minister in 2006, which preceded the economic crisis. The freefall of the government's popularity might have been followed by a recovery, but then the Great Recession hit Hungary particularly hard and made such developments all but impossible. In Slovakia, finally, it was the protracted political crisis in the aftermath of the clash within the governing centre-right coalition over Slovakia's participation in the EFSF that led SMER-SD to an unprecedented victory in the 2012 elections.

In addition, the experience of populism in CEE countries provides maybe the most clear-cut evidence for Moffitt's (2014) thesis that crises are not just triggers of populism, but that populism also 'attempts to act as a trigger of crisis'. In line with this claim, Enyedi maintains that the case of *Fidesz* reminds us that political crises are, by definition, constructed, and that populists can have an important role in framing political crises. Similarly, the Polish case draws our attention to a more reciprocal relationship between political crisis and populism: the politicisation of the Smolensk disaster by PiS and the recurrence of identity-based populist mobilisation that occurred in its wake suggest that populists may choose to create political crises through the manipulation of the meaning and significance of events. More generally, Stanley (this volume) suggests that populists 'both exploit crises and seek to provoke them in order to benefit from the ensuing sense of elite incompetence and loss of control. They discern an all-pervading and chronic state of crisis across all domains of public life which exists due to elite incompetence and/or conspiracy'. Finally, the unprecedented victory for SMER-SD in the 2012 Slovak elections is, as Učeň suggests, a result of SMER-SD's masterful management of the political crisis.

With respect to the behaviour of populists in office, the CEE cluster of cases is a mixed bag. While the Czech and Slovak populists tuned down their populism after election campaigns and, especially, after having assumed office as coalition government partners, their Polish and Hungarian counterparts showed exactly the opposite behaviour. In Poland, PiS became more populist when in power in an effort to challenge the older, transition elites. In Hungary, too, *Fidesz* stepped up its populist discourse and polarising tactics once in power. Like any other populist party exercising power single-handedly (think of Europe's two other examples, the Greek PASOK during its long rule since the early 1980s and Berlusconi's governance in Italy – to say nothing about populist parties in power in Latin America), *Fidesz* thrived on intense polarisation. For, according to its political discourse and majoritarian logic, it is only *Fidesz* and none of its political opponents who can fully represent the Hungarian nation. Therefore, to be against it, is simply to oppose Hungary.

The Anglo-Celtic countries: Similar crises, contrasting outcomes

Contrary to the other regions, before the Great Recession, populism was virtually non-existent in both the United Kingdom (UK) and Ireland. The economic crisis hit Ireland particularly hard, but the UK was not spared either. However, the outcomes of the crisis on these countries' respective politics could not be more diverse. The UK saw the emergence of the United Kingdom Independence Party (UKIP) that grew fast during the crisis years, and made an impressive showing in the 2014 elections for the European Parliament. In Ireland, in contrast, no populist party emerged despite the severe crisis (which, incidentally, points to the need of further examining this country as a valuable negative case in the field of populist studies). In the absence of any Irish populist party, Table 18.5 shows, only the electoral results of British populism, which, importantly, have been rather negligible at the national level but quite momentous if also considering the 2014 elections for the European Parliament.

UKIP was founded in 1993 specifically as a reaction to the Maastricht Treaty (February 1992), which led to the creation of the euro and provided for further integration of the EU member states in a number of key areas such as foreign policy or military cooperation. The party remained for many years on the domestic political fringe, but had some successes in second-order elections, such as those for the European Parliament (it elected three MEPs in 1999, twelve in 2004, and thirteen in 2009). Still, in the 2010 general elections, UKIP polled a rather poor 3.1 per cent of the vote, and gained no parliamentary seat. Soon thereafter, Nigel Farage assumed the leadership of the party making it clear that his intention was

Table 18.5: Populism in the UK

	A. Pre-crisis	B. Post-crisis	Difference B/A	EU2014
UKIP	2.2 (2005)	3.1 (2010)	0.9	27.5

to overtake the Liberal Democrats for third party. During the crisis, the UKIP emerged as the dominant expression of Euroscepticism, anti-immigration, and anti-establishment populism (Goodwin, this volume). In a fashion similar to the True Finns, it became particularly vocal against immigration from Central and Eastern Europe, which it promised to halt – a promise that was strongly resonant with the fears of the economically disadvantaged and socially conservative sectors of the electorate Farage had expected to woo. In 2013, UKIP performed well in a number of local elections and, indeed, it came third in nationwide vote share. In the 2014 EU elections, UKIP won seats in every region of Great Britain, including Scotland. It received the greatest number of votes of any British party and elected twenty-four deputies in the European Parliament.

Although several of its parties have occasionally borrowed from the populist toolbox, Ireland has never had a real populist formation. In recent decades, *Fianna Fáil* mostly distinguished itself for its nationalist rather than populist discourse, which also was notably absent from the appeals of all the other significant parties. During the Great Recession, and despite the tumult it caused to Ireland's party system, no new populist party emerged. What occurred in Ireland, instead, was the belated appearance of several populist themes (about corruption, anti-elitism, and even some Euroscepticism) that became diffuse in the party and political competition. As put by O'Malley and FitzGibbon (this volume), a populist narrative thus 'began to emerge during and after the 2011 general election that sought to characterise Ireland's economic woes as an unjust action brought about by a corrupt political elite beholden to a cabal of bankers and EU politicians'. For all the severity of its crisis, then, Ireland stands unique among the countries examined here for not experiencing the rise of a populist party since all major Irish parties chose responsibility over responsiveness.

The effects of the economic crisis on the UK were severe. GDP growth suffered a great contraction – the greatest since 1958. Unemployment did not increase as sharply as elsewhere in Europe, and it remained below the EU average throughout the Great Recession. Meanwhile, government debt as a percentage of GDP more than doubled, increasing from 44 per cent in 2007 to 91 per cent in 2013. With regard to our political crisis indicators, public trust in parliament decreased, but, on the whole, such distrust fluctuated well above EU average during the crisis, while satisfaction with democracy remained at sufficiently acceptable levels. A major scandal that erupted in 2009 revealed that many MPs across the mainstream party spectrum had abused parliamentary expenses. And yet, the party and political systems remained by and large stable. There was no breakdown or even major rupture in the party system. In typical politically moderate fashion, the 2010 general elections caused the replacement in power of Labour by the Conservatives, who subsequently formed a coalition government with the Liberal Democrats. UKIP only managed to collect a very small share of the vote, but gained no parliamentary seat. And yet, Euroscepticism had gathered new momentum during the crisis, and became the main reason for UKIP's victory at the recent European Parliament elections.

Along with Greece, Ireland was the country most badly hit by the Great Recession (for a comparison of the two crisis-ridden countries, *see* Pappas and O'Malley 2014). In January 2009, a banking crisis erupted in Ireland compelling the government to intervene, imposing extraordinary burdens to an already stagnating economy and rising borrowing costs. In the course of the events and as the crisis gathered steam across Europe, Ireland registered negative growth rates, a large increase in unemployment rates (which remained above the EU average), and, most importantly, as a result of the bank bailout government debt rose more than eight-fold from 11 per cent in 2007 to 94 per cent in 2011. At the same time, public trust in parliament decreased, but remained above the EU average. Most important have been the effects of the crisis on the Irish party system, which has traditionally been characterised by the predominance of two large parties, *Fianna Fáil* and *Fine Gael*. That pattern was broken in the 2011 general election, which saw formerly mighty *Fianna Fáil* crumbling into third place. The winner was *Fine Gael*, a conservative liberal and pro-European party, with the Labour Party finishing second.

With regard to our original hypotheses, the case of UKIP seems, indeed, to confirm the causal relation between economic crisis and the increase in populist discourse. Ireland, on the other hand, most firmly refutes it. Here is one of Europe's most severely hit economies, but with almost no trace of a populist party. How can we make sense of this 'anomaly'? As O'Malley and FitzGibbon point out in their analysis of the Irish case, there are at least three possible explanations: In addition to the high electoral threshold for aspiring new party entrants (especially for securing political funding) and to Ireland's high rate of success for independent or non-party politicians, it is above all the diffusion of populism across all major parties in Ireland (a situation recalling US party politics, which is also characterised by intense populism in the absence of a purely populist party), which is characteristic of the Irish case. As O'Malley and FitzGibbon suggest, the populist rhetoric that emerged during and after the 2011 general election in Ireland is diffuse, not attributable to a specific party, but part of the anti-government discourse more generally shared by the opposition parties (and independent challengers). More specifically, the Irish populist reaction to the crisis was rather a left populist one, where the issues of the property taxes and water charges finally provided the means by which to mobilise populism.

European populism in the aggregate: A notable but uneven surge during crisis

The most general question we sought to answer in this volume is whether, and to what extent the Great Recession contributed to a populist ascendancy across Europe. After having examined the relevant developments at individual country- and region-specific levels, we are now in a position to aggregate our findings and test our original hypotheses at the overall European level. Table 18.6, a compound itself of the foregoing tables for each region and based on the electoral results before and after the crisis of all populist parties that have been examined in this

Table 18.6: Aggregate European populism

	A. Pre-crisis	B. Post-crisis	Difference B/A	EU2014
25 parties in 17 countries*	19.0	23.1	4.1	24.6

Notes: *Including Ireland, a case of negative populism.

volume, shows that during the Great Recession populism in Europe increased notably by 4.1 per cent. Moreover, as indicated by the result the same group of parties achieved as a whole in the recent elections of the European Parliament (i.e. over a quarter of all ballots cast across the EU), populism's upward tendency in Europe is non-negligible and probably enduring.

The populist surge has been particularly strong in Southern and Central-Eastern Europe. The two types of surges show, however, different patterns: while the more recent wave of CEE populism and anti-establishment mobilisation more generally is partly (but certainly not exclusively) related to the emergence of 'purifier' parties promising better and scandal-free governance, Southern European populism is generally highly polarising, often anti-systemic, and thriving on the left as well as on the right of the political spectrum. Nordic populism was also on the rise during the Great Recession, but, with the possible exception of the Swedish SD, this region's populist parties have been consistently systemic and, at times, even supportive of their mainstream competitors' policies. The only region where populism contracted, albeit slightly, during the crisis was Western Europe – with the exception, of course, of France. Finally, the duo of Anglo-Celtic countries, the UK and Ireland, contrasts sharply in that, while both experienced grave crises, only the former saw the development of a strong anti-European populist force. Ireland stands out as the rare case without a significant populist party in spite of the severity of its economic and political crisis. As we have seen, this does, however, not mean that Ireland did not see a rise in populism: As a matter of fact, it experienced the rise of a diffuse populism that manifested itself across all opposition parties and independent challengers.

With regard to the validity of our initial hypotheses at the European aggregate level, we have first of all found partial confirmation of the expected relationship between an economic crisis and populist leaps. On the one hand, this hypothesis has been confirmed in the cases of countries heavily affected by the crisis – Greece, Italy, the UK, Hungary, and, to a lesser extent, the Czech Republic and Slovakia – where populism, indeed, grew considerably. On the other hand, this hypothesis has also been confirmed by the countries that were less affected by the economic crisis and, accordingly, did not experience a populist surge: Poland, Norway, as well as the Western European countries (except for France) belong to this group. The French exception, as well as the Danish and Finnish cases, suggest that whether there is an economic crisis or not may be a question of a combination of perception and agency: while France (at least at first) got better through the Great Recession than others, compared to its main standard of comparison, Germany, it lost in competitiveness, which gave rise to the specific version of the French malaise. Marine Le Pen seized the opportunity offered to her by this malaise both to establish herself as a serious, professional politician and to forge a new image for the FN, which were at the origin of her success. The Finnish exception similarly suggests that the perception of an economic crisis may be decisive and may be exploited/created by able populists in unexpected ways. The Danish exception (as well as the Dutch and the Austrian case) remind us that populist parties in or close to government may just as well be punished by economic voting as regular incumbents. The most glaring exception, the diffuse populism across all opposition parties in Ireland, also points to the importance of agency and to the different ways populism can manifest itself: in this case, too, populist politicians seized the opportunity offered by the crisis, but not in the expected way. Finally, the Swedish case of a slow rise of populism in spite of a lack of economic hardship is, as we have argued, best explained by the belated manifestation of long-term trends, which have had a hard time to impose themselves in this country because of a generally inauspicious opportunity structure.

In what concerns our second hypothesis about a nexus between rising populism and political crisis, confirmation comes from the Southern and Central- and Eastern European countries, as well as from Finland, where the political crisis was important (in relative terms in Finland) and contributed to the rise of populism. This hypothesis has met with difficulties in Belgium, Austria and Switzerland, where political crises (important again in relative terms) did not contribute to the strength of populists. As we have seen, however, in all three cases, there were country-specific reasons concerning the internal difficulties of populist parties and competition by functionally equivalent challengers, which account for this lack of success. This hypothesis is disconfirmed by the case of Ireland (major political crisis with no rising populist party).

Our third hypothesis, stating that populism becomes more intense when there is a coincidence between economic and political crises finds robust empirical support among the cases examined. Indeed, as shown most prominently by the cases of Greece, Italy, Hungary, and to a lesser extent Slovakia and the Czech Republic, it is where there is a tandem of economic and political crisis that populism emerges the strongest. Ireland is again the exception that disconfirms this hypothesis.

Finally, regarding our last hypothesis stating that populists tend to soften their discourse when they are in office (or have a good chance of it), the most confirmatory evidence comes from the Nordic populist parties, which are fully integrated in their respective countries' party systems and tend to behave systemically as well as responsibly. The Austrian FPÖ and the Swiss People's Party are also cases of a populist party moderating its populism while in coalition government – but also of relapsing to populism when removed from office. Significantly, when populist parties control power either as dominant coalition partner or singlehandedly – as indicated by the cases of PASOK and ND in pre-crisis Greece, FI/PdL in Italy, PiS in pre-crisis Poland, and *Fidesz* in Hungary – they tend to step up their populism and issue highly polarising messages. This surprising result, together with several other issues that this volume has raised, certainly deserves more empirical analysis.

At the time of writing in late 2014, the specter of financial and economic disintegration in Europe is not yet over. There are currently serious worries that the Eurozone will remain in relative recession and that it may fall into deflation, while the proportion of loans in default is rising in many countries, especially in the European South. At the same time, populism also continues to be on the rise, and even appears strong in places that previously had no such experience. Thus, 2014 witnessed the emergence of Podemos in Spain, a leftist populist party proclaiming to transform Spanish politics in a majoritarian direction. In the May 2014 elections for the European Parliament, Podemos won almost 8 per cent of the Spanish vote and, by November of the same year, public opinion polls showed it to have overtaken both of Spain's mainstream parties.

Clearly, then, as difficulties with the economy persist, and become deeply felt by Europeans, populism seems to be posing great challenges for Europe's liberal democracy. The crisis has left behind disgruntled electorates, delegitimised policies, ineffectual – and even outright incompetent – leaders, unworkable institutions, old ideas that now seem obsolete. On the other hand, it has brought the people massively – and occasionally violently – out into the streets, most commonly led by new political entrepreneurs who, whether standing on the left or on the right of the political spectrum, proclaim to express the genuine popular will. One of them, Hungary's Prime Minister Victor Orbán, has even announced his intention to transform his country into an 'illiberal state'. In a much-noted speech in Transylvania in July 2014, Orbán disparaged the 'failed liberal Western system' and promised to work towards replacing welfare society with a 'workfare state'. What he seems to have in mind is a centrally controlled state, capable of confronting multinational companies, such as banks and energy firms, and that can escape from 'debt slavery' and avoid becoming a 'colony' of the EU. In the aftermath of Europe's Great Recession, it is an open question whether other countries will follow Hungary's example of populism in power.

Bibliography

Aardal, B., Bergh, J. and Hennum Haugsgjerd, A. (2014) 'Velgervandringer og valgdeltakelse ved stortingsvalget 2013. De første resultater fra Valgundersøkelsen' Institutt for samfunnsforskning, Oslo.

Aarts, K. and Thomassen, J. (2008) 'Dutch voters and the changing party space 1989–2006', *Acta Politica* 43 (2–3): 203–234.

Abts, K. (2011) 'Maatschappelijk onbehagen en etnopopulisme. Burgers, ressentiment, vreemdelingen, politiek en extreem rechts', *Proefschrift*, Katholieke Universiteit Leuven.

Åkesson, J. (2013) *Satis politico*, Stockholm: Asp & Lycke.

Akkerman, T. (2005) 'Anti-immigration parties and the defence of liberal values: The exceptional case of the List Pim Fortuyn', *Journal of Political Ideologies* 10 (3): 337–354.

Albertazzi, D. (2008) 'Switzerland: Yet another populist paradise', in Albertazzi, D. and McDonnell, D. (eds) *Twenty-first century populism: The spectre of Western European democracy*, Basingstoke: Palgrave, pp. 100–118.

— (2009) 'Reconciling "voice" and "exit": Swiss and Italian populists in power', *Politics* 29(1): 1–10.

Albertazzi, D. and McDonnell, D. (2005) 'The Lega Nord in the second Berlusconi government: in a league of its own', *West European Politics* 28 (5): 952–972.

— (2007) 'Introduction: The sceptre and the spectre', in Albertazzi, D. and McDonnell, D. (eds) *Twenty-First Century Populism: The spectre of Western European democracy*, Basingstoke: Palgrave.

— (2010) 'The Lega Nord back in government', *West European Politics* 33 (6): 1318–1340.

— (2015) *Populists in Power*, London: Routledge (forthcoming).

Albertini, D. and Doucet, D. (2013) *Histoire du Front National*, Paris: Tallandier.

Alho, K. (2010) 'Lama, rakennekriisi ja elvytys – näkökohtia toimialoittaisesta sopeutumisesta ja talouspolitiikan mitoituksesta talouskriisin jälkeen' *The Research Institute of the Finnish Economy (ETLA) Discussion Papers*, No. 1215.

Altares (2014) *'Bilan 2013: défaillances et sauvegardes d'entreprises en France'*. Online. Available http://www.altares.fr/wpcontent/uploads/2014/01/AltaresDefaSauvBilan2013.pdf (accessed 15 May 2014).

Ames, P. (2014) 'The Scary Return of a Radical, Far-right Europe and What It Means' *GlobalPost* 21 May. Online. Available http://www.globalpost.com/dispatch/news/regions/europe/france/140520/european-parliament-elections-far-right (accessed 21 May 2014).

Andersen, J. G. (2011) 'From the edge of the abyss to bonanza - and beyond: Danish economy and economic policies 1980–2011', *Comparative Social Research* 28: 89–186.

— (2013) 'Den økonomiske udvikling op til 2011-valget', in Stubager, R., Hansen, K. M., and Andersen, J. G. (eds) *Krisevalg. Økonomien og Folketingsvalget 2011*, København, Jurist- og Økonomforbundets Forlag, pp. 45–60.

Andersen, J. G. and Bjørklund, T. (1990) 'Structural changes and new cleavages: the Progress Parties in Denmark and Norway', *Acta Sociologica* 33 (3): 195–217.

Andersen, J. G. and Borre, O. (2007) 'Partiledere gør en forskel', in Andersen, J. G., Andersen, J., Borre, O., Hansen, K. M., and Nielsen, H. J. (eds) *Det nye politiske landskab. Folketingsvalget 2005 i perspektiv*, Århus: Academica, pp. 289–306.

Andersen, J. G. and Møller Hansen, K. (2013) 'Vælgernes krisebevidsthed' in Stubager, R., Hansen, K. M. and Andersen, J. G. (eds) *Krisevalg. Økonomien og Folketingsvalget 2011*, København, Jurist– og Økonomforbundets Forlag, pp. 137–162.

ANO (2011) *Výzva ANO 2011*, ANO 2011. Online. Available http://www.anobudelip.cz/file/edee/ke-stazeni/ostatni/ano-vyzva-ano.pdf (accessed 15 March 2014).

— (2013a) *Naše prohlášení k současné politické situaci*. Online. Available http://www.anobudelip.cz/cs/o-nas/aktuality/novinky/tiskove-prohlaseni-hnuti-ano-k-soucasne-politicke-situaci-12266.shtml

— (2013b) *Volební program*. ANO 2011. Online. Available http://www.anobudelip.cz/cs/o-nas/program/ (accessed 15 March 2014).

Anopress. Online. Available http://www.anopress.cz (accessed 5 May 2015).

Anti-Austerity Alliance (2014) 'Petition against water charges to be launched', Press release 23 April 2014.

APRI (2014) *Finance v Česku nikdo neřídil, řekl Andrej Babiš*. APRI. Online. Available http://www.asociaceppp.cz/?action=ventire&n_id=1513&page=0&nonotify=0 (accessed 15 March 2014).

Art, D. (2008) 'The organizational origins of the contemporary radical right: the case of Belgium', *Comparative Politics* 40 (4): 421–440.

— (2011) *Inside the Radical Right: The development of anti-immigrant parties in Western Europe*, Cambridge: Cambridge University Press.

Arter, D. (2010) 'The breakthrough of another West European populist radical right party? The case of the True Finns', *Government and Opposition* 45 (4): 484–504.

— (2012) 'Analysing "successor parties": the case of the True Finns', *West European Politics* 35 (4): 803–825.

Arter, D. and Kestilä-Kekkonen, E. (2014) 'Measuring the extent of party institutionalisation: the case of a populist entrepreneur party', *West European Politics* 37 (5): 932–956.

Arzheimer, K. and Carter, E. (2006) 'Political opportunity structures and right-wing extremist party success', *European Journal of Political Research* 45: 419–443.

Aslanidis, P. (2014) 'Social Movements of the Great Recession: a populist wave of mobilization?', unpublished manuscript.

Aspinwall, M. (2000) 'Structuring Europe: powersharing institutions and British preferences on European integration', *Political Studies* 48: 415–442.

Babiš, A. (2013) *Podporuje levici, proto volím* pravici? Online. Available http://www.andrejbabis.blog.idnes.cz/c/369510/Podporuje-levici-proto-volim-pravici.html (accessed 5 May 2015)

Bakker, R. *et al.* (2012) 'Measuring party positions in Europe: The Chapel Hill Expert Survey Trend File', 1999–2010. Online. Available http://www.chesdata.eu/Papers/PP_2012.pdf (accessed 15 March 2014).

Bale, T. and Bergman, T. (2006) 'Captives no longer, but servants still? Contract parliamentarism and the new minority governance in Sweden and New Zealand', *Government and Opposition* 41(3): 422–449.

Balík, S. (2010) 'Neuskutečněné předčasné volby 2010', in Balík, S. *et al. Volby do Poslanecké sněmovny vroce*, Brno: CDK, pp. 39–68.

Bank of Greece (2014) 'The saga of the Great Crisis: the Bank of Greece 2008–2013' (Το Χρονικό της Μεγάλης Κρίσης: Η Τράπεζα της Ελλάδος 2008–2013). Online. Available http://www.bankofgreece.gr (accessed 24 June 2014).

Bartlett, J., Froio, C. and McDonnell, D. (2013) *New Political Actors in Europe: Beppe Grillo and the M5S*, Demos UK. Online. http://www.demos.co.uk/files/Beppe_Grillo_and_the_M5S_-_Demos_web_version.pdf?1360766725 (accessed 6 March 2014).

Becuwe, S., Blancheton, B. and Charles, L. (2013) 'First globalization: Why did France miss the boat? Université Montesquieu Bordeaux IV', *Cahiers du GREThA*, 2013–17. Online. Available http://halshs.archives-ouvertes.fr/docs/00/87/99/96/PDF/2013-17.pdf (accessed 15 May 2014).

Bellone, F. and Schiappini, R. (2014) 'Le déclin de la compétitivité française: états des lieus', *Cahiers français*, 380, May–June: 2–9.

Benoit, K. and Laver, M. (2006) *Party Policy in Modern Democracies*, London: Routledge.

Bergh, J. and Bjørklund, T. (2013) 'Lokalvalget i skyggen av 22. Juli', in Bergh, J. and Christensen, D. A. (eds) *Et robust lokaldemokrati – lokalvalget i skyggen av 22 juli*, Oslo: Abstrakt forlag.

Bernhard, L. (2012) *Campaign Strategy in Direct Democracy*, Basingstoke: Palgrave Macmillan.

Bernier, A. (2014) *La gauche radicale et ses tabous: Pourquoi le Front de gauche échoue face au Front National*, Paris: Éditions du Seuil.

Betz, H. G. (1993) 'The new politics of resentment: radical right-wing populist parties in Western Europe', *Comparative Politics* 25 (4): 413–427.

Betz, H. G. and Johnson C. (2004) 'Against the current-stemming the tide: the nostalgic ideology of the contemporary radical populist right', *Journal of Political Ideologies* 9(3): 311–327.

Bíber, J. (2009) 'Gypsy-crime is a Zionist biological weapon' ('A cigánybűnözés a cionisták biológiai fegyvere'). Online. Available https://www.kuruc. info/r/7/23568/ (accessed 30 June 2014).

Bjørklund, T. (1981) 'Anders Lange og Fremskrittspartiet: Norges svar på Glistrupianismen', Oslo: Institutt for samfunnsforskning.

Bjørklund, T. and Andersen, J. G. (2002) 'Anti-Immigration Parties in Denmark and Norway: The Progress Party and Danish People's Party' in Schain, M. A., Zolberg, A. and Hossay, P. *Shadows over Europe: The development and impact of the extreme right in Western Europe*, New York: Palgrave Macmillan.

Blomquist, M. and Slätt, R. (2004) 'Sverigedemokraterna från insidan: berättelsen om Sveriges största parti utanför riksdagen', 1. uppl. Stockholm: Hjalmarson & Högberg.

Blot, Y. (2012) 'Un livre néo marxiste? Quand Marine le Pen devient Marine la rouge...', Online. Available http://www.atlantico.fr/decryptage/marine-pen-pour-que-vive-france-livre-marxisme-rouge-yvan-blot-301601.html (accessed 12 March 2014).

Bordignon, F. and Ceccarini, L. (2013) 'Five stars and a cricket: Beppe Grillo shakes Italian politics', *South European Society and Politics*, http:// www.democraziapura.altervista.org/wp-content/uploads/2013/09/2013-Bordignon-Ceccarini.pdf (accessed 18 April 2015).

Borg, S. (2012a) 'Perussuomalaiset', in Borg, S. (ed.) *Muutosvaalit 2011*. Oikeusministeriön selvityksiä ja ohjeita 16/2012, Oikeusministeriö (Ministry of Justice), pp. 191–210.

— (2012b) 'Tärkeimmät asiakysymykset ja vakavimmat ongelmat,' in Borg, S (ed.) *Muutosvaalit 2011*. Oikeusministeriön selvityksiä ja ohjeita 16/2012, Oikeusministeriö (Ministry of Justice), pp. 240–252.

Borg, S. and Paloheimo, H. (2009a) in *Vaalit yleisödemokratiassa. Eduskuntavaalitutkimus 2007,* Tampere: Tampere University Press, pp. 13–27.

— (2009b) in *Vaalit yleisödemokratiassa. Eduskuntavaalitutkimus 2007*, Tampere: Tampere University Press, pp. 13–27.

Bornschier, S. (2010) *Cleavage Politics and the Populist Right: The new cultural conflict in Western Europe*, Philadelphia: Temple University Press.

Bosco, A. and McDonnell, D. (2013) 'The Monti Government and the Downgrade of Italian Parties', in Bosco, A. and McDonnell, D. (eds), *From Berlusconi to Monti*, New York: Berghahn, pp. 37–56.

Boulhol, H. and Sicari, P. (2014) 'The Declining Competitiveness of French Firms Reflects a Generalised Supply-Side Problem', *OECD Economics Department Working Papers*, 1029, Online. Available http://dx.doi. org/10.1787/5k4c0dldmgr2-en (accessed 18 May 2014).

Bovens, M. and Wille, A. (2011) 'Politiek vertrouwen in Nederland: tijdelijke dip of definitieve daling?', in Andeweg, R. and Thomassen, J. (eds) *Democratie Doorgelicht, het functioneren van de Nederlandse democratie*, Leiden: Leiden University Press, pp. 21–43.

Bruhn, K. (2012) 'To hell with your corrupt institutions!', AMLO and populism in Mexico', in C. Mudde and C. Rovira Kaltwasser (eds) *Populism in Europe and the Americas: Threat or corrective for democracy?*, Cambridge: Cambridge University Press, pp. 88–112.

Budge, I. and Farlie, D. (1983) 'Party competition – selective emphasis or direct confrontation? An alternative view with data', in Daalder, H. and Mair, P. (eds) *Western European Party Systems: Continuity and change,* Beverly Hills: Sage, pp. 267–305.

Burdziej, S. (2008) Radio Maryja a społeczeństwo obywatelskie. Znak, (640), pp. 17–28.

BVA (2013) 'Impact des affaires sur la classe politique'. Online. Available http://www.bva.fr/data/sondage/sondage_fiche/1481/fichier_bva_pour_i_tele-cqfd-le_parisien_-_limpact_des_affaires_sur_la_classe_politique3978a.pdf (accessed 27 May 2014).

BZÖ (2010) *Bündnis Zukunft Österreich – BZÖ Pressedient Parlamentsklub,* (1 April 2010–31 May 2010). Online. Available http://www.ots.at (accessed 15 March 2015).

— (2012) *Bündnis Zukunft Österreich – BZÖ Pressedient Parlamentsklub,* (a: 1 February 2012–31 March 2012; b: 1 June 2012–31 July 2012). Online. Available http://www.ots.at (accessed 15 March 2015).

Čadová, N. (2006) *Důvěra k ústavním institucím a spokojenost s politickou situací* http://www.cvvm.soc.cas.cz/media/com_form2content/documents/c1/a3334/f3/100607s_pi61030.pdf (accessed 15 March 2015).

Canovan, M. (1999) 'Trust the people! Populism and the two faces of democracy', *Political Studies* 47 (1): 2–16.

— (2002) 'Taking Politics to the People: Populism as the ideology of democracy', in Mény, Y. and Surel, Y.(eds) *Democracies and the Populist Challenge*, Basingstoke: Palgrave, pp. 25–44.

Cappelen, Å. and Torbjørn, E. (2010) '2000–tallet: Fra optimisme til krise', *Statistisk Sentralbyrå*, Oslo.

Carter, E. (2005) *The Extreme Right in Western Europe: Success or failure?*, Manchester: University of Manchester Press.

Carty, R. K. (1981) *Electoral Politics in Ireland: Party and parish pump,* Waterloo, Ontario: Wilfrid Laurier University Press.

Cassely, J. L. (2013) 'Le populisme "vintage" de Jean-Luc Mélenchon, trop élaboré pour être efficace' slate.fr, 15 April. Online. Available http://www.slate.fr/story/70687/melenchon-populisme-vintage (accessed 20 August 2014).

CBOS (2008) Opinie o działalności prezydenta, parlamentu i NBP, Warszawa: Centrum Badania Opinii Społecznej.

— (2009) Opinie o działalności prezydenta, parlamentu, ZUS, ABW i CBA, Warszawa: Centrum Badania Opinii Społecznej.

— (2010) Oceny działalności parlamentu i prezydenta, Warszawa: Centrum Badania Opinii Społecznej.

— (2011) Ocena działalności parlamentu i prezydenta, Warszawa: Centrum Badania Opinii Społecznej.

— (2012) Oceny instytucji publicznych w grudniu, Warszawa: Centrum Badania Opinii Społecznej.

— (2013) Oceny instytucji publicznych, Warszawa: Centrum Badania Opinii Społecznej.

— (2014) Trendy. http://www.cbos.pl. Online. Available http://www.cbos. pl/PL/trendy/trendy.php (accessed 01 March 2014).

CBS, SKON, Brinkman, M., van der Kolk, H., Aarts, C. and Rosema, M. (2007) *Dutch Parliamentary Election Study 2006*, The Hague: DANS.

Česká pozice (2011) *Babiš se s výzvou ANO 2011 obrátil na občany, chce znovu zaplnit 'Václavák'* Česká pozice. Online. Available http://ceskapozice. lidovky.cz/babis-se-s-vyzvou-ano-2011-obratil-na-obcany-chce-znovu-zaplnit-vaclavak-12w-/tema.aspx?c=A111104_061044_pozice_42754 (accessed 15 March 2014).

Česká televize (2010) *Otázky Václava Moravce – Speciál*. Česká televize. Online. Available http://www.ceskatelevize.cz/ivysilani/10252839638-hyde-park-ct24/210411058080423/ (accessed 15 March 2014).

— (2013a) *Babiš chystá Občanské fórum proti korupci a hledá lídra*. Česká televize. Online. Available http://www.ceskatelevize.cz/ct24/ domaci/136958-babis-chysta-obcanske-forum-proti-korupci-a-hleda-lidra/ (accessed 15 March 2014).

— (2013b) *Tomio Okamura hostem Interview DD*. Česká televize. Online. Available http://www.ceskatelevize.cz/ct24/predvolebni-interview-dd/predvolebni-interview-dd/244543-tomio-okamura-hostem-interview-dd/ (accessed 15 March 2014).

Český rozhlas (2009a) *Kulatý stůl na téma veřejných financí*, 21 September 2009.

— (2009b) *Interview Studia Stop*, 20 August 2009.

— (2010a) *Dvacetiminutovka Český rozhlasu*, 26 April 2010.

— (2010b) *Rozhovor s Radkem Johnem, předsedou strany Věci veřejné*, 3 June 2010.

Chevènement, J.-P. (2008) 'Un grand parti de gauche pour le New Deal', *Le Monde* 24 April. Online. Available http://www.lemonde.fr/idees/ article/2008/04/23/un-grand-parti-de-gauche-pour-un-new-deal-par-jean-pierre-chevenement_1037449_3232.html (accessed 22 February 2014).

— (2011) 'Contre Marine Le Pen, la République, la vraie!' Chevenement.fr, 25 March. Online. Available http://www.chevenement.fr/Contre-Marine-Le-Pen-la-Republique-la-vraie-_a1104.html (accessed 22 February 2014).

Chiaramonte, A. and Emanuele, V. (2013) 'Volatile e tripolare: il nuovo sistema partitico italiano'. Online. Available http://cise.luiss.it/cise/2013/02/27/volatile-e-tripolare-il-nuovo-sistema-partitico-italiano/ (accessed 15 October 2013).

Christiansen, F. J. (2012) 'Raising the stakes: passing state budgets in Scandinavia', *World Political Science Review* 8 (1): 184–200.

Church, C. H. (2004) 'The Swiss elections of October 2003: two steps to system change?', *West European Politics* 27 (3): 518–534.

— (2008) 'The Swiss elections of 21 October 2007: consensus fights back', *West European Politics* 31(3): 608–623.

— (2000) 'The Swiss elections of October 1999: learning to live in more interesting times', *West European Politics* 23(3): 215–30.

Church, C. H. and Vatter, A. (2009) 'Opposition in consensual Switzerland: a short but significant experiment', *Government and Opposition* 44 (4): 412–437.

Clerc, D. (2014) 'La décennie maudite des inégalités en France', *Alternatives économiques* March, 37–39.

Coffé, H. (2005) 'Do individual factors explain the different success of the two Belgian extreme right parties', *Acta Politica* 40(1): 74–93.

Cohen, D. (2012) *Homo economicus, Prophète (égaré) des temps nouveaux*, Paris: Albin Michel.

Corbetta, P. and Gualmini, E. (2013) (eds) '*Il Partito di Grillo*', Bologna: Il Mulino.

Courtois, G. (2014) 'En France, l'euroscepticisme marque des points', *Le Monde*, 20 May.

Cowen, B. (2012) 'The Euro: From Crisis to resolution? Some reflection from Ireland on the road thus far' Speech to BMW Center for German and European Studies, Georgetown University, Washington DC., 21 March 2012.

CPB (2014) 'CPB: Slight economic recovery and EMU balance under 3 per cent', CPB Netherlands Bureau for Economic Policy Analysis, Press release, 4 March 2014. Online. Available http://www.cpb.nl/en/pressrelease/3214615/cpb-slight-economic-recovery-and-emu-balance-under-3-cent (accessed 5 March 2014).

Cranmer, M. (2011) 'Populist communication and publicity: an empirical study of contextual differences in Switzerland', *Swiss Political Science Review* 17 (3): 286–307.

Creighton, L. (2014) 'Party Whip system in Irish Politics' Speech to Irish Times Debating Final, The Law Society. Online. Available http://www.lucindacreighton.ie/whip-system-in-irish-politics/ (accessed 30 May 2014).

CSA (2014) 'Français, ce qui vous rassemble est-il plus fort que ce qui vous divise?' *Cahier CSA 2014*. Online. Available http://www.csa.eu/media/cahiercsa2014/files/assets/common/downloads/CSA-CAHIER-2014.pdf (accessed 19 May 2014).

Curtice, J., Fisher, S. D. and Ford, R. (2010) 'Appendix 2: An Analysis of the Results' in Kavanagh, D. and Cowley, P. (eds) *The British General Election of 2010*, Basingstoke: Palgrave Macmillan.

Cutts, D., Ford, R. and Goodwin, M. J. (2011) 'Anti-immigrant, politically disaffected or still racist after all? Examining the attitudinal drivers of extreme right support in Britain in the 2009 European elections', *European Journal of Political Research* 50(3): 418–440.

Czapiński, J. (2006) 'Stosunek do przemian systemowych i ocena ich wpływu na życie badanych', in Czapiński, J. and Panek, T. (eds) *Diagnoza Społeczna 2005: Warunki i jakość życia Polaków*, Warszawa: Wyższa Szkoła Finansówi Zarządzania w Warszawie, pp. 182–189.

Dachs, H. *et al.* (eds) *Politik in Österreich. Ein Handbuch,* Vienna, ManzVerlag.

Dalongeville, G. (2013) *Pen Perdue*, Paris: Éditions Jacob-Duvernet.

Debreczeni, J. (2009) *Image* (Arcmás), Budapest: Noran Libro.

Deegan-Krause, K. (2004) 'Uniting the enemy: politics and the convergence of nationalisms in Slovakia', *East European Politics and Societies* 18(4): 651–96.

— (2006) '*Elected Affinities: Democracy and party competition in Slovakia and the Czech Republic*', Palo Alto: Stanford University Press.

— (2012) 'Populism, democracy and nationalism in Slovakia' in Mudde, C. and Kaltwasser, R. C. (eds) *Populism in Europe and the Americas: Threat or corrective to democracy?*, Cambridge: Cambridge University Press, pp. 182–204.

Deegan-Krause, K. and Haughton, T. (2009) 'Toward a more useful conceptualization of populism: types and degrees of populist appeals in the case of Slovakia', *Politics and Policy* 37(4): 821–841.

De Lange, S. and Art, D. (2011) 'Fortuyn versus Wilders: an agency-based approach to radical right party building', *West European Politics* 34(6): 1229–1249.

De Lange, S. and Rooduijn, M. (2011) 'Een populistische Zeitgeist in Nederland? Een inhoudsanalyse van de verkiezingsprogramma's van populistische en gevestigde politieke partijen', in Andeweg, R. and Thomassen, J. (eds) *Democratie Doorgelicht, het functioneren van de Nederlandse democratie,* Leiden: Leiden University Press, pp.319–334.

Delwit, P. (2014) *PTB- Nouvelle gauche, vieille recette,* Liège: Editions Luc Pire.

Demker, M. (2012) 'Positiv attityd till invandring trots mobilisering av invandringsmotstånd', in Weibull, L., Oscarsson, H and Bergström, A. (eds) *I framtidens skugga*, Göteborgs universitet: SOM-institutet.

Demker, M. and Oscarsson, M. (2013) in Rydgren, J. (ed.) *Class Politics and the Radical Right*, London: Routledge.

De Montvallon, D. and Denis, T. (2011) 'Marine Le Pen : "Dix millions de fausses cartes Vitale circulent"', *France-Soir*, 11 July. Online. Available http://www.francesoir.fr/actualite/politique/marine-pen-dix-millions-fausses-cartes-vitales-circulent-117496.html (accessed 14 March 2014).

Dézè, A. (2012) *Le Front national: À la conquête du pouvoir?* Paris: Armand Colin.

Dowling, M. (1997) 'The Ireland that I would have': De Valera and the creation of an Irish national image', *History Ireland* 5 (2 Spring).

Downs, W. M. (2001) 'Pariahs in their midst: Belgian and Norwegian parties react to extremist threats', *West European Politics* 24 (3): 23–42.

Dudek, A. (2013) *Historia polityczna Polski 1989-2012*, Kraków: Wydawnictwo Znak.

Eatwell, R. (2000) 'The Extreme Right and British Exceptionalism: The primacy of politics', in Hainsworth, P. (ed.) *The Politics of the Extreme Right: From the margins to the mainstream*, London: Pinter, pp. 72–92.

— (2006) 'Explaining fascism and ethnic cleansing: the three dimensions of charisma and the four dark sides of nationalism', *Political Studies* 4 (3): 263–78.

Eatwell, R. and Goodwin, M. J. (eds) (2010) *The New Extremism in Twenty-First Century Britain*, London: Routledge.

Edelman, M. (1988) *Constructing the Political Spectacle*, Chicago: University of Chicago Press.

Eggers, A. and Fischer, A. (2011) 'Electoral accountability and the UK parliamentary expenses scandal: did voters punish corrupt MPs?', *Political Science and Political Economy Working* Paper 8/11.

Eibl, O. (2010) 'Volební programy', in Balík, S. *et al. Volby do poslanecké sněmovny 2010*, Brno: CDK, pp. 69–96.

— (2014) 'Volební programy', in V. Havlík *et al., Volby do poslanecké sněmovny 2013*, Brno: Munipress, pp. 21–52.

Elinkeinoelämän keskusliitto, Confederation of Finnish Industries 2014. Trust indicator. Online. Available http://www.ek.fi/avainsanat/luottamusindikaattori/ (accessed 13 March 2013).

Ekeland, A., Nærsheim, H., Rønningen, D. and Berge, C. (2009) 'Hvordan påvirkes innvandrerne av omslaget i arbeidsmarkedet?', *Statistisk sentralbyrå*, Oslo.

Ekman, M. and Poohl, D. (2010) 'iUt ur skuggan En kritisk granskning av Sverigedemokraterna', Stockholmi: *Natur & Kultur*.

Ekström von Essen, U. (2003) 'Folkhemmets kommun: socialdemokratiska idéer om lokalsamhället 1939–1952', Diss. Stockholm: Univ.

Erlingsson, G, Vernby, K. and Öhrvall, R. (2013) 'The single-issue party thesis and the Sweden Democrats', *Acta Politica* (early view).

Ennser-Jedenastik, L. (2014) 'The politics of patronage and coalition: how parties allocate managerial positions in state-owned enterprises', *Political Studies* 62: 398–417.

Eurobarometer, Standard (2010) Eurobarometer 73, Brussels: European Commission.

— (2013) Eurobarometer 80, Brussels: European Commission.

— (2014) 'Macroeconomic Imbalances, France 2014', Occasional Papers, 178, March. Online. Available http://ec.europa.eu/economy_finance/publications/occasional_paper/2014/pdf/ocp178_en.pdf (accessed 10 March 2014).

European Commission (2013a) 'Macroeconomic Imbalances, France 2013', *Occasional Papers* 136, April. Online. Available http://ec.europa.eu/economy_finance/publications/occasional_paper/2013/pdf/ocp136_en.pdf (accessed 10 March 2014).

— (2013b) 'Public Opinion in the European Union. First Results', *Standard Eurobarometer* 79, Spring. Online. Available http://ec.europa.eu/public_opinion/archives/eb/eb79/eb79_first_en.pdf (accessed 6 June 2014).

— (2014) 'Macroeconomic Imbalances, France 2014', *Occasional Papers* 178, March. Online. Available http://ec.europa.eu/economy_finance/publications/occasional_paper/2014/pdf/ocp178_en.pdf (accessed 10 March, 2014).

Eurostat (2014a) General government gross debt, annual data. Online. Available http://epp.eurostat.ec.europa.eu/tgm/table.do?tab=table&plugin=1&language=en&pcode=teina225 (accessed 26 June 2014).

— (2014b) Eurostat Statistical Database. Online. Available http://epp.eurostat.ec.europa.eu/portal/page/portal/statistics/search_database (accessed 26 June 2014).

Evans, G. (1998) 'Euroscepticism and Conservative electoral support: how an asset became a liability', *British Journal of Political Science* 28: 573–590.

Fabbrini, S. and Lazar, M. (2013) 'Still a difficult democracy? Italy between populist challenges and institutional weakness', *Contemporary Italian Politics* 5 (2): 106–112.

Ferrand, O. and Jeanbart, B. (2011) 'Gauche: Quelle majorité pour 2012?' Paris, Fondation Terra Nova. Online. Available http://www.tnova.fr/essai/gauche-quelle-majorit-lectorale-pour-2012 (accessed 22 January 2014).

Fiala, P. (2010) 'Rozpad politiky', *Kontexty* 1 (2): 3–10.

Fine Gael (2011) '*Fine Gael* Getting Ireland Working', Dublin: *Fine Gael*.

FitzGibbon, J. (2013) 'Citizens against Europe? Civil society and Eurosceptic protest in Ireland, the United Kingdom and Denmark', *Journal of Common Market Studies* 51 (1): 105–22.

Fœssel, M. (2012) 'Marine Le Pen ou la captation des "invisibles"', *Esprit* 382: 20–31.

Foltýn, T. and Havlík, V. (2006) 'Teorie a praxe sestavování vlády vČeské republice', in Čaloud, D. *et al.* (eds) *Volby do Poslanecké sněmovny vroce*, Brno: CDK, pp. 188–202.

Ford, R. (2010) 'Who Might Vote for the BNP? Survey evidence on the electoral potential of the extreme right in Britain, in Eatwell, R. and Goodwin, M. (eds) *The New Extremism in Twenty-First Century Britain*, London: Routledge.

Ford, R. and Goodwin, M. J. (2010) 'Angry white men: individual and contextual predictors of support for the British National Party', *Political Studies* 58: 1–25.

— (2014) *Revolt on the Right: Explaining public support for the radical right in Britain*, London: Routledge.

Ford, R., Goodwin, M. J., and Cutts, D.C. (2012) 'Strategic Eurosceptics and polite xenophobes: support for the United Kingdom Independence Party (UKIP) in the 2009 European Parliament elections', *European Journal of Political Research* 51: 204–234.

Forster, A. (2002) *Euroscepticism in British Politics*, New York: Routledge.

Fortuyn, P. (2002) *De Puinhopen van acht jaar paars. Een genadeloze analyse van de collectieve sector en aanbevelingen voor een krachtig herstelprogramma*, Uithoorn-Rotterdam: Karakter Uitgevers-Speakers Academy.

FPÖ (2010) *FPÖ Pressedient -Freiheitlicher Parlamentsklub*, (1 April 2010–31 May 2010). Online. Available http://www.ots.at/pressemappe/4468/ freiheitlicher-parlamentsklub-fpoe (accessed 26 June 2014).

—   (2012) *FPÖ Pressedient -Freiheitlicher Parlamentsklub*, (a: 1 February 2012–31 March 2012; b: 1 June 2012–31 July 2012). Online. Available http://www.ots.at/pressemappe/4468/freiheitlicher-parlamentsklub-fpoe (accessed 26 June 2014).

Frachon, A. (2014) 'Européennes : nostalgique, le FN veut ramener la France à l'ère prémondialisation', *Le Monde*, 29 May. Online. Available http://www. lemonde.fr/europe/article/2014/05/29/europeennes-2014-nostalgique-le-fn-veut-ramener-la-france-a-l-ere-premondialisation_4428371_3214. html (accessed 29 May 2014).

Freeden, M. (1998) 'Is Nationalism a Distinct Ideology?', *Political Studies*, 46: 748–765.

Frekvence 1 (2010) *Rozhovor s Radkem Johnem, předsedou Věcí veřejných*, 4 April 2010.

Fressoz, F. (2012) 'Présidentielle: le message de la "France des invisibles"', *Le Monde*, 23 April. Online. Available http://www.lemonde.fr/election-presidentielle-2012/article/2012/04/23/score-de-marine-le-pen-le-message-de-la-france-des-invisibles_1689734_1471069.html (accessed 15 May 2014).

Front National (1993) *300 mesures pour la renaissance de la France*, Paris: Editions nationales.

—   (2010) 'Contribution du Front National', in Boutin, C. (ed.) *De la mondialisation à l'universalisation: une ambition sociale*, Paris, La documentation Française, pp. 312–15.

Gallagher, M. (2010) 'The Oireachtas: President and parliament', in Coakley, J. and Gallagher, M. (eds.) *Politics in the Republic of Ireland*, 5th ed., London: Routledge.

—   (2011) 'Ireland's Earthquake Election: Analysis of the results', in Gallagher, M. and Marsh, M. (eds) *How Ireland Voted 2011*, London: Palgrave.

Gatinois, C. (2013) 'La France, championne d'Europe du pessimisme', *Le Monde*, 6 May. Online. Available http://www.lemonde.fr/europe/article/2013/05/06/ la-france-championne-d-europe-du-pessimisme_3171535_3214.html (accessed 15 May 2014).

Gatinois, C. and Guélaud, C. (2013) 'Competitivité : l'Allemagne distance toujours plus la France', *Le Monde*, 14 September. Online. Available http://www. lemonde.fr/economie/article/2013/09/04/competitivite-l-allemagne-distance-toujours-plus-la-france_3470940_3234.html (accessed 12 March 2014).

Gazeta W. (2006) 'The Fall of Post-Communism: Transformation in Central and Eastern Europe heritage.org. Online. Available http://www.heritage.org/about/speeches/the-fall-of-post-communism-transformation-in-central-and-eastern-europe (accessed 8 March 2014).

— (2009) 'Tusk o wzroście: nie ulegliśmy namowom histeryków', Gazeta. pl. Online. Available http://wiadomosci.gazeta.pl/wiadomosci/1,11487 3,6665217,Tusk_o_wzroscie__nie_uleglismy_namowom_histerykow. html (accessed 2 March 2014).

Geddes, A. (2003) *The European Union and British Politics*, London: Palgrave Macmillan.

Goertz, G. (2006) *Social Science Concepts*, Princeton: Princeton University Press.

Goodwin, M. J. (2007) 'The extreme right in Britain: still an "ugly duckling" but for how long?', *Political Quarterly* 78 (2): 241–250.

— (2011) *New British Fascism: Rise of the British National Party*, London: Routledge.

— (2013) *The Roots of Extremism: The English Defence League and the counter-Jihad challenge*, London: Chatham House.

— (2014) 'Forever a false dawn? Explaining the electoral collapse of the British National Party', *Parliamentary Affairs* forthcoming.

Gregor, M. and Macková, A. (2014) 'Předvolební kampaně 2013: prohloubení trendů, nebo nástup nových', in Havlík V. *et al.*: *Volby do poslanecké sněmovny,* Brno: Munipress, pp. 53–72.

Guilluy, C. (2013) 'Exclues, les nouvelles classes populaires s'organisent en "contre-société"', *Le Monde*, 2 February. Online. Available http:// www.lemonde.fr/idees/article/2013/02/19/exclues-les-nouvelles-classes-populaires-s-organisent-en-contre-societe_1835048_3232.html (accessed 12 March 2014).

Hanley, S. (2012) 'The Czech Republicans 1990–1998: A populist outsider in a consolidating democracy', in Mudde, C. and Kaltwasser, C. R. (eds) *Populism in Europe and the Americas*, Cambridge: Cambridge University Press, pp. 68–87.

Hanley, S. and Sikk, A (2013) 'Economy, corruption or promiscuous voters? Explaining the success of anti-establishment reform parties in Eastern Europe', COMPASSS Working Paper 2013–75. Online. Available http:// www.compasss.org/wpseries/HanleySikk2013.pdf (accessed 26 June 2014).

Haughton, T., Novotná, T. and Deegan-Krause, K. (2011) 'The 2010 Czech and Slovak parliamentary elections: red cards to the "Winners"', *West European Politics* 34 (2): 394–402.

Havlík, V. (2011) 'Česká republika', in Balík, S. *et al.* (eds) *Koaliční vládnutí ve střední Evropě (1990–2010)*, Brno: Munipress, pp. 39–90.

—   (2014) 'Výsledky voleb', in V. Havlík *et al.* (eds) *Volby do poslanecké sněmovny 2013*, Brno: Munipress, pp. 145–164.

Hawkins, K. A. (2009) 'Is Chavez populist?: Measuring populist discourse in comparative perspective', *Comparative Political Studies* 42 (8): 1040–67.

Helander, V. (1971) (ed.) *Vennamolaisuus populistisena joukkoliikkeenä.* Hämeenlinna: Karisto. HS = Helsingin Sanomat 18 April 2012. *Nova-yhtiöiden Merisalo ja Yli-Saunamäki saivat vuosien vankeustuomiot.* Online. Available http://www.hs.fi/kotimaa/a1305560125364 (accessed 9 July 2012).

Hellström, A. (2010) 'Vi är de goda: den offentliga debatten om Sverigedemokraterna och deras politik', Hägersten: Tankekraft.

Hermann, M. (2014) 'Elite und Basis im Spannungsfeld, l' in Scholten, H. and Kamps, K. (eds) *Abstimmungskampagnen: Politikvermittlung in der Referendumsdemokratie*, Wiesbaden: Springer VS, pp. 123–137.

Hinnfors, J. and Spehar, A. (2012) 'The missing factor: why social democracy can lead to restrictive immigration policy', *Journal of European Public Policy* 19 (4): 585–603.

Hloušek, V. (2012) 'Věci veřejné: politické podnikání strany typu firmy', *Politologický časopis/Czech Journal of Political Science* 19 (4): 322–340.

Hloušek, V. and Kopeček, L. (2012) *Záchrana státu? Úřednické a polopolitické vlády v České republice a Československu*, Brno: Barrister & Principal.

Holstein, E. (2014) 'Regeringen får smæk for EU-politikken, men går frem på økonomi', Altinget.dk April 22. København: Altinget.dk. Online. Available http://www.altinget.dk/christiansborg/artikel/regeringen-faar-smaek-for-eu-politikken-men-gaar-frem-paa-oekonomi (accessed 15 March 2014).

Hooghe, M., Marien, S. and Pauwels, T. (2011) 'Where do distrusting voters turn if there is no viable exit or voice option? The impact of political trust on electoral behaviour in the Belgian regional elections of June 2009', *Government and Opposition*, 46 (2): 245–273.

HS 21 August 2011, *Perussuomalaiset otti käyttöön englanninkielisen nimen.* Online. Available http://www.hs.fi/politiikka/artikkeli/1135268708128 (accessed 16 March 2012).

HS 18 August 2014, Kokoomus repii kaulaa – perussuomalaisten kannatus alhaisimmillaan kahteen vuoteen. Online. Available http://www.hs.fi/kotimaa/a1408247044769 (accessed 27 August 2014).

Ifop (2012) 'Regards internationaux sur la crise et la situation économique'. Online. Available http://www.ifop.com/media/poll/1769-1-study_file.pdf (accessed 13 March 2014).

Ignazi, P. and Ysmal, Y (1992) 'New and old extreme right parties. The French Front National and the Italian Movimento Sociale', *European Journal of Political Research* 22 (1): 101–121.

Igounet, V. (2014) *Le Front National*, Paris: Seuil

INSEE (2013) 'In May 2013, households' confidence declined again (-4 points)' *Informations rapides* 28 May. Online. Available http://www.insee.fr/en/indicateurs/ind20/20130528/cam_mai_eng.pdf (accessed 14 March 2014).

—   (2014) 'Monthly Consumer Confidence Index: Methodology'. Online. Available http://www.insee.fr/en/indicateurs/ind20/Cam_m-EN.pdf (accessed 12 March 2014).

Instinkt (2010) *Kateřina Klasnová – Lidé vědí, kdo jsou dinosauři*, 3 June 2010.

Ipsos (2014) 'Fractures françaises vague 2: 2014'. Online. Available http://www.ipsos.fr/ipsos-public-affairs/actualites/2014-01-21-nouvelles-fractures-francaises-resultats-et-analyse-l-enquete-ipsos-steria (accessed 12 March 2014).

Ivaldi, G. (2013) 'Vers un nouveau chauvinisme du welfare? La transformation du programme économique du Front National (1984–2012)', paper presented at the annual conference of the French Political Science Association, Paris, 9–11 July. Online. Available http://www.congres-afsp.fr/st/st27/st27ivaldi.pdf (accessed 20 February 2014).

Ivarsflaten, E. (2006) 'Reputational Shields: Why Most Anti-immigrant Parties Failed in Western Europe, 1980–2005', paper presented at the Annual Meeting of the American Political Science Association, Philadelphia, PA.

—   (2008) 'What unites the populist right in Western Europe? Reexamining grievance mobilization models in seven successful cases', *Comparative Political Studies* 41 (1): 3–23.

Jakobsson, N. and Blom, S. (2014) 'Did the 2011 terror attacks in Norway change citizens' attitudes toward immigrants?', *International Journal of Public Opinion Research*. Online. Available http://www.ijpor.oxfordjournals.org/content/early/2014/01/09/ijpor.edt036.full.pdf?keytype=ref&ijkey=0Hg4wgRjJ5a6OzG (accessed 18 April 2015).

Jagers, J. (2006) 'De Stem van het Volk! Populisme als Concept Getest bij Vlaamse Politieke Partijen', Universiteit Antwerpen, Antwerpen.

Jagers, J. and Walgrave, S. (2007) 'Populism as political communication style: an empirical study of political parties' discourse in Belgium', *European Journal of Political Research* 46: 319–345.

Janda, K. (1970) 'A conceptual framework for the comparative analysis of political parties', in Eckstein, H. and Gurr, T. R. (eds) *Sage Professional Papers in Comparative Politics*, vol. 1, Beverly Hills: Sage Publications, pp. 75–126.

Jansen, R. S. (2011) 'Populist mobilization: a new theoretical approach to populism', *Sociological Theory* 29 (2): 75–96.

Jenssen, A. T. and Kalstø, Å. M. (2012) 'Did the financial crisis save the red-green government in the 2009 Norwegian election–the dissatisfaction with rising expectations superseded by a grace period?', *World Political Science Review* 8 (1): 70–100.

Jobbik (2010) Radical Change. Party program of *Jobbik* for election 2010. Online. Available http://www.jobbik.hu/sites/jobbik.hu/down/Jobbik-program2010OGY.pdf (accessed 30 June 2014).

Joffrin, L. (2014) 'Européennes: le choc est terrible. Sera-t-il salutaire?' *Nouvel Observateur,* May 25. Online. Available http://tempsreel.nouvelobs.com/politique/20140525.OBS8451/le-choc-est-terrible-sera-t-il-salutaire.html (accessed 25 May 2014).

John, P. and Margetts, H. (2009) 'The latent support for the extreme right in British politics', *West European Politics,* 32 (3): 496–513.

Jones, E. (2012) 'The Berlusconi government and the sovereign debt crisis' in Bosco, A. and McDonnell, D. (eds) *From Berlusconi to Monti,* New York: Berghahn, pp 172–190.

Jungar, A. -C. (2013) 'Det reformerade kommunala folkinitiativet' *Erfarenheter* 2011–2013, Report, *Sveriges kommuner och landsting.*

— (2014) 'Sweden Democrats: Party organisation' chapter prepared for edited volume on PRR party organisation (ed.) Heinisch, R. and Mazzoleni, O.

Jungar, A.-C. and Backlund, A. (2014) 'Radical right representation on socio-cultural issues: Patterns of party-voter congruence in Western and Central-Eastern Europe', unpublished paper.

Jungar, A.-C. and Jupskås, A. (2014) 'Populist radical right parties in the Nordic Region: a new and distinct party family?' *Scandinavian Political Studies* 37 (3): 215–238.

Jupskås, A. R. (2013) 'The Progress Party: a fairly integrated part of the Norwegian Party System?', in Grabow, K. and Hartleb, F. *Exposing the Demagogues: Right-wing and national populist parties in Europe,* Brussels/Berlin: Centre European Studies/Konrad Adenauer Stiftung, pp. 205–236.

— (2014) 'Between a business firm and a mass party: the organization of the Norwegian Progress Party', paper presented at How Populist Parties Organize, Salzburg, March 14.

Jupskås, A. R. and Tore, W. (2012) 'One year after terrorism struck Norway: taking stock' *openDemocracy* July 24, 2012. Online. Available https://www.opendemocracy.net/anders-ravik-jupsk%C3%A5s-tore-wig/one-year-after-terrorism-struck-norway-taking-stock (accessed 18 July 2014).

Kammenos, P. (2012) Speech at the opening of the ANEL Athens office, April 2, 2012, Online. Available http://www.youtube.com/watch?v=IuoWaANGMrw (accessed 10 March 2014).

— (2014) Radio interview, January 10, 2014. Online. Available http://www.anexartitoiellines.gr/post.php?post_id=3911 (accessed 1 March 2014).

Kantola, A. (ed.) (2011) *Hetken hallitsijat. Julkinen elämä notkeassa yhteiskunnassa,* Helsinki: Gaudeamus.

Kantola, A., Vesa, J. and Hakala, S. (2011) 'Notkean myrskyn silmässä: vaalirahaskandaali,' in Kantola, A. (ed.) *Hetken hallitsijat. Julkinen elämä notkeassa yhteiskunnassa,* Helsinki: Gaudeamus, pp. 65–88.

Karácsony, G. and Róna, D. (2010) 'The secret of *Jobbik*'. (A *Jobbik* titka), *Politikatudományi Szemle,* 19 (1): 31–66.

Kestilä, E. (2006) 'Is there demand for radical right populism in the Finnish electorate?', *Scandinavian Political Studies* 29 (3): 169–191.

Kestilä-Kekkonen, E. and Söderlund, P. (2014) 'Party, leader or candidate? Dissecting the right-wing populist vote in Finland', *European Political Science Review*, FirstView Article, January 2014.

Kitschelt, H.and McGann, A.-J. (1995) *The Radical Right in Western Europe: A comparative analysis*, Ann Arbor: University of Michigan Press.

Klasnja, M. and Tucker, J. (2013) 'The economy, corruption, and the vote: evidence from experiments in Sweden and Moldova', *Electoral Studies* 32 (3): 536–543.

Klíma, M. (2013) 'Koncept klintelistické strany, Případová studie – Česká republika', *Politologický časopis/Czech Journal of Political Science* 20 (3): 215–235.

Kmenta, J. (2011) *Superguru Bárta. Všehoschopní*. Praha: JKM – Jaroslav Kmenta.

Knigge, P. (1998) 'The ecological correlates of right-wing extremism inWestern Europe', *European Journal of Political Research* 34: 249–279.

Koivulaakso, D., Brunila, M. and Andersson, L. (2012) *Äärioikeisto Suomessa. Vastarintamiehiä ja metapolitiikkaa*, Helsinki: Into Kustannus.

Koopmans, R. and Muis, J. (2009) 'The rise of right-wing populist Pim Fortuyn in the Netherlands: a discursive opportunity approach', *European Journal of Political Research* 48: 642–664.

Koopmans, R. and Olzak, S. (2004) 'Discursive opportunities and the evolution of right-wing violence in Germany', *American Journal of Sociology* 110 (1): 198–230.

Kriesi, H. (2007) 'The role of European integration in national election campaigns'. *European Union Politics* 8 (1): 83–108.

—— (2014) 'The populist challenge', *West European Politics* 37 (3): 361–378.

Kriesi, H., Grande, E., Dolezal, M., Helbling, M., Höglinger, D., Hutter, S. and Wüest, B. (eds) (2012) *Political Conflict in Western Europe,* Cambridge: Cambridge University Press.

Kriesi, H., Grande, E., Lachat, R., Dolezal, M., Bornschier, S. and Frey, T. (eds) (2006) 'Globalization and the transformation of the national political space: six European countries compared', *European Journal of Political Research* 45, 6: 921–957.

—— (2008) *West European Politics in the Age of Globalization*, New York: Cambridge University Press.

Kriesi, H., Lachat, R., Selb, P., Bornschier, S. and Helbling, M. (2005) *Der Aufstieg der SVP: Acht Kantone im Vergleich*, Zürich: NZZ Verlag.

Kriesi, H. and Sciarini, P. (2004) 'The impact of issue preference on voting choice in the Swiss federal elections, 1999', *British Journal of Political Science* 34 (4): 726–747.

Kriesi, H. and Trechsel, A. H. (2008) *The Politics of Switzerland: Continuity and change in a consensus democracy,* Cambridge: Cambridge University Press.

Kritzinger, S., Zeglovits, E., Lewis-Beck, M. S. and Nadeau, R. (2013) *The Austrian Voter*, Vienna: Vienna University Press.

Kritzinger, S., Müller, W.C. and Schönbach, K. (ed.) (2014) *Die Nationalratswahl Wie Parteien, Medien und Wählerschaft zusammenwirken*, Vienna: Böhlau Verlag.

Kumlin, S. and Esaiasson, P. (2011) 'Scandal fatigue? Scandal elections and satisfaction with democracy in Western Europe, 1977–2007', *British Journal of Political Science* 42 (2): 263–82.

Kunštát, D. (2012) *Důvěra ústavním institucím v prosinci 2012*, CVVM. Online. Available http://cvvm.soc.cas.cz/media/com_form2content/documents/c1/a6937/f3/pi130103.pdf (accessed 15 March 2014).

— (2013a) *Důvěra ústavním institucím v lednu 2013*, CVVM. Online. Available http://cvvm.soc.cas.cz/media/com_form2content/documents/c1/a6948/f3/pi130205.pdf (accessed 15 March 2014).

— (2013b) *Důvěra ústavním institucím v listopadu 2013*, CVVM. Online. Available http://cvvm.soc.cas.cz/media/com_form2content/documents/c1/a7140/f3/pi131202.pdf (accessed 15 March 2014).

Kucharczyk, J. and Wysocka, O. (2008) 'Poland', in Mesežnikov, G., Gyárfášová, O. and Smilov, D. (eds) *Populist Politics and Liberal Democracy in Central and Eastern Europe*, Bratislava: Institute for Public Affairs, pp. 71–100.

Laclau, E. (1977) *Politics and Ideology in Marxist Theory: Capitalism—Fascism—Populism*, London: Verso.

— (2005a) *On Populist Reason*, London: Verso.

— (2005b) 'Populism: What's in a name?' in *Populism and the Mirror of Democracy*, Panizza, F. (ed.), London: Verso, pp. 32–49.

Ladner, A., Felder, G., Gerber, S. and Fivaz, J. (2010) 'Die politische Positionierung der europäischen Parteien im Vergleich: Eine Analyse der politischen Positionen der europäischen Parteien anlässlich der Wahlen des Europäischen Parlaments 2009 mit besonderer Berücksichtigung der Schweizer Parteien' Lausanne, *Cahier de l'IDHEAP* 252.

Lane, P. R. (2012) 'The European sovereign debt crisis', *Journal of Economic Perspectives* 26 (3): 49–68.

Le Bras, H. and Todd, E. (2013) *Le mystère français*, Paris: Éditions du Seuil/La République des Idées.

Leefbaar Nederland komt er nu aan, Leefbaar Nederland parliamentary election manifesto 2002, in: Documentatiecentrum Nederlandse politieke partijen. Online. Available http://www.dnpp.eldoc.ub.rug.nl/FILES/root/programmas/vp-per-partij/ln/ln02.pdf (accessed 24 August 2013).

Le Goff, J.-P. (2013a) 'Du gauchisme culturel et de ses atavars', *Le Débat*, 176: 39–55.

— (2013b) 'Briser l'influence du gauchisme culturel', *Le Monde*, 24 October. Online. Available http://www.lemonde.fr/idees/article/2013/10/24/briser-l-influence-du-gauchisme-culturel_3501777_3232.html (accessed 10 March 2014).

Legrain, P. (2014) *European Spring: Why our economics and politics are in a mess, and how to put them right,* London: Phillipe Legrain.

Le Pen, J.-M. (1985) *Pour la France*, Paris: Éditions Albatros.

Le Pen, M. (2012a) 'Mon projet pour la France et les Français'. Online. Available http://www.frontnational.com/pdf/projet_mlp2012.pdf (accessed 12 March 2014).

— (2012b) *Pour que vive la France*, Paris: Éditions Grancher.

Lepper, A. (2002) *Lista Leppera*, Warszawa: Wydawnictwo KAMEA.

Letty, E. (2011) 'Le virage à gauche de *Front National*', *Le choc du mois*, May: 36–37.

Leven, B. (2011) 'Avoiding crisis contagion: Poland's case', *Communist and Post-Communist Studies*, 44 (3): 183–187.

Lewica i Demokraci (2011) 'Nowa polityka, nowa nadzieja. Program wyborczy Lewicy i Demokratów', in Słodkowska, I. and Dolbakowska, M. (eds) Wybory 2007, Partie i ich programy. Warszawa: Instytut Studiów Publicznych PAN, pp. 368–421.

Lidové noviny (2013) *Úsvit podpoří jakoukoliv vládu, která bude pro obecné referendum.* Lidovky. Online. Available http://www.lidovky.cz/usvit-podpori-jakoukoliv-vladu-ktera-bude-pro-obecne-referendum-px2-/zpravy-domov.aspx?c=A131026_205726_ln_domov_ebr (accessed 15 March 2014).

Liga Polskich Rodzin (2006) 'Skrót programu gospodarczego' in Słodkowska, I. and Dolbakowska, M. (eds) Wybory 2005: Partie i ich programy, Warszawa, pp. 66–76.

Liga Prawicy Rzeczypospolitej (2011) 'Deklaracja wyborcza 2007' in Słodkowska, I. and Dolbakowska, M. (eds) Wybory 2007: Partie i ich programy, Warszawa, pp. 66–67.

Linde, J. (2012) 'Why feed the hand that bites you? Perceptions of procedural fairness and system support in post-communist democracies', *European Journal of Political Research* 51: 410–434.

Linek, L. (2010) *Zrazení snu? Struktura a dynamika postojů k politickému režimu a jeho institucím a jejich důsledk*, Praha: SLON.

LPF (2002) Lijst Pim Fortuyn. Zakelijk met een hart. Lijst Pim Fortuyn parliamentary election manifesto 2002, in: Documentatiecentrum Nederlandse politieke partijen. Online. Available http://dnpp.eldoc.ub.rug.nl/FILES/root/programmas/vp-per-partij/lpf/lpf02.pdf (accessed 24 August 2013).

Lucardie, P. (2000) 'Prophets, purifiers and prolocutors: towards a theory on the emergence of new parties', *Party Politics* 6 (2): 175–186.

— (2008) 'The Netherlands: Populism versus pillarization', in Albertazzi, D. and McDonnell, D. (eds) *Twenty-First Century Populism: The spectre of Western European democracy*, Basingstoke: Palgrave MacMillan, pp. 151–165.

Lucardie, P. and Voerman, G. (2012) *Populisten in de Polder*, Amsterdam: Boom.

Lupu, N. (2012) 'Brand Dilution and the Breakdown of Political Parties in Latin America', unpublished manuscript.

Luther K. R. (1991) 'Die Freiheitliche Partei Österreichs', in Dachs, H., Gerlich, P., Gottweis, H., Horner, F., Kramer, H., Lauber, V., Müller, W. C. and Tálos, E (eds) *Handbuch des politischen Systems Österreichs*, Vienna: Manz.

— (1999) 'A framework for the comparative analysis of parties and party systems in consociational democracy', in Luther, K. R. and Deschouwer, K. (eds) *Political Elites in Divided Societies: Political parties in consociational democracy,* London: Routledge, pp. 3–19.

— (2008) 'Electoral Strategies and Performance of Austrian Right-Wing Populism, 1986–2006', in Bischof, G. and Plasser, F. (eds) *The Changing Austrian Voter*, New Brunswick, NJ, Transaction Publishers, pp. 104–122.

— (2009) 'The revival of the radical right: The Austrian parliamentary election of 2008', *West European Politics* 32: 1049–1061.

— (2011) 'Of goals and own goals: a case study of right-wing populist party strategy for and during incumbency', *Party Politics* 17 (4): 453–470.

McDonnell, D. (2006) 'A weekend in Padania: regionalist populism and the *Lega Nord*', *Politics*, 26 (2): 126–132.

— (2007) 'The Republic of Ireland: the dog that hasn't barked in the night', in Albertazzi, D. and McDonnell, D. (eds) *Twenty-First Century Populism: The spectre of western European democracy,* Basingstoke: Palgrave.

— (2013) 'Silvio Berlusconi's personal parties: from *Forza Italia* to the *Popolo Della Libertà*', *Political Studies* 61 (1): 217–233.

McLaren, L. M. and Johnson, M. (2007) 'Resources, group conflict and symbols: explaining anti-immigration hostility in Britain', *Political Studies* 55: 709–732.

Maghalhães, P. C. (2012) 'Economy, Ideology and the Elephant in the Room: A research note on the elections of the Great Recession in Europe'. Online. Available http://papers.ssrn.com/sol3/papers.cfm?abstract_id=2122416 (accessed October 2013).

Mainwaring, S., Bejarano, A. M. and Pizarro Lengómez, E. (2006) 'The crisis of democratic representation in the Andes: an overview' in Mainwaring, S., Bejarano, A. M. and Pizarro Lengómez, E. (eds) *The Crisis of Democratic Representation in the Andes*, Stanford: Stanford Univ. Press, pp. 1–44.

Mair, P. (1998) *Party System Change: Approaches and interpretations*, Oxford: Oxford University Press.

— (2000) 'Partyless democracy and the "paradox" of New Labour', *New Left Review* 2: 21–35.

— (2002) 'Populist Democracy versus Party Democracy' in Mény, Y. and Surel, Y. (eds) *Democracies and the Populist Challenger*, Basingstoke: Palgrave, pp. 81–98.

— (2007) *Populist Radical Right Parties in Europe*, Cambridge: Cambridge University Press.

— (2008) 'Electoral volatility and the Dutch party system: a comparative perspective', *Acta Politica* 43 (2–3), 235–253.

—   (2009) *Representative versus Responsible Government*, Max Planck Institute for the Study of Societies Working Paper, MPIfG Working Paper 09/8. Online. Available http://www.mpifg.de/pu/workpap/wp09-8.pdf (accessed 22 June 2014).

—   (2011a) 'The election in context', in Gallagher, M. and Marsh, M. (eds) *How Ireland Voted 2011: The full story of Ireland's earthquake election*, Basingstoke: Palgrave.

—   (2011b) 'Bini Smaghi vs. the parties: Representative government and institutional constraints', EUI Working Papers RSCAS 2011/22, Florence, Italy: Robert Schuman Centre for Advanced Studies & EUDO – European Union Democracy Observatory.

—   (2013) *Ruling the Void: The hollowing of Western democracy*, London: Verso.

Manifesto data project. Online. Available https://manifesto-project.wzb.eu/ (accessed 5 May 2015).

Manifesto Project Main Dataset (2013). Manifesto Project Database. Online. Available https://manifesto-project.wzb.eu/datasets (accessed 15 March 2014).

Manzetti, L. and Wilson, C. J. (2007) 'Why do corrupt governments maintain public support?' *Comparative Political Studies* 40 (8): 949–970.

March, L. (2011) *Radical Left Parties in Europe,* Oxon: Routledge.

—   (2012) 'Towards an understanding of contemporary left-wing populism', paper presented at the Political Studies Association (PSA), Annual International Conference, Belfast, 3–5 April 2012.

Marsh, M. and Cunningham, K. (2011) 'A Positive Choice, or anyone but *Fianna Fáil*?', in Gallagher, M. and Marsh, M. (eds) *How Ireland Voted 2011: The full story of Ireland's earthquake election,* Basingstoke: Palgrave.

Mareš, M. (2003) *Pravicový extremismus a radikalismus v ČR*, Brno: Barrister & Principal.

—   (2005) 'Sdružení pro republiku – Republikánská strana Československa' in Malíř, J. and Marek, P. (eds) *Politické strany. Vývoj politických stran a hnutí v českých zemích a Československu. Díl II. 1938–2004*, Brno: Doplněk, pp. 1593–1604.

Markowski, R. (2008) 'The 2007 Polish parliamentary election: some structuring, still a lot of chaos', *West European Politics* 31 (5): 1055–1068.

Mastropaolo, A. (2008) 'From centrism to bipolarism (and back?)', *Modern Italy* 13 (4): 399–414.

Mattila, M. and Sundberg, (2011)'Vaalirahoitus ja vaalirahakohu', in Borg, S. (ed.) Muutosvaalit 2011. Oikeusministeriön selvityksiä ja ohjeita 16/2012, Oikeusministeriö (Ministry of Justice).

Matušková, A. (2010) 'Volební kampaně' in Balík, S. *et al.* (eds) *Volby do Poslanecké sněmovny vroce 2010*, Brno: CDK pp. 99–118.

Mayer, N. (2012) 'De Jean-Marie Le Pen à Marine Le Pen: l'électorat du Front National a-t-il changé?', in Delwitt, P. (ed.) *Le Front National – Mutations de l'extrême droite française,* Brussels, Editions de l'Université de Bruxelles, pp. 143–59.

—   (2013) 'Les effets politiques de la crise: le vote des personnes pauvres et précaires en 2012', in Klein, T. (ed.) *Crises et politiques sociales, Informations sociales,* 180.

Mény, Y. and Surel, Y. (2000) *Par le peuple, pour le peuple. Le populisme et les démocraties.* Paris: Fayard.

—   (2002) 'The constitutive ambiguity of populism', in Mény, Y. and Surel, Y. (eds) *Democracies and the Populist Challenge*, Basingstoke: Palgrave, pp. 1–21.

Meret, S. (2010) 'The Danish People's Party, the Italian Northern League and the Austrian Freedom Party in a Comparative Perspective: Party Ideology and Electoral Support', PhD Thesis, Institute of History and International Social Studies AMID, Academy for Migration Studies in Denmark, Aalborg University, Aalborg.

Mergier, A. (2011) 'Le vote FN donne une valeur politique à ce que les gens vivent', *La Croix*, 27 March. Online. Available http://www.la-croix.com/Actualite/France/Alain-Mergier-Le-vote-FN-donne-une-valeur-politique-a-ce-que-les-gens-vivent-_NG_-2011-03-27-606508 (accessed 12 March 2014).

Mergier, A. and Fourquet, J. (2011) 'Le point de rupture: Enquête sur les ressorts du vote FN en milieux populaires', *Fondation Jean Jaurès*, Paris. Online. Available http://www.jean-jaures.org/Publications/Essais/Le-point-de-rupture (accessed 10 March 2014).

Mestre, A. (2012). 'Le FN n'est plus le même, mais a-t-il vraiment changé? *Le Monde*, 20 September. Online. Available http://www.lemonde.fr/culture/article/2012/09/20/le-front-national-n-est-plus-le-meme-mais-a-t-il-vraiment-change_1763234_3246.html (accessed 12 March 2014).

—   (2014) '34% des Français "adhèrent aux idées du Front National"', *Le Monde*, 12 February. Online. Available http://www.lemonde.fr/politique/article/2014/02/12/le-front-national-de-marine-le-pen-confirme-son-enracinement_4364586_823448.html (accessed 13 March 2014).

Metron Analysis (2012) Exit Poll – National Election 6 May 2012: Results Report. Online. Available http://www.metronanalysis.gr/gr/polls/ziped/pub1651_expol.pdf (accessed 23 June 2014).

Mesežnikov, G. *et al.* (eds.) (2008) 'Slovakia' in *Populist Politics and Liberal Democracy in Central and Eastern Europe*, Bratislava: Institute for Public Affairs, pp. 99–130.

Mihaely, G. and Boughezala, D. (2012) 'Florian Philippot: "Chevènement est polus proche de Marine Le Pen que de Hollande"', *Causeur*, November: 30–32.

Minkenberg, M. (2001) 'The radical right in public office: Agenda setting and policy effects', *West European Politics* 24 (4): 1–21.

Mladá fronta Dnes 7/5/2010, 5/10/2013.

Moatti, S. (2014) 'L'illusionisme économique du FN', *Alternatives économiques*, February: 58–61.

Moffitt, B. (2014) 'How to Perform Crisis: A Model for Understanding the Key Role of Crisis in Contemporary Populism', *Government and Opposition*.

Moring, T. and Mykkänen, J. (2009) 'Vaalikampanja', in Borg, S. and Paloheimo, H. (eds) *Vaalit yleisödemokratiassa. Eduskuntavaalitutkimus 2007*, Tampere: Tampere University Press, pp. 28–59.

Mossuz-Lavau, J. (2012) 'Mélenchon ne parle pas à "ceux qui sont dans la dèche"' *Slate.fr*, 23 April. Online. Available http://www.slate.fr/story/53897/presidentielle-marine-le-pen-classes-populaires-mossuz-lavau (accessed 10 March 2014).

Moynihan, M. G. (1980) *Speeches and Statements by Eamon de Valera – 1917–1973*, Dublin: Gill & Macmillan.

Mudde, C. (2000) *The Ideology of the Extreme Right*, Manchester: Manchester University Press.

— (2007) *Populist Radical Right Parties in Europe*. Cambridge: Cambridge University Press.

— (2014) 'Marine Le Pen, femme de paroles plus que d'action', *Le Monde*, 13 February: 9.

— (2010) 'The populist radical right: a pathological normalcy', *West European Politics* 33 (6): 1167–1186.

Mudde, C. and Kaltwasser, R. C. (2013) 'Exclusionary vs. inclusionary populism: comparing the contemporary Europe and Latin America', *Government & Opposition* 48 (2): 147–174.

Müller, W. C. and Tálos, E. (eds) *Politik in Österreich: Ein Handbuch*, Vienna: ManzVerlag.

Muzet, D. and Perrineau, P. (2004) 'The populist zeitgeist', *Government and Opposition*, 39 (4): 542–63.

Narud, H. M. (2011) 'Et regjeringsvalg i skyggen av finanskrisen,' in Aardal, B. (ed.) *Det politiske landskap. En studie av stortingsvalget 2009*, Oslo: Cappelen Damm akademisk, pp. 225–258.

Näsström, S. (2007) 'The legitimacy of the people', *Political Theory* 35 (5): 624–658.

Neuendorf, K. (2002) *The Content Analysis Guidebook*, Thousand Oaks, California: Sage Publications.

Nordsieck, W. (2013) 'Parties and Elections in Europe'. Online. Available http://www.parties-and-elections.eu/index.html (accessed 16 December 2013).

N-VA (2014) 'Verandering voor Vooruitgang', Election Manifesto.

Oikeusministeriön selvityksiä ja ohjeita 16/2012, Oikeusministeriö (Ministry of Justice), January 2012, pp. 227–238.

OECD (2001) OECD Economic Surveys: Greece. Paris: OECD.

— (2011) Restoring Public Finances – Country Notes, Ireland. Paris: OECD.

— (2014) OECD.Stat.

Oesch, D. (2008) 'Explaining workers' support for right-wing populist parties in Western Europe: evidence from Austria, Belgium, France, Norway and Switzerland', *International Political Science Review*, 29 (3): 349–373.

Okamura, T. (2011) *Umění vládnout*, Praha: Fragment.

—   (2013a) *"Novoroční projev"* Tomia Okamury 2014. Online. Available http://www.okamura.blog.idnes.cz/c/389928/Novorocni-projev-Tomia-Okamury-2014.html (accessed 6 March 2015).

—   (2013b) *Proč chtít skutečnou demokracii.* Online. Available http:// okamura.blog.idnes.cz/c/338639/Proc-chtit-skutecnou-demokracii.html (accessed 6 March 2015).

—   (2013c) *'Buďme politicky nekorektní!'.* Online. Available http://okamura. blog.idnes.cz/c/177377/Budme-politicky-nekorektni.html (accessed 6 March 2015).

—   (2013d) *Chtějme demokracii – chtějme konec korupčního politického systému.* Online. Available http://okamura.blog.idnes.cz/c/317420/ Chtejme-demokracii-chtejme-konec-korupcniho-politickeho-systemu. html (accessed 6 March 2015).

O'Malley, E. (2008) 'Why is there no radical right party in Ireland?', *West European Politics* 31 (5): 960–977.

OpinionWay (2014) 'Baromètre de la confiance politique', *vague 5*, January. Online. Available http://www.opinion-way.com/pdf/barometre_de_la_ confiance_cevipof_opinionway_-_13_janvier_2014.pdf (accessed 14 March 2014).

Orbán, V. (2007) 'Speech at the XXII' Tusnádfürdő camp. Online. Available http:// www.mno.hu/migr/orban-viktor-tusnadfurdoi-beszede-+-video-432398 (accessed 30 June 2014).

—   (2010) 'Speech in front of the Hungarian Chamber of Commerce and Industry on 18 February, 2010'. Online. Available http://www.2007-2010.orbanviktor.hu/beszedek_list.php?item=113 (accessed 30 June 2014).

ORF (2009–2012) *Sommergespräche.* Online. Available http://www.apa.at (accessed 6 March 2015).

Oscarsson, H. (2012) Blogg. Online. Available http://www.henrikoscarsson. com/2012/03/varfor-litar-vi-allt-mer-pa-vara.html (accessed 30 June 2014).

Paloheimo, H. (2012) 'Populismi puoluejärjestelmän vedenjakajana', in Borg, S. (ed.) *Muutosvaalit 2011.* Oikeusministeriön selvityksiä ja ohjeita 16/2012. Oikeusministeriö (Ministry of Justice), pp. 324–346.

Państwowa Komisja Wyborcza., Wybory Sejm/Senat. Online. Available http:// www.pkw.gov.pl/wybory-sejm-senat/ (accessed March 08 2014).

Papandreou, N. (2014) 'Life in the First Person and the Art of Political Storytelling: The Rhetoric of Andreas Papandreou', *Hellenic Observatory Papers on Greece and Southeast Europe*, E. I. Hellenic Observatory, London: LSE.

Pappas, T. S. (2003) 'The transformation of the Greek party system since 1951', *West European Politics* 26 (2): 90–114.

—   (2013) 'Why Greece failed', *Journal of Democracy* 24 (2): 31–45.

—   (2014a) 'Populist democracies: post-authoritarian Greece and post-communist Hungary', *Government and Opposition* 49 (1): 1–23.

—   (2014b) *Populism and Crisis Politics in Greece*, Houndmills, Basingstoke: Palgrave Macmillan.

Pappas, T. S. and O'Malley, E. (2014) 'Civil compliance and "political Luddism": explaining variance in social unrest during crisis in Ireland and Greece', *American Behavioral Scientist*, 58 (12): 1592–1613.

Parlament (2010) *Stenographisches Protokoll. Sitzung des Nationalrates der Republik Österreich, XXIV. Gesetzgebungsperiode* (Sessions 57, 64 & 66), Vienna. Online. Available http://www.parlament.gv.at/ (accessed 18 July 2014).

—   (2012) *Stenographisches Protokoll. Sitzung des Nationalrates der Republik Österreich, XXIV. Gesetzgebungsperiode* (Sessions 140, 143, 161 & 164), Vienna. Online. Available http://www.parlament.gv.at/ (accessed 18 July 2014).

Pasquino, G. (2008) 'Populism and Democracy in *Twenty-First Century Populism: The Spectre of Western European Democracy*' in Albertazzi, D. and McDonnell, D. (eds), Houndmills, Basingstoke: Palgrave Macmillan, pp. 15–29.

Pattie, C. and Johnston, R. (2012) 'The electoral impact of the UK 2009 MPs' expenses scandal', *Political Studies*, 730–750.

Pauwels, T. (2010) 'Explaining the success of neoliberal populist parties: the case of *Lijst Dedecker* in Belgium', *Political Studies* 58 (5): 1009–1029.

—   (2011a) 'Explaining the strange decline of the populist radical right Vlaams Belang in Belgium: The impact of permanent opposition', *Acta Politica* 46 (1): 60–82.

—   (2011b) 'Measuring populism: A quantitative text analysis of party literature in Belgium. Journal of Elections', *Public Opinion and Parties* 21 (1): 97–119.

Pedersen, M. (1979) 'The dynamics of European party systems: changing patterns of electoral volatility', *European Journal of Political Research* 7 (1): 1–26.

Pelinka, A. (2013) 'Right-Wing Populism: Concept and typology', in Wodak, R. (ed.) *Right-Wing Populism in Europe: Politics and discourse*, London: Bloomsbury Academic, pp. 3–22.

Pellikaan, H., van der Meer, T. and de Lange, S. (2007) 'Fortuyn's legacy: party system change in the Netherlands', *Comparative European Politics* 5 (3): 282–302.

Pernaa, V. (2007) 'Mistä nämä vaalit muistetaan', in Pernaa, V., Niemi, M. K. and Pitkänen, V. (eds) *Mielikuvavaalit. Kevään 2007 eduskuntavaalien mediailmiöt,* Turku: Kirja-Aurora, pp. 15–34.

—   (2012a) 'Vaalikamppailu mediassa' in Borg, S. (ed.) *Muutosvaalit 2011.* Oikeusministeriön selvityksiä ja ohjeita 16/2012, Oikeusministeriö (Ministry of Justice), pp. 29–42.

—   (2012b) Kevään 2011 'Eduskuntavaaliasetelman pitkät juuret', in Pernaa, V. and Railo, E. (eds) *Jytky. Eduskuntavaalien 2011 mediajulkisuus.* Turku: Kirja-Aurora, pp. 9–30.

Pernaa, V., Niemi, M. K. and Pitkänen, V. (eds.) (2007): *Mielikuvavaalit. Kevään 2007 eduskuntavaalien mediailmiöt.* Turku: Kirja-Aurora.

Pernaa, V. and Railo, E. (eds) (2012) *Jytky. Eduskuntavaalien 2011 mediajulkisuus*, Turku: Kirja–Aurora.

Perrineau, P. (2012) 'La renaissance électorale de l'électorat frontiste', Paris, CEVIPOF. Online. Available http://www.cevipof.com/rtefiles/File/AtlasEl3/NotePERRINEAU.pdf (accessed 10 March 2014).

— (2014) *La France au Front*, Paris: Fayard.

Perussuomalaiset 2007: *Oikeudenmukaisuuden, hyvinvoinnin ja kansanvallan puolesta!* Perussuomalaisten eduskuntavaaliohjelma 2007. Online. Available http://www.perussuomalaiset.fi//wp-content/uploads/2013/04/Perussuomalaisten_eduskuntavaaliohjelma_2007.pdf (accessed 20 July 2013).

— (2011) *Suomalaiselle sopivin*. Perussuomalaisten eduskuntavaaliohjelma 2011 Online. Available http://www.perussuomalaiset.fi//wp-content/uploads/2013/04/Perussuomalaisten_eduskuntavaaliohjelma_2011.pdf (accessed 18 July 2013).

Petrocik, J. R. (1996). 'Issue ownership in presidential elections with a 1980 case study', *American Journal of Political Science* 40 (3): 825–850.

Piros, P. (2006) 'The only faulty man', (Egyetlen hibás ember), *Hetek*, 2006, pp. 10–27.

Platforma Obywatelska (2011) 'Polska zasługuje na cud gospodarczy', Program wyborczy.

Platformy Obywatelskiej, (2007) in Słodkowska, I and Dolbakowska, M. (eds) Wybory 2007, *Partie i ich programy*, Warszawa, Instytut Studiów Publicznych PAN, pp. 195–260.

Pop-Eleches, G. (2010) 'Throwing out the bums: protest voting and unorthodox parties after communism', *World Politics* 62 (2): 221–60.

Pokorný, J. (2010) *'John už si diktuje vládní podmínky'*, Mladá fronta Dnes, 5 May 2010.

Portheault, N. and Portheault, T. (2014) *Revenus du Front*, Paris: Grasset.

Powell, E. N. and Tucker, J.-A. (2014) 'Revisiting electoral volatility in post-communist countries: new data, new results and new approaches', *British Journal of Political Science* 44 (1): 123–47.

Právo J. (2009) *Doufám, že voliči nebudou "blbá telata", která si vyberou svého řezníka*, 12 October 2009.

Prawo i Sprawiedliwość (2009) Nowoczesna Solidarna Bezpieczna Polska. Program Prawa i Sprawiedliwości, Warszawa: Prawo i Sprawiedliwość.

— (2011) Dbamy o Polskę. Dbamy o Polaków. Program Prawa i Sprawiedliwości in Słodkowska I and Dolbakowska M (eds), Wybory 2007: Partie i ich program, Warszawa, Wydawca Instytut Studiów Publicznych, pp. 125–171.

Prima TV (2009) *Nedělní partie*. 25 October 2009.

PTB (2014) Notre Avenir est Social.

PVV (2010) Partij voor de Vrijheid: De agenda van hoop en optimisme. Een tijd om te kiezen. Partij voor de Vrijheid parliamentary election manifesto, 2010.
— (2012) Hún Brussel, óns Nederland, Partij voor de Vrijheid parliamentary election manifesto, 2012.
Rafter, K. (2005) *Sinn Féin 1905–2005: In the shadow of gunmen*, Dublin: Gill & Macmillan.
Railo, E. (2012) 'Euroopan unionin talouskriisin julkisuus – kritiikistä konsensukseen' in Pernaa, V. and Railo, E. (eds.) *Jytky. Eduskuntavaalien 2011 mediajulkisuus*, Turku: Kirja-Aurora, pp. 231–263.
Railo, E. and Välimäki, M. (2012a) 'Vaalikevään media-agenda' in Pernaa, V. and Railo, E. (eds) *Jytky. Eduskuntavaalien 2011 mediajulkisuus*, Turku: Kirja-Aurora, pp. 32–66.
— (2012b) 'Kamppailu julkisuuden hallinnasta' in Pernaa, V. and Railo, E. (eds.) *Jytky. Eduskuntavaalien 2011 mediajulkisuus*, Turku: Kirja-Aurora, pp. 100–161.
Reeskens, T. (2014) 'Politiek Vertrouwen: Een Sleutelfactor', in Devos, C. (ed.) *België 2014. Een politieke geschiedenis van morgen*, Borgerhoff & Lamberigts.
Reyniér, D. (2011) 'Le tournant ethno-socialiste du Front National', *Études*, November, pp. 463–72.
Riché, P. (2011) 'La France des "invisibles" et des "oubliés" de Marine Le Pen', *Le Monde*, 19 December. Online. Available http://www.rue89.com/rue89-presidentielle/2011/12/19/la-france-des-invisibles-et-des-oublies-de-marine-le-pen-227631 (accessed 10 March 2014).
Rihoux, B., Dumont, P., De Winter, L., Deruette, S. and Bol, D. (2011) 'Belgium', *European Journal of Political Research* 50 (7–8): 913–921.
Ringsmose, J. and Pedersen K. (2005) 'Fra Protest til Indflydelse: Organisatoriske forskelle mellem Fremskridtspartiet og Dansk Folkeparti', *Politik* 8 (3): 68–78.
Roberts, K. M. (1995) 'Neoliberalism and the transformation of populism in Latin America: the Peruvian case', *World Politics* 48, October: 82–116.
— (2003) 'Social correlates of party system demise and populist resurgence in Venezuela', *Latin American Politics and Society* 45 (32): 35–57.
— (2013) 'Market reform, programmatic (de)alignment, and party system stability in Latin America', *Comparative Political Studies* 46 (11): 1422–1452.
Rooduijn, M. (2013) 'The nucleus of populism: in search of the lowest common denominator', *Government and Opposition*, FirstView, 1–27.
— (2014) 'Van protest- naar pluchepartij? Een analyse van de ontwikkeling van de SP', Stuk Rood Vlees, 23 June 2014. Online. Available http://www.stukroodvlees.nl/populisme/van-protest-naar-pluchepartij-een-analyse-van-de-ontwikkeling-van-de-sp/ (accessed 30 June 2014).
Rooduijn, M., De Lange, S. and Van der Brug, W. (2014) 'A populist Zeitgeist? Programmatic contagion by populist parties in Western Europe', *Party Politics* 20 (4): 563–575.

Rooduijn, M. and Pauwels, T. (2011) 'Measuring Populism: Comparing Two Methods of Content Analysis', *West European Politics* 34 (6): 1272–1283.

Rouvinen, P. and Ylä-Anttila, P. (eds) (2010) *Kriisin jälkeen*, Helsinki, Taloustieto Oy.

Ruch Na Rzecz Demokracji (2007) Deklaracja Programowa Ruchu Na Rzecz Demokracji.

Russell, A. and Fieldhouse, E. (eds) (2005) *Neither Left Nor Right: The Liberal Democrats and the Electorate*, Manchester, Manchester University Press.

— (2008) 'Immigration sceptics, xenophobes or racists? Radical right wing voting in six West European countries', *European Journal of Political Research* 47 (6): 737–765.

Rydgren, J. (2002) 'Radical right populism in Sweden: still a failure, but for how long?' *Scandinavian Political Studies* 25 (1): 27–56.

— (2005a) 'Is extreme right-wing populism contagious? Explaining the emergence of a new party family', *European Journal of Political Research* 44: 413–437.

— (2005b) 'Från skattemissnöje till etnisk nationalism Högerpopulism och parlamentarisk högerextremism i Sverige', Lund, Studentlitteratur.

Saarikko, A. (2007) 'Haastaja, hyökkääjä, populisti ja puolustaja television vaalikeskusteluissa' in Pernaa, V., Niemi, M. K. and Pitkänen, V. (eds) *Mielikuvavaalit. Kevään 2007 eduskuntavaalien mediailmiöt* Turku: Kirja-Aurora, pp. 55–74.

Samoobrona Rzecypospolitej Polskiej (2011) Samoobrona w rządzie koalicyjnym. Realizacja programu społeczno-gospodarczego (wrzesień 2006) in Wybory 2007: Partie i ich programy. Warszawa: Wydawca Instytut Studiów Publicznych, pp. 331–343.

Saukkonen, P. (2003) 'Suomalaisen yhteiskunnan historia, rakenne ja poliittinen kulttuuri' in Saukkonen, P. (ed.) *Paikkana politiikka. Tietoja ja tulkintoja Suomen poliittisesta järjestelmästä*. Helsinki, University of Helsinki, Department of Political Science, pp. 9–42.

SCB (2011) Åttapartivalet 2010 Allmänna valen Valundersökning, Stockholm, SCB.

Sejm Rzeczypospolitej Polskiej (2007) Sprawozdanie stenograficzne z posiedzeń Sejmu RP V kadencji. Online. Available http://orka2.sejm.gov.pl/Debata5.nsf (accessed 14 March 2014).

Shambaugh, J. C. (2012) 'The Euro's Three Crises', *Brookings Papers on Economic Activity* 2012 (1): 157–231.

Sikk, A. (2009) *Parties and Populism*, London: UCL School of Slavonic and East European Studies.

Sinardet, D. (2010) 'From consociational consciousness to majoritarian myth. Consociational federalism, multi-level politics and the Belgian case of Brussels-Halle-Vilvoorde', *Acta Politica* 45 (3): 346–369.

Singer, M. M. (2013) The global economic crisis and domestic political agendas, *Electoral Studies* 32: 404–410.

Sinn Féin (2009) *European Election Manifesto 2009*, Dublin: *Sinn Féin*.

—   (2011) *There is a better way (Tá belach níos fear ann) Sinn Féin General Election Manifesto 2011*, Sinn Féin: Dublin.

—   (2014) *Putting Ireland First (Éire Chun Cinn) EU Election Manifesto 2014*, Dublin, Sinn Féin.

Sjöblom, G. (2008) *Party Strategies in a Multiparty System*, Lund political studies. Vol 7, Department of Political Science, University of Lund.

Skadhede, J. (2014) 'DF skovler vælgere ind fra Løkke og Thorning', in Altinget. dk January 27. København, Altinget.dk. Online. Available http://www. altinget.dk/artikel/131809-df-skovler-vaelgere-ind-fra-loekke-og-thorning (accessed 18 July 2014).

SKON, CBS, van der Kolk, H., Aarts, C. and Tillie, J. (2012) *Dutch Parliamentary Election Study 2010*, The Hague: DANS.

SKON, CBS, van der Kolk, H., Tillie, J., Van Erkel, P., van der Velden, M. and Damstra, A. (2013) *Dutch Parliamentary Election Study 2012*, The Hague: DANS.

Sládek, M. (1992) *...a tak to vidím já*. Electronic document.

—   (1996) *Právě váš hlas rozhodne*! Electronic document.

Smilov, D. (2013) 'Populism of Fear: Eastern European perspectives' in Giusto, H., Kitching, D., Rizzo, S. (eds) *The Changing Faces of Populism: Systemic challengers in Europe and the U.S.,* Bruxelles: FEPS, pp. 227–254.

Smith, R. M. (2003) *Stories of Peoplehood: The Politics and morals of political memberships*, Cambridge: Cambridge University Press.

Socialist Party (2013) 'Merkel's & Irish Establishment's gross hypocrisy over Anglo tapes', Online. Available http://www.socialistparty.ie/2013/07/ merkels-a-irish-establishments-gross-hypocrisy-over-anglo-tapes/ (accessed on 27 May 2014).

Sørensen, C. (2014) 'Stigende dansk EU-skepsis er en myte in Politiken' (feature article) April 14. København: Politiken. Online. Available http://www. politiken.dk/debat/kroniken/ECE2262845/stigende-dansk-eu-skepsis-er-en-myte/#tocomment (accessed 18 July 2014).

SP (1994) *Stem tegen*, Stem SP. Verkiezingsprogramma Socialistische Partij, Socialistische Partij parliamentary election manifesto, 1994.

—   (2006) *Een beter Nederland, voor hetzelfde geld. Verkiezingsprogramma van de SP*, 2006–2010, Socialistische Partij parliamentary election manifesto, 2006.

—   (2010) *Een beter Nederland, voor minder geld. Verkiezingsprogramma SP 2011–2015*, Socialistische Partij parliamentary election manifesto, 2010.

—   (2012) *Nieuw Vertrouwen. Verkiezingsprogramma SP 2013–2017*, Socialistische Partij parliamentary election manifesto, 2012.

Spektorowski, A. (2003a) 'Ethnoregionalism: the intellectual New Right and the *Lega Nord*', *The Global Review of Ethnopolitics* 2 (3): 55–70.

—   (2003b) 'The New Right: ethno-regionalism, ethno-pluralism and the emergence of a neo-fascist "third way"', *Journal of Political Ideologies* 8 (1): 111–130.

Stanley, B. (2008) 'The thin ideology of populism', *Journal of Political Ideologies* (13) 1: 95–110.

Stanley, B. and Učeň, P. (2008) 'The 'thin ideology' of populism in Central and Eastern Europe: theory and preliminary mapping', unpublished manuscript

Stavrakakis, Y. and Katsambekis, G. (2014) 'Left-wing populism in the European periphery: the case of *SYRIZA*', *Journal of Political Ideologies* 19 (2): 119–142.

Ström, K. and Mueller, W. (1999) *Policy, Office, or Votes?: How political parties in Western Europe make hard decisions*, Cambridge: Cambridge University Press.

Stubager, R., Hansen, K. M. and Andersen, J. G. (2013) 'It's the Economy, Stupid!', in Stubager, R., Hansen, K.M. and Andersen, J. G. (eds) *Krisevalg. Økonomien og Folketingsvalget 2011*, København: Jurist- og Økonomforbundets Forlag, pp. 17–44.

Suomen Sisu principles (2006). Online. Available http://www.suomensisu.fi/2006Periaateohjelma.pdf (accessed 26 August 2014).

Sverigedemokraterna (2011) Sverigedemokraternas principprogram 2011.

— (2012a) Inriktningsprogram för en Sverigedemokratisk kommunalpolitik, Sverigedemokraterna 2012. Online. Available http://www.sverigedemokraterna.se/wp-content/uploads/2013/08/riktlinjer_sd_kommunalpolitik_04_02.pdf (accessed 6 March 2015).

— (2012b) Sverigedemokraternas principprogram 2012.

— (2013a) Sverigedemokraterna 25 år Jubileumsskrift 2013.

— (2013b) Sverigedemokraternas EU valplattform 2013.

Swiss Political Yearbook (2009) *Année Politique Suisse*, Berne: Institute of Political Science.

Szczerbiak, A. (2002) 'Poland's unexpected political earthquake: the September 2001 parliamentary election, *Journal of Communist Studies and Transition Politics* 18 (3): 41–76.

— (2008) 'The birth of a bipolar party system or a referendum on a polarizing government? The October 2007 Polish parliamentary election, *The Journal of Communist Studies and Transition Politics* 24 (3): 415–443.

Szczerbiak, A. and Taggart, P. (2004) 'The politics of European Referendum outcomes and turnout: two models', *West European Politics* 27 (4): 557–83.

— (eds) (2008) *Opposing Europe? The comparative party politics of Euroscepticism*, Oxford: Oxford University Press.

Taggart, P. (1996) *The New Populism and New Politics: New protest parties in Sweden in a comparative perspective*, London: MacMillan Press.

— (1998) 'A touchstone of dissent: Euroscepticism in contemporary Western European party systems', *European Journal of Political Research* 33: 363–388.

— (2000) *Populism*, Buckingham: Open University Press.

—   (2002) 'Populism and the Pathology of Representative Democracy', in Mény, Y. and Surel, Y. (eds) *Democracies and the Populist Challenge*, Houndmills, Basingstoke: Palgrave, pp. 62–100.

—   (2004) 'Populism and representative politics in contemporary Europe', *Journal of Political Ideologies* 9 (3): 269–288.

Taggart, P. and Szczerbiak, A. (2002) 'The Party Politics of Euroscepticism in EU Member and Candidate States', *Sussex European Institute Working Paper* No.51.

Taguieff, P.-A. (1993) 'From race to culture: the New Right's view of European identity', *Telos* December 21: 99–125.

—   (2003) *L'illusione populista*, Milan: Mondadori.

Team Stronach (2013) *Grundsatzprogramm*, Vienna.

Tellér, G. (2014) 'Was an "Orban-regime" born between 2010 and 2014?' (Született-e 'Orbán-rendszer' 2010–2014 között), *Nagyvilág*, 59 (3): 346–367.

TNS-Sofres (2011) 'Les Français, la mondialisation et le protectionisme', November. Online. Available http://www.tns-sofres.com/etudes-et-points-de-vue/les-francais-et-la-mondialisation-2011 (accessed 14 March 2014).

—   (2014a) 'Baromètre politique Baromètre politique – février 2014'. Online. Available http://www.tns-sofres.com/etudes-et-points-de-vue/barometre-politique-fevrier-2014 (accessed 12 March 2014).

—   (2014b) 'Baromètre d'image du Front national', February. Online. Available http://www.tns-sofres.com/etudes-et-points-de-vue/barometre-2014-dimage-du-front-national (accessed 13 March 2014).

Tsakatika, M. and Eleftheriou, K. (2013) 'The radical Left's turn towards civil society in Greece: one strategy, two paths', *South European Society and Politics* 18 (1): 81–99.

Tsipras, A. (2012) Athens campaign speech, May 3, 2012.

Tsiras, S. (2012). Έθνος και ΛΑΟΣ: Νέα άκρα δεξιά και λαϊκισμός (Nation and LAOS: New far right and populism), Athens: Epikentro.

Učeň, P. (1999) 'Decade of Conflict within Slovak polity: Party politics perspective', in Dvořáková, V. (ed.) *Success or Failure? Ten years after*, Prague: Czech Political Science Association and Slovak Political Science Association, pp. 80–103.

—   (2003) 'Centrist Populism Parties and the Ingredients of their Success' in Mesežnikov, G. *et al.* (ed.) *Slovak Elections 2002: Results, implications, context*, Bratislava: Institute for Public Affairs, pp. 49–62.

—   (2004) 'Centrist Populism as a New Competitive and Mobilization Strategy in Slovak Politics', in Gyárfášová, O. and Mesežnikov, G. (ed.) *Party Government in Slovakia: Experience and perspectives*, Bratislava: Institute for Public Affairs, pp. 45–73.

—   (2007a) 'Parties, populism, and anti-establishment politics in East Central Europe', *SAIS Review* 27 (1): 49–62.

— (2007b) 'Populist Appeals in Slovak Politics before 2006 Elections', in Bútora, M., Gyárfášová, O., Mesežnikov, G. and Skladony, T. W. (eds) *Democracy and Populism in Central Europe: The Visegrad elections and their aftermath*, Bratislava: Institute for Public Affairs 2007, pp. 131–47.

— (2010) 'Approaching National Populism' in Petőcz, K. (ed.) *National Populism in Slovakia and Slovak-Hungarian Relations 2006–2009*, Šamorín-Somorja: Forum Minority Research Institute, pp. 13–38.

— (2011) 'Competitive Lines in the 2010 Slovak Parliamentary Elections' in Gyárfášová, O. and Mesežnikov, G. (eds) *Visegrad Elections 2010: Domestic impact and European consequences*, Bratislava: Institute for Public Affairs, pp. 79–96.

— (2012) 'Populism in Slovakia' in Bachrynowski, S.(ed.) *Populism in Central and Eastern Europe – Challenge for the Future?*, Warsaw, European Green Foundation, pp. 34–42. Online. Available http://www. gef.eu/uploads/media/Populism_in_CEE_-_Challenge_for_the_Future. pdf (accessed 3 August 2014).

UKIP (2010) *Empowering the People: UKIP Manifesto 2010*, Devon: UK Independence Party.

— (2014) *Create an Earthquake: UKIP Manifesto 2014*, Heathfield: UK Independence Party.

Urbinati, N. (2014). *Democracy Disfigured: Opinion, truth, and the people*, Cambridge, Mass: Harvard University Press.

Úsvit (2013a) *Nemakačenka, paraziti a podvodníci – svět kolem nás*. Online. Available http://www.hnutiusvit.cz/blog/nemakacenka-paraziti-a-podvodnici-svet-kolem-nas (accessed 6 March 2015).

— (2013b) *Program hnutí*. Online. Available http://www.hnutiusvit.cz/ program-hnuti/ (accessed 6 March 2015).

— (2013c) *Konec zvyšování daní, práce a příležitost*. Online. Available http://www.hnutiusvit.cz/blog/konec-zvysovani-dani-prace-a-prilezitost/ (accessed 6 March 2015).

— (2013d) *Radim Fiala: Chystají podraz na živnostníky*. Online. Available http://www.hnutiusvit.cz/tiskove-zpravy/radim-fiala-chystaji-podraz-na-zivnostniky/ (accessed 6 March 2015).

Vaitilingham, R. (2009) 'Britain in Recession: Forty Findings from Social and Economic Research', Swindon: Economic and Social Research Council.

Väliverronen, J. (2011) 'Kansalaisuus liikkeessä' in Kantola, A. (ed.) *Hetken hallitsijat. Julkinen elämä notkeassa yhteiskunnassa*, Helsinki: Gaudeamus, 142–163.

Van Aelst, P.and Louwerse, T. (2013) 'Parliament without Government: The Belgian Parliament and the Government Formation Processes of 2007–2011' *West European Politics* 37 (3): 475–496.

Van der Brug, W., Fennema, M., and Tillie, J. (2005) 'Why some anti-immigrant parties fail and others succeed: a two-step model of aggregate electoral support', *Comparative Political Studies* 38 (5): 537–573.

—	(2000) 'Anti-immigrant parties in Europe: Ideological or protest vote?', *European Journal of Political Research* 37 (1): 77–102.

Van der Brug, W., van der Eijk, C. and Franklin, M. (2007) *The Economy and the Vote: Economic conditions and elections in fifteen countries*, New York: Cambridge University Press.

Van der Eijk, C.and Franklin, M. (2009) *Elections and Voters*, Basingstoke: Palgrave Macmillan.

Van der Meer, T., Lubbe, R. van Elsas, E., Elff, M. and van der Brug, W. (2012) 'Bounded volatility in the Dutch electoral battlefield: A panel study on the structure of changing vote intentions in the Netherlands during 2006–2010' *Acta Politica*, Advance online publication.

Van der Steen, P. (1995) 'De doorbraak van de 'gewone mensen'-partij. De SP en de Tweede-Kamerverkiezingen van 1994, in *Jaarboek DNPP 1994*, Groningen: DNPP, pp. 172–189.

Van Heerden, S., de Lange, S., Van der Brug, W. and Fennema, M. (2013) 'The immigration and integration debate in the Netherlands: discursive and programmatic reactions to the rise of anti-immigration parties', *Journal of Ethnic and Migration Studies* 40 (1): 119–136.

Van Holsteyn, J. and Irwin, G. (2003) 'Never a Dull Moment: Pim Fortuyn and the Dutch Parliamentary Election of 2002', *West European Politics* 26 (2): 41–66.

Van Holsteyn, J., Irwin, G. and den Ridder, J. (2003) 'In the eye of the beholder: the perception of the *List Pim Fortuyn* and the parliamentary elections of 2002', *Acta Politica* 38 (1): 69–87.

Van Kessel, S. (2010) 'The Dutch General Election of June 2010', European Parties Elections and Referendums Network, *Election Briefing Paper* no. 54.

—	(2011) 'Explaining the electoral performance of populist parties: the Netherlands as a case study', *Perspectives on European Politics and Society* 12 (1): 68–88.

—	(2013) 'A matter of supply and demand: the electoral performance of populist parties in three European countries', *Government and Opposition* 48 (2): 175–199.

—	(2014) 'The populist cat-dog: applying the concept of populism to contemporary European party systems', *Journal of Political Ideologies* 19 (1): 99–118.

Van Kessel, S. and Castelein, R. (2014) 'Who is the enemy? Analysing the anti-establishment discourse of populist parties through Twitter', paper prepared for the 64th Annual ICA Conference, Seattle WA, 22–26 May 2014.

Van Kessel, S. and Hollander, S. (2012) 'Europe and the Dutch Parliamentary Election, September 2012', European Parties Elections and Referendums Network, Election Briefing Paper, No. 71.

Van Spanje, J. and Van der Brug, W. (2007) 'The party as pariah: the exclusion of anti-immigration parties and its effect on their ideological positions', *West European Politics* 30 (5): 1022–104.

—   (2009) 'Being intolerant of the intolerant: The exclusion of Western European anti-immigration parties and its consequences for party choice', *Acta Politica* 44 (4): 353–384.

Věci veřejné. The Journal of the Public Affairs Party (April 2009–February 2012). Online. Available http://www.volby.cz (accessed 6 March 2015).

Verney, S. (2011) 'An Exceptional Case? Party and Popular Euroscepticism in Greece, 1959–2009', *South European Society and Politics* 16 (1): 51–79.

Vibjerg, T., Cordsen, C. and Rytgaard, N. (2014) 'Vælgerne vil trodse EU i striden om børnecheck', in *Jyllands-Posten* March 13. København: Jyllands-Posten. Online. Available http://www.jyllands-posten.dk/politik/ECE6577744/vaelgerne-vil-trodse-eu-i-striden-om-boernecheck/ (accessed 18 July 2014).

Viavoice (2013) 'France 2013: crise économique, psychologies collectives et "Marques France"', Online. Available http://www.institut-viavoice.com/docs/Observatoire-WCie-Marque-France_2013.pdf (accessed 12 March 2014).

Visnot, M. (2014) 'Attractivité: la France se fait distancer par l'Allemagne et le Royaume-Uni', *Le Figaro*, 27 May, p. 24.

Vivyan, N., Wagner, M. and Tarlov, J. (2012) 'Representative misconduct, voter perceptions and accountability: evidence from the 2009 House of Commons expenses scandal', *Electoral Studies* 31 (4): 750–763.

Voerman, G. (2009) 'Van Mao tot marketing. Over het populisme van de SP', *Socialisme & Democratie*, 1 September 2009. Online. Available http://www.wbs.nl/system/files/voerman_gerrit_van_mao_tot_marketing_sd2009_9.pdf (accessed 28 August 2013).

Voerman, G. and Lucardie, P. (2007) 'De Sociaal-Democratisering van de SP' in Becker, F. and Cuperus, R. (eds) *Verloren Slag. De PvdA en de verkiezingen van november 2006*, Amsterdam: Mets and Schilt/Wiardi Beckman Stichting, pp. 139–164.

—   (2012) *Populisten in de polder*, Groningen: University of Groningen Press.

von Beyme, K. (1988) 'Right-wing extremism in post-war Europe', *West European Politics* 11 (2): 1–18.

Vona, G. (2009) 'Nobody talks about holocaust-approvers', (A holokausztigenlőkről még nem esett szó), *Barikád*, 2009, 5, 4. Online. Available http://www.barikad.hu/node/28493 (accessed 7 March 2015).

—   (2012) 'Born on 20 August' (Született augusztus 20-án), Budapest: *Magyar Hírek*.

—   (2013) 'Black sheep, white raven' (Fekete bárány, fehér holló), Budapest: *Magyar Hírek*.

Vossen, K. (2011) 'Classifying Wilders: The Ideological Development of Geert Wilders and His Party for Freedom', *Politics* 31 (3): 179–189.

Vouillazère, A. (2013) 'La "mutation marxiste" de Marine Le Pen', *Minute*, 16 January, 7.

VRT (2014) Werkloosheid in Wallonië stijgt, maar minder snel Retrieved 16 July. Online. Available http://www.deredactie.be/cm/vrtnieuws/economie/1.1826822 (accessed 22 June 2014).

VV (2009) *'Nejdůležitější je omezit dopady krize na každého z nás,' tvrdí Radek John*. Online. Available http://www.veciverejne.cz/domaci-politika/clanky/nejdulezitejsi-je-omezit-dopady-krize-na-kazdeho-z-nas-tvrdi-rad.html (accessed 6 March 2015).

— (2009a) *Stanovy strany Věci veřejné*, printed document.

— (2009b) *Hrozí ČR státní bankrot*. Online. Available http://www.veciverejne.cz/ekonomika/clanky/hrozi-cr-statni-bankrot.html (accessed 6 March 2015).

— (2010a) *Politický program*, printed document.

— (2010b) *Volební spot s kandidáty Věci veřejných*. Online. Available http://www.youtube.com/watch?v=w8pHuO4WXMY (accessed 15 March 2014).

— (2012) *Výsledky referend*. Online. Available http://www.veciverejne.cz/vysledky-referend.html (accessed 6 March 2015).

Walgrave, S., Lefevere, J. and Tresch, A. (2012) 'The associative dimension of issue ownership', *Public Opinion Quarterly* 76 (4): 771–782.

Walsh, D. and O'Malley, E. (2013) '*Sinn Féin*: from minor player to centre stage?' in Clark, A. and Weeks, L. (eds) *Radical or Redundant: The politics of small parties in Ireland*, Dublin: The History Press.

Weeks, L. (2010) 'Parties and the party system', in Coakley, J. and Gallagher, M. (eds) *Politics in the Republic of Ireland*, 5th edn. London: Routledge.

Weyland, K. (2001) 'Clarifying a contested concept: populism in the study of Latin American politics', *Comparative Politics* 34 (1): 1–22.

Widfelt, A. (2008) 'Party change as a necessity: the case of the Sweden Democrats', *Representation* 44 (3): 265–276.

Wieviorka, M. (2013) 'The Front National's new clothes', *openDemocracy*, 15 April. Online. Available https://www.opendemocracy.net/michel-wieviorka/front-national%E2%80%99s-new-clothes (accessed 25 January 2014).

Wilders, G. (2005) *Groep Wilders. Onafhankelijkheidsverklaring*, Party Document, Groep Wilders, The Hague.

Wiles, P. (1969) 'A Syndrome, Not a Doctrine', in Ionescu, G. and Gellner, E. (eds) *Populism: Its meanings and national characteristics*, London: Weidenfeld and Nicolson pp. 166–79.

Wollebæk, D., Enjolras B., Steen-Johnsen, K., and Ødegård G. (2012a) 'After Utøya: how a high-trust society reacts to terror—trust and civic engagement in the aftermath of July 22', *PS: Political Science & Politics* 45 (1): 32–37.

— (2012b) Ett år etter 22. Juli' Institutt for samfunnsforskning, Oslo.

Wren, K. (2001) 'Cultural racism: something rotten in the state of Denmark?', *Social & Cultural Geography* 2 (2), 141–162.

Ylä-Anttila, T. (2012) 'What is Finnish about the Finns Party? Political Culture and Populism', Master's thesis, University of Helsinki. Online. Available https://helda.helsinki.fi/handle/10138/37445 (accessed 10 March 2015).

— (2014) 'Perussuomalaisten sisäiset poliittiset suuntaukset: Julkisen oikeuttamisen analyysi', *Politiikka* 56 (3): 191–209.

Yle (6 Oct 2008) *Perussuomalaiset pitävät vahvuutenaan avoimuutta*. Online. Available http://www.yle.fi/vaalit/2008/id103692.html (accessed 10 March 2015).

— (26 October 2008) Voitonjuhlat ravintola Zetorissa. Online. Available http://www.yle.fi/elavaarkisto/artikkelit/perussuomalaisten_vaalivoitto_2008_34660.html#media=34666 (accessed 6 March 2014).

— (9 February 2012) *KMS-vaalirahoituksen koreografia alkaa kirkastua*. Online. Available http://www.yle.fi/uutiset/kotimaa/2012/02/kms-vaalirahoituksen_koreografia_alkaa_kirkastua_3246164.html (accessed 27 February 2012).

Zaslove, A. (2008) 'Here to stay? Populism as a new party type', *European Review* 16, 3: 319–336.

Zechmeister, E. J. and Zizumbo-Colunga, D. (2013) 'The varying political toll of concerns about corruption in good versus bad economic times', *Comparative Political Studies* 46, 10: 1190–1218.

Index